JOYCE'S CHOICES

Joyce's Choices

New Textual Parallels in James Joyce's *Dubliners*,
A *Portrait of the Artist as a Young Man*, and *Ulysses*

R. H. Winnick

https://www.openbookpublishers.com
©2025 R.H. Winnick

This work is licensed under a Creative Commons Attribution-NonCommercial 4.0 International (CC BY-NC 4.0) license. This license allows you to share, copy, distribute and transmit the text; to adapt the text for non-commercial purposes providing attribution is made to the author (but not in any way that suggests that the author endorses you or your use of the work). Attribution should include the following information:

R.H. Winnick, *Joyce's Choices: New Textual Parallels in James Joyce's 'Dubliners', 'A Portrait of the Artist as a Young Man', and 'Ulysses'*. Cambridge, UK: Open Book Publishers, 2025, https://doi.org/10.11647/OBP.0429

Further details about CC BY-NC licenses are available at https://creativecommons.org/licenses/by-nc/4.0/

All external links were active at the time of publication unless otherwise stated and have been archived via the Internet Archive Wayback Machine at https://archive.org/web

Digital material and resources associated with this volume are available at https://doi.org/10.11647/OBP.0429#resources

Information about any revised edition of this work will be provided at https://doi.org/10.11647/OBP.0429

ISBN Paperback 978-1-80511-414-7
ISBN Hardback 978-1-80511-415-4
ISBN PDF 978-1-80511-416-1
ISBN HTML 978-1-80511-418-5
ISBN EPUB 978-1-80511-417-8

DOI: 10.11647/OBP.0429

Cover image: James Joyce (1915), photo by Alex Ehrenzweig, https://commons.wikimedia.org/wiki/File:James_Joyce_by_Alex_Ehrenzweig,_1915_cropped.jpg

Cover design: Jeevanjot Kaur Nagpal

For Margot Norris

Table of Contents

About the Author   ix

Preface   xi

I. DUBLINERS   1

The Sisters   3

An Encounter   5

Araby   7

Eveline   9

After the Race   11

Two Gallants   15

A Little Cloud   19

Counterparts   27

A Painful Case   29

Ivy Day in the Committee Room   33

A Mother   39

Grace   43

The Dead   47

II. A PORTRAIT OF THE ARTIST AS A YOUNG MAN   49

Portrait, Chapter 1   51

Portrait, Chapter 2   61

Portrait, Chapter 3   71

Portrait, Chapter 4	73
Portrait, Chapter 5	75

III. ULYSSES — 81

1. 'Telemachus'	83
2. 'Nestor'	89
3. 'Proteus'	95
4. 'Calypso'	111
5. 'Lotus-Eaters'	121
6. 'Hades'	131
7. 'Aeolus'	151
8. 'Lestrygonians'	167
9. 'Scylla and Charybdis'	181
10. 'Wandering Rocks'	201
11. 'Sirens'	217
12. 'Cyclops'	227
13. 'Nausicaa'	245
14. 'Oxen of the Sun'	301
15. 'Circe'	335
16. 'Eumaeus'	363
17. 'Ithaca'	371
18. 'Penelope'	379
Select Bibliography	387
Index of Antecedent Writers and Works Discussed	389

About the Author

R. H. Winnick earned his Ph.D. in English and American Literature from Princeton University in 1976, receiving dissertation credit for his co-authorship, as a graduate student, of *Robert Frost: The Later Years, 1938–1963* (Holt, Rinehart and Winston, 1977), vol. 3 of the late Lawrance Thompson's Pulitzer Prize-winning (for vol. 2) 'official' Frost biography. He next researched an authorized biography of the American poet, playwright, educator, journalist, and statesman Archibald MacLeish and edited *Letters of Archibald MacLeish, 1907 to 1982* (Houghton Mifflin, 1983). Winnick's third book, *Tennyson's Poems: New Textual Parallels*, published in 2019 by Open Book Publishers, documented more than a thousand previously unrecognized, unidentified, or misidentified textual parallels in the work of that poet. He has also published sixteen article-length studies on Chaucer, Sidney, Shakespeare, Melville, Clough, Hardy, and Larkin, appearing in, among other journals, *The Chaucer Review*, *Nineteenth-Century Literature*, *Literary Imagination*, *The Hardy Review*, and *About Larkin*.

Preface

Over the past half century, James Joyce's three most widely read works—*Dubliners* (1914), *A Portrait of the Artist as a Young Man* (1916), and *Ulysses* (1922)—have been the subject of four major book-length studies entirely devoted to annotating one or more of them: Weldon Thornton's *Allusions in 'Ulysses': An Annotated List* (Chapel Hill: University of North Carolina Press, 1968); Don Gifford's *Joyce Annotated: Notes for 'Dubliners' and 'A Portrait of the Artist as a Young Man'*, second edition, revised and enlarged (Berkeley: University of California Press, 1982); Gifford's (with Robert J. Seidman) *Ulysses Annotated: Notes for James Joyce's 'Ulysses'*, second edition, revised and enlarged (Berkeley: University of California Press, 1988); and, most recently and comprehensively, the nearly fourteen-hundred-page *Annotations to James Joyce's 'Ulysses'* (Oxford: Oxford University Press, 2022), by Sam Slote, Marc A. Mamigonian, and John Turner (hereinafter, 'SMT'). One might reasonably suppose, after these four studies plus several extensively annotated editions of the works themselves, not to mention a century of other book- and article-length Joyce scholarship, that little remains to be found and said about the textual parallels—otherwise known as allusions, borrowings, echoes, and the like—that *Dubliners*, *Portrait*, and *Ulysses* contain.[1] Further

---

1 Annotated editions of *Dubliners* include those edited by Terence Brown (1992), John Wyse Jackson and Bernard McGinley (1993), Robert Scholes and A. Walton Litz (1996), Jeri Johnson (2000), and Margot Norris (2006). Annotated editions of *A Portrait of the Artist as a Young Man* include those edited by Chester G. Anderson (1968), Seamus Deane (1992), Jeri Johnson (2000), John Paul Riquelme (2007), and Marc A. Mamigonian and John Turner (2018). Annotated editions of *Ulysses* include *The Cambridge Centenary 'Ulysses': The 1922 Text with Essays and Notes*, edited by Catherine Flynn (2022). Further bibliographical details on these and other editions and studies may be found in the Select Bibliography that begins on p. 387.

examination of the three works at the level of phrases as short as two or three to as many as several words, however, coupled with a far-ranging search of the printed works that came before, facsimiles of which are now widely available in digitized and searchable form, together reveal a total of more than eight hundred previously unrecognized, unidentified, or (in my view) misidentified textual parallels—including some sixty in *Dubliners*, some forty in *Portrait*, and just over seven hundred in *Ulysses*, all of them matching Joyce's language verbatim or very nearly so—which singly and together shed new light on Joyce's reading, thematic intentions, and creative technique.

The main title of this study reflects my belief that the textual parallels to antecedent works found in such abundance in *Dubliners*, *Portrait*, and *Ulysses*,[2] far from being accidental and incidental, were largely if not entirely conscious and deliberate, reflecting Joyce's voracious reading from an early age, at home, in school and college, at the bookshops and bookstalls he patronized and the libraries he frequented in Dublin, Trieste, Zurich, Paris, and elsewhere in Europe;[3] his ear for and interest in the Anglo-Irish speech patterns and expressions of his family, friends, acquaintances, and community; his prodigious memory;[4] and, no less

---

2 Among the many apposite comments on that abundance: Stuart Gilbert, in *James Joyce's 'Ulysses': A Study* (London: Faber & Faber, 1930; repr. New York: Knopf, 1952), refers on p. 22 of the latter edition to 'the thousand and one correspondences and allusions with which the book is studded'; and R. Brandon Kershner, in 'Dialogical and Intertextual Joyce', *Palgrave Advances in James Joyce Studies*, ed. Jean-Michel Rabaté (Basingstoke: Palgrave Macmillan, 2004), 183–202, p. 183, writes: 'It is arguable that, more than the work of any other major author, Joyce's writings are permeated by quotations, citations, literary allusions, and other traces of texts and voices.'

3 A voracity suggested by Joyce's letter dated 28 February 1905 to his brother Stanislaus from Pola, Austria, reading in part (titles italicized, bracketed details and some commas moved or added): 'I have read the *Sorrows of Satan* [by Marie Corelli (London, 1895)], *A Difficult Matter* (Mrs Lovett Cameron) [(London, 1898)], *The Sea Wolves* (Max Pemberton) [(London, 1894)], *Resurrection* and *Tales* (Tolstoy)[the former as translated by Louise Maude (London, 1900); the latter possibly referring to *Tales from Tolstoi* and/or *More Tales from Tolstoi*, both as translated by R. Nisbet Bain, both published in London in, respectively, 1901 and 1902], *Good Mrs Hypocrite* (Rita [Mrs Desmond Humphreys (London, 1899)]), [*The*] *Tragedy of Korosko* (Conan Doyle)[(London, 1898)], *Visits of Elizabeth* (Elinor Glyn) [(London, 1900)], and *Ziska*[, *The Problem of a Wicked Soul*, by Marie Corelli (London, 1897)]—all these read, it may be supposed, since his previous surviving letter to Stanislaus dated 7 February 1905. See *Letters of James Joyce* (New York: The Viking Press, 1966), ed. Richard Ellmann—hereinafter, *Letters*—vol. 2, pp. 82–83.

4 In his 'Introduction: Composition, Text, and Editing' to the Norton Critical Edition of Joyce's *Portrait*—a revised excerpt from the 'Introduction' to *A Portrait of the Artist as*

important, his longtime practice of jotting down on the slips of paper he always carried with him any word, phrase, or passage he came across—in antecedent texts ranging from major and minor works of English, Irish, Scottish, French, German, Italian, Latin, Norwegian, Russian, and other literatures to the poems, plays, popular songs, street ballads, comic operas, triple-deckers, dime novels, penny dreadfuls, print advertisements, and other genres of his own day, as well as in any number of literary anthologies, general encyclopedias, and phrase dictionaries—that he found note-worthy and thought he might find use for in something he was then writing or might someday write.

These slips of paper, which must once have numbered in the tens of thousands,[5] were organized over time into subcategories by various criteria, and were subsequently reorganized into successively smaller, more usable groupings.[6] As the Joyces traveled from country to country across Europe in search of a safe haven, needed income, and a congenial environment in the years before, during, and after the so-called Great War, many of these noteslips, notesheets, and notebooks were lost or left behind, with only a fraction of the total believed to have survived. But much that he had read, remembered, and recorded found its way into his fiction.

Similarly, what is known of Joyce's personal libraries in Dublin, Trieste, Zurich, Paris, and elsewhere, which must once have totaled

---

a Young Man, ed. by Hans Walter Gabler with Walter Hettche (New York and London: Garland, 1993)—Gabler writes, on p. xix: 'In Zurich, within neutral Switzerland, he was cut off from all the notes and manuscripts he had left behind in war-embroiled Trieste. Yet from a prodigious memory—a faculty that was essential to Joyce's writing throughout his life—he reprovided flawlessly words and sentences missing in the *Egoist* installments [of *Portrait*]; with great determination, he insisted on an entirely uncensored text for the book publication.'

5 Richard Ellmann writes in his biography *James Joyce* (New York: Oxford University Press, 1959), p. 558, that Joyce's friend the American artist Myron Nutting (1890–1972), then living in Paris, 'was surprised to see Joyce sorting out old notes for *Ulysses* in February 1923, especially when Joyce announced proudly that the unused notes weighed twelve kilos'—equal to more than 26 pounds.

6 In 'The Economy of Joyce's Notetaking'—chap. 9, pp. 163–70, of *New Quotatoes: Joycean Exogenesis in the Digital Age*, ed. by Ronan Crowley and Dirk Van Hulle (Leiden: Brill Rodopi, 2016), https://doi.org/10.1163/9789004319622—Sam Slote writes, on p. 164: '[W]e can see that Joyce's notetaking progressed through various discrete stages: notes taken directly from his reading would then be selected and copied into other notebooks, where they would be categorised under various headings (either by subject or by episode), and then these might be further re-copied and re-sorted into other notebooks or notesheets before eventually winding up in a draft of the text.'

thousands of volumes, has been published in catalogues issued by the libraries owning them (or what remains of them) in those cities or elsewhere.[7] But here again, many of the titles Joyce once owned were sold, lost, or left behind,[8] as a result of which one of the best available ways to reconstruct his reading—apart from mentions of particular titles in his (again) surviving correspondence, sales receipts, and other documentary material—is from verbatim or nearly verbatim echoes of phrases of various lengths from that reading in his own published works, including (among others) *Dubliners*, *Portrait*, and *Ulysses*.

As for the subtitle of this book, I first employed the term 'textual parallel', which had previously occurred from time to time mostly in exegetical and linguistic studies, as an alternative to the more common but less clearly defined 'allusion' six years ago at the suggestion of Christopher Ricks, in whose definitive edition of the complete poems of Tennyson I had found more than a thousand previously undocumented instances.[9] In the Prefatory Note to his *Allusion to the Poets* (Oxford:

---

[7] See Tristan Power, 'Joyce's *Ulysses* Library' in *Studies in Bibliography*, vol. 60 (2018), 229–250, https://doi.org/10.1353/sib.2018.0005, and especially note 1 on p. 229, which lists the principal repositories of Joyce materials and the publications describing them as of its year of publication. For a book-length discussion of Joyce's personal library while he lived in Trieste, see Michael Patrick Gillespie, *Inverted Volumes Improperly Arranged: James Joyce and His Trieste Library* (Ann Arbor: UMI Research Press, 1983). In *The Cambridge Companion to 'Ulysses'*, edited by Sean Latham (Cambridge: Cambridge University Press, 2014), https://doi.org/10.1017/cco9781139696425.003, Michael Groden observes in chap. 1, 'Writing Ulysses', pp. 4–5: 'The surviving material covers an extraordinarily wide range. Major collections exist at the British Library, the University at Buffalo, the National Library of Ireland, and Cornell and Yale universities, with smaller collections at Harvard, Princeton, and Southern Illinois universities; the universities of Texas, Tulsa, and Wisconsin-Milwaukee; the Rosenbach Museum and Library; the Huntington Library; the New York Public Library; and University College Dublin.'

[8] See Power, 'Joyce's *Ulysses* Library', p. 229: 'There is a great amount of evidence for the books read by Joyce from 1914 to 1922 while he was writing *Ulysses*. [...] Six hundred items survive in the Nelly Joyce collection [at the Harry Ransom Humanities Research Center (The University of Texas at Austin)], almost all of which are genuine works belonging to Joyce from his Trieste library. Besides these, ninety further titles have been obtained from the external evidence of Joyce's shelf inventory and bookstore bills during this period, but estimates of the library suggest that it contained at least another five hundred books, which have left few if any documentary traces that are external to the novel itself.'

[9] See R. H. Winnick, *Tennyson's Poems: New Textual Parallels* (Open Book Publishers, 2019), available for downloading or accessing online at https://doi.org/10.11647/OBP.0161

Oxford University Press, 2002), Ricks had earlier written, on pp. 3–4 (italics in the original):

> There are distinctions to be philosophized about: borrowings, parallels, sources, echoes, allusions. If you ask a philosopher whether there exists any indispensable account of allusion, he or she has a way of implicating you in implicatures, or of referring you to his or her work on referring—which is not the same as allusion. And although to speak of an allusion is always to predicate a source (and you cannot call into play something of which you have never heard), a source may not be an allusion, for it may not be called into play; it may be scaffolding such as went to the building but does not constitute any part of the building.[10] Readers always have to decide—if they accept that such-and-such is indeed a *source* for certain lines—whether it is also more than a source, being part not only of the making of the poem but of its meaning.

And so, in my discussion of Joyce's prose as in Ricks's discussion of poetry, while I often have occasion to speak of a phrase in Joyce echoing, or possibly being borrowed from or pointing to, an antecedent work of prose or poetry that may or may not have been its source, I have consistently refrained from declaring unequivocally that any given phrase in Joyce is from, or is an allusion to, a similar or even identical phrase in an antecedent work or that any such antecedent work was necessarily Joyce's source. Readers of this study are, of course, free to decide for themselves which, if any, of the textual parallels discussed in it may or do constitute allusions on Joyce's part, and which, if any, of the antecedent texts discussed, even when they match Joyce's language verbatim (as most of them do) and even when they appear to be the only antecedent to do so, were necessarily his source, but it is always possible that Joyce came up with the phrase out of the blue, or heard it somewhere, or read it in some work which has not yet found its way into searchable and findable form.

---

10   Ezra Pound, in his 'Paris Letter' to *The Dial*, vol. 72, no. 6 (June 1922), 623–29—rpt. in *Literary Essays of Ezra Pound*, ed. T. S. Eliot (Norfolk, Conn.: New Directions, 1954), 403–09—employed a similar metaphor in discussing the Homeric framework of *Ulysses*: 'These correspondences are part of Joyce's medievalism and are chiefly his own affair, a scaffold, a means of construction, justified by the result, and justifiable by it only.' See also A. Walton Litz, *The Art of James Joyce: Method and Design in 'Ulysses' and 'Finnegans Wake'* (London: Oxford University Press, 1961), p. 21.

I should add that in many instances I have found more than one antecedent text perfectly or all but perfectly matching Joyce's language. If two or more such antecedent texts have what appear to me to be roughly equal claims to have been the one Joyce had in mind, I note them both or all, in chronological order. I generally ignore, or mention only in passing, antecedent phrases that occur more than three or four times; being so common, any such phrase may have become so familiar that Joyce was as likely to have picked it up at a neighborhood park or pub as in anything he chanced or chose to read.

Beyond his practice of jotting down notes by the thousand to remind himself later of words, phrases, and passages he had found of interest when he first read or heard them, what else has been and can be said about Joyce's reading habits?

In *My Brother's Keeper: James Joyce's Early Years* (New York: Viking Press, 1958), his brother and confidant Stanislaus Joyce (1884–1955) writes, on p. 79 of the 2003 Da Capo Press edition:

> He devoured books, while I was a slow reader. It sometimes surprised me, however, to find both that my brother remembered little or nothing of most of the books he read so voraciously and that at need he could make good use of the one or two things he did remember from his reading. He read quickly, and if the book or author did not appeal to him he forgot them both. If a book did, on the contrary, make some impression on him, he tried to read as many by the same writer as he could lay his hands on.

In 'James Joyce and the Middlebrow', chap. 8 of *New Quotatoes* (see note 6 above), Wim Van Mierlo observes on p. 142 (italics in the original):

> Although his consumption of *belles-lettres* may have slowed down somewhat in later life, [Joyce's] reading habits never substantially changed: he read widely and eclectically. Despite this, I cannot claim to see any specific strategy in his book collecting habits. What is certain is that he did not always acquire books with a view of using them for his writing. Like most of us, he purchased books on impulse simply because they spoke to him in one way or another. [...] The writers we encounter in his libraries and notebooks, many of whom enjoyed wide popularity, produced for the most part unchallenging, realistic prose; the sort of writing that can be classed as middlebrow.

In 'A Library of Indistinction', chap. 1 of the same volume, Daniel Ferrer writes on p. 11 (italics in the original):

> It was particularly important for the young Joyce, as a *déclassé*, to build what [the French sociologist Pierre] Bourdieu calls "cultural capital" as a compensation for the loss of other forms of capital. Erecting a library, a virtual library of distinction, was a way to restore his status or acquire a new one. As (former) bluffers, we can sympathize with Stephen Dedalus (who probably represents Joyce adequately in this respect): "reading two pages apiece of seven books every night" (*U* 3.136) is a quick and easy way to acquire a vast field of quotable references.

Ferrer adds, on p. 14:

> Whereas Stephen Dedalus was "Reading two pages apiece of seven books every night" ("I was young", he tells us [*U* 3.136–37]), Joyce often read books very superficially, as his notetaking proves: skimming, reading only the bold or the italicized words, or the footnotes.

It goes without saying, or should, that—notwithstanding whatever shortcuts he employed to amass the word- and phrase-hoard which provided raw materials for much of his art—Joyce was extraordinarily well read, did have a prodigious memory, knew the Bible (both the King James and Douay-Rheims versions), Shakespeare's plays, and other canonical and theological works of Western literature backwards and forwards, and had clearly read carefully and thoughtfully, cover to cover, hundreds of other major and minor works of prose, poetry, and drama, among them—as the present study suggests or appears further to confirm—works by (among others) Alcott, Arnold, Austen, Balzac, Baudelaire, Charlotte Brontë, Emily Brontë, Burns, Byron, Carlyle, Cervantes, Conrad, Cowper, Dante, Defoe, Dickens, Dostoevsky, Dryden, George Eliot, Goethe, Goldsmith, Hardy, Hawthorne, Hugo, Ibsen, Samuel Johnson, Ben Jonson, Keats, George Macdonald, Malory, Marlowe, Milton, Schiller, Sir Walter Scott, Shelley, Smollett, Sterne, Stevenson, Swift, Swinburne, Tennyson, Thackeray, Tolstoy, Trollope, Turgenev, Wordsworth, Yeats, Zola—and doubtless those by hundreds of others, canonical and noncanonical, from which he crafted, with consummate artistry, some of the twentieth century's most masterful, memorable, and original literary works.

Interestingly, notwithstanding that originality—*Ulysses* and *Finnegans Wake* are surely among the most imaginative and original novels ever written—Ellmann notes in the 1982 edition of his Joyce biography, p. 661, that Joyce 'often agreed with [the Italian philosopher Giambattista] Vico [1668–1744] that "imagination is nothing but the working over of what is remembered"', and that he said to his friend the English painter and writer Frank Budgen (1882–1971), as Budgen himself reports in *Myselves When Young* (London: Oxford University Press, 1970), p. 187, 'Imagination is memory'. Hugh Kenner observes, in the revised edition of his seminal study *Ulysses* (Baltimore: The Johns Hopkins University Press, 1987), p. 50: 'Joyce writes nothing that is not already written. Like the Homer of Samuel Butler's imagination he does not like inventing, chiefly because he thinks human beings seldom invent, and the painful scene is unwritten because its silences will have outscreamed its speeches.' As has been noted by SMT and others, Joyce observed in a letter of 3 January 1931 to his friend the American modernist composer George Antheil (1900–1959) that he was 'quite content to go down to posterity as a scissors and paste man for that seems to me a harsh but not unjust description.'[11] And Ellmann, on p. xv of his Introduction to Stanislaus Joyce's *My Brother's Keeper* (2003 edition), writes: 'Inspired cribbing was always part of James's talent; his gift was for transforming material, not for originating it, and Stanislaus was the first of a series of people on whom he leaned for ideas.' Ellmann then quotes (misquotes, actually) a remark of Joyce's mentioned on p. 364 of Budgen's *James Joyce and the Making of 'Ulysses' and Other Writings* (London, 1972): 'When you get an idea, have you ever noticed what I can make of it?'

On p. xxiii of their Introduction, SMT observe:

In *Ulysses*, Joyce's covert citations and borrowings come from a wide variety of sources, from the obscure to the mundane: from Queen Victoria's published diaries to numerous advertisements to a Hopalong Cassidy novel to a fetish magazine for transvestites. It is not within the scope of the present volume to comprehensively catalogue all of Joyce's known borrowings, but we hope to provide a wide enough range in order to help illustrate the variety of Joyce's aesthetics of 'stolentelling'.[12]

---

11 *Letters*, I, 297.

12 The final word, a play on 'storytelling', occurs in the sentence 'The last word in stolentelling!' on p. 424 of the first edition of *Finnegans Wake* published by Faber and Faber, London, and The Viking Press, New York, 4 May 1939, and on the same page of all subsequent editions based on it.

The variety of textual parallels reported and discussed in this study is comparably wide, ranging from a six-word phrase in the story 'Grace' in *Dubliners*, a 'young man in a cycling suit', that previously and apparently uniquely occurred (twice) in the first English-language edition of the Russian writer Leo Tolstoy's (1828–1910) last major novel, *Resurrection* (London, 1900)—which, as indicated above, Joyce is known to have read—to another six-word phrase in episode 15 ('Circe') of *Ulysses*, 'little jobs that make mother pleased', which previously and apparently uniquely occurred in a print advert for the Fluxite Soldering Set. As was the case for SMT in their volume, a comprehensive catalogue of all of Joyce's previously identified textual parallels in addition to those newly identified here was beyond the scope of my study. My primary objective, as stated above, has been to document as many new textual parallels as I have been able to identify, including both the several hundred whose possible sources have never been adduced and the considerable number of others in which the sources previously adduced seem to me less plausible than those I have since found.

Like Thornton in several respects, I do not discuss difficult, archaic, slang, foreign, or other words, phrases, or passages unless they figure in a specific textual parallel; nor, with the same proviso, do I discuss for their own sake any political, historical, cultural, religious, theological, Theosophical, or other references, or any characters in one or more of the three books in question, whether or not based on real people. I do not trace Stephen's, Bloom's, or any other character's steps in and around Dublin, or seek to demonstrate Joyce's exacting verisimilitude in his representation of that city. Like Thornton, Gifford, SMT, and other annotators of Joyce's works, I have little to say about how the textual parallels discussed in this study may bear upon one or another literary theory, past or present, beyond noting that Joyce's allusive practices, particularly in *Ulysses* and *Finnegans Wake*, have often been cited in critical discussions of intertextuality, one of the core concepts of such theory.[13]

---

13 Book-, chapter-, and article-length discussions of intertextuality—a term coined in 1966 by the Bulgarian-French philosopher and literary critic Julia Kristeva (b. 1941) that defined every text as a 'mosaic of quotations'—include, among many others, Graham Allen, *Intertextuality*. Third edn (London and New York: Routledge, 2022), https://doi.org/10.4324/9781003223795; Scarlett Baron, *The Birth of Intertextuality: The Riddle of Creativity* (London and New York: Routledge, 2020), https://doi.org/10.4324/9780203711057; William Irwin, 'Against Intertextuality', *Philosophy and*

My attention here is entirely focused on textual, not literary, parallels; so, for example, I have nothing to say about the many literary parallels linking Joyce's *Ulysses* to Homer's *Odyssey*. With few exceptions, I offer no interpretive comments.[14] Also with few exceptions, I do not claim to know which textual parallels are allusive, which ones Joyce expected some or many of his readers to recognize, and which ones he crafted for the purpose of stumping most or all of those readers or solely for his own private amusement.

Many of the textual parallels discussed in this study involve antecedent works likely to be deemed noncanonical. To spare readers, to the extent possible, the task of tracking down hard or digitized copies of such relatively minor, rare, and/or hard to find works, I have generally provided longer excerpts from such works than I do for more familiar, more readily available canonical ones.

Since (as discussed above) so many of the noteslips, notesheets, and notebooks Joyce created, and so many of the books and other printed material he once owned, were subsequently sold, lost, or left behind—and since Joyce is believed to have owned and/or read hundreds of books for which there is no documentary record—I do not infer from the absence of such documentary evidence that he could not have owned and/or read any work in which a textual parallel occurs. The textual parallels linking Joyce's writings to such antecedent texts are, as stated above, themselves in my view a powerful form of documentary evidence. As Michael Groden observes in his *Ulysses in Focus: Genetic, Textual, and Personal Views* (Gainesville: University of Florida Press, 2010), p. 127: 'Many of [Joyce's]

Literature vol. 28, no. 2 (Oct. 2004), 227–42; R. Brandon Kershner, 'Intertextuality', chap. 12 in *The Cambridge Companion to 'Ulysses'*, ed. Sean Latham (Cambridge: Cambridge University Press, 2014), 171–83, https://doi.org/10.1017/cco9781139696425.017; and Mary Orr, *Intertextuality: Debates and Contexts* (Cambridge: Polity, 2003).

14   In this regard, I commend and concur with SMT's comment on p. xx of their introductory section 'On the Uses and Disadvantages of Annotations for *Ulysses*': '*Ulysses* is a work of art, its annotations are a work of scholarship. And so, by definition, annotations alone will never fully comprehend Joyce's novel: they are simply an aid for the reader to do so. In annotating, we have tried to follow Fritz Senn's comment [in his *Inductive Scrutinies*, ed. Christine O'Neill (Dublin: Lilliput, 1995), p. 234] that "[n]otes should enable interpretations, not predispose them". It is thus not the place of the annotations to offer interpretations of the text, but rather to simply provide information and enable readers to find their own interpretations without predisposing or ordaining them.'

notes for *Ulysses* point to his reading, and scholars have also determined much of his reading from the published text alone.'

Similarly, I am often inclined to take with a grain of salt claims that a particular surviving noteslip or notesheet definitively establishes the source of a given Joycean phrase, particularly when the content of the noteslip or notesheet bears little or no resemblance to the purported source text—and even more particularly when a Joycean phrase or short passage perfectly or all but perfectly matches a phrase occurring in one or more antecedent works not represented in any surviving noteslip, notesheet, or notebook.

I have not knowingly made, and have deliberately avoided making, use of any Artificial Intelligence or Digital Humanities tools in preparing this study—my principal research tool has been the pre-AI version of Google Advanced Search; my principal online resources: HathiTrust Digital Library and the Internet Archive (at archive.org)—and I have in every instance repeatedly checked facsimile copies of first editions or the earliest available editions wherever applicable, but never including transcriptions, of the antecedent works I cite to ensure the accuracy of all quotations, including the spelling, punctuation, and spacing of all quotations as they originally appeared. Beginning but by no means ending with careful readings and rereadings of Thornton, Gifford, and SMT, as well as of every annotated edition of *Dubliners*, *Portrait*, and *Ulysses* and of every major study discussing textual parallels in Joyce to prior works of song, fiction, poetry, drama, and other genres, I have done my best to ensure that every textual parallel offered as new in this study is indeed new. If any of the new textual parallels discussed herein are found to be, in fact, old, I offer my apologies for any such errors.

After comparing, on p. xxxix of the introductory section mentioned above, the differing approaches of Thornton and Gifford, SMT continue (italics in the original): 'We have decided to refrain from indicating mistakes in the earlier volumes of annotation because such critical vituperation would ultimately be unhelpful (and probably uninteresting) to our readers. In places where our annotations differ from Gifford and Seidman's and Thornton's, it can be assumed that such differences are *considered*.'

My own approach, in instances where one or more of the antecedents I cite perfectly or more nearly match a phrase in Joyce than does an antecedent previously cited based on a perceived verbal resemblance, a surviving noteslip, or otherwise, I so state in my commentary, not in a spirit of 'critical vituperation' but simply for the information and convenience of my readers, by enabling them to more easily compare and consider which of the adduced antecedents is more likely to have been the one Joyce had in mind.

Thornton writes on p. 4 of his Introduction:

> In compiling this list [of allusions in *Ulysses*], I have aimed at completeness in the areas of literature, philosophy, theology, history, the fine arts, and popular and folk music. Inadequately as this aim may be realized, such an attempt is now possible because of the prior work of such scholars as Stuart Gilbert, Joseph Prescott, William Schutte, William York Tindall, M. J. C. Hodgart and Mabel Worthington, and Robert M. Adams. My debt to these and to many others is obvious. The present list, however, is more than a compilation of previously discovered allusions, for it attempts to be complete, and consequently it contains many allusions never listed before as well as some which have been only partially or mistakenly identified by earlier scholars.

Six decades after Thornton published those words in the first book-length study of what he called allusions in *Ulysses*, three years after the publication of the mammoth and enormously valuable volume produced by Slote, Mamigonian, and Turner, and even with the addition of the several hundred new textual parallels reported in this study, it seems clear to me that more, perhaps many more, textual parallels in Joyce's *Dubliners*, *A Portrait of the Artist as a Young Man*, *Ulysses*, and no doubt in other of his works, remain to be found. Doing so will require continued study of those works and continuing exploration of the universe of printed works that came before, aided but not supplanted by whatever technological tools and resources are available to scholars of this and future generations.

R. H. Winnick
Princeton, New Jersey

I.

DUBLINERS

The Sisters[1]

Dub, Sisters, line 181: solemn and copious

From a passage in which the story's nameless boy narrator describes the body of the now-coffined Father Flynn, and a sentence in that passage reading 'There he lay, solemn and copious, vested as for the altar, his large hands loosely retaining a chalice', the highlighted phrase had previously occurred in *Thirty Sermons, on the Life of David, and on the Twenty-Third and Thirty-Second Psalms* (Dublin, 1847), by the Rev. C[harles]. M[arlay]. Fleury, preached by the author, he notes in the book's dedicatory letter, before the congregation of the Molyneux Asylum Chapel, Dublin. The passage containing the phrase occurs in Fleury's Sermon III, which takes as its text 1 Samuel xvi 19 ('Wherefore Saul sent messengers unto Jesse, and said, Send me David thy son, which is with the sheep') and, as its theme, 'the formal induction of David into the office for which he was selected'. It reads in part, on pp. 28–30:

> Here is a volume of wisdom opened to us. We have a double calling—one to future dignity in God's set time, another to present duty in our earthly state. [...] Our wisdom, then, our duty, our religion, is to realise, by sober contemplation, the heaven that awaits us. We have not here to follow the guidance of mere fancy ; we have not here the deceitful rule of passion, to observe which will paint a paradise, according to each man's peculiar lust. We have the solemn and

---

[1] This first-written of the stories in *Dubliners* was published in *The Irish Homestead*, a Dublin weekly, on 13 August 1904, and before its inclusion in *Dubliners* was extensively revised. All dates of composition indicated herein for the *Dubliners* stories are based on those provided in the 'Notes to the Stories' section on pp. 457–92 of the Scholes-Litz edition.

copious narrative of revelation ; the history of successive periods yet to come ; of gradation above gradation in eternal glory for the saints ; of resurrection joy, millennial glory with Christ, abiding favour with the Father ; of physical happiness, as well as filial consolations ; of a promised land, a better country, a heavenly city, of many mansions.

If, as seems at least possible and at most likely, Joyce chose to borrow and reuse Fleury's phrase in this passage describing the boy-narrator's encounter with the body of his late friend, he may have done so as an implicit reproach if not condemnation of Flynn for 'follow[ing] the guidance of mere fancy', for observing 'the deceitful rule of passion', and for allowing his 'peculiar lust' for the boy to interfere with his priestly duty to lead him not into a pederastic relationship but to salvation, heaven, and God.

An Encounter

Dub, Encounter, line 50: one of my consciences

Completed by 18 September 1905, this ninth-composed, second-placed of *Dubliners'* fifteen tales revolves around the planned adventure of three schoolboys—the unnamed narrator, Leo Dillon, and 'a boy named Mahony'—to skip school for a day and make their way east across Dublin toward the Pigeon House Generation Station off Sandymount. Before the appointed day, Dillon—who fails to show up for the adventure and thereby forfeits the sixpence he had paid in advance to participate in it— is scolded by the schoolmaster-priest Father Butler for having hidden in his pocket an issue of a weekly children's story-paper, *The Halfpenny Marvel*, featuring a tale Joyce refers to as *The Apache Chief*.[2] The boy narrator later reflects, in lines 48–50 of the story as published in Margot Norris's Norton Critical Edition (on which all line references in the *Dubliners* section of this study are based): 'This rebuke during the sober hours of school paled much of the glory of the wild west for me and the confused puffy face of Leo Dillon awakened one of my consciences.'

The phrase 'one of my consciences' seems to have occurred only once before Joyce's use of it, in 'The Canon with Two Consciences', a short story by the English author and editor Edward Howard (1793–1841)

---

2 The story has been tentatively identified as 'Cochise the Apache Chief: The Perils and Adventures of Dudley Fraser and his Chum in the Wilds of Arizona', published in *The Halfpenny Marvel* (London), vol. 4, no. 86 (25 June 1895), 1–14. See Greg Winston, '"Cochise the Apache Chief," by Paul Herring', *James Joyce Quarterly*, vol. 46, no. 2 (2009), 239–54, https://doi.org/10.1353/jjq.0.0154, which reprints and discusses the story.

published in *The New Monthly Magazine* (London)[3], vol. 55 (Mar. 1839), 366–79. The paragraph in which the phrase occurs, on p. 374, and for context the one immediately preceding it, read:

> " Let the palings be coloured with any hue you like, my children, but the red ochre must be procured ; for such is the wicked degeneracy of this world, that something beside the palings must also be coloured. When you have done this, Scipio, you will repair to the Pope's vicar at the cathedral town, and take him this letter, which is to request that his holiness will condescend to acquaint me in what manner he would have the wealth disposed that I have collected in the service of the church. " I have now," he continued, but abstractedly, as if he were speaking only to himself, " got well rid of one of my consciences, and the one that remains to me is a good pillow-smoother, and a healthy opiate [...]."[4]

---

3 Hereinafter referred to as such, though this periodical's full name changed several times between 1814 and 1884: from 1814 to 1820 appearing as *The New Monthly Magazine and Universal Register*; from 1821 as *The New Monthly Magazine and Literary Journal*; from 1837 as *The New Monthly Magazine and Humorist*; from 1853 as *The New Monthly Magazine*; and from 1882 to 1884 as, simply, *The New Monthly*.

4 As mentioned in the Preface (see p. xxi), in this and all subsequent passages from antecedent works quoted in this study, I have preserved wherever possible the spelling, punctuation, and spacing of all quotations as they originally appeared. Thus, for example, as here, double opening quotes were commonly followed from the late eighteenth to the early twentieth centuries by one character space; semicolons and colons commonly preceded by one character space and followed by two; question marks and exclamation points commonly preceded by one and followed by two character spaces; etc. My principal purpose in doing so is to demonstrate that all quotations herein, unless otherwise indicated, are based wherever possible on the first editions of the works quoted and not on later, possibly inaccurate, editions or transcriptions. My secondary purpose is to replicate, again wherever possible, the 'look and feel' of the antecedent texts quoted as Joyce himself would have seen them.

Araby

Dub, Araby, line 219: driven and derided by vanity

Completed in October 1905, this eleventh-written, third-placed of *Dubliners'* fifteen tales ends, at lines 218–20, with the (again) unnamed boy who is its protagonist and narrator bitterly disappointed by the failure of the bazaar—to which he travels alone with very little money and at which he arrives near closing time—to meet his high expectations, and by his own failure to bring back from it a promised souvenir to give to his friend Mangan's also unnamed sister, for whom he feels the first powerful stirrings of adolescent love. The story's final paragraph reads in its entirety: 'Gazing up into the darkness I saw myself as a creature driven and derided by vanity: and my eyes burned with anguish and anger.'

Critical comment on the quoted passage has tended to focus on the boy's 'anguish and anger', with relatively little attention paid to his sense of being 'driven and derided by vanity'. As to the latter phrase, 'driven and derided' seems to have occurred only twice before Joyce's use of it: first, in a review signed 'T. P. K.' of the third edition of Thomas Taylor's *Life of William Cowper, Esq.* (London, 1833), published in the Dublin-based *Christian Examiner and Church of Ireland Magazine*, vol. 3, no. 28 (Feb. 1834), 73–88, the second paragraph of which, condemning Taylor's all-too-faithful representation of Cowper's long struggle with mental illness, reads in part:

> But his friends and admirers will not have it so ; they are determined that a monument shall be raised to his honour ; they have erected a pillar on his grave, and have sculptured thereon more frightful forms than any that ever barbarous superstition daubed upon

the legend of her savage, self-tormenting, and fiend-encountering saints ; sullen and haggard Melancholy ; Madness with eyes outbursting from his shaven head, with foaming mouth and chained and writhing limbs ; deep-damned Despair and Suicide, driven and derided by torturing demons ; and many monstrous and mysterious things, that the heart sickens to look upon, and the tongue refuses to describe !

and next, in chap. 9 of the triple-decker novel *Folle-Farine* (London, 1871), by the English author Maria Louise Ramé (1839–1908) as 'Ouida', with, in vol. 3 (of 3), 211–12:

The wondrous promise swept her fancy for the moment on the strong current of its imagery, as a river sweeps a leaf. This empire hers ?—hers ?—when all mankind had driven and derided her and shunned her sight and touch, and cursed and flouted her, and barely thought her worthy to be called " thou dog ! "

Eveline

Dub, Eveline, lines 1–2: watching the evening invade the avenue

First published in *The Irish Homestead* (Dublin) for 10 September 1904, this second-composed, fourth-placed of *Dubliners'* tales memorably begins with a striking and much-remarked metaphor: 'She sat at the window watching the evening invade the avenue.' Joyce may himself have found the metaphor memorable and striking, for a version of it had previously appeared in the second paragraph of a story by Charles Ollier (1788–1859)—the English publisher (of Keats and Shelley, among others) and author—published in the London edition of *Bentley's Miscellany*, vol. 10 (Dec. 1841), 564–75, under the title 'The Night-Shriek: A Tale for December'. The story begins:

> Few aspects of external nature are more impressive than a wintry landscape. In the morning, the sun's gleam over a wide expanse of unsullied snow, its rays glittering on the rime-loaded branches of trees, which, as the wind stirs them, nod and wave fantastically like plumes of white feathers,—the lustrous icicles that droop from the eaves of barns and sheds,—the congealed and glassy streams,—and the merry sportsman and his dog,—all these give a joyous effect to a country prospect, even when the year is dying of age and cold.
> But this cheerful appearance is very brief. Noon has not long passed before the sullen shades of evening invade the landscape : the sun, like a meagre ghost, fades away in a pale and vapoury gloom, leaving to the world nothing but the blank, dark, and dumb night.

After the Race

This third-composed, fifth-placed of *Dubliners'* tales, first published in the 17 December 1904 issue of *The Irish Homestead*, begins with a paragraph describing the reaction of 'clumps'—scornfully pejorative word—of onlookers as a succession of motorcars returning from a multinational competition in Bally Shannon, Ireland (based on an actual race which took place there on 2 July 1903), speed past them on their way back to Dublin:

> The cars came scudding in towards Dublin, running evenly like pellets in the groove of the Naas Road. At the crest of the hill at Inchicore sightseers had gathered in clumps to watch the cars careering homeward and through this channel of poverty and inaction the continent sped its wealth and industry. Now and again the clumps of people raised the cheer of the gratefully oppressed.

As discussed below, two of the paragraph's phrases—'poverty and inaction' and 'gratefully oppressed'—occur verbatim in previously published works.

Dub, Race, lines 4–5: poverty and inaction

Joyce could have encountered this phrase in any of several antecedent works, the earliest of which may have been the book-length entry on the history of Scotland in the 1796 and subsequent editions of the *Encyclopædia Britannica*. In vol. 17 of Moore's Dublin Edition of the *Encyclopædia* (Dublin, 1796), a section discussing the so-called Ridolphi plot of 1571–72—a failed Catholic conspiracy to overthrow Queen Elizabeth I and replace her with Mary, Queen of Scots—reads in part, on p. 81:

> Ridolphi, whose ability was inspirited by motives of religion and interest, exerted all his eloquence and address to engage the duke [of Norfolk] to put himself at the head of a rebellion against his sovereign. He represented to him, that there could not be a season more proper than the present for atchieving the overthrow of Elizabeth. Many persons who had enjoyed authority and credit under her predecessor were much disgusted ; the Roman Catholics were numerous and incensed ; the younger sons of the gentry were languishing in poverty and inaction in every quarter of the kingdom ; and there were multitudes disposed to insurrection from restlessness, the love of change, and the ardour of enterprise.

One of the many subsequent instances of the same phrase occurs in the English historian John Richard Green's (1837–1883) *A Short History of the English People* (London, 1874), where chap. 7 ('The Reformation'), section 5 ('The England of Elizabeth'), reads in part, on p. 386:

> But in the reign of Elizabeth the poverty and inaction to which the North had been doomed since the fall of the Roman rule begins at last to be broken. We see the first signs of the coming revolution which has transferred English manufactures and English wealth to the north of the Mersey and the Humber, in the mention which now meets us of the friezes of Manchester, the coverlets of York, and the dependence of Halifax on its cloth-trade.

Dub, Race, lines 6–7: the cheer of the gratefully oppressed

Commenting on this phrase, Jackson and McGinley, on p. 35 of their edition of *Dubliners*, note that 'This sardonic detail recalls that when Queen Alexandra visited Dublin with Edward VII in 1904, she observed of the crowds that "the poorer they are the more they cheer".'[5] Perhaps so, but it appears that the only pre-*Dubliners* instance of 'gratefully oppressed' is the one found in the anonymous essay 'Social Prayer'

---

5 This comment seems first to have been reported in *The Sphere: An Illustrated Newspaper for the Home* (London), vol. 14, no. 184 (1 Aug. 1903), p. 95, where the caption to a series of sketches on that page by M. Paul Thiriat reads: 'Our special artist with the King in the Irish capital has here caught some side incidents of typically Irish character in connection with the events from July 20–24. The King and Queen have been touched by the affectionate demonstration of the people. " The poorer they are," said the Queen, " the more they cheer."'

published in *The Christian Witness and Church Members' Magazine* (London), a Protestant (Congregational) journal, vol. 18 (1861), 150–52, with, on p. 151:

> In all ages and countries the outpouring of the Holy Spirit has been accompanied with special regard to the ordinance of social prayer. The effect of such outpouring has everywhere been the establishment of prayer meetings. Whether in the regions of Paganism or of Popery, whether among Episcopalian or Presbyterian Protestants, the result has been uniformly the same—a result requiring neither law, nor precept, nor persuasion, to bring it about, and which nothing could delay or prevent. This fact is admirably exemplified in the history of Methodism, both in Britain and America. The Spirit of God has ever been a Spirit of prayer in the souls of men ; and, when largely imparted, always a Spirit of social as well as private prayer. When men are baptized with the Holy Ghost, they are drawn together by a power which they cannot resist, and gratefully oppressed by a feeling of gracious emotion which seeks relief in the exercise of social supplication.

Dub, Race, line 96: the machinery of human nerves

In lines 95–97 of this tale the narrator writes: 'The journey laid a magical finger on the genuine pulse of life and gallantly the machinery of human nerves strove to answer the bounding courses of the swift blue animal'— that is, of Ségouin's motorcar. Coincidentally or not, 'the machinery of human nerves' had previously and apparently uniquely occurred pre-Joyce in chap. 21, p. 206, of *Mr. Salt: A Novel*, by the American financial journalist and author Will Payne (1865–1954), published in Boston and New York in October 1903 (though the date on the title page was 1904), just over a year before Joyce's story was itself first published:

> Esther had seen two or three of these periods of stress in the office, when the machinery of human nerves, driven by the president's ruthless will, quivered and strained to the breaking point. She understood it was no time for her little affair.

Two Gallants

Dub, Gallants, line 19: cunning enjoyment

Written in the winter of 1905–06, sixth-placed in the volume, this tale of the womanizer Corley (whose name, the narrator indicates, was locally pronounced 'Whorely') and his friend the leech Lenehan contains, in its second paragraph, a sentence that includes the highlighted phrase: '[Lenehan's] eyes, twinkling with cunning enjoyment, glanced at every moment towards his companion's face.' The first of what appear to be two pre-Joyce instances of the phrase occurs in the novel *Speculation* (London, 1834) by the English poet, novelist, historian, and travel writer Julia Pardoe (1806–1862), vol. 1 (of 3), chap. 15, whose first paragraph, on pp. 262–63, reads in part:

> Two or three individuals whom they passed, looked towards the young barrister with a low smile of cunning enjoyment, as though they comprehended his employment, and felt no disposition to interfere with it ; and even while Harcourt loathed the look of vulgar understanding which they cast on him, he nevertheless felt more assured in his impertinence.

The phrase recurs in the popular and prolific Scottish novelist Mrs Margaret Oliphant's (1828–1897) *Young Musgrave* (London, 1877),[6] vol. 1 (of 3), chap. 23 ('Mary'), where a passage on p. 33 finds Mary Musgrave, the unmarried forty-year-old daughter of Squire Musgrave and manager

---

6   Oliphant's novel was also serialized from January to December 1877 in *Macmillan's Magazine* (London).

of his estate, thinking about the country parson, Mr. Pennithorne, whose love for her is as mild and hopeless as the man himself:

> Her own existence had no exciting source of joy in it, but how far it was from being unhappy ! Had she been unhappy she would have scoffed at herself. What ! so many things to enjoy, so many good and pleasant circumstances around, and not happy ! Would not that have been a disgrace to any woman ? So she was apt to think Mr. Pennithorne extracted a certain cunning enjoyment from that vain love for herself which had been so visionary at all times, and which he persuaded himself had saddened his life.

Dub, Gallants, lines 328–29: pangs and thrills

At lines 326–29 of the story, Lenehan is waiting pensively to see if Corley has succeeded in getting an unnamed slavey whom he has apparently seduced to steal a gold coin—perhaps on Lenehan's behalf—from her elderly and well-to-do employer: 'His mind became active again. He wondered had Corley managed it successfully. He wondered if he had asked her yet or if he would leave it to the last. He suffered all the pangs and thrills of his friend's situation as well as those of his own.'

The phrase 'pangs and thrills' seems to have occurred only twice before Joyce's use of it: first in the tale entitled 'Dumb Friends' from the English children's author Frances Freeling Broderip's (1830–1878) story collection *Way-side Fancies* (London, 1857), with, on p. 189:

> And then the little cot, where the round rosy face lay at night, when you made your usual pilgrimage to it. The coverlet thrown half off, and showing the round, mottled, healthy limbs of the little sleeper. And, oh ! if that white nest was afterwards exchanged for a deeper and colder one, beneath the green sod of the churchyard, by its little tenant, with what pangs and thrills of memory did you afterwards look on it, and yet love it too well to part with it.

and next in the English journalist, author, and publisher's reader S[tephen]. W[atson]. Fullom's (1818–1872) *The Mystery of the Soul: A Search into Man's Origin, Nature, and Destiny* (London, 1865), chap. 7 of which ('Of Man's Sensations, Emotions, Qualities, and Passions, Exhibiting the Distinctness of the Body and Mind, and the Nature of Their Association') has, on p. 136, a paragraph containing same phrase:

I. DUBLINERS

The first quality of life is sensation. It is as necessary to brutes as to man, to the beetle as the giant, and impresses all organisms in a greater or less degree, the higher having a full measure, and the lowest barely a touch. It forms the backbone of Man, his frame's pillar, and spreads conductors through its every part ; whence the operation is so thorough that the whole system may be convulsed by a sound. Indeed, the same effect may be produced by a thought ; for the thread of our sensations is as the web of a spider, and " feels along the line "—feels with a delicacy reached in no other being, either in pain or pleasure. Nor could we expect less ; for our pangs and thrills are more than bodily : they penetrate to the mind.

A Little Cloud

Dub, Cloud, line 21: a shabby and necessitous guise

In lines 20–22 of this fourteenth-composed, eighth-placed tale, which Joyce wrote in Trieste in the first half of 1906, the law clerk known as Little Chandler awaits the arrival from London of the newspaperman Ignatius Gallaher (another self-proclaimed womanizer), whom he has not seen in eight years: 'The friend whom he had known under a shabby and necessitous guise had become a brilliant figure on the London press.'

The first of what seem to be the only two pre-Joyce instances of 'shabby and necessitous' occurred in the Scottish writer, colonial entrepreneur, and political and social commentator John Galt's (1779–1839) novel *The Majolo: A Tale* (London, 1816), vol. 2 (of 2), chap. 5, p. 39:

" The interior squalor of the town was suitable to its physiognomy. A promiscuous multitude of the meanest and ugliest of the human race sweltered in the streets. The military had a shabby and necessitous look ; the reverse of every thing I had heard of English soldiers ; who, whatever was subtracted from their military qualities, were generally supposed to resemble the pampered Prætorians of the Romans more than any other troops in modern Europe.["]

and the second, in the penny dreadful *Boys of the World Story-Teller* (London), vol. 1, no. 11 (1 Dec. 1869), in which chap. 2 ('The Fence's Crib') of the anonymous tale 'The Coiner's Fate' has, on p. 50, the following passage:

Within, however, a quarter of an hour after the departure of her husband, Mrs. Sugden, disguised in very shabby and necessitous-looking clothes, hurriedly left the Camberwell villa by the garden-gate, and hurrying to the nearest cab-stand, entered a four-wheeler, and whispering her instructions to the driver, was driven rapidly away.

Joyce's 'guise', which follows 'shabby and necessitous' in his tale's quoted phrase, may have been suggested by 'disguised' in the passage above from 'The Coiner's Fate'.

Dub, Cloud, lines 52–53: a present joy

In lines 48–53, having walked past '[a] horde of grimy children' (lines 45–46) on his way to meet Gallaher, Little Chandler, Joyce writes, 'gave them no thought. He picked his way deftly through all that minute verminlike life and under the shadow of the gaunt spectral mansions in which the old nobility of Dublin had roistered. No memory of the past touched him, for his mind was full of a present joy.'

For the phrase 'memory of the past' Gifford and others cite the song 'There Is a Flower That Bloometh' from Act 3 of the opera *Maritana* (1845), libretto by the English playwright Edward Fitzball (1793–1873) and music by the Irish composer and pianist William Vincent Wallace (1812–1865). Neither Gifford nor anyone else seems to have noted, however, that the phrase 'a present joy' in the same passage had also occurred previously, most often in evangelical works, but also including in the English poet William Wordsworth's (1770–1850) *The Prelude; Or, Growth of a Poet's Mind*, reading, in Book First ('Introduction: Childhood and School-time'), lines 46–50 of the 1850 version:

> Thus far, O Friend ! did I, not used to make
> A present joy the matter of a song,
> Pour forth that day my soul in measured strains
> That would not be forgotten, and are here
> Recorded[.]

and in the English novelist and poet Mary Ann Evans's (1819–1880), as 'George Eliot', novella *The Lifted Veil*, first published anonymously in *Blackwood's Edinburgh Magazine*, vol. 86, no. 525 (July 1859), 24–48, republished two decades later in *The Works of George Eliot: Silas Marner, The Lifted Veil, Brother Jacob* (Edinburgh and London, 1878), and containing the following paragraph spoken by the clairvoyant Latimer at the beginning of chap. 2 on p. 310 of the latter version:

Before the autumn was at an end, and while the brown leaves still stood thick on the beeches in our park, my brother and Bertha were engaged to each other, and it was understood that their marriage was to take place early in the next spring. In spite of the certainty I had felt from that moment on the bridge at Prague, that Bertha would one day be my wife, my constitutional timidity and distrust had continued to benumb me, and the words in which I had sometimes premeditated a confession of my love, had died away unuttered. The same conflict had gone on within me as before—the longing for an assurance of love from Bertha's lips, the dread lest a word of contempt and denial should fall upon me like a corrosive acid. What was the conviction of a distant necessity to me ? I trembled under a present glance, I hungered after a present joy, I was clogged and chilled by a present fear. And so the days passed on : I witnessed Bertha's engagement and heard her marriage discussed as if I were under a conscious nightmare—knowing it was a dream that would vanish, but feeling stifled under the grasp of hard-clutching fingers.

The phrase 'present joy' minus the indefinite article also previously occurred in a poem by Queen Elizabeth I (1533–1603), written sometime between 1568 and 1571, that begins 'The doubt of future foes exiles my present joy'; in the elegy on Queen Elizabeth entitled 'Our Present Sorrow, and Our Present Joy' (1603) by Robert Fletcher (fl. 1603), the English 'Yeoman purveyor of carriages' to Queen Elizabeth and later to James VI and I, and author of *The Nine English Worthies; or Famous and Worthy Princes of England* (London, 1606); and in the Scottish poet Robert Pollok's (1798–1827) *The Course of Time: A Poem, in Ten Books* (London, 1827), book 1, line 464: 'Sorrows remembered sweeten present joy.'

Dub, Cloud, line 70: low fugitive laughter

In lines 67–71, still making his way toward Corless's and his rendezvous there with Gallaher, Little Chandler, the narrator reports, 'chose the darkest and narrowest streets and, as he walked boldly forward, the silence that was spread about his footsteps troubled him, the wandering silent figures troubled him, and at times a sound of low fugitive laughter made him tremble like a leaf.' The phrase 'low fugitive laughter' in that passage may have been suggested by the English writer and essayist Thomas De Quincey's (1785–1859) *Suspiria de Profundis*, a collection of short essays, first published in *Blackwood's* in the spring and summer of 1845 and later that year in book form, as a sequel to his *Confessions of an*

English Opium-Eater, which had first been published anonymously in the September and October 1821 issues of *The London Magazine* before its publication in book form (London, 1822). The paragraph in which the phrase occurs, in the section of the *Suspiria* called (in the *Blackwood's* version) "The Palimpsest of the Human Brain," reads on pp. 741–42 of the June 1845 issue of *Blackwood's* (with its *how*, its *why*, and its *had* italicized in the original):

> Fancy not, reader, that this tumult of images, illustrative or allusive, moves under any impulse or purpose of mirth. It is but the coruscation of a restless understanding, often made ten times more so by irritation of the nerves, such as you will first learn to comprehend (its *how* and its *why*) some stage or two ahead. The image, the memorial, the record, which for me is derived from a palimpsest, as to one great fact in our human being, and which immediately I will show you, is but too repellent of laughter ; or, even if laughter *had* been possible, it would have been such laughter as oftentimes is thrown off from the fields of ocean—laughter that hides, or that seems to evade mustering tumult ; foam-bells that weave garlands of phosphoric radiance for one moment round the eddies of gleaming abysses ; mimicries of earth-born flowers that for the eye raise phantoms of gaiety, as oftentimes for the ear they raise echoes of fugitive laughter, mixing with the ravings and choir-voices of an angry sea.

Dub, Cloud, line 88: my considering cap

As he awaits Ignatius Gallaher's return from his rendezvous with the slavey, Little Chandler recalls that when Gallaher in former days 'was in a tight corner', he would sometimes say lightheartedly 'Half time now, boys. Where's my considering cap?' In a note on the latter phrase, Margot Norris defines it as 'a metaphorical hat or cap to confer wisdom or sharpen concentration—also called a "thinking cap."' It may be added that considering caps had made a number of prior literary appearances: once in the comedy or farce *Foole upon Foole, or, Six sortes of sottes* (London, 1605), by the English comic actor, author, and member of the Lord Chamberlain's Men Robert Armin (c. 1568–1615); again in the Jacobean playwright John Fletcher's (1579–1625) tragicomedy *The Loyal Subject, or, The Faithful General*, first performed in 1618 and first published in the Beaumont and Fletcher folio of 1647; and again in *The History of Little Goody Two-Shoes* (London, 1765), a children's story anonymously published but generally thought to have been written by Oliver Goldsmith.

But the instance Joyce seems most likely to have had in mind occurs in Dickens's thirteenth and next-to-last completed novel *Great Expectations* (London, 1861), vol. 2 (of 3), chap. 18, p. 290, where Wemmick is speaking with Pip:

> " You are right," he returned. " You hit the nail on the head. Mr. Pip, I'll put on my considering-cap, and I think all you want to do, may be done by degrees. Skiffins (that's her brother) is an accountant and agent. I'll look him up and go to work for you."
> " I thank you ten thousand times."

Dub, Cloud, line 101: bid them arise, shake themselves and begone

In lines 95–101, midway through a paragraph in which Little Chandler fantasizes about writing a poem if only he could find a suitable topic and publishing it in London if only Gallaher could help him do so, the narrator relates Chandler's pathetic-fallacy-laden thoughts:

> As he crossed Grattan Bridge he looked down the river towards the lower quays and pitied the poor stunted houses. They seemed to him a band of tramps huddled together along the river banks, their old coats covered with dust and soot, stupefied by the panorama of sunset and waiting for the first chill of night to bid them arise, shake themselves and begone.

Pathetic fallacies aside, Joyce seems to have infused the passage with echoes of Isaiah lii 2—echoes as applicable to the feckless Chandler himself as to the 'poor stunted houses' past which he walks: 'Shake thyself from the dust; arise, and sit down, O Jerusalem: loose thyself from the bands of thy neck, O captive daughter of Zion.'

Dub, Cloud, line 106: infant hope

In lines 104–06 of the same paragraph, continuing to record what is passing through Chandler's mind, the narrator continues: 'Could he write something original? He was not sure what idea he wished to express but the thought that a poetic moment had touched him took life within him like an infant hope.' Seemingly unremarked, the phrase 'infant hope' previously occurred, among other instances, in at least three poems and one novel.

The earliest of the three poems: the English poet and literary critic Samuel Taylor Coleridge's (1772–1834) Petrarchan sonnet 'On Receiving An Account That His Only Sister's Death Was Inevitable' (1794):

> The tear which mourn'd a brother's fate scarce dry—
> Pain after pain, and woe succeeding woe—
> Is my heart destin'd for another blow ?
> O my sweet sister ! and must thou too die ?
> Ah ! how has Disappointment pour'd the tear
> O'er infant Hope destroy'd by early frost !
> How are ye gone, whom most my soul held dear !
> Scarce had I lov'd you, ere I mourn'd you lost ;
> Say, is this hollow eye—this heartless pain
> Fated to rove thro' life's wide cheerless plain—
> Nor father, brother, sister meet its ken—
> My woes, my joys unshar'd ! Ah ! long ere then
> On me thy icy dart, stern Death, be prov'd ;—
> Better to die, than live and not be lov'd !

Next of the three, the English novelist and poet Charlotte Smith's (1749–1806) 'Sonnet XLV. On Leaving A Part Of Sussex', from her *Elegiac Sonnets*, fifth edn, with additional sonnets and other poems (London, 1789), the opening lines of which read:

> FAREWELL Aruna !—on whose varied shore
> My early vows were paid to Nature's shrine,
> When thoughtless joy, and infant hope were mine,
> And whose lorn stream has heard me since deplore
> Too many sorrows !

And last of the three, the English poet and future Poet Laureate Alfred, Lord Tennyson's (1809–1892) early poem 'Ode to Memory' (1830), the third of whose five sections reads in its entirety:

> Whilome thou camest with the morning mist,
>   And with the evening cloud,
> Showering thy gleaned wealth into my open breast,
> (Those peerless flowers which in the rudest wind
>   Never grow sere,

When rooted in the garden of the mind,
   Because they are the earliest of the year).
      Nor was the night thy shroud.
In sweet dreams softer than unbroken rest
Thou leddest by the hand thine infant Hope,
The eddying of her garments caught from thee
The light of thy great presence ; and the cope
   Of the half-attain'd futurity,
   Though deep not fathomless,
Was cloven with the million stars which tremble
O'er the deep mind of dauntless infancy.
Small thought was there of life's distress ;
For sure she deem'd no mist of earth could dull
Those spirit-thrilling eyes so keen and beautiful :
Sure she was nigher to heaven's spheres,
Listening the lordly music flowing from
      The illimitable years.
   Oh strengthen me, enlighten me !
   I faint in this obscurity,
   Thou dewy dawn of memory.

As for the phrase's apparently only pre-Joyce appearance in fiction, that occurs in the English novelist Lady Emily Ponsonby's (1817–1877) *Oliver Beaumont and Lord Latimer* (London, 1873), vol. 3 (of 3), chap. 17, p. 282:

Nothing so easy to live upon, nothing so animating and inspiriting, as a hope. But then it must be a real hope—a hope full-grown and strong, not a feeble, infant hope, whose fragile life seems daily passing away. And almost any hope which, though bright at first, instead of coming nearer, seems, as time passes, to become more distant, turns to this fragile infant thing, and makes the heart sick.

Counterparts

Dub, Counterparts, line 179: impertinent ruffian

In lines 179–82 of this sixth-composed, ninth-placed tale, which Joyce wrote almost simultaneously with 'The Boarding House' and completed by 12 July 1905, Mr Alleyne's rage against the nominally professional but persistently unprofessional copyist Farrington culminates in a final diatribe: '—You impertinent ruffian! You impertinent ruffian! I'll make short work of you! Wait till you see! You'll apologise to me for your impertinence or you'll quit the office instanter! You'll quit this, I'm telling you, or you'll apologise to me!' Previously unremarked, Mr Alleyne's 'impertinent ruffian' had a number of literary antecedents.

One of these, a story signed 'D. C.' called 'Recollections of an Old Umbrella' and published in *The New Monthly Magazine*, vol. 29, no. 119 (Nov. 1830), 459–65, has the following exchange on p. 463 (italics in the original):

> " A likely thing," I exclaimed, " that I am to empty my pockets to satisfy your impertinent curiosity ! Pray *who* are you, that you should stop me in this manner ? let me pass, fellow, I am desirous to leave the gardens."
>
> " I dare say you are, my shy cock ; but if you don't know who I am, perhaps this will tell you—I'm not only ranger, but special constable."
>
> So saying, he displayed his official baton. The thing was now carried too far for a joke, and I began to get in " a towering passion."[7] Pulling out the luckless ring from my pocket, I exclaimed,

---

7   The narrator's phrase echoes *Hamlet* V ii 79–80, Hamlet to Horatio, referring to Laertes: 'But sure the bravery of his grief did put me | Into a tow'ring passion.'

" You impertinent ruffian, this is what I picked up, it fell from my own umbrella ; now stop me if you dare !"

Another instance, lacking only the personal pronoun, occurs in the English writer W[illiam]. Somerset Maugham's (1874–1965) second novel, *The Making of a Saint: A Romance of Mediaeval Italy* (London, 1898), in which the following exchange occurs in chap. 15 between Checco d'Orsi and his cousin Matteo, on one side, and on the other, a captain in the employ of Ercole Piacentini, Duke of Calabria, who will not let them pass:

> " You insolent fellow ! What do you mean by stopping me like this ? "
> " I have a right to refuse passage to any one I choose."
> " Take care ! " I said. " I swear the count shall be told of your behaviour, and nowadays the count is in the habit of doing as the Orsi tell him."
> " He shall hear of this," growled the Piacentini.
> " Tell him what you like. Do you think I care ? You can tell him that I consider his captain a very impertinent ruffian. Now, let me go."

A Painful Case

Dub, Painful, lines 71–72: sing to empty benches

In this seventh-written (around July 1905), eleventh-placed of *Dubliners'* tales, which concerns the intimate, chaste, ultimately tragic friendship of James Duffy and Emily Sinico, nearly all of Mrs Sinico's remarks to Mr Duffy over the course of their relationship are reported by indirect address. The sole exception: her very first words to him when, still complete strangers, they sit side by side in a 'thinly peopled and silent' concert hall at the Rotunda, on London's Rutland Square, waiting for the evening's scheduled performance to begin, and, turning to him, she says (in lines 71–72): 'What a pity there is such a poor house tonight! It's so hard on people to have to sing to empty benches.'

Mrs Sinico's phrase 'sing to empty benches', while perhaps new to Mr Duffy, was not without precedent. One early instance of the phrase appeared in an essay by the Anglo-Irish writer Oliver Goldsmith (1728–1774) called 'Of the Opera in England', first published in the short-lived literary magazine *The Bee: Being essays on the most interesting subjects* (London), of which Goldsmith was himself founder and editor, and reprinted in several subsequent editions of Goldsmith's works. The essay, in issue no. 8 for 24 November 1759, reads in a passage on pp. 292–93:

> The rise and fall of our amusements pretty much resemble that of empire. They this day flourish without any visible cause for such vigour ; the next they decay without any reason that can be assigned for their downfall. Some years ago the Italian opera was the only fashionable amusement among our nobility. The managers of the playhouses dreaded it as a mortal enemy, and our very poets listed themselves in the

opposition ; at present the house seems deserted, the castrati sing to empty benches, even Prince Vologese himself, a youth of great expectations, sings himself out of breath, and rattles his chain to no purpose.

A century later, another instance of the phrase occurred in the Dublin-born Anglo-Irish novelist and raconteur Charles Lever's (1806–1872) popular novel *A Day's Ride: A Life's Romance* (London, 1863)—first published alongside Dickens's *Great Expectations* in the latter's weekly magazine *All the Year Round* (London) in 1860 and 1861—in which chap. 42 ('A Glimpse of an Old Friend') begins, on p. 376 of the 1863 edition:

> If there be anything in our English habits upon which no difference of opinion can exist, it is our proneness to extend to a foreigner a degree of sympathy and an amount of interest that we obstinately deny to our own people. The English artist struggling all but hopelessly against the town's indifference has but to displace the consonants or multiply the vowels of his name to be a fashion with and a success. Strange and incomprehensible tendency in a nation so overwhelmingly impressed with a sense of its own vast superiority ! But so it is. Mr. Brady may sing to empty benches, while il Signor Bradini would " bring down the house."[8]

Dub, Painful, line 145: the soul's incurable loneliness

The friendship of Mr Duffy and Mrs Sinico abruptly and effectively ends in lines 141–50:

> He thought that in her eyes he would ascend to an angelical stature; and as he attached the fervent nature of his companion more and more closely to him he heard the strange impersonal voice, which he recognized as his own, insisting on the soul's incurable loneliness. We cannot give ourselves, it said: we are our own. The end of these discourses was that one night, during which she had shown every sign of unusual excitement, Mrs Sinico caught up his hand passionately and pressed it to her cheek.
> Mr Duffy was very much surprised.

---

8   An earlier—perhaps among the earliest—instance(s) of the same phrase, to similar effect, occurred in an item in the 'General Intelligence' column of *The Courier* (Hobart, Tasmania) for 15 Feb. 1858, which began, on p. 2: 'MADAME CARANDINI's CONCERT. Where were the sons of the soil and the daughters of the land on Thursday, when they permitted their native nightingale [that is, Madame Carandini] to sing to empty benches ?'

One of the several, mostly evangelical, prior instances and versions of Joyce's phrase occurred in a sermon by the Anglican cleric and historian Rev. Alexander H. Craufurd (1843–1917) collected in his *Seeking for Light. Sermons.* (London, 1879), chap. 4 of which, 'Spiritual Loneliness and Its Remedy', begins on pp. 46–47 with the following paragraph:

> It is well for us all to realise the loneliness of life. There is much truth in the saying that corporations have no consciences. Guilt shared with many others does not cause us much dismay. It is only when we realise our spiritual loneliness, and feel the burden of our individual responsibility, that we become fully conscious of our difficulties and dangers in the religious life. Realised loneliness is a strange quickener of the conscience. All true and deep religion is the product of solitary thought. In a crowd we think that we can do without God. Loneliness scares us and drives us to the Father's arms. We cannot sustain the heavy weight of our individual responsibility. We yearn for someone to share it with us; but our yearning is wholly vain, and at last we realize our incurable loneliness of spirit, and feel and know that we live in a vast wilderness, far from all real human companionship, and alas ! as it often seems, far from our Father also.

Dub, Painful, line 338: like a worm with a fiery head

From a sentence in the story's penultimate paragraph reading 'Beyond the river he saw a goods train winding out of Kingsbridge Station, like a worm with a fiery head winding through the darkness obstinately and laboriously.', the highlighted phrase in Mr Duffy's fevered imagination may have been suggested by a passage in the British novelist and dramatist Charles Reade's (1814–1884) best-known work, the historical novel *The Cloister and the Hearth: A Tale of the Middle Ages* (first, four-volume edn, London, 1861; new, three-volume edn, London, 1862), with, in vol. 1 of the latter, chap. 14, p. 115:

> No sooner was the haunted tower visible, than a sight struck their eyes that benumbed them as they stood. More than half way up the tower, a creature with a fiery head, like an enormous glowworm, was steadily mounting the wall : the body was dark, but its outline visible through the glare from the head, and the whole creature not much less than four feet long.

An earlier version of Reade's novel was serialized under the title "A Good Fight" in *Once a Week* (London) from 2 July to 1 October 1859.

Ivy Day in the Committee Room

Dub, Ivy Day, line 206: a hissing protest

Largely completed by 29 August 1905, this eighth-written, twelfth-placed of *Dubliners'* tales reads, at lines 205–06: 'Mr Henchy snuffled vigorously and spat so copiously that he nearly put out the fire which uttered a hissing protest.' Unlikely though it may seem, the latter phrase may have been inspired by an otherwise forgettable and forgotten story by the prolific American children's (mostly boy's) book author J[ames]. O[tis]. Kaler (1848–1912) called 'A Journey On Snowshoes: The Adventures of Two Boys in an Arctic Clime', serialized in the Dublin-based *Young Ireland: An Irish Magazine of Entertainment and Instruction*. Chapter 5 ('A Renewal of Hope') of that story, appearing on pp. 219–21 of *Young Ireland*, vol. 7, no. 14 (2 Apr. 1881), has the following paragraph on p. 220:

> There was no doubt about the smaller and drier of his firewood burning, for they soon flamed up in a way which actually looked cheerful, and, by judicious treatment, the boards so fortunately discovered also did their part toward the fire, although they sent out many a hissing protest at being thus obliged to serve as firewood.

Joyce's ironic tale of Dublin's political inertia nears its end with a recitation, by Joe Hynes, of 'The Death of Parnell, 6th October 1891', which, Mr Crofton declares—or perhaps concedes—in the story's final line 'was a very fine piece of writing'. Though nominally written by Hynes, the poem is a pastiche of clichés and other phrases borrowed by Joyce from an assortment of prior, mostly obscure poems with an occasional phrase from a canonical poet and poem added to the mix.[9]

Dub, Ivy Day, line 523: mourn with grief and woe

The poem's second line, 'O, Erin, mourn with grief and woe', may have been suggested by a line from book 7, chap. 1 ('How WALLACE burnt the Barns of Air, put Bishop Beik out of Glasgow, and killed Lord Piercy') of the Scottish poet William Hamilton of Gilbertfield's (c. 1665–1751) verse translation of the fifteenth-century Scottish bard Blind Harry's *The Wallace* as *The Life and Heroick Actions of the Renoun'd Sir William Wallace, General and Governour of Scotland*, several editions of which were published in Edinburgh beginning in 1722: 'Therefore his Friends did mourn, with Grief and Woe, | Till his proud Breast was like to burst in two.'

The same phrase occurs a century later in *The Mosiad, or Israel Delivered; a Sacred Poem, in Six Canticles, with Notes, &c.* (London, 1815), by one Charles Smith, reading, in canticle 3, lines 98–99: 'Long, long, did Egypt mourn with grief and woe, | The dreadful day of Pharaoh's overthrow'.

Dub, Ivy Day, line 526: coward hounds

Line 5 of the Hynes poem, 'He lies slain by the coward hounds', echoes a phrase, 'coward hounds', that occurs in several nineteenth-century works. One of these, the Scottish novelist, poet, and travel writer Robert Louis Stevenson's (1850–1894) historical adventure and romance novel *The Black Arrow*, was serialized in *Young Folks; A Boys' and Girls' Paper of Instructive and Entertaining Literature* (London), vols. 22 and 23, between June and October 1883 (with the subtitle 'A Tale of Tunstall Forest'); then published as *The Black Arrow: A Tale of the Two Roses* (London, 1888), in the latter of which, chap. 5, 'The "Good Hope" (*continued*)', reads on p. 179: 'Thereupon,

---

9 Another Joycean instance of similar technique occurs in Gabriel Conroy's after-dinner speech in *Dubliners'* 'The Dead'. As Jackson and McGinley note on p. 180 of their edition of *Dubliners*, 'Stanislaus said that Gabriel's speech was an exact pastiche of the orations of John Joyce.'

Lawless sheathed his dagger, and turning to his next neighbour, " I have left my mark on them, gossip," said he, " the yelping, coward hounds."'

Another instance: in 'To England', a poem by the British novelist, poet, and journalist Francis William Lauderdale Adams (1862–1893) posthumously collected in his *Songs of the Army of the Night* (London, 1894), in which the last four lines of the first stanza read: ' O that, if struck, then struck with glorious wounds, | I bore apart | (Not torn with fangs of leprous coward hounds) | My bleeding heart !'

Dub, Ivy Day, line 529: her monarch's pyre

The phrase 'monarch's pyre' in lines 7–8 of the Hynes poem, 'And Erin's hopes and Erin's dreams | Perish upon her monarch's pyre', may echo any of a handful of antecedent instances of the phrase. One such occurs on p. 17 of 'King Ethelbert of Kent and Saint Augustine' in the Irish poet and critic Aubrey Thomas De Vere's (1814–1902) *Legends of the Saxon Saints* (London, 1879), based on Bede's *Ecclesiastical History of the English People* (written c. 731):

> In graver mood
> That chief resumed : ' A Norland King dies well !
> His bier is raised upon his stateliest ship ;
> Piled with his arms ; his lovers and his friends
> Rush to their monarch's pyre, resolved with him
> To share in death, and with becoming pomp
> Attend his footsteps to Valhalla's Hall.[']

and another, in *Beowulf, An Epic Poem, Translated from the Anglo-Saxon into English* (London, 1849), by A. Diedrich Wackerbarth, canto 41, p. 116:

> And at the noble Monarch's Pyre
> No Hero's Gold shall melt in Fire,
> For here are Treasures all untold,
> A grimly purchas'd Hoard of Gold
> And now with his own Life at last
> He bought the Rings, which shall be cast
> To greedy Fire-brand to devour
> And for the Flame to cover o'er.

Dub, Ivy Day, line 533: wrought her destiny

The third stanza of the Hynes poem reads: 'In palace, cabin or in cot | The Irish heart where'er it be | Is bowed with woe—for he is gone | Who would have wrought her destiny.'—the last three words of which occur in several mostly forgettable nineteenth-century works of poetry and prose. One such instance occurs in stanza 9 of the Scottish Indian Army officer and poet Major Calder Campbell's (1798–1857) 'The Phantasmal Reproof', published in *Hood's Magazine and Comic Miscellany* (London), vol. 1, no. 4 (Apr. 1844), pp. 381–84:

> " There was no falsehood in her heart—
>   No perfidy to thee ;
> But thy words unkind, like a sudden wind
>   That charmeth the summer sea,
> Awoke in her that fearful stir
>   Which wrought her destiny.["]

and another instance, in the American author Virginia F[rances]. Townsend's (1836–1920) short story 'The Temptation and the Triumph' published in the May 1857 issue of *The Lady's Companion, and Monthly Magazine* (London), vol. 2, second series, 255–59, with, on p. 257:

> " It would afford me unspeakable pleasure to carry your daughter over in my buggy, with your permission, my dear madam," very diplomatically concluded the urbane gentleman.
> " Thank you, Mr. Abbott," was the flattered mother's response ; " I shall be very happy to place Bertha in your care ; and she will enjoy the ride so much better than in that lumbering old stage – poor child !" And Bertha went ; and that visit wrought her destiny.

Dub, Ivy Day, line 535: The green flag gloriously unfurled

Although flags are gloriously unfurled in other, mostly nationalistic poems, Joyce's line may have been suggested by stanza 4 (of 6), line 2, of the widely circulated poem 'The Final Toast: A Masonic Song'—written in the 1840s by the Calcutta-based officer of the East India Company, Freemason, poet, literary editor, and educator David Lester Richardson (1801–1865), and, as set to music by Richardson's Calcutta-based musician friend the Dublin-born William Henry Hamerton (1795–1853)—first printed in *The Masonic Vocal Manual* (Hebden Bridge, Yorkshire, 1852). Stanza 4 of the poem reads:

> Amidst our mirth we drink " To all poor Masons o'er the world"—
> On every shore our flag of love is gloriously unfurled;
> We prize each brother, fair or dark, who bears no moral stain—
> " Happy to meet—sorry to part—happy to meet again!"

Dub, Ivy Day, line 538: He dreamed (alas, 'twas but a dream!)

Although an early poetic instance of the phrase 'Alas ! 'twas but a dream' occurred in an anonymous poem published in *The Scots Magazine* (Edinburgh), vol. 54, in 1792, this seventeenth line of the Hynes poem was probably inspired (as were countless other lines over the course of the nineteenth century) by the first line of a Wordsworth sonnet, written and first published in 1819, that begins: 'I heard (alas, 'twas only in a dream) | Strains—which, as sage Antiquity believed, | By waking ears have sometimes been received, | Wafted adown the wind from lake or stream'.

Dub, Ivy Day, line 542: coward caitiff

The phrase 'coward caitiff' in the first line of stanza 6, 'Shame on the coward caitiff hands', seems first to have occurred in the Bristol poet and satirist—a working-class contemporary, schoolmate, and rival of Thomas Chatterton (1752–1770)—James Thistlethwaite's (b. 1751) THE CONSULTATION. *A Mock Heroic, In Four Cantos*, 'The Second EDITION, with *large* ADDITIONS' (Bristol, 1775), where the closing lines of canto 2, on p. 52, read: 'The coward caitiff deaf to Wisdom's cry, | (His fatal purpose pregnant in his eye,) | Tir'd of existence dares his maker's frown, | And plunges headlong to a world unknown.'

The phrase recurs in 'The Dunciad of To-day, A Satire', a long poem published in the short-lived weekly periodical *The Star Chamber* (London), no. 5 for Wednesday, 10 May 1826, believed to have been written by the British author, statesman, Conservative politician, and future Prime Minister Benjamin Disraeli (1804–1881), and reading, in lines 401–12:

> And deem not ye, who kneel at SHAKSPEARE's throne,
> From Britain's stage her last of poets flown.
> KNOWLES yet survives, the OTWAY of his age,
> Sole prop and honour of our falling stage ;
> Let British eyes Rome's mighty moral view,
> And British tears confess that moral true.
> The Tribune's lust,—he feels and feeds its growth,—
> The slave—the pander—shall they scorn an oath ?
> The virgin's fall—this, this alone, could save,—
> Th' avenging parent claims the life he gave ;
> Stifles in death the coward caitiff's cries,
> Bewilder'd clasps his frantic brain, and dies !

It recurs yet again late in the century in Samuel Ferguson's *Hibernian Nights' Entertainments, Third Series: The Rebellion of Silken Thomas* (Dublin and London, 1887, repr. 1897), reading, on p. 68 of both printings:

> " Let him curse ! " cried Talbot ; " I dread no malediction of a dishonest man !—is not this he whose forged report of the old Earl's death has driven us all into rebellion without a cause ? Ay, Archibishop Alan, you were the man, who to gratify the spite you cherished against the noble house of Kildare, first spread that most insidious and destructive falsehood ; raising the rumour of a murder that had never been committed, nor in danger of commission now, but for the fatal belief that men too easily deceived, put in your dishonourable devices ; and, now, like a coward caitiff, you fly from the war you have yourself thus basely succeeded in enflaming !["]

Dub, Ivy Day, line 545: fawning priests

As a final example of the poem's apparent borrowings, the highlighted phrase occurs, among a considerable number of other instances, in the Irish actor, poet, and dramatist Francis Gentleman's (1728–1784) *Royal Fables* (London, 1766), where 'Fable XI. The BIRTH DAY', reads in part, on p. 56 (italics in the original):

> The BIRTH DAY levee now were come,
> And marshall'd in the drawing room ;
> A medly of most curious creatures,
> As diff'rent in designs as features.
>
> Here fawning *Priests*, with looks demure,
> In hopes to get a better *cure*,
> Appear'd to grace the friendly croud ;
> And very low——for livings bow'd——

A Mother

Dub, Mother, line 2: walking up and down

This tenth-composed, thirteenth-placed tale of a concert series gone badly awry, which Joyce finished writing by late September 1905, begins with the narrator reporting that, in connection with the series, Mr Holohan, assistant secretary of a society promoting Irish culture, 'had been walking up and down Dublin for nearly a month', a phrase to which Joyce calls further attention by repeating it later in the same paragraph: 'He walked up and down constantly, stood by the hour at street corners arguing the point'—though what the point is and with whom he argued it is not indicated—'and made notes: but in the end it was Mrs Kearney who arranged everything.'

That Mrs Kearney—whose piano-playing daughter Kathleen Mr Holohan had himself *arranged*, as in engaged, to serve as an accompanist at the concerts—ultimately demonizes Holohan for his society's failure to pay Kathleen her fee in full, despite poor turnout at the first two concerts and the cancellation of the third (of four), suggests that the repeated phrase in the first paragraph was deliberate and meaningful: it had first occurred in Job ii 2, reading, in most scriptural versions including the King James: 'And the Lord said unto Satan, From whence comest thou? And Satan answered the Lord, and said, From going to and fro in the earth, and from walking up and down in it.'

Dub, Mother, line 150: that doesn't alter the contract

Another echo in the tale, also seemingly unremarked, is not scriptural but Shakespearean. Mrs Kearney's demand that her daughter be paid in full the eight guineas stipulated in the contract 'for her services as accompanist at the four grand concerts' (lines 67–68) regardless of the concerts' total proceeds or whether all four concerts were actually performed, recurs several times in the story: in lines 150–51, when Mrs Kearney learns that, based on the poor turnout at the first two concerts, the third has been cancelled: '—But, of course, that doesn't alter the contract, she said [to Holohan]. The contract was for four concerts.'; in lines 154–58: 'She called Mr Fitzpatrick away from his screen and told him that her daughter had signed for four concerts and that, of course, according to the terms of the contract she should receive the sum originally stipulated for whether the Society gave the four concerts or not.'; and, in the most extended and heated exchange regarding the payment due her daughter, in lines 259–74:

> —Mr Holohan, I want to speak to you for a moment, she said.
> They went down to a discreet part of the corridor. Mrs Kearney asked him when was her daughter going to be paid. Mr Holohan said that Mr Fitzpatrick had charge of that. Mrs Kearney said that she didn't know anything about Mr Fitzpatrick. Her daughter had signed a contract for eight guineas and she would have to be paid. Mr Holohan said that it wasn't his business.
> —Why isn't it your business? asked Mrs Kearney. Didn't you yourself bring her the contract? Anyway, if it's not your business it's my business and I mean to see to it.
> —You'd better speak to Mr Fitzpatrick, said Mr Holohan distantly.
> —I don't know anything about Mr Fitzpatrick, repeated Mrs Kearney. I have my contract and I intend to see that it is carried out.

Given the tone and content of Mrs Kearney's iterated demand that her daughter be paid in full, it seems likely Joyce had in mind that other famously injured and irate party, the money-lender Shylock, as he speaks to Antonio in *The Merchant of Venice*, III iii 12–17:

> I'll have my bond; I will not hear thee speak.
> I'll have my bond, and therefore speak no more.
> I'll not be made a soft and dull-ey'd fool

> To shake the head, relent, and sigh, and yield
> To Christian intercessors. Follow not,
> I'll have no speaking, I will have my bond.

Note, too, that in *Dubliners'* next story, 'Grace,' at lines 315–16, the narrator refers obliquely to Shylock and directly to 'the jewish ethical code'.

Dub, Mother, line 310: the moral umbrella

In lines 310–11 of the story, the narrator, speaking of Mr O'Madden Burke, writes: 'His magniloquent western name was the moral umbrella upon which he balanced the fine problem of his finances.' Among other pre-Joyce instances of 'moral umbrella', the earliest seems to have occurred in *The Spectator* (London), vol. 35, no. 1776, for the week ending 12 July 1862, in an anonymous essay entitled 'The British Umbrella' that begins, on p. 768, with the following:

> The umbrella is not strictly a British institution. Its germ or embryo, the parasol, was at least as popular in Greece and Rome as in England, but then the parasol has none of the exclusive and insular effect of the umbrella. It is not our climate nor our rain alone which has made the umbrella peculiarly British ; it is the intense insularity and exclusiveness which the umbrella carries with it. It shuts out all the world except oneself, and transforms a trudging nation into a visible multiple of units. Only consider that peculiar British word " umbrage." When a Briton " takes umbrage," he does in fact take to a moral umbrella, shutting out earth and skies with a temporary individual erection of his own.

Another, more nearly contemporary instance of the phrase occurred in *Popular American Readings in Prose and Verse* (London, 1893), edited by Robert Ford. In that collection—placed between Charles F. Browne's (as 'Artemus Ward') 'Lecture on the Mormons' and Samuel L. Clemens's (as 'Mark Twain') 'The Celebrated Jumping Frog'—is an anonymous poem on pp. 88–90 entitled 'The Moral Umbrella', the penultimate stanza of which reads:

> Just then the minister said, says he,
> " And now I come to the fellers
> Who've lost this shower, by usin' their friends
> As a sort o' ' Moral Umbrellers.'

> Go home," says he, " and find your faults,
>   In place o' huntin' your brothers' ;
> Go home," says he, " and wear the coats
>   You've tried to fit on others ! "

A third instance occurs in the novel *Guenn. A Wave on the Breton Coast* (Boston and New York, 1883; London, 1884), by the American-born writer Blanche Willis Howard (1847–1898), with, in chap. 2 ('Everett Hamor'), pp. 28–29 of the London edition, 'If a dense cloud of feeling seemed to threaten him from any quarter, he would discreetly shelter himself under his moral umbrella.'

Joyce may or may not have been aware of any of these pre-*Dubliners* instances of the phrase, but I have found no others occurring before 1907, in which year the last of the tales in the collection are believed to have been written.

Dub, Mother, line 339: struggle of tongues

In lines 339–40, Joyce writes of the continuing altercation between Mr Holohan and Mrs Kearney over the payment due to her daughter: 'After a swift struggle of tongues Mr Holohan hobbled out in haste.' A rare instance of the highlighted phrase occurs in an essay by the English historian, architectural artist, and Liberal politician E[dward]. A[ugustus]. Freeman (1823–1892) entitled 'Saalburg and Saarbrücken' published in *Macmillan's Magazine*, vol. 27, no. 162 (Nov. 1872), 29–40, where, on pp. 30–31, Freeman writes:

> But Wiesbaden and Rambach together supply enough to set any one thinking, to make any one who feels an interest in the great struggle of tongues and races which has gone on for so many ages along the line of the great river, feel specially eager to learn something more of any traces which the earlier stages of that great struggle may have left behind them.

Grace

Begun in October 1905, this twelfth-composed, fourteenth-placed of the fifteen stories that would ultimately comprise *Dubliners*, and originally intended—before Joyce wrote 'The Dead'—to be the final tale in the volume, 'Grace' is generally thought, based on Stanislaus Joyce's account in *My Brother's Keeper*, to have been structured with the hell-purgatory-paradise pattern of Dante's *Divine Comedy* in mind. As with *Dubliners'* other stories, it is also laced with often thematically relevant textual parallels to prior works, some not previously identified.

Dub, Grace, lines 42 and 172–73: young man in a cycling suit

The 'young man in a cycling suit' whose first aid revives the unconscious Mr Kernan after his fall down the stairs leading to the pub's lavatory at the beginning of the story is referred to as such three times, but is never seen again or identified by name. Coincidentally or not, what seems to have been the only prior literary reference to a 'young man in a cycling suit' occurs in a book Joyce is known to have read by September 1905 and greatly admired: Tolstoy's last major novel, *Voskresenie* (1899), the first English-language edition of which, under the title *Resurrection* and translated by Louise Maude, was, as noted above, published in London the following year.

Specifically, the reference occurs in the first paragraph of the final (forty-second) chapter of book 2 ('Le Vrai Grand Monde.'), in which, on p. 414, Nekhlúdoff—Prince Dmitry Ivanich Nekhlúdoff, the novel's central character—sees disembark from the first-class carriage of his

©2025 R.H. Winnick, CC BY-NC 4.0 https://doi.org/10.11647/OBP.0429.10

Siberia-bound train (in which, by choice, he is riding third-class) the wealthy and aristocratic Korchágin family on its way to one of the family's several estates. The paragraph reads in its entirety:

> Before Nekhlúdoff got out he had noticed in the station yard several elegant equipages, some with three, some with four, well-fed horses, with tinkling bells on their harness. When he stepped out on the wet, dark-coloured boards of the platform, he saw a group of people in front of the first-class carriage, among whom were conspicuous a stout lady with costly feathers on her hat, and a waterproof, and a tall, thin-legged young man in a cycling suit. The young man had by his side an enormous, well-fed dog, with a valuable collar. Behind them stood footmen, holding wraps and umbrellas, and a coachman, who had also come to meet the train.

Though he is the only son of Prince and Princess Korchágin, whose daughter, Missy, Nekhlúdoff is expected eventually to marry, Tolstoy's young man in a cycling suit can hardly be called even a minor character in the novel, saying and doing nothing and playing no role in the story. It might thus be thought that the appearance of the six-word phrase in both Tolstoy's *Resurrection* and Joyce's 'Grace' is merely coincidental and of no consequence.

Interestingly, however, another key phrase in the latter work, 'turn over a new leaf' in lines 172–73, also plays a key role in the former, where it appears—in English—in Tolstoy's otherwise Russian- and occasionally French-language novel and, of course, in the Maude translation, book 1, chap. 28 ('The Awakening') of which reads, on p. 112:

> More than once in Nekhlúdoff's life there had been what he called a " cleansing of the soul." By ' cleansing of the soul' he meant a state of mind in which, after a long period of sluggish inner life, a total cessation of its activity, he began to clear out all the rubbish that had accumulated in his soul, and was the cause of the cessation of the true life. His soul needed cleansing as a watch does. After such an awakening Nekhlúdoff always made some rules for himself which he meant to follow for ever after, wrote his diary, and began afresh a life which he hoped never to change again. " Turning over a new leaf," he called it to himself in English. But each time the temptations of the world entrapped him, and without noticing it he fell again, often lower than before.

The same phrase occurs in Joyce's story in the passage beginning at line 172:

> —O now, Mrs Kernan, said Mr Power, we'll make him turn over a new leaf. I'll talk to Martin [Cunningham]. He's the man. We'll come here one of these nights and talk it over.
> [...]
> —We'll make a new man of him, he said. Goodnight, Mrs Kernan.

'Turn(ing) over a new leaf' is, of course, a common phrase that has been around for centuries—since the sixteenth century, to be more nearly precise. But the appearance of that phrase and the iterated references to a 'young man in a cycling suit' in both Tolstoy's novel and Joyce's story, and the major thematic role that turning over a new leaf plays in both works, together suggest that, in an unusually clear Joycean instance of thematically relevant intertextuality, Joyce had the Maude translation of Tolstoy's *Resurrection* in mind when he wrote the tale he called, no doubt ironically, 'Grace'.

Dub, Grace, line 443: calm enmity

Referring to Mr Kernan, lines 441–44 read: 'He took no part in the conversation for a long while but listened, with an air of calm enmity, while his friends discussed the Jesuits.' The phrase 'calm enmity' seems first to have occurred on p. 3 of a book-length essay bearing the title *An Appeal from the New to the Old Whigs, In Consequence of Some Late Discussions in Parliament, Relative to the 'Reflections on the French Revolution'* (London, 1791), published anonymously, written in the third person, referring throughout to the Anglo-Irish statesman, economist, and philosopher Edmund Burke (1729–1797), but actually written by Burke himself. The phrase itself is part of an aphorism, much quoted and paraphrased thereafter, that reads: 'Angry friendship is sometimes as bad as calm enmity.'

Dub, Grace, line 797: spiritual accountant

As Father Purdon's sermon/talk—or as much of it as Joyce or his narrator chooses to record—nears an end, lines 796–800 read: 'If he might use the metaphor, he said, he was their spiritual accountant and he wished each and every one of his hearers to open his books, the books of his spiritual life, and see if they tallied accurately with conscience.'

As crass and worldly as Father Purdon's 'spiritual accountant' may seem, it was not without precedent in evangelical literature. A sermon by the prominent Congregational minister Rev. E[noch]. Mellor, D.D. (1823–1881), of Liverpool, England, published in the London-based *Evangelical Magazine and Missionary Chronicle*, vol. 7 (Mar. 1877), 125–33, under the title 'Paul's Computation', begins with an epigraph quoting Romans viii 18 ('I reckon that the sufferings of this present time are not worthy to be compared with the glory which shall be revealed in us.'), followed by a paragraph employing the same metaphor:

> This is the language of careful and accurate computation. The
> " reckon " is not here employed in its loose, colloquial signification,
> as if the Apostle were simply delivering his opinion formed on very
> insufficient grounds. Its import is of the strictest kind, and calls up to our
> imagination the Apostle as a spiritual accountant who has been carefully
> and profoundly calculating all the various items of his spiritual life in
> order to ascertain whether Christianity is attended with the greater loss
> or gain. We see before him a balance sheet, and this is the general result,
> " I reckon that the sufferings of this present time are not worthy to be
> compared with the glory which shall be revealed in us."

A sermon that Joyce may have read before writing 'Grace', and that Father Purdon might himself have preached.

The Dead

Dub, The Dead, line 945: a less spacious age

In lines 943–46 of his after-dinner speech, Gabriel says: 'Listening tonight to the names of all those great singers of the past it seemed to me, I must confess, that we were living in a less spacious age. Those days might without exaggeration be called spacious days'. In a note on the passage, Gabler defines 'spacious age' as 'A time of great expansiveness, when people had a wide and generous outlook'—which, so far as it goes, is no doubt true. As to where in prior works Joyce may have crossed paths with the phrase itself, two possible instances present themselves.

The first of these: in *Macmillan's Magazine*, vol. 64, no. 383 (Sept. 1891), 392–400, where an essay by 'W. P. J.' entitled 'The Great Work' reads on p. 394: 'Or to come to our own less spacious age, consider the magnificence of fixed resolve with which Mr. Herbert Spencer announced already in a prospectus of 1860 the whole mighty scheme of his System of Philosophy.'

The second, in the London- and New York-based *Cosmopolis, An International Monthly Review*, vol. 5, no. 15 (Mar. 1897), 684–701, where an essay entitled 'Current German Literature' by the Scottish philologist John George Robertson (1867–1933)—then Lecturer at the University of Strasbourg, later Professor of German at the University of London—reads on p. 699 in the subsection on 'Literary Criticism and Biography', and referring to the German-Swiss poet and author Gottfried Keller (1819–1890): 'His fine aristocratic nature was too good to be classed among the *Epigoni* of the great age, his pride too strong to allow him to write down to the less spacious age into which he was born.'

©2025 R.H. Winnick, CC BY-NC 4.0   https://doi.org/10.11647/OBP.0429.11

Joyce may or may not have seen either or both of these essays. At a minimum, it can reasonably be assumed that the phrase 'less spacious age' was abroad in the land and available for his use in the decade before he wrote 'The Dead'.

As for 'spacious days', that phrase may ultimately be traceable to Tennyson's 'A Dream of Fair Women', first published in 1832 but much revised as republished a decade later, where the third line of the second stanza has not 'The spacious days' but 'The spacious times of great Elizabeth'. Nevertheless, between 1842 and 1907, the year in which Joyce wrote 'The Dead', there were numerous instances, some citing Tennyson, of 'the spacious days of great Elizabeth', 'the spacious days of Good Queen Bess', and simply 'the spacious days', so that Joyce could have and probably did encounter the phrase in any number of works and in general parlance any number of ways.

II.

A PORTRAIT OF THE ARTIST AS A YOUNG MAN

Portrait, Chapter 1[1]

Por 1.1: Once upon a time and a very good time it was

The phrase with which Joyce's *Portrait* begins, after an epigraph quoting a line from Ovid's *Metamorphoses*, occurs verbatim in at least two pre-*Portrait* works, the first of these vol. 3 (of 3) of the study by Henry Mayhew (1812–1887)—the English journalist, playwright, and co-founder (with Ebenezer Landells) of the humorous and satirical magazine *Punch, or The London Charivari*—entitled *London Labour and the London Poor* (London, 1851), a study, its subtitle declares, 'of the Condition and Earnings of Those That *Will* Work, Those That *Cannot* Work, and Those That *Will* Not Work'. In a section on the lives of the boy inmates of the so-called casual wards of London's workhouses, Mayhew quotes a story told by one such inmate 'to show what are the objects of admiration of these vagrants'. It begins, on pp. 389–90:

> " You see, mates, there was once upon a time, and a very good time it was, a young man, and he runned away, and got along with a gang of thieves, and he went to a gentleman's house, and got in, because one of his mates sweethearted the servant, and got her away, and she left the door open.["]

Later in the section, the same boy adds:

---

1 All quotations and line numbers in the *Portrait* section of this study are based on the text of *A Portrait of the Artist as a Young Man*, ed. John Paul Riquelme, text ed. by Hans Walter Gabler with Walter Hettche (New York: W. W. Norton, 2007).

> " Some [of us] told long stories, very interesting ; some were not fit to be heard ; but they made one laugh sometimes. I've read ' Jack Sheppard ' through, in three volumes ; and I used to tell stories out of that sometimes. We all told in our turns. We generally began,—' Once upon a time, and a very good time it was, though it was neither in your time, nor my time, nor nobody else's time.' The best man in the story is always called Jack."

The second of the two works, *English Fairy Tales* (London, 1890), collected by the New South Wales-born Australian-American folklorist, translator, literary critic, social scientist, historian, and writer Joseph Jacobs (1854–1916), contains two tales with the same opening phrase, the first of the two 'Jack and his Golden Snuff-Box', which begins, on p. 81:

> Once upon a time, and a very good time it was, though it was neither in my time nor in your time nor in any one else's time, there was an old man and an old woman, and they had one son, and they lived in a great forest. And their son never saw any other people in his life, but he knew that there was some more in the world besides his own father and mother, because he had lots of books, and he used to read every day about them.

and the second an Anglo-Scottish Border fairy tale called 'The Well of the World's End' that begins, on p. 215, with:

> Once upon a time, and a very good time it was, though it wasn't in my time, nor in your time, nor any one else's time, there was a girl whose mother had died, and her father had married again. And her stepmother hated her because she was more beautiful than herself, and she was very cruel to her.

Clearly, then, whether Joyce knew the phrase from a tale of his father's or another's telling, or from his own reading of Mayhew, Jacobs, or some other work or works, it was not a phrase of his own invention.

Por 1.427–28: the black dog [...] with eyes as big as carriage-lamps

Gifford, p. 140, writes: 'May have been borrowed from Hans Christian Andersen's (1805–75) fairy tale, "The Tinder Box," though the dogs in that short tale are benign.' It may be added that while the 1835 translation of Andersen's tale features three dogs and their eyes, the dogs have, respectively, 'eyes as large as teacups', 'eyes as big as mill-wheels', and eyes 'as big as a tower', but none 'eyes as big as carriage-lamps'.

Joyce's phrase may, however, recall a similar one in *The Wife's Stratagem: A Story for Fireside and Wayside* (New York and London, 1862), by the American author Frances Elizabeth Barrow (1822–1894), whose books for children were published under the pen name 'Aunt Fanny'. Chapter 4 ('Little Sister') of Barrow's novel has, on p. 57, the following exchange between two of its principal characters (italics in the original):

> " Well, Frank," said Kitty, " your eyes *are* as big as carriage lamps ! sister Tiny was right."
> Frank's face fell to zero. " Did you say that, Miss Stanley ? " he asked.
> " Oh ! good gracious, no I didn't, yes, I did, but (oh ! you goblin") [*sic*] pinching the child ; " but, that don't prevent your eyes being *handsome*," she said with a sideways glance at his angry face ; " dear Frank, I say such things sometimes, you know, to hide how much I really—really—"

Joyce's phrase and a similar one later on the same page—'O how cold and strange it was to think of that! All the dark was cold and strange. There were pale strange faces there, great eyes like carriage-lamps. They were the ghosts of murderers, the figures of marshals who had received their deathwound on battlefields far away over the sea.'—may also owe something to another novel, *The Haunted Room. A Tale.* (London, 1876) by the English writer and poet for children and adults Charlotte Maria Tucker (1821–1893), as 'A.L.O.E.', with, in chap. 3 ('Gossip Downstairs'), the following passage on p. 32: '" Mrs. Jael Jessel, the old lady's attendant, told me that she had twice passed a ghost in the corridor, and once on the stairs. It was a tall figure in white,—at least seven feet high,—and it had great round eyes like carriage-lamps staring upon her."'; and the same metaphor on p. 37 of the same chapter: '" If miss screams when a puppy-dog barks at her, and hides her face under her bed-clothes if there's a peal o' thunder, how will she face ghosts ten feet high, with eyes like carriage-lamps ? " cried the cook.'

Por 1.823: pity the poor blind

Reminded by his wife at Christmas dinner that he has not yet given Dante Riordan any sauce, Simon Dedalus cries 'Haven't I?' and adds, by way of apology, 'Mrs Riordan, pity the poor blind.' Simon's phrase had previously occurred, among other instances, in *The Irish Sketch-Book* (London, 1843) by the English novelist, author, and illustrator William Makepeace Thackeray (1811–1863), as 'Mr. M. A. Titmarsh', where the first paragraph of chap. 23 ('Ballinasloe to Dublin')—quoting from vol. 2 (of 2), chap. 8, pp. 116–17, of the second (London, 1845) edition—reads in part:

> I think the beggars were more plenteous and more loathsome here than almost anywhere ; to one hideous wretch I was obliged to give money to go away, which he did for a moment, only to obtrude his horrible face directly afterwards, half eaten away with disease. " A penny for the sake of poor little Mery," said another woman, who had a baby sleeping on her withered breast ; and how can any one who has a little Mery at home, resist such an appeal ? " Pity the poor blind man !" roared a respectably dressed grenadier of a fellow. I told him to go to the gentleman with the red neckcloth and fur cap, (a young buck from Trinity College,) [*sic*]—to whom the blind man with much simplicity immediately stepped over ; and as for the rest of the beggars, what pen or pencil could describe their hideous leering flattery, their cringing swindling humour !

A similarly cynical view is expressed by the English author Richard Rowe (1828–1879) in his *Picked Up in the Streets, or, Struggles for Life Amongst the London Poor* (London, 1880)—reissued the following year under the title *Life in the London Streets: or, Struggles for Daily Bread* (London, 1881) but with an identical text—where chap. 22 ("Pity the Poor Blind") reads in part on pp. 308–09 of both editions:

> Under the head of " Pity the poor blind," blind beggars first suggest themselves. There are still some literal blind beggars, men who stand by the highway side begging either verbally or by the mute appeal of a label inscribed " I am blind " pinned upon their breast ; their dogs, with pleading eyes and anxiously-wagging tails, seconding the appeal. Some of the talkers merely toll out " Pity the poor blind," in a funereal tone, very much as the railway porters at Tring announce the name of that station : others indulge in little harangues.

Rowe continues:

> One day in a " Nelson " omnibus I fell in with a tall man, dressed in clerical-looking clothes [...]. Misunderstanding, or pretending to misunderstand, some remark I had made to a companion, the tall

man began to lecture me loftily on the ignorance and inhumanity I had displayed in sneering at those whom it had pleased the Almighty to deprive of sight, quoting Scripture largely against me. I had said nothing about blind people, and did not know, until I looked at him closely, that the man was blind. However, as I thought that I had wounded his feelings, I apologised for the unintentional offence I had given him, and we got into conversation, throughout which he maintained a *de haut en bas* tone towards me, laying down the law most oracularly, but throwing out hints now and then about money, which when I heard them I could not understand.

At last the 'bus pulled up in Deptford Broadway, and the blind man got out, graciously allowing me to shake hands with him, in token that he bore no malice, before he departed. When he was gone, a man at the top of the 'bus burst into a roar of laughter.

" Do you know who it is," he said to me, " you've been talking so respectfully to all this time ? The old rogue's a blind beggar. He lodges somewhere about here,—not in Mill Lane, he's a cut above that. He's got a pitch just now in the New Kent Road, and rides to business and back again just like any City man."

A few weeks afterwards I came upon my blind friend holding forth in his professional capacity to a congregation of half-a-dozen at a street corner in Camberwell, and found that he had given me a good bit of his street sermon in the omnibus.

It may be inferred from both Thackeray's and Rowe's accounts, and from others of similar tone and content published over the course of the eighteenth and nineteenth centuries, that Mr Dedalus's seeming apology to Mrs Riordan for forgetting to offer her sauce has a more sardonic edge than might otherwise be supposed.

Por 1.840–41: *I'll pay you your dues* [...] *house of God into a pollingbooth*

Gifford (p. 143) comments: 'Source unknown, but an obvious reference to the Irish Catholic clergy's condemnation of Parnell from the pulpit and its active intervention against Parnellite candidates after the split.' Joyce's 'I'll pay you your dues' did, however, previously and, it seems, uniquely occur in print pre-*Portrait* in the weekly Irish literary newspaper *The Shamrock* (Dublin), vol. 15, no. 592 (16 Feb. 1878), in a serialized comic novel, *Mick M'Quaid's Spa*, by the Irish author

Captain (later Major) William Francis Lynam (1833–1894) of the Royal Lancashire Militia. Chapter 81 of Lynam's novel ('Father O'Flanigan gives Mick Advice that he Doesn't Take—Renewal of the Devotions at the Well—Mr. Bulger Reconciles Mr. Gowan with our Hero—A Visitor Mick could Dispense with, &c.') reads, on p. 306:

> " Oh, blood alive, your Riverence," broke forth Mick, " don't do nothin' iv the kind. Bekase then I'd have to throw myself into the hands iv the Protestan's, and Quakers, and them soort, and I wouldn't like to do that, bekase iv the rispect I always had and have for your cloth. I'll pay you your dues, never fear, if I make anythin' by the place, whether I'm a Pagan or no."
>
> Here the priest could not help smiling, but he immediately checked himself and said, " I cannot take any money for dues from a Pagan, and when you are converted it will be time enough to think of that.["]

Por 1.985–86: O, come all you Roman catholics | That never went to mass.

Gifford writes (on p. 145): 'Parodies the conventional opening to a *come-all-you* or Irish street ballad: "Come all you loyal [or gallant] Irish / And listen to my song".' To this may be added that the first line, which Simon Dedalus 'began to sing in a grunting nasal tone' at his family's contentious Christmas dinner, had several verbatim antecedents in eighteenth- and nineteenth-century Irish balladry; the second line, apparently, none. One representative example of the opening lines of such ballads, collected by the Irish doctor, writer, abolitionist, and historian R[ichard]. R[obert]. Madden (1798–1886) in his *Literary Remains of The United Irishmen of 1798, and Selections from Other Popular Lyrics of Their Times* (Dublin, 1887), reads, on p. 17: 'Come all you Roman Catholics, | That is both just and true, | I hope you'll pay attention | To those lines I write to you.' Another, from an undated broadside in a university collection, begins: 'Come all you Roman Catholics, | Throughout the British land, | Come join to crush the Tories down, | They're nearly at a stand.' A third example in another such collection, 'The Lamentation of the Rev. Father Campbell', begins: 'Come all you Roman Catholics, | That's in your native home, | Beware of those who do oppose | The holy church of Rome.'

Por 1.1052: *I'm blinded entirely!*

This punch line, so to speak, of Mr Casey's anecdote about his encounter with a virulently anti-Parnellite woman, not unlike Mrs Riordan, into whose eye he purportedly spat a mouthful of tobacco juice seems to have occurred in print only once pre-*Portrait*, in the American journalist and author Ralph D[elahaye]. Paine's (1871–1925) 'Corporal Sweeney, Deserter', first published in *The Century Magazine* (New York and London), vol. 68 (n.s. vol. 46), no. 5 (Sept. 1904)—later collected as chap. 3 of Paine's *The Praying Skipper and Other Stories* (New York, 1906)—with the following passage on pp. 149–50 of the latter version:

> It did not seem possible that the danger of death was menacing in this absurdly small theater of action, yet it could not have been many moments before the deserter began to realize where lay the odds in another hour's exposure to such a storm. All sense of direction had been snatched from him, and he fought only for breath. You Han had no knowledge of desert storms in his home on the bank of the Pei-ho. He gasped whatever prayers came to him, but placed his active faith, still unshaken, in the ability of his master to save him from the choking, freezing terror. The man and the boy were not only stifled, but soon benumbed, for neither had ever felt anything to compare with the searching cold of this blast. They stumbled from one hill to another, sometimes keeping their feet, falling oftener, rising more slowly, the little mule trying in vain to turn tail to the storm.
> There could be no conversation. At length the deserter muttered drowsily to the storm such fragments as these:
> "No place like home. It's the finish that's comin' to me. Cudn't take me medicine like a man. P'rhaps this'll blow over soon. I'm blinded entirely. Good God! forgive me poor cowardly sowl! I niver meant to go wrong. Had to bring that poor fool You Han into this mess."

Por 1.1075–76: an unfortunate priest-ridden race

One of the recorded handful of nearly verbatim, pre-*Portrait* instances of Joyce's phrase occurs in *Hansard's Parliamentary Debates* (London), new series, vol. 20, for 13 Mar. 1829, when the House of Lords took up the question of 'Roman Catholic Claims — Petitions For and Against.' Hansard's entry begins, at column 1006, 'The [Sixth] Duke of *Devonshire* [William George Spencer Cavendish] said, he had two petitions to present to their lordships, praying for the removal of all Civil Disabilities on account of Religious Opinions.' In the course of his remarks, as reported by Hansard, the Duke observed that the proportion of criminal indictments per capita in Ireland was far lower than the comparable figure in England, and continued, at column 1010:

> He felt the more satisfaction in stating this, because he was aware that there were some persons in this country whose imaginations might have been led to conceive that in those countries of Europe where Roman Catholics were admitted to the privileges of the constitution, nothing but persecution and bloodshed prevailed, and they might, therefore, suppose that the same persons would act, in unfortunate and priest-ridden Ireland, nothing but a scene of perpetual lawlessness, vice, and crime. So far from such being really the case, Ireland, as he had stated, exhibited at present comparatively a much more favourable condition than England, with respect to the general state of morality; and he was justified in stating, that if their lordships had before them a comparative statement of the amount of convictions in the two countries, they would find it still more favourable as respected Ireland.

Another such instance occurs in a letter to the editor, signed 'No Peace with Rome', in *The Gospel Magazine* (London), vol. 8, no. 88 (Apr. 1848), 187–88, which begins: 'A great outcry has been set up, and is going the rounds of all the newspapers in England and Ireland, relative to priestly denunciations from the altars of the Roman Catholic chapels in this unfortunate priest-ridden country ; but few seem to have hit on the true merits of the case.'

Por 1.1325–28: *It can't be helped;* | *It must be done.* | *So down with your breeches* | *And out with your bum.*

This schoolboy rhyme, which Athy recites in anticipation of the flogging two of his schoolmates are liable to suffer for a serious departure from proper conduct, begins with two lines that echo verbatim or very nearly so passages in three prior works.

The first of the three, and the least likely to have come to Joyce's notice: 'Swallowing a Fortune', a short story by Howard W. James published in *The Dollar Monthly Magazine* (Boston), vol. 21, no. 6 (June

1865), 481–87, the opening lines of chap. 1 ('Rich or Poor') of which read (italics in the original):

> " It *is* awkward, isn't it? I shall look such a fool !"
> These words were uttered by a young man in a room in one of the principal hotels in Liverpool.
> " It can't be helped. It must be done," was the rejoinder.

The second: a passage in Oliphant's *The Ladies Lindores* (Edinburgh and London, 1883)—about (among others) two sisters the elder of whom, Lady Caroline, is forced to marry a crude, brutish, but wealthy man against her wishes—vol. 1 (of 3), chap. 14, p. 286:

> As for Lord Rintoul, he declared that he understood his father perfectly. " If Beaufort were left out, he'd fill Millefleur's mind with all sorts of prejudices. I'd rather not meet the fellow myself ; but, as it can't be helped, it must be done, I suppose," he said.

As noted in its front matter, Oliphant's novel had originally been serialized in *Blackwood's*—specifically, in the fourteen monthly issues published from April 1882 to May 1883.

The third: in *Vailima Letters, Being Correspondence Addressed By Robert Louis Stevenson to Sidney Colvin, November 1890—October 1894* (London and Chicago, 1895), in which a letter dated 1 January 1892 reads in part, on p. 128:

> For a day or two I have sat close and wrought hard at the *History*, and two more chapters are all but done. About thirty pages should go by this mail, which is not what should be, but all I could overtake. Will any one ever read it ? I fancy not ; people don't read history for reading, but for education and display—and who desires education in the history of Samoa, with no population, no past, no future, or the exploits of Mataafa, Malietoa, and Consul Knappe ? Colkitto and Galasp are a trifle to it. Well, it can't be helped, and it must be done, and, better or worse, it's capital fun.

Sidney Colvin (1845–1927), a British curator and literary and art critic, was Stevenson's friend, literary advisor, and editor. Stevenson died in Vailima, Upolu, Samoa, in December 1894.

As for the third line of Athy's schoolboy rhyme, 'So down with your breeches', that phrase occurs verbatim in, and apparently only in, chap. 1 ('Early Experiences') of the late Lt. Col. Joseph Anderson's *Recollections of a Peninsular Veteran* (London, 1913)—referring to the Peninsular War of 1807–1814, a conflict on the Iberian Peninsula involving Spain, Portugal, and the United Kingdom of Great Britain and Ireland versus Napoleonic France—the first paragraph of which reads in part, on pp. 1–2:

> But before I go any further I must mention an amusing incident which took place before I left Banff Academy to join my regiment, and as in the present day it may not appear much to my credit, I beg my dear ones who may read this to remember I was still a boy, and with less experience of the world than most of the youths of the present day. Out of my pocket money I managed to save six shillings, with which I purchased an old gun to amuse myself, and to shoot sparrows during our play hours ; and this being contrary to all rules and positive standing orders, I kept my dangerous weapon at an old woman's house a little way from town. A few chosen companions knew of my secret and accompanied me one evening to enjoy our sport, but there was one amongst them to whom I refused a shot, so next day he reported me and my gun to the second master. I was called up and questioned on his evidence, when I stoutly and boldly denied every word he said. The good master, Mr. Simpson, then said, " You have told a lie, sir, and I must punish you ; so down with your breeches."

I have found no literary or other antecedent for the rhyme's fourth line, 'And out with your bum', but perhaps it was suggested by the poem-like scansion and rhyme in the last sentence of the quoted passage in Stevenson's letter to Colvin: 'Well, it can't be helped, and it must be done, and, better or worse, it's capital fun.'

Portrait, Chapter 2

Por 2.20: *Blue eyes and golden hair*

Matthew J. C. Hodgart and Mabel P. Worthington, on p. 176 of their *Song in the Works of James Joyce* (New York, 1959), list Joyce's phrase as the title of a song by the Irish composer James L. Molloy (1837–1909). Commenting on that citation, Gifford notes that while Molloy did write a song entitled 'Blue Eyes'—the lyrics of which Gifford quotes at length—'the golden hair seems to be missing'.

In fact, two pre-*Portrait* songs, both of American origin, do contain the phrase 'blue eyes and golden hair'. The earlier of the two, 'Kate O'Shane', with words by Dexter Smith (1839–1909), music by J[ohn]. R[ogers]. Thomas (1829–1896), published by S. Brainard & Sons, Cleveland, in 1858—and not to be confused with the song of the same name (1842) with words and music by the English verse-writer and musical composer George Linley (1797–1865)—reads:

> 1.
> There's a lass of beauty rare,
> With blue eyes and golden hair
> One who meets me often in the shady lane;
> And she loves me well I know,
> Tho' she's never told me so,
> And I know I dearly love sweet Kate O'Shane,
> There's a charm about the girl,
> More than dainty eye or curl;
> More than all that lover's fancies may beguile,
> 'Tis a good and loving heart
> That from me will never part

I can read it in her happy truthful smile.

Chorus
There's a lass of beauty rare,
With blue eyes and golden hair,
One who meets me often in the shady lane,
And she loves me well I know,
Tho' she never told me so,
And I know I dearly love sweet Kate O'Shane.

2.
Come there sunshine or come storm
There's a gentle fairy form
That will ever cheer life's path as forth we go;
Come then sadness or come joy,
There's a peace without alloy,
For the hearts that ever trust each other so,
Those blue eyes may gently fade,
As we go down earth's fair glade,
And the soft hair lose its tint of brightest gold,
Yet along life's varied strand
As we wander hand in hand
We shall never, never let our hearts grow old.

Chorus

The later of the two—cited by Marc A. Mamigonian and John Turner in their annotated edition of *Portrait* (Richmond, Surrey: Alma Classics, 2018), p. 233—is the minstrel song 'Blue Eyes and Golden Hair: Double Song and Dance', with words and music by J. M. Thatcher (Nashville, Tennessee), published by Jas. A. McClure of that city in 1871, and with Joyce's phrase occurring both as the song's main title and at the beginning and end of its chorus. But the references in that chorus to 'A brownstone front on Broadway' and 'A cottage at Cape May' would seem to make it less likely that this was the song Joyce had in mind.

Although Joyce refers to 'Blue eyes and golden hair' *as* a song, the phrase also occurs in several works of prose and poetry, among them the English novelist and social critic Charles Dickens's (1812–1870) historical novel *A Tale of Two Cities* (London, 1859), book 3 ('The Track of a Storm'), chap. 44 ('The Knitting Dome'); and the Irish physician and poet Richard D'Alton Williams's (1822–1862) poignant and much-reprinted poem 'The Dying Girl' (1851), based on his experience as a medical student at St. Vincent's Hospital, Dublin, and specifically on his encounter there with a fatally ill patient named Jessy, a victim—as Dr Williams would himself be two decades later—of tuberculosis.

Por 2.92: dark avenger

While the phrase is applicable, as Gifford (p. 159) suggests, to Edmond Dantès as represented in the French novelist and playwright Alexandre Dumas *père*'s (1802–1870) adventure novel *The Count of Monte Cristo* (Paris, 1846)—and while the phrase occurs in several nineteenth-century poems and plays—Joyce may also have encountered it in the English poet and peer George Gordon Lord Byron's (1788–1824) early poem 'Childish Recollections', recounting his friends and friendships as a student at Harrow beginning in 1801, and included during his lifetime in (and only in) the first, private edition of his first volume of poetry, *Hours of Idleness* (London, 1807).[2] The lines containing the phrase, near the end of the poem, read:

> Mix'd in the concourse of the thoughtless throng,
> A mourner midst of mirth, I glide along ;
> A wretched, isolated, gloomy thing,
> Curst by reflection's deep-corroding sting ;
> But not that mental sting which stabs within,
> The dark avenger of unpunish'd sin[.]

Por 2.93: strange and terrible

The sentence in *Portrait* in which 'dark avenger' occurs reads in its entirety: 'The figure of that dark avenger stood forth in his mind for whatever he had heard or divined in childhood of the strange and terrible.' And indeed, stories of strange and terrible creatures and events were a staple of the popular fiction of the day, including in such sensation novels as Marie Corelli's *The Soul of Lilith* (London, 1892) and Lord Lytton's *A Strange Story* (London, 1901). But even when Stephen and his creator

---

[2] Passages from 'Childish Recollections' were, however, included in several posthumous collections of Byron's works, among them Thomas Moore's seventeen-volume edition (London, 1833), where the poem's concluding lines are reprinted in vol. 7, pp. 145–46.

developed a taste for more serious literature, they did not need to leave their taste for the strange and terrible behind. Shakespeare's *Antony and Cleopatra*, Act 4, scene 15—midway through which Antony enters and dies—begins with Cleopatra and her maid Charmian engaged in a grim conversation on a familiar topic:

> Cleo.   O Charmian, I will never go from hence.
> Char.   Be comforted, dear madam.
> Cleo.   No, I will not.
> All strange and terrible events are welcome,
> But comforts we despise; our size of sorrow,
> Proportion'd to our cause, must be as great
> As that which makes it.[3]

And in the Maude translation of Tolstoy's *Resurrection*—which, as discussed above (see p. 43), may have inspired Joyce's inclusion of the 'young man in a cycling suit' in his short story 'Grace'—we find as the heading of chapter 35 another reference to the strange and terrible, 'Not Men But Strange and Terrible Creatures?', after which, in the chapter itself, in which Prince Nekhlúdov visits the prison in which the innocent Maslova is confined, the phrase recurs in the third paragraph:

> On they went, all dressed alike, moving a thousand feet all shod alike, swinging their free arms as if to keep up their spirits. There were so many of them, they all looked so much alike, and they were all placed in such unusual, peculiar circumstances, that they seemed to Nekhlúdoff to be not men but some sort of strange and terrible creatures.

Por 2.105: a long train of adventures

While young Stephen Dedalus associates the phrase with the adventures of Edmond Dantès in *The Count of Monte Cristo*, Joyce himself may have borrowed it from another work of romantic fiction: *The Arabian Nights' Entertainments*—also commonly known as *One Thousand and One Nights* or simply the *Arabian Nights*—in which, in the several English-language

---

3   All Shakespeare quotations herein, and all associated line numbers, are based on the text in *The Riverside Shakespeare*, ed. by G. Blakemore Evans (Boston: Houghton Mifflin, 1997).

editions of the work published over the course of the eighteenth and nineteenth centuries, the tale for the 184th night reads in part, with minor variations:

> Thus the sultaness finished this long train of adventures, to which the pretended death of Hump-back gave occasion ; then held her peace, because day appeared. Upon which her sister Dinarzade says to her, My princess, my sultaness, I am so much the more charmed with the story you just now told, because it concludes with an incident I did not expect. I verily thought Hump-back was dead.

Another, less familiar instance of the phrase occurs in the novel *Hannah Hewit: or, The Female Crusoe* (London, 1792)—'supposed to be written by herself', the title page asserts, but actually written by the English composer, musician, dramatist, novelist, singer, and actor Charles Dibdin (1745–1814)—with, in vol. 3 (of 3), book 6 ('The Adventures of Hannah Hewit from the Moment She Had a Glimpse of Hope to the Completion of Her Happiness'), chap. 1 ('In Which Hannah Hewit and the Reader Are Introduced to Some Old Acquaintance'), pp. 137–38: 'Binns took the sailors with him, and I was left with my brother, Walmesley, and Hewit ; who now, at my earnest desire, proceeded to relate a long train of adventures, having, in answer to my anxious enquiry, first satisfied me that my son was alive and in perfect health.'

Por 2.118: taking counsel with his lieutenant

The sentence in which this phrase occurs, in lines 116–19, reads in its entirety: 'Stephen, who had read of Napoleon's plain style of dress, chose to remain unadorned and thereby heightened for himself the pleasure of taking counsel with his lieutenant before giving orders.' What appears to be the sole nearly verbatim antecedent of the highlighted phrase occurred in a serialized story of school life called 'The Dis-Order of the Bath', by the Anglican cleric, schoolmaster, and author Rev. A[rthur]. N[oel]. Malan (1846–1933), as published in *The Boy's Own Paper* by the London-based Religious Tract Society, where chap. 5, in vol. 14, no. 668 (31 Oct. 1891), begins on p. 67 with the following two paragraphs:

> The appearance of such an unaccustomed visitor as a fire-engine occasioned no small interest among the scattered inhabitants of that rural district. It may possibly be remembered that the school was

situated at some distance from the village of Deepwells, but there were galaxies of cottages dotted about in the more immediate vicinity, and from these all the inmates who could find leisure came out to see the sight. Old men with sticks, old women with babies, young men and young women, boys and girls, soon mustered in troops on the shores of the pond.

Captain Blazer made a cursory inspection of the ground, and a look of puzzled anxiety brooded on his swarthy countenance. He took counsel with his lieutenant and corporal. He told the doctor that it was a formidable job—but they would do their best ; and then he proceeded to practical operations.

Por 2.245: embittered silence

Joyce's phrase occurs in a sentence, beginning at line 243, that reads: 'He went once or twice with his mother to visit their relatives: and, though they passed a jovial array of shops lit up and adorned for Christmas, his mood of embittered silence did not leave him.'

One of the several prior instances of the phrase that Joyce is likely to have seen occurred in the French novelist and playwright Honoré de Balzac's (1799–1850) short story 'La Paix du ménage'—first published in 1830 as one of his *Scènes de la vie privée* (Scenes of private life), later as one of the many tales gathered in Balzac's *La Comédie humaine* (1842)—where the tale as translated by Ellen Marriage and Clara Bell and published under various titles including 'Domestic Peace', 'Household Peace', and 'Peace in the House', reads under the last of these titles, in vol. 10 (of 34) of *La Comédie humaine* (London: 1896), edited by George Saintsbury, at pp. 349–50:

> ["]Why do you look at me with so much amazement ? Listen to me. If you want to play with men, do not try to wring the hearts of any but those whose life is not yet settled, who have no duties to fulfill ; the others do not forgive us for the errors that have made them happy. Profit by this maxim, founded on my long experience. —That luckless Soulanges, for instance, whose head you have turned, whom you have intoxicated for these fifteen months past, God knows how ! Do you know at what you have struck ? —At his whole life. He has been married these two years ; he is worshiped by a charming wife, whom he loves, but neglects ; she lives in tears and embittered

II. A PORTRAIT OF THE ARTIST AS A YOUNG MAN

silence.⁴ Soulanges has had hours of remorse more terrible than his pleasure has been sweet. And you, you artful little thing, have deserted him. —Well, come and see your work."

Another occurred in the Polish-British novelist and short story writer Joseph Conrad's (1857–1924) novella 'Typhoon', serialized in *The Pall Mall Magazine* (London) from January to March 1902, later published in Conrad's *Typhoon and Other Stories* (London, 1903), and reading, in chap. 4, p. 60, of the latter:

> The boatswain found himself overwhelmed with reproaches of all sorts. They seemed to take it ill that a lamp was not instantly created for them out of nothing. They would whine after a light to get drowned by—anyhow ! And though the unreason of their revilings was patent—since no one could hope to reach the lamp-room, which was forward—he became greatly distressed. He did not think it was decent of them to be nagging at him like this. He told them so, and was met by general contumely. He sought refuge, therefore, in an embittered silence.

And a third, in the English novelist, playwright, and journalist Arnold Bennett's (1867–1931) *Clayhanger* (London, 1910)—the first of four coming-of-age novels comprising The Clayhanger Family series whose central character is Edwin Clayhanger—where the first paragraph of vol. 2, chap. 17 ('Challenge and Response') ends:

> The potters were on strike, and a Bursley contingent was returning in embittered silence from a mass meeting at Hanbridge. When the sound of the steam-car subsided, as the car dipped over the hill-top on its descent towards Hanbridge, nothing could be heard but the tramp-tramp of the procession on the road.

Por 2.313–14: the feverish agitation of his blood

This six-word phrase occurs midway through a long sentence that begins, at *Portrait* 2.311: 'The mirth, which in the beginning of the evening had seemed to him false and trivial, was like a soothing air to him, passing gaily by his senses, hiding from other eyes the feverish agitation of his blood'. The same phrase had previously occurred verbatim in *Marceau's Prisoner*, a novella by Alexandre Dumas *père* anonymously translated

---

4 This sentence translating Balzac's 'elle vit dans les larmes et dans le silence le plus amer'.

from the French original, *Blanche de Beaulieu, ou la vendéenne* (1826), first published in *The Strand Magazine* (London), vol. 4, June to Dec. 1892, set in Napoleonic France in 1793, featuring as protagonist the young republican general Alexandre Marceau, and reading in issue 19 (June 1892), chap. 3, pp. 11–12: 'Yet from time to time a vague uneasiness tormented him ; a sudden chill struck cold upon his heart. He spurred on the postillions by lavish promises of gold, and the horses flew along the road. Everything seemed to partake of the feverish agitation of his blood.'

Por 2.622: gloomy tenderness

Joyce's phrase appeared in print several times over the course of the nineteenth and early twentieth centuries, but the two instances he seems most likely to have read occurred in the English novelist and poet Thomas Hardy's (1840–1928) last-completed novel *Jude the Obscure* (London, 1895) and the English novelist, poet, and literary critic D. H. Lawrence's (1885–1930) novel *The Trespasser* (London, 1912).

In the former, the passage containing the phrase, in part 5 ('At Aldbrickham and Elsewhere'), chap. 3, reads:

> He found the way to the little lane, and knocked at the door of Jude's house. Jude had just retired to bed, and Sue was about to enter her chamber adjoining when she heard the knock and came down.
> " Is this where father lives ?" asked the child.
> " Who ?"
> " Mr. Fawley, that's his name."
> Sue ran up to Jude's room and told him, and he hurried down as soon as he could, though to her impatience he seemed long.
> " What—is it he—so soon ?" she asked, as Jude came.
> She scrutinized the child's features, and suddenly went away into the little sitting-room adjoining. Jude lifted the boy to a level with himself, keenly regarded him with gloomy tenderness, and telling him he would have been met if they had known of his coming so soon, set him provisionally in a chair whilst he went to look for Sue, whose super-sensitiveness was disturbed, as he knew. He found her in the dark, bending over an arm-chair. He enclosed her with his arm, and putting his face by hers, whispered,
> " What's the matter?"
> " What Arabella says is true — true ! I see you in him !"

In the latter, the phrase occurs in chap. 5, p. 38:

> When Helena entered the room his eyes sought hers swiftly, as sparks lighting on the tinder. But her eyes were only moist with tenderness. His look instantly changed. She wondered at his being so silent, so strange.
> Coming to him in her unhesitating, womanly way—she was only twenty-six to his thirty-eight—she stood before him, holding both his hands and looking down on him with an almost gloomy tenderness. She wore a white dress that showed her throat gathering like a fountain-jet of solid foam to balance her head. He could see the full white arms passing clear through the dripping spume of lace, towards the rise of her breasts. But her eyes bent down upon him with such gloom of tenderness that he dared not reveal the passion burning in him.

Por 2.839: intangible phantoms

The sentence in which Joyce's phrase occurs reads in its entirety: 'While his mind had been pursuing its intangible phantoms and turning in irresolution from such pursuit he had heard about him the constant voices of his father and of his masters, urging him to be a gentleman above all things and urging him to be a good catholic above all things.' Among the several instances of the phrase appearing in print in the second half of the nineteenth century, one that Joyce is likely to have seen occurs in the translation of Goethe's *Faust* by Anna Swanwick (London, 1879), in which the Chorus of captive Trojan women sings, in part 2, Act 3, lines 623–34, of Faust's approaching doom:

> All itself over-shrouds,
> Wrapt in vapour and mist :
> Gaze on each other can we not !
> What befalls ? Do we walk ?
> Hover we now,
> Tripping with light steps over the ground ?
> Seest thou naught ? Floats not us before
> Hermes perchance ? Gleams not his golden wand,
> Bidding, commanding us back to return,
> Back to yon joyless realm, dusky and grey,
> With intangible phantoms teeming,
> The o'ercrowded, yet aye-empty Hades ?

If Joyce did not see it there, he could also have seen it in Albert G. Latham's translation of the same work (London, 1905), where the corresponding lines read, on p. 211:

> Now already with mist
> All is shrouded about.
> Nay, but we see each other not !
> What betides ? Do we walk ?
> Hover we but
> Lightsomely tripping along the ground ?
> Seest thou naught ? Floateth haply e'en
> Hermes before ? Gleams not the golden wand,
> Bidding, commanding us backward again,
> To the undelectable, gray-glimmering,
> With intangible phantoms crowded,
> Over-crowded, ever-empty Hades ?

Portrait, Chapter 3

Por 3.849: antlike men

Joyce's phrase occurs in a passage of *Portrait* reading: 'What did it profit a man to gain the whole world if he lost his soul? At last he had understood: and human life lay around him, a plain of peace whereon antlike men laboured in brotherhood, their dead sleeping under quiet mounds.' The first quoted sentence, as has been noted, is a nearly verbatim echo of two familiar scriptural verses: Matthew xvi 26 and Mark viii 36. Less familiar is the possible source of the highlighted phrase in the second sentence: a novella by Joseph Conrad entitled 'Gaspar Ruiz: The Story of a Guerilla Chief' first serialized in *The Pall Mall Magazine*, vol. 38 (July to Oct. 1906), later collected as the first tale in Conrad's *A Set of Six* (London, 1908), and reading, on p. 26 of the latter:

> A red and unclouded sun setting into a purple ocean looked with a fiery stare upon the enormous wall of the Cordilleras, worthy witnesses of his glorious extinction. But it is inconceivable that it should have seen the antlike men busy with their absurd and insignificant trials of killing and dying for reasons that, apart from being generally childish, were also imperfectly understood. It did light up, however, the backs of the firing party and the faces of the condemned men. Some of them had fallen on their knees, others remained standing, a few averted their heads from the levelled barrels of muskets. Gaspar Ruiz, upright, the burliest of them all, hung his big shock head. The low sun dazzled him a little, and he counted himself a dead man already.
>
> He fell at the first discharge. He fell because he thought he was a dead man. He struck the ground heavily. The jar of the fall surprised him. "I am not dead apparently," he thought to himself, when he heard

the execution platoon reloading its arms at the word of command. It was then that the hope of escape dawned upon him for the first time. He remained lying stretched out with rigid limbs under the weight of two bodies collapsed crosswise upon his back.

Gaspar Ruiz's miraculous survival, without injury, from all but certain death by firing squad may have struck Joyce as an apt metaphor for Stephen's hope to be saved from the gulf of death for his sins through the intercession of the Virgin Mary—a hope expressed in the short paragraph immediately preceding the one partially quoted above—possibly explaining the presence of 'antlike men' in both works. Without the presence of 'antlike men' where the phrase occurs in the two works, however, any suggestion that the two passages may have been thematically and, by Joyce, deliberately linked would have seemed dubious at best.[5]

---

5 A note dated 9 March 1910 that Joyce sent to Stanislaus when both were living in Trieste (*Letters*, II, 282–83) reads in part: 'I wish you would save me these continual rows as I have already too many worries. I will take *A Set of Six*. Leave it out for me and Bartoli's magazine.'

Portrait, Chapter 4

Por 4.783–84: an ecstasy of fear

The passage in which Joyce's phrase occurs reads: 'His heart trembled; his breath came faster and a wild spirit passed over his limbs as though he were soaring sunward. His heart trembled in an ecstasy of fear and his soul was in flight.' Among the several prior instances of the phrase, the earliest may have been in Coleridge's play *Remorse: A Tragedy, in Five Acts* (1813), Act 4, scene 1, where a stage direction referring to the character Isidore reads 'He goes out of sight, opposite to the patch of moonlight: returns after a minute's elapse, in an ecstasy of fear.'

One subsequent instance of the phrase occurs in the American essayist and poet Ralph Waldo Emerson's (1803–1882) *Society and Solitude: Twelve Chapters* (London, 1870), where the essay entitled 'Art', on pp. 31–49, reads on p. 32:

> The utterance of thought and emotion in speech and action may be conscious or unconscious. The sucking child is an unconscious actor. The man in an ecstasy of fear or anger is an unconscious actor. A large part of our habitual actions are unconsciously done, and most of our necessary words are unconsciously said.

Another instance: in the British writer and physician Sir Arthur Conan Doyle's (1859–1930) detective novel—the second featuring Sherlock Holmes—*The Sign of Four* (London, 1890), with, in chap. 4, 'The Story of the Bald-Headed Man', on p. 49: 'I listened to his heart, as requested, but was unable to find anything amiss, save, indeed, that he was in an ecstasy of fear, for he shivered from head to foot.'

Portrait, Chapter 5

Por 5.213: great dull stone

Joyce's phrase, in a sentence beginning 'The grey block of Trinity on his left, set heavily in the city's ignorance like a great dull stone set in a cumbrous ring, pulled his mind downward [...]', had occurred previously and possibly uniquely pre-*Portrait* in, and may thus have been suggested by, the English author and traveller Frances Mary Peard's (1835–1923) 'Under the Mountain', a story first published in *The Cornhill Magazine* (London), vol. 24, no. 139 (July 1871), 63–85; in several other periodicals also that year; and later collected in Peard's *A Madrigal and Other Stories* (London, 1876), 51–98. The sentence by Peard in which the phrase occurs, on p. 72 of *The Cornhill* (minus the word 'grave') and p. 70 of *A Madrigal*, reads: '["]Look," he said, smiling a little grave sad smile, "thou art like the beautiful clear water that rushes down, evermore down to the lake, and I am like the great dull stone it dashes over."'

Por 5.1299: benevolent malice

The oxymoron occurs in a sentence referring to the 'fat young man' named Donovan who is a classmate of Stephen's and who provides him with a report on the just-released results of the university's civil service exams: 'His pallid bloated face expressed benevolent malice and, as he had advanced through his tidings of success, his small fatencircled eyes vanished out of sight and his weak wheezing voice out of hearing.' The same phrase had already appeared at least three times pre-*Portrait*: first, in *Clan-Albin: A National Tale* (London, 1815), anonymously published but by the Scottish journalist and editor Christian Isobel Johnstone (1781–1857), reading, in vol. 2 (of 4), chap. 22, on pp. 59–60 of that edition, and p. 114 of the Edinburgh edition also published that year:

> Meanwhile, Montague gave her the warmest assurances of kindness and protection ; and, as she firmly refused all pecuniary obligation, he could only contribute to what he thought her happiness, by expensive and useless presents, and by throwing around her, as far as he could, the same appearance of splendour which had distinguished her during the life of his brother. These, and some other circumstances, excited suspicion in her mind ; she formed conjectures not very far from the truth, and anticipated, with benevolent malice, her future triumphant refutation of the calumnies of her relations, and the pride she would feel in showing them, that he who made her rich, had also made her happy by well-judged concealment.

It seems next to have occurred in the Irish novelist and short story writer George Moore's (1852–1933) *Vain Fortune*, 'new edition completely revised' (London, 1895), in which, on pp. 64–65, its central character, the aspiring playwright Hubert Price, scans an article about his latest work in the (fictitious) periodical *The Modern Review*, reading in part:

> The article began with a sketch of the general situation, and in a tone of commiseration, of benevolent malice, the writer pointed out how inevitable it was that the critics should have taken Mr. Price, when *Divorce* was first produced, for the new dramatic genius they were waiting for. 'There comes a moment,' said this caustic writer, 'in the affairs of men when the new is not only eagerly accepted, but when it is confounded with the original.[']

Its apparently third pre-*Portrait* instance occurred in an essay by the British poet, critic, and magazine editor Arthur Symons (1865–1945) on the novels of the French writer and art critic Joris-Karl Huysmans (1848–1907) published in the March 1892 issue of *The Fortnightly Review* (London) and later excerpted in Symons's *The Symbolist Movement in Literature* (London, 1899), pp. 191–92:

> " To realise how faithfully and how completely Huysmans has revealed himself in all he has written, it is necessary to know the man. ' He gave me the impression of a cat,' some interviewer once wrote of him ; ' courteous, perfectly polite, almost amiable, but all

nerves, ready to shoot out his claws at the least word.' And, indeed, there is something of his favourite animal about him. The face is grey, wearily alert, with a look of benevolent malice. At first sight it is commonplace, the features are ordinary, one seems to have seen it at the Bourse or the Stock Exchange. But gradually that strange, unvarying expression, that look of benevolent malice, grows upon you, as the influence of the man makes itself felt.["]

Por 5.1329–30: a strong suspicion, amounting almost to a conviction

Taking leave of Stephen, his portly, rather arrogant classmate Donovan says 'softly and benevolently' that he must go: 'I have a strong suspicion, amounting almost to a conviction, that my sister intended to make pancakes today for the dinner of the Donovan family.' By the time Joyce wrote *Portrait*, the phrase 'amounting almost to a conviction' was a well-worn cliché, usually preceded by I had or have a fear, feeling, foreboding, impression, or the like. A rare pre-*Portrait* instance in which the cliché is preceded, as in *Portrait*, by 'I have a suspicion', with or without the modifier 'strong', occurs in the Scottish author, poet, and Christian Congregational minister George MacDonald's (1824–1905) novel *The Vicar's Daughter: An Autobiographical Story* (London, 1872), vol. 1 (of 3), chap. 18 ('Miss Clare'), p. 285: '" Describe the place to me, Wynnie," he said, when I had ended. " I must go and see her. I have a suspicion amounting almost to a conviction that she is one whose acquaintance ought to be cultivated at any cost. There is some grand explanation of all this contradictory strangeness."'

Por 5.2218–19: the grey spouse of Satan

In his comment on the phrase (subsequently echoed by Riquelme and others) Gifford (on p. 274) writes: 'In Milton's *Paradise Lost*, book 2, Satan encounters his daughter-wife Sin and the son of their incest, Death, at the gates of Hell', but adds: 'she is not described [there] as "grey" but as "fair" above and "foul" below.' In fact, Joyce's 'grey spouse of Satan' seems to point not to *Paradise Lost* but to the English poet, playwright, novelist, and critic Algernon Charles Swinburne's (1837–1909) poem 'Giordano Bruno 9 June 1889'—written upon the erection on that date, in

Rome's Campo dei Fiori, of a statue of the Dominican friar, philosopher, poet, and cosmological theorist burned at the stake for heresy in 1600 by the Roman Inquisition, and retitled 'The Monument of Giordano Bruno' when the poem was collected in Swinburne's *Astrophel and Other Poems* (London, 1894)—where the highlighted phrase occurs, on p. 182, in the second line of the second, fourteen-line stanza:

> Cover thine eyes and weep, O child of hell,
>   Grey spouse of Satan, Church of name abhorred.
>   Weep, withered harlot, with thy weeping lord,
> Now none will buy the heaven thou hast to sell
> At price of prostituted souls, and swell
>   Thy loveless list of lovers. Fire and sword
>   No more are thine : the steel, the wheel, the cord,
> The flames that rose round living limbs, and fell
> In lifeless ash and ember, now no more
>   Approve thee godlike. Rome, redeemed at last
>   From all the red pollution of thy past,
> Acclaims the grave bright face that smiled of yore
>   Even on the fire that caught it round and clomb
>   To cast its ashes on the face of Rome.

Por 5.2729: from dreams to dreamless sleep

The passage in which this phrase occurs, dated 10 April, begins: 'Faintly, under the heavy night, through the silence of the city which has turned from dreams to dreamless sleep as a weary lover whom no caresses move, the sound of hoofs upon the road.' Mamigonian and Turner note (on p. 311 of their Alma Books edition) that the passage in its entirety 'reproduces with minor variations Joyce's Epiphany no. 27 (*Workshop of Daedalus*, p. 37)'; Gifford (on p. 286), that in 'a curious and probably anachronistic coincidence', Joyce's 'from dreams to dreamless sleep' anticipates a passage in the Irish poet, dramatist, writer, and politician W[illiam]. B[utler]. Yeats's (1865–1939) *A Vision* (privately published, 1925). In another possible—though not anachronistic—coincidence, Joyce's phrase had previously occurred verbatim in the novel *Wilfred Montressor: or the Secret Order of the Seven. A Romance of Life in the New York Metropolis* (New York, 1848), by the American author and publisher Charles Jacobs Peterson (1819–1887), the final chapter (8) of which, 'The Triennial Meeting', begins:

> Curious and fantastical are the dreams of the dreamer. He digs in the ground, like a mole ; he roams over the earth, like a deer ; he flies through the air, like an eagle. He laughs with the daughters of mirth—he weeps with the children of sorrow. Coffers of gold and precious stones are his, and a kingly crown and thrones of ivory ; also rags, and muck, and noisome distempers. He flies from dreams to dreamless sleep—when a thousand years are as a moment, and a moment as a thousand years—from dreamless sleep to waking. Like sparks of golden fire sculptured into the likenesses of angels, are the dreams of the dreamer at the moment of waking.

The phrase 'dreamless sleep' alone occurred, among many other instances, in Byron's 'Elegy On Thyrza' (1811)—thought, despite the feminine name in the title, to have been written for his late friend John Edleston—stanza 4 of which reads:

> The better days of life were ours ;
>   The worst can be but mine :
> The sun that cheers, the storm that lours
>   Shall never more be thine.
> The silence of that dreamless sleep
> I envy now too much to weep ;
>   Nor need I to repine
> That all those charms have pass'd away
> I might have watch'd through long decay.

and in the first English translation, by William Archer (London, 1900), of the Norwegian playwright Henrik Ibsen's (1828–1906) last-written play *When We Dead Awaken: A Dramatic Epilogue in Three Acts* (1899), where in Act 1, p. 57, its central character, the sculptor Professor Rubek, having been unexpectedly reunited after several years with the now half-mad and homicidal woman, Irene, who had been the model for and inspiration of the masterpiece responsible for his subsequent fame and fortune, tells her:

> Thanks and praise be to you, I achieved my great task. I wanted to embody the pure woman as I saw her awakening on the Resurrection Day. Not marvelling at anything new and unknown and undivined ; but filled with a sacred joy at finding herself unchanged—she, the woman of earth—in the higher, freer, happier region—after the long, dreamless sleep of death. [*More softly*] Thus did I fashion her.—I fashioned her in your image, Irene.[6]

---

[6] See my note on *Uly* 10.1074–75 for further details on William Archer.

III.

ULYSSES

1. 'Telemachus'

Uly 1.6: Halted, he peered down the dark winding stairs

Dark winding stairs have made many literary appearances since the early eighteenth century, from the Anglo-Irish author, poet, and cleric Jonathan Swift's (1667–1745) satirical treatise *A Tale of a Tub, Written for the Universal Improvement of Mankind* (London, 1704) with, in 'The Bookseller's Dedication to Lord Somers': 'From thence I went to several other Wits of my Acquaintance, with no small Hazard and Weariness to my Person, from a prodigious Number of dark, winding Stairs'; to the American novelist, essayist, and short story writer F. Scott Fitzgerald's (1896–1940) story 'May Day', first published in the New York-based monthly literary magazine *The Smart Set*, vol. 62 (July 1920), then collected in his *Tales of the Jazz Age* (New York, 1922), with, on p. 81: 'They followed him out the far door, through a deserted pantry and up a pair of dark winding stairs, emerging finally into a small room chiefly furnished by piles of pails and stacks of scrubbing brushes, and illuminated by a single dim electric light.'

One instance in particular that may have recommended the phrase to Joyce for use in the opening lines of *Ulysses* occurs in Charles Dickens's *Little Dorrit* (London, 1857). There, in the final paragraph of book 2 ('Riches'), chap. 20 ('Introduces the next'), speaking of Arthur Clennam—the kindly, middle-aged man who loves and will ultimately marry the novel's heroine, Amy Dorrit—Dickens describes Clennam's state of mind in a way perfectly matching that of Stephen Dedalus even before Stephen has climbed the dark winding stairs of the Martello tower he shares with Mulligan and first stepped into the novel: 'He came down the dark winding stairs into the yard, with an increased sense upon him of the gloom of the wall that was dead, and of the shrubs that were dead, and of the fountain that was dry, and of the statue that was gone.'

Uly 1.152–53: He fears the lancet of my art as I fear that of his. The cold steel pen.

An early instance of 'cold steel pen' was collected in *George Cruikshank's Table-Book* (London, 1845), edited by Gilbert Abbott à Beckett, a compendium of etchings by Cruikshank (1792–1878), the English caricaturist and book illustrator whose work often appeared in *Punch, or the London Charivari,* and in the novels of his friend Charles Dickens. In 'A Cold Love Letter', an anonymous entry on pp. 89–90 of that collection, two drawings by Cruikshank illustrate a playful letter to 'My Dearest Alice' from 'Your own Horatio' replete with references to the cold, coldness, frost, and the like, and ending with a paragraph reading:

> I would have written the above [poem, entitled 'A Sonnet to the Frost'] in your album with my own hand, but I'm sure you would be the last person to expect me to come out for the purpose of fetching the book. You ask me to write to say when I am coming. I know you will excuse my writing when I tell you it is very uncomfortable to have to hold a cold steel pen between my fingers. The thermometer, dearest, will indicate to you when you may expect to see [signed] Your own HORATIO.

Another instance of the phrase, and one more apposite in tone to Stephen's remark on himself and Mulligan, occurs in the London-based weekly humorous magazine *Fun*, founded in 1861 as a competitor to *Punch*. In vol. 34, new series, no. 861 (9 Nov. 1881), p. 190, the anonymous column 'Floats and Flies' for that date begins: 'The notion that the theatrical critic is an inhuman savage, with an insatiable thirst for prey, and with a heart as hard and cold as his hard and cold steel pen, and bitter as the ink he dips it in, is an erroneous notion.'

But Joyce could also have had in mind the phrase as it appears in Thomas Hardy's *The Woodlanders* (London, 1887), vol. 1 (of 3), chap. 8, p. 148—after the novel's serialization in *Macmillan's Magazine* from May 1886 to April 1887—in which Mrs Charmond confides to Grace Melbury:

> " Now I am often impelled to record my impressions of times and places. I have often thought of writing a *New Sentimental Journey*. But I cannot find energy enough to do it alone. When I am at different places in the south of Europe I feel a crowd of ideas and fancies thronging upon me continually ; but to unfold writing materials, take up a cold steel pen, and put these impressions down systematically on cold smooth paper—that I cannot do.["]

Uly 1.198–99: *O, it's only Dedalus whose mother is beastly dead.*

As noted by SMT, p. 14, Turner and Mamigonian had previously written: 'We can deduce that Gogarty really did say this to Joyce from a bitter remark of Joyce's in a 1907 letter to Stanislaus: "The news is that O. G.'s mother is 'beastly dead' and that O. G. is very rich" (*Letters*, vol. 2, p. 206).'[1] If so, Gogarty, Joyce, or both may have borrowed the phrase from the American bibliographer, editor, and translator George Burnham Ives's (1856–1930) translation of the French naturalist writer Alphonse Daudet's (1840–1897) novel *L'Immortel* (Paris, 1888), as *The Immortal* (Boston, 1899), chap. 5, p. 101: 'It is as if some one were amusing himself, during his absence, by pulling down what he has built. — Who can it be? — The dead man, of course ! that beastly dead man. It is absolutely necessary to be there by her side, from morning till night ; but how is one to do it, with the demands of life, work to be done, and so much running about after money?'

That the expression 'beastly dead' was in common usage around the time of Ives's translation is suggested by its occurrence in another book published four years later: *Debonnair Dick* (London and Sydney, 1892), by the English novelist Anne Florence Louisa Patton-Bethune (1865–1894), as 'Florence Patton-Bethune', chap. 4, pp. 63–64:

> " Bah ! " said Hugh Mitford, making a very wry face one day, after a desperate hand-to-hand encounter during a reconnaissance ; " I saw three or four beastly dead Egyptians floating in the canal when I went to get a drink."

---

1 Turner, John and Marc A. Mamigonian, 'Solar Patriot: Oliver St. John Gogarty in *Ulysses*', *James Joyce Quarterly*, vol. 41, no. 4 (Summer 2004), 639–40.

" How very unpleasant," answered Macpherson. " However, it's the only water we've got, and one's jolly glad to get a drink of any description out here."

Patton-Bethune, a family history states, died at the age of twenty–nine, shortly after the publication of her second novel, Bachelor to the Rescue (London, 1894), 'from injuries after being thrown from her dog-cart in Hyde Park.'

Uly 1.273–74: Her glazing eyes, staring out of death, to shake and bend my soul. On me alone.

Commenting on the latter phrase, both Gifford and SMT cite Horatio's words to Hamlet regarding his father's ghost: 'It beckons you to go away with it, | As if it some impartment did desire | To you alone.' (I iv 58–60). But the phrase 'On me alone' occurs both verbatim and often in English literature, including (among other instances) in the English poet, literary critic, translator, and playwright John Dryden's (1631–1700) 'Annus Mirabilis' (1667), stanza 265: '"Or if my heedless youth has stepped astray, | Too soon forgetful of Thy gracious hand, | On me alone Thy just displeasure lay, | But take Thy judgments from this mourning land.["]'; and in the English poet, painter, and printmaker William Blake's (1757–1827) poem 'The Rime of the Ancient Mariner' (1834 version), part 6, lines 51–54: 'Swiftly, swiftly flew the ship, | Yet she sailed softly too : | Sweetly, sweetly blew the breeze— | On me alone it blew.'

Uly 1.449: Pay up and look pleasant

This cliché occurred widely in England from the mid-nineteenth to and beyond the early twentieth centuries, as often in general-interest as in trade publications. One notable instance: in *The Chequers: Being the Natural History of a Public-house, set forth in A Loafer's Diary* (London, 1888), by the English schoolmaster, author, and journalist James Runciman (1852–1891), chap. 1 ('The Wanderer'), pp. 11–12, where the passage ending with the phrase reads:

> My man spoke with a deep voice that contrasted oddly with his air of debility, and I noticed that he not only had a good accent, but his

words were uttered with a deliberate attempt at formal and polished elocution. We talked of horse-racing, and he mouthed out one speech after another with a balanced kind of see-saw, which again and again ran into blank verse. I said, " You have something good for Lincoln, I hear. Any chance of being on ?" He replied, " I heed no fairy tales or boasting yarns. When a man says he has a certainty, I tell him to his face that he's a liar. The ways of chance are far beyond our ken, and I can but say that I try. Information I have. From Newmarket I receive daily messages, and I have as much chance of being right as other men have ; but you know what the Bard says. Ah ! what a student of human nature that man was ! What an intellect ! In apprehension how like a god ! You know what he says of prophecy and chance ? I only fire a bolt at a venture, and if my venture don't come off, then I say, ' Pay up and look pleasant.' "

and another in *Punch*, vol. 108 (30 Mar. 1895), p. 150, where a poem under the title 'Quarter-Day ; or, Demand and No Supply' and the subtitle '*Resentful Ratepayer loquitur*' reads, in stanza 5, lines 1–4: 'Pay up, and look pleasant ? Ah yes, that's my rule | For every impost, from Poor Rate to Income. | But paying for what you don't get fits a fool, | Besides, you old Grampus-Grab, whence will the tin come ?'

2. 'Nestor'

Uly 2.16: From a hill above a corpse-strewn plain

Reflecting the increasing deadliness of Western armaments from the mid-nineteenth through the early-twentieth centuries, 'corpse-strewn plain' had become a gruesome cliché by the time Joyce used it in *Ulysses*. One early instance of the phrase occurred in the final line of a poem called 'Curfew' signed by 'H. A.' and published in the August 1843 issue of *The Illuminated Magazine* (London), p. 205, the last of whose four stanzas reads:

> By lamplight conning still the lettered page,
>   (Day all too short his studies to illume)
> The Saxon monk, with mingled grief and rage,
>   Heard in his lonely cell those sounds of gloom
> Swinging their measured tones " with sullen roar
>   O'er wizard stream and fountain," and in haste
> He closed the brass-clasped tomes of monkish lore,
>   And while his darkened cell in ire he paced,
> He gave a sigh to Harold's happier reign,
>   And wept at thought of Hastings' corpse-strewn plain.

Seven decades and several instances later, a writer signing himself Wm. Cameron of Gavin Street, Motherwell, in Lanarkshire, Scotland, published on p. 3 of *The Motherwell Times* for Friday, 18 March 1910, a poem called 'Speak Not to Me of War' containing the same phrase in its fifth line:

> Speak not to me of sword or gun,
>   Of bloody war and strife,

Laud not the inhuman brutes who've won
    And split their brother's life.
See yonder bloody corpse-strewn plain
    Where man has butchered man,
Then write upon your scroll of fame,
    Write 'glorious,' if you can.

Ask of some nation's crippled son,
    Who for his country bled,
Ask him to show the prize he's won,
    A medal made of lead.
Poor pay, indeed, for such as he
    Mere trifle it would cost,
Admit the fact, you can't but see
    In winning, he has lost.

See yonder lonely woman weep,
    The heart-felt silent tear ;
It slowly trickles down her cheek,
    For one she loved so dear.
Come, ask the reason of her sigh,
    Why weeps she what's her care,
She mourns a slaughtered son, that's why,
    Show me the glory there.

Stay, here those children cry for bread,
    Poor mites, they've naught to eat ;
Their father's numbered with the dead,
    Does fame to them taste sweet ?
Is not the horror of it plain,
    Does the example serve
A grateful nation lauds his name
    And leaves his young to starve.

Why should the toiler seek the fray,
    Unto what good what end,
Defend his native land, you say,
    What has he to defend ?
I say to those who own the land,
    Those purse-proud pampered elves,
Be men, go, face the foemen, and
    Defend your land yourselves.

No no, they say war's not for us,
    We're made of too fine clay,

> Indeed it has been ever thus,
>   They always shirk the fray.
> You toiler, are so big and strong,
>   'Twould cost you little trouble,
> Poor dupe, they merely fool you on,
>   And reward you with a bubble.
>
> War's not for them, I'm not for war,
>   So here we make an end,
> They will not fight, I fight not for,
>   I've nothing to defend.
> So let them fight who needs must fight,
>   I will not fight, I say,
> Until you prove that might is right,
>   Take, take your sword away.[2]

Uly 2.16–17: a general speaking to his officers, leaned upon his spear

See 2 Samuel i 6: 'And the young man that told him said, As I happened by chance upon mount Gilboa, behold, Saul leaned upon his spear; and, lo, the chariots and horsemen followed hard after him.' 2 Samuel i 1–27 relates how the young man, an Amalekite soldier who had survived the just-ended battle between his army and the Israelites, claimed to have come upon the wounded King Saul, slew him at Saul's own request, and brought Saul's crown back to the Israelite camp in hopes of clemency or a reward—an act for which now-King David ordered the regicide to himself be slain.

As with 'corpse-strewn plain', the phrase 'leaned upon his spear', by the time Joyce used it, had occurred several times, including in the Scottish writer, poet, and politician James Macpherson's (1736–1796) *Fingal*, purportedly 'an Ancient Epic Poem [...] Composed by Ossian, the Son of Fingal' (1762), duan 4, line 329: 'Dark he leaned upon his spear'; from *The Cornish Ballads And Other Poems* (Oxford and London, 1869), pp. 21–22, the Anglican priest, poet, and antiquarian Robert

---

2   Various print and online sources claim that Cameron's poem was first published in the Glasgow-based socialist newspaper *Forward* on 15 August 1914. I have not been able to verify, in a search of the British Newspaper Archive, that the poem or a version of it appeared in that publication on that or any other date.

Stephen Hawker's (1803–1875) poem 'Dupath Well', the third of whose six stanzas reads: 'Upright he sate within the bed, | The helm on his unyielding head : | Sternly he leaned upon his spear, | He knew his passing hour was near.'; and in the English novelist H[enry]. Rider Haggard's (1856–1925) *The People of the Mist* (London, 1894), chap. 35 ('Be Noble or Be Base'), p. 294: 'And once more he bowed his head, leaned upon his spear, and was silent.'

Uly 2.17: They lend ear.

Joyce's 'lend ear' occurs three times in Shakespeare, two of them verbatim: the most familiar—not verbatim—Antony's 'Friends, Romans, countrymen, lend me your ears!' in *Julius Caesar*, III ii 73; in *Coriolanus*, V iii 17–19, the general's 'Fresh embassies and suits, | Nor from the state nor private friends, hereafter | Will I lend ear to.'; and, with George Wilkins, in *Pericles, Prince of Tyre*, V i 82, Marina's 'Hail, sir! my lord, lend ear.'

It also occurs in the Scottish historian, novelist, poet, and playwright Sir Walter Scott's (1771–1832) historical novel *Ivanhoe: A Romance* (Edinburgh, 1819), chap. 28: 'Wherefore I will lend ear to thy counsel'; and in the English novelist and poet George Meredith's (1828–1909) novel *Diana of the Crossways* (London, 1885), chap. 23 ('Records a Visit to Diana from One of the World's Good Women'): 'You will not lend ear to an intercession ?'

Uly 2.39: Kingstown pier, Stephen said. Yes, a disappointed bridge.

Nineteenth-century travel literature is replete with references to ruined bridges, one example of which, published in the Palestine Exploration Fund's Quarterly Statement for 1907 (London), is 'Diary of a Visit to Safed' by R. A. Stewart Macalister and Dr. E. W. G. Masterman. It reads in part, on p. 106:

> Our route was now all the way within sight of the Jordan. We passed a ruined bridge (*Jisr es-Sidd*), the piers of which still stand in the bed of the river : near it is a weir across the river, diverting much of the water into a canal on the west bank.

But Stephen's memorably witty definition of 'pier' as 'a disappointed bridge' may owe something to a paper by the Oxford geologist and anthropologist W[illiam]. J[ohnson]. Sollas (1849–1936) 'On the Cranial and Facial Characters of the Neanderthal Race', published in *Philosophical Transactions of the Royal Society* (London), vol. 199 (1 Jan. 1908), 281–339, which concludes on p. 337 in the last sentence before the Appendix: 'Looked at from this point of view, the Neanderthal and Pithecanthropus skulls stand like the piers of a ruined bridge which once continuously connected the kingdom of man with the rest of the animal world.' As such, Joyce's and/or Stephen's witticism may ironically comment on the evolutionary status of the mentally lazy children from well-to-do Anglo-Irish families enrolled in Mr Deasy's private school.

Uly 2.83–85: Here also over these craven hearts his shadow lies and on the scoffer's heart and lips and on mine.

Immediately preceded and followed by the scriptural echoes noted by Thornton, Gifford, and SMT, this passage may point to 2 Peter iii 3: 'Knowing this first, that there shall come in the last days scoffers, walking after their own lusts'—and to the perils such willfully ignorant scoffers face in the world's coming destruction.

3. 'Proteus'

Uly 3.2–3: Signatures of all things I am here to read, seaspawn and seawrack, the nearing tide, that rusty boot.

The phrase with which this second sentence of 'Proteus' ends seems simply to denote an item washed up or abandoned on the shore of Sandymount strand. But Stephen could have read the phrase 'rusty boot' itself: it had previously occurred (along with a handful of passing references in nineteenth-century periodical fiction) in *A Comedy of Masks* (London, 1893), the first of two collaborative novels by the English poet and novelist Ernest Dowson (1867–1900) and his Queen's College, Oxford, friend the English author Arthur Moore (1866–1952), vol. 3 (of 3), chap. 28, p. 46:

> He pointed his words, which Rainham found meaningless enough, with an impatient dig of his rusty boot against the fragrant wood, and his friend considered him curiously in the light of the blaze which his gesture had provoked.
> ' Is there anything wrong ?' he asked. ' More wrong than usual, I mean.'

Uly 3.9: Shut your eyes and see.

In *Imaginary Conversations of Greeks and Romans* (London, 1853), by the English writer, poet, literary reformer, and political activist Walter Savage Landor (1775–1864), the remarks of Landor's Lucian in his conversation with Landor's Timotheus include the following, on p. 304:

" Open your mouth and shut your eyes and see what Zeus shall send you," says Aristophanes in his favourite metre. In this helpless condition of closed optics and hanging jaw, we find the followers of Plato. It is by shutting their eyes that they see, and by opening their mouths that they apprehend.

The Canadian science writer and novelist Grant Allen (1848–1899) seems clearly to have had this passage in mind when he wrote, in *Post-Prandial Philosophy* (London, 1894), section 17 ('On the Casino Terrace'), pp. 143–44, 'You needn't risk a louis on the tables [at Monte Carlo] unless you choose, but, like it or lump it, if you're bound for Nice or Cannes or Mentone, you must open your mouth and shut your eyes and see what P.L.M. will send you.'—'P.L.M.', he writes on pp. 142–43, being 'the curt and universal abbreviation for the Paris, Lyon, Méditerranée Railway Company—in all probability the most gigantic and wickedest monopoly on the face of this planet.'

Uly 3.19–20: Dominie Deasy kens them a'.

Thornton writes that the phrase 'suggests a Scottish song' but adds: 'Hodgart and Worthington take no note of it, and I have not been able to identify it.' Gifford: 'Source unknown.' SMT cite the title of the nineteenth-century ballad 'D'ye Ken John Peel'. The phrase *kens them a'* itself occurs verbatim, however, in many collections of Scottish poems, songs, and tales, among them the Glasgow-born engineer, poet, author, and journalist Alex[ander]. G.[regor] Murdoch's (1841–1891) *Lilts on the Doric Lyre: A Collection of Humorous Poems and Versified Sketches of Scottish Manners and Character* (Glasgow, 1873), with, in 'The Flittin' Day', pp. 33–37, stanza 3, lines 1–2: 'There's Mrs Hardnieves wi' her trash— | The pawnshop kens them a'— '; the Northumberland-born James Armstrong's (1823–1909) *Wanny Blossoms: A New Book of Border Songs and Ballads. With a Brief Treatise on Fishing, Fly, Worm, and Roe* (Carlisle, 1876), where, in 'The Kielder Hunt', pp. 64–67, stanza 5, lines 3–4, read: 'The Key-Heugh an' the Cloven-Crags, the Cove, an' Darnaha', | Chatlehope-Spout an' the Wily-holes, auld foxy kens them a'.'; and, by the Scottish poet, novelist, and essayist James Hogg (1770–1835) *Tales and Sketches, by The Ettrick Shepherd*, vol. 3 (of 6), (Glasgow, Edinburgh, and London, 1837), with 'The Brownie of the Black Haggs', reading, on p. 355:

" Alack-a-day! we get the blame o' muckle that we little deserve. But, Wattie, keep ye a geyan sharp lookout about the cleuchs and the caves o' our hope; for the Leddy kens them a' geyan weel; and gin the twenty hunder merks wad our way, it might gang a waur gate. It wad tocher a' our bonny lasses."

Uly 3.21–22: *Won't you come to Sandymount, | Madeline the mare?*

Thornton comments: 'This seems to be an Irish song or poem, or a parody of one, but I have not been able to locate it.' Gifford sees in the second line 'a play on one of two names: Madeleine Lemaire [...] or Philippe-Joseph Henri Lemaire', but is otherwise silent on the possible reference to an actual song. SMT, echoing Thornton, write: 'This seems to be from a song, with perhaps some alteration of the lyrics, but no source has yet been found.'

SMT's surmise, as far as it goes, appears to be correct, but the song on which Joyce's lines are based may now be deemed identified: 'Won't you come to Margate?', from the long-running musical comedy *Gentleman Joe*, with words by the English dramatist and lyricist Basil Hood (1864–1917) and music by the English conductor and composer Walter Slaughter (1860–1908)—'Sung with immense success at the Prince of Wales Theatre', the sheet music as published (London, 1895) proclaims—and with its three verses and chorus reading as follows:

> You may talk of leaving England
> For a change of air and scene,
> Going miles from home
> To Paris or Rome,
> Or perhaps the Engadine.
> But there isn't one of those places
> Nor any place under the sun,
> Comes up to a spot
> That licks the lot,
> And Margate is the one!
>
> We'll go by cheap excursion
> A dollar for there and back,
> Just full of delight
> No matter how tight

The passengers have to pack !
The carriage may be a bit crowded,
But the party will be select,
And if there's a squeeze,
You can sit on my knees,
And be sure I won't object !

And in mem'ry of our visit,
We will each have our photograph
Took there on the beach,
And wouldn't I screech
If you happen'd to move or laugh !
You shall be standing like this here,
And mind you've a happy smile
And with me by your side,
Like a duke and his bride,
Something in this here style !

Chorus
So won't you come to Margate,
O, won't you come with me ?
To sit on the sand and hear the band
In the beautiful hall by the sea ?
Oh! won't you come to Margate,
How rollicking it will be
Sitting side by side for a donkey ride
O, won't you come with me ?

That Joyce chose to echo the title and a line from the chorus of 'Won't you come to Margate?' in his 'Won't you come to Sandymount...?' is not surprising, given how prominently Margate figures in *Ulysses* as a whole. The word 'Margate' itself occurs four times in the novel: once in 'Lestrygonians', at line 8.1065; twice in 'Eumaeus', at lines 16.519–20; once in 'Penelope', at line 18.1346. And, as Bowen and others have noted, echoes of the phrase 'seaside girls' from the title of the popular song so-named (London, 1899), with words and music by Harry B. Norris—a song that begins 'Down at Margate looking very charming you are sure to meet | Those girls, dear girls, those lovely seaside girls'—occur in *Ulysses* a total of eight times: four in 'Calypso', in lines 4.281–82, 4.408–09, 4.437–39, and 4.442–43; and once each in 'Hades' (as 'seaside gurls'), in lines 6.784–85); 'Lestrygonians', in lines 8.1065–66; 'Sirens', in line 11.939; and 'Nausicaa', in line 13.906.

Uly 3.88: Lump of love.

Commenting on this phrase—which is derisively echoed in Simon Dedalus's 'papa's little lump of dung' at 6.52–53—SMT write that it comes 'From the song "Irish Hearts for the Ladies": "'Twas stuff'd too with large lumps of love, sir!"' But Joyce's phrase—an early instance of which occurs in the Scottish minister and theologian Samuel Rutherford's (1600–1661) *Christ Dying and Drawing Sinners to Himselfe* (London, 1647), with, on p. 281 (italics in the original): 'Christ not onely teacheth *how to love*, or *modum rei*, but hee teacheth *Love it selfe*, he draweth a lumpe of love out of his owne heart, and casts it in the sinners heart'[3]—may also owe something to the English writer M[ary]. E[lizabeth]. Braddon (1835–1915), whose *The Christmas Hirelings* (London, 1894), chap. 4, pp. 114–15, records a brief conversation between the lonely, long-widowed Sir John Penlyon and his friend Thomas Danby, who has hired three young siblings—the youngest of whom is a little girl named Moppet— to brighten Sir John's Christmas. "Have you forgiven the children," Danby asks Sir John, "for being so much smaller than you expected ? ", to which Sir John replies:

> " I could forgive that youngest mite anything—smashing the
> Portland vase, if I owned it. She is what your friends over yonder"
> (with a nod westward) " would call an amusing little cuss."
> " She is a little lump of love," answered Danby. " One has to know
> that child well to know how much there is in her."

As noted by Thornton, Gifford, and SMT, the phrase recurs in 9.1039, 'Lizzie, grandpa's lump of love,' referring there to Elizabeth Hall, Shakespeare's only granddaughter, born in 1608.

---

3 A similarly worded and contemporary instance occurs in the English Puritan divine Isaac Ambrose's (1604–1664) theological treatise 'Looking unto Jesus', book 10, chap. 2, section 6, p. 697: 'it is Christ's way of winning hearts, he draws a lump of love out of his own heart, and casts it into the sinners heart, and so he loves him.' See *The Compleat Works* (London, 1701). Like the chicken and the egg, and given the verbal similarity, it is difficult to tell which of the two works came first.

Uly 3.132–33: More tell me, more still!

Joyce's phrase may owe something to a line in Act 4 of Henrik Ibsen's verse drama *Brand* (1866)—whose title character, a rural vicar, is both saint-like hero and moral monster—a line in which Agnes, Brand's wife, still mourning the death of their child and after Brand has insisted that she give the dead child's cherished clothes away, at length asks him, following 'a severe inward struggle', in the play as first published in English in a prose translation by William Wilson (London, 1891), 'Tell me, Brand, is it fair for still more to be asked?'—the line in the original Dano-Norwegian reads: 'Sig mig, Brand, om det er billigt, at der kræves mer endnu?'—and shortly thereafter dies of a broken heart.

Or perhaps owe something to a hymn called 'Tell Me More, Still More of Jesus', by the prominent American Congregational minister, abolitionist, hymnist, and educator J[eremiah]. E[ames]. Rankin (1828–1904), published in (among other American hymnals) *Gospel Bells: A Collection of New and Popular Songs for the Use of Sabbath Schools and Gospel Meetings*, edited by J. W. Bischoff, Otis F. Presbrey, and Rankin himself (Chicago, 1880 et seq.). The title phrase of Rankin's hymn, with which the book begins, is repeated in each of the hymn's six verses and in its chorus.

Uly 3.153–54: isle of dreadful thirst

As Thornton notes, Stuart Gilbert, in the second, revised edition of his *James Joyce's 'Ulysses': A Study* (London, 1952), compares Joyce's 'isle of dreadful thirst' to the 'isle of dreadful hunger' of Pharos, where Menelaus and his men stay while searching for Proteus in book 4 of the *Odyssey*. Gifford further and reasonably notes that, for Joyce, the 'isle of dreadful thirst' also signifies Ireland. It may also be noted that Joyce's phrase echoes nearly verbatim the title of the Australian bush poet, journalist, and author A[ndrew]. B[arton]. 'Banjo' Paterson's (1864–1941) poem 'The City of Dreadful Thirst'—itself echoing the title of the Scottish journalist and poet James 'B.V.' Thomson's (1834–1882) long and dark poem 'The City of Dreadful Night' (1874)—first published in the 9 December 1899 issue of *The Bulletin* (Sydney); later collected in

Paterson's *Rio Grande's Last Race and Other Verses* (Sydney, 1902; London, 1904). The possible appeal to Joyce of Paterson's poem may best be suggested by quoting it in full:

THE CITY OF DREADFUL THIRST

The stranger came from Narromine and made his little joke—
' They say we folks in Narromine are narrow-minded folk.
' But all the smartest men down here are puzzled to define
' A kind of new phenomenon that came to Narromine.

' Last summer up in Narromine 'twas gettin' rather warm—
' Two hundred in the water-bag, and lookin' like a storm—
' We all were in the private bar, the coolest place in town,
' When out across the stretch of plain a cloud came rollin' down,

' We don't respect the clouds up there, they fill us with disgust,
' They mostly bring a Bogan shower—three rain-drops and some dust ;
' But each man, simultaneous-like, to each man said, " I think
' " That cloud suggests it's up to us to have another drink ! "

' There's clouds of rain and clouds of dust—we'd heard of them before,
' And sometimes in the daily press we read of " clouds of war :"
' But—if this ain't the Gospel truth I hope that I may burst—
' That cloud that came to Narromine was just a cloud of thirst.

' It wasn't like a common cloud, 'twas more a sort of haze ;
' It settled down about the streets, and stopped for days and days,
' And not a drop of dew could fall and not a sunbeam shine
' To pierce that dismal sort of mist that hung on Narromine.

' Oh, Lord ! we had a dreadful time beneath that cloud of thirst !
' We all chucked-up our daily work and went upon the burst.
' The very blacks about the town that used to cadge for grub,
' They made an organised attack and tried to loot the pub.

' We couldn't leave the private bar no matter how we tried ;
' Shearers and squatters, union-men and blacklegs side by side
' Were drinkin' there and dursn't move, for each was sure, he said,
' Before he'd get a half-a-mile the thirst would strike him dead !

' We drank until the drink gave out, we searched from room to room,
' And round the pub, like drunken ghosts, went howling through the gloom.
' The shearers found some kerosene and settled down again,
' But all the squatter chaps and I, we staggered to the train.

' And, once outside the cloud of thirst, we felt as right as pie,
' But while we stopped about the town we had to drink or die.
' But now I hear it's safe enough, I'm going back to work
' Because they say the cloud of thirst has shifted on to Bourke.

' But when you see those clouds about—like this one over here—
' All white and frothy at the top, just like a pint of beer,
' It's time to go and have a drink, for if that cloud should burst
' You'd find the drink would all be gone, for that's a cloud of thirst ! '

We stood the man from Narromine a pint of half-and-half ;
He drank it off without a gasp in one tremendous quaff ;
' I joined some friends last night,' he said, ' in what *they* called a spree ;
' But after Narromine 'twas just a holiday to me.'

And now beyond the Western Range, where sunset skies are red,
And clouds of dust, and clouds of thirst, go drifting overhead,
The railway-train is taking back, along the Western Line,
That narrow-minded person on his road to Narromine.

Uly 3.157: Human shells.

Passed over without comment by Thornton, Gifford, and SMT, Joyce's phrase previously occurred in the Russian mystic and Theosophist H[elena]. P[etrovna]. Blavatsky's (1831–1891) *The Secret Doctrine: The Synthesis of Science, Religion and Philosophy* (London, 1888), vol. 1 (of 2), book 2, chap. 13 ('Cosmogenesis'), p. 457, in a footnote commenting on 'the Dhyanis' (italics in the original): 'They may indeed mark a "special" or extra *creation*, since it is they who, by incarnating themselves within the senseless human shells of the two first Root-races, and a great portion of the Third Root-race — create, so to speak, a *new race*: that of thinking, self-conscious and *divine* men.'

That Joyce here has Madame Blavatsky and her followers in mind is further suggested by lines 3.155–56 with 'and on the higher beach a dryingline with two crucified shirts': 'higher' being an adjective frequently found in Theosophical writings in such phrases as 'higher consciousness', 'higher self', 'higher plane', 'higher worlds', and 'higher life'.

Uly 3.177: Eating your groatsworth of *mou en civet*

As noted by SMT, the *OED* defines 'groatsworth' as 'a small amount'. Given the iconoclastic passage of 'Proteus' in which the word occurs, however—including Stephen's mention, in line 167, of the anti-Catholic and anti-clerical comic novel *La Vie de Jésus* (Paris, 1882) by Marie Joseph Gabriel Antoine Jogand-Pagès (1854–1907) as 'Léo Taxil'—'groatsworth' here may be a passing reference to the Elizabethan dramatist and pamphleteer Robert Greene's (1558–1592) posthumously published *Greene's Groats-Worth of witte, bought with a million of Repentance* (London, 1592), best known for its presumed reference to William Shakespeare as an 'vpstart Crow, beautified with our feathers' who 'is in his owne conceit the onely Shake-scene in a countrey.'

Uly 3.212–13: In Rodot's Yvonne and Madeleine newmake their tumbled beauties

What seems to be the only pre-*Ulysses* instance of 'tumbled beauties' occurs in the American feminist scholar and historian Evangeline Wilbour Blashfield's (1858–1918) *Portraits and Backgrounds: Hrotsvitha, Aphra Behn, Aïssé, Rosalba Carriera* (New York, 1917)—published five months before the 'Proteus' episode was first serialized—where, in the long chapter on the French letter-writer Charlotte Elisabeth Aïssé (1695?–1733), spanning pp. 287–379, the first section reads in part, on p. 290:

> But where was the new Venus to be found ? Not among the tumbled beauties of the court. Mesdames de Parabère, de Sabran, d'Averne, d'Argentan were the roses of yester-years. The actresses Demares and Grandval were cast-off puppets; even the wonderful dancing doll, Florence of the Opera, had ceased to please. The pretty English girls, seductive agents of the Pretender, had been bowed out of the presence by one who saw the hook quite as plainly as the bait. The task of leading him by the nose was no easy one even for such adroit players upon human frailty as the future cardinal and the ex-nun.

Joyce's phrase may also have been suggested by 'tumbled beauty' singular in the English author and poet Richard Le Gallienne's (1866–1947)

'London Beautiful', first published in his *New Poems* (London and New York, 1910), on pp. 132–34. It begins:

> LONDON, I heard one say, no more is fair,
> London whose loveliness is everywhere,
> London so beautiful at morning light
> One half forgets how fair she is at night,
> London as beautiful at set of sun
> As though her beauty had but just begun;
> London, that might sob, that splendid tear,
> That jewel hanging in the great world's ear.
> Strange queen of all this grim romantic stone,
> Paris, say some, shall push you from your throne,
> And all the tumbled beauty of your dreams
> Submit to map and measure, straight cold schemes
> Which for the loveliness that comes by chance
> Shall substitute the conscious streets of France,
> A beauty made for beauty that has grown,
> An alien beauty, London, for your own.

For the rather insipid romanticism of Le Gallienne's London, however, Joyce substitutes the raw naturalism of Paris as Stephen Dedalus recalls it after his return to Dublin: seated in Rodot's, a patisserie (Gifford notes) at 9 Boulevard Saint-Michel (c. 1902), are two prostitutes, Yvonne and Madeleine, who while devouring with gold-capped teeth their breakfast of *flan Breton* are putting on fresh makeup and fixing their hair in preparation for another day working the streets of that city.

Uly 3.279: Take all, keep all.

The Oxford Dictionary of Proverbs (2008), edited by John Simpson and Jennifer Speake, reports as a proverbial expression traceable to Northern England of the early fifteenth century: 'Hear all, see all, say nowt, tak' all, keep all, gie nowt, and if tha ever does owt for nowt do it for thysen.'

Joyce's phrase also occurs in the English journalist and author Ernest Alfred Vizetelly's (1853–1922) translation of the French novelist Émile Zola's (1840–1902) psychological thriller *La Bête Humaine* (Paris, 1890) as *The Monomaniac* (London, 1901), chap. 9, p. 270:

> When the clock struck three she felt mortally sorry that she had
> refused to share. A thought, indeed, came to her, still confused, and far

from being determined on : supposing she were to get up, and search
beneath the parquetry, so that he might have nothing more. Only she
was seized with such icy coldness that she would not dream of it. Take
all, keep all, without him daring to complain !

Uly 3.308–09: I spoke to no-one: none to me.

Thornton writes: 'Hodgart and Worthington list this as an allusion to the
English folk song "The Miller of the Dee" (also "There Was a Jolly Miller
Once" and "The Jolly Miller"), but there is no line in the song closely
similar to Stephen's statement.' Gifford and SMT cite the same song—
the latter referring to it as a nursery rhyme—both quoting versions of
its final lines: 'I care for nobody, no not I | And nobody cares for me.'
(Gifford); 'I care for nobody, no! not I, | If nobody cares for me.' (SMT)

An all-but–verbatim match with Joyce's phrase may be found,
however, in *The Boy's Own Paper*, vol. 8, no. 362 (19 Dec. 1885), where
chap. 12 ('A Nocturnal Alarm') of a story called 'A Great Mistake' by the
Rev. T. S. Millington reads on p. 178:

> Ben Chalmers conversed with him freely, and interpreted to us
> afterwards. Andy said " Comment ? " with a fine accent (acquired
> on the Continent), every time the good man spoke to him ; and I was
> so overpowered with fatigue that I spoke to no one and no one spoke
> to me. Only I remember asking for café, and being supplied with the
> delicious and refreshing beverage, and being led away afterwards
> and pushed up a ladder, and then dropped down through a hole
> somewhere.

Another antecedent that Joyce may also have had in mind: a novel
by the Irish poet, novelist, historian, and Anglican priest George Croly
(1780–1860) first published anonymously, in two volumes, as *Salathiel. A
Story of the Past, the Present, and the Future.* (New York and Philadelphia,
1828; London, 1829); then as *Salathiel. The Immortal. A History.* New
Edition Revised. (London, 1855); then, in a posthumous edition, as
Tarry Thou Till I Come, or Salathiel, The Wandering Jew (London and New
York, 1901). In the 1855 edition, chap. 46 begins, on p. 312, with the
following paragraph:

> My first object was, to ascertain the fate of my family. From Constantius
> I could learn nothing ; for the severity of his wound had reduced

him to such a state, that he recognized no one. I sat by him, day after day ; watching with bitter solicitude, for the return of his senses. He raved continually of his wife, and of every other name that I loved. The affecting eloquence of his appeals sometimes plunged me in the deepest depression ; sometimes drove me out, to seek relief from them even in the horrors of the streets. I was the most solitary of men. In those melancholy wanderings, none spoke to me ; I spoke to none. The kinsmen whom I had left under the command of my brave son, were slain or dispersed ; and, on the night when I saw him warring, with his native ardour; the men whom he led to the foot of the rampart were an accidental band, excited by his brilliant intrepidity to choose him at the instant for their captain. In sorrow, indeed, had I entered Jerusalem.

Uly 3.412: walking beneath a reign of uncouth stars

The rare phrase 'uncouth stars' previously—and perhaps first—occurred, as 'vnkouth sterris', in the English monk and poet John Lydgate's (c. 1370–c. 1451) thirty-six-thousand-line poem *The Fall of Princes*, written in 1431–38, based on Italian writer and poet Giovanni Boccaccio's (1313–1375) *De Casibus Virorum Illustrium* (1373) [On the fates of famous men] as translated from Boccaccio's Latin prose into French by Laurent de Premierfait (1380–1418) as *Du cas des nobles hommes et femmes* [Concerning the fates of illustrious men and women]. Book 6, lines 2283–89, of Lydgate's poem read:

> At the gyn*n*yng of thes woful werris,
> In the heuene wer seyn dreedful siht*es* —
> Sparklyng brondis, cometis, vnkouth sterris,
> With flawme of fyr many feerful liht*es*
> Lik lau*m*pis bren*n*yng al the longe niht*es*,
> Castyng of speres, dartis in the hair,
> Wherbi Romey*ns* fill in gret dispair.

The quoted passage appears post-*Ulysses* in the poem as printed in *Lydgate's Fall of Princes*, edited by Dr Henry Bergen, 'Presented to the Early English Text Society by the Carnegie Institution of Washington' (London, 1924), part 3, p. 736, where a marginal translation reads: 'At their beginning strange comets and uncouth stars were seen in the sky, burning like lamps all night long, and spears and darts flew about in the air.' But since Bergen's edition of Lydgate's poem was published six years after the 'Proteus' episode was first serialized in *The Little Review*, vol. 5, no. 1 (May 1918) and two years after the publication of *Ulysses*, Joyce could not have based his use of the phrase 'uncouth stars' on a reading of that edition. So he may have encountered it elsewhere—in some earlier version or edition of Lydgate's poem, in Boccaccio's *De Casibus Virorum Illustrium*, in de Premierfait's *Du Cas des nobles hommes et femmes*, or in some other work.

That other work could possibly have been *The Historie of Great Britaine Vnder the Conqvests of the Romans, Saxons, Danes and Normans*, second edition, revised and enlarged by John Speed (London, 1623), p. 464, where the phrase 'Vncouth Stars' occurs as a marginal note alongside a passage describing two or more comets seen together in the sky in 1096 during the reign of William Rufus, grandson of William the Conqueror and King of England from 1087 to 1100.

Uly 3.452: All or not at all.

Thornton writes of the passage in which this phrase occurs—'He now will leave me. And the blame? As I am. As I am. All or not at all.'—'John Z. Bennett has suggested that this, too, involves an allusion to Oscar Wilde. In *The Picture of Dorian Gray* [...] Dorian says to Basil Hallward, "Don't leave me, Basil, and don't quarrel with me. I am what I am. There is nothing more to be said."' Gifford sees in the phrase an allusion to Ibsen's *Brand*, where, at the end of Act 2, scene 2 (and several times thereafter) Brand announces (in G. M. Gathorne-Hardy's 1966 translation, which Gifford cites), 'My claim is "nought or all."'[4] SMT comment: 'Follows the sentiment of Jesus's line: "He that is not with me, is against me" (Matthew 12:30)', adding that 'similar catchphrases can be traced back to the sixteenth century in English (Dent)'.

To this may be added that Joyce's phrase also matches nearly verbatim two lines, including the final line, of the song sung by the cunning Vivien as she seduces the aged Merlin—before imprisoning him forever

---

4   Gifford's suggestion is perfectly reasonable. In the first English translation, by William Wood, of Ibsen's *Brand* (see note for lines 3.132–33 above), Wood renders the passage in which the phrase occurs, spoken by Brand to Agnes: 'Remember, I am stern in my demand—I require All or nothing.' (In the original Dano-Norwegian: 'Husk at jeg er streng i Kravet | fordrer intet eller alt'.)

in an old oak tree—on pp. 113–17 of the 'Merlin and Vivien' episode of Tennyson's *Idylls of the King* (London, 1859):

> " In Love, if Love be Love, if Love be ours,
> Faith and unfaith can ne'er be equal powers :
> Unfaith in aught is want of faith in all.
>
> " It is the little rift within the lute,
> That by and by will make the music mute,
> And ever widening slowly silence all.
>
> " The little rift within the lover's lute,
> Or little pitted speck in garner'd fruit,
> That rotting inward slowly moulders all.
>
> " It is not worth the keeping : let it go :
> But shall it ? answer, darling, answer, no.
> And trust me not at all or all in all."
>
> [. . . .]
>
> " My name, once mine, now thine, is closelier mine,
> For fame, could fame be mine, that fame were thine,
> And shame, could shame be thine, that shame were mine.
> So trust me not at all or all in all."

Uly 3.490: All days make their end.

Thornton writes: 'This recalls the proverb known in several languages. The [*Oxford Dictionary of English Proverbs*] lists "The longest day hath an end," and lists nine instances from c. 1340 to 1841, including John Ray's *Proverbs* (1670).' He adds: 'Compare Brutus' statement in *Julius Caesar*, V, i, 125: "But it sufficeth that the day will end."' Another antecedent, not it seems previously cited, occurs in a passage in book 3, chap. 9 ('Of Vanitie'), in *The Essayes of Michael Lord of Montaigne*, as translated in 1603 by the Renaissance linguist and humanist John Florio (1552–1625) and reading in part at p. 500 of the edition published by Henry Morley (London, 1893): 'My dessigne is everywhere divisible, it is not grounded on great hopes : each day makes an end of it. Even so is my lifes voiage directed.'

Uly 3.501: For the rest let look who will.

Near the end of the 'Proteus' episode, Joyce, speaking of Stephen Dedalus, writes in lines 3.500–01: 'He laid the dry snot picked from his nostril on a ledge of rock, carefully. For the rest let look who will.' The second of the two sentences matches verbatim one occurring in chap. 8 ('Good Friday') of *Lent and Holy Week: Chapters on Catholic Observance and Ritual*, by Herbert Thurston, S.J. (London, 1904)—and ultimately in the writings of the English abbot Ælfric of Eynsham (c. 955–c. 1010) as translated from Ælfric's Anglo-Saxon by Benjamin Thorpe in 1840. Thurston writes, on pp. 367–68 of his book:

> It may be interesting in concluding this chapter to quote a popular description of the Good Friday ritual written nine hundred years ago, in Anglo-Saxon, by Abbot Ælfric. It brings home to us how little change there has been in all that interval:
>
>> I pray you (he says) that you take heed of yourselves, so as your books instruct you, how you should do in these days to come. Housel may not be hallowed on Good Friday, because Christ suffered on that day for us ; but there must, nevertheless, be done what appertains to that day : so that two lessons be read, with two expositions, and with two collects, and Christ's passion ; and afterwards, the prayers. And let them pray to the holy rood, so that they all greet the rood of God with kiss. Let the priest then go to the altar of God, with the housel bread that he hallowed on Thursday, and with unhallowed wine mixed with water, and conceal it with his corporale, and then immediately say: 'Oremus preceptis salutaribus moniti ;' and 'Pater noster' to the end. And then let him say to himself : 'Libera nos quæso Domine ab omnibus malis,' and aloud : 'Per omnia secula seculorum.' Let him then put a part of the housel into the chalice, as it is, however, usual ; then let him go silently to the housel ; and for the rest, let look who will.'[5]

'And for the rest, let look who will.' If Joyce, Stephen, or both had this passage from Ælfric in mind in lines 500–01 as quoted above, one or both of them may have intended the snot Stephen carefully places on the rock—recall Matthew xvi 18, 'And I say also unto thee, That thou art Peter, and upon this rock I will build my church'—as a sign of their distance from, and disdain for, the Roman Catholic rites both had been taught so long and so rigorously to faithfully and piously observe.

---

5   Thurston's citation identifies his source as 'The Canons of Ælfric' in the English scholar of Anglo-Saxon literature Benjamin Thorpe's (1782–1870) *Ancient Laws and Institutes of England* (1840), p. 449. Where Thurston's transcription of 'The Canons' differs from Thorpe, I have followed Thorpe's text.

4. 'Calypso'

Uly 4.112–13: my bold Larry

Based on the reference to Larry O'Rourke as 'bold Larry O' later in the novel, Thornton suspects an allusion to an Irish ballad called 'Bold Traynor O' mentioned by John Hand in an article entitled 'Street Songs and Ballads and Anonymous Verse' in *Irish Literature: Irish Authors and Their Writings in Ten Volumes*, vol. 3 (New York, 1904), pp. 3265–71. Noting that 'Larry is a faintly comic name to the Dublin ear', Gifford cites the eighteenth-century Irish ballad that begins 'The night before Larry was stretched', but Joyce's phrase does not occur in it. SMT write: 'Perhaps after the finale of the anonymous ballad "Larry MacHale",' where, they continue, in *Dublin Saturday Magazine*, vol. 1, no. 16 (1 Jan. 1865), p. 3, the phrase 'bold Larry MacHale' occurs.

Joyce's phrase 'my bold Larry' may, however, have originated elsewhere. As discussed by John C. Greene in *Theatre in Belfast* (Bethlehem, Pennsylvania: Lehigh University Press, and London: Associated University Presses, 2000), pp. 200–02, an actor by the name of Lawrence Kennedy, born in Dublin around 1729, married Elizabeth Orfeur, an actress and singer herself, in 1749. Returning to Ireland after an extended engagement in Edinburgh, Kennedy planned to rejoin Dublin's Smock Alley company, where Orfeur was then performing at a salary of £4 a week. But when Smock Alley's managers at first refused to pay him a salary of more than 30s. a week, the enraged Kennedy soon returned to the theatre 'with a pistol in each hand and demanded satisfaction.' He was immediately signed at £3 a week, and was thereafter known in and around Dublin's theater community as 'Bold Larry' Kennedy.

While Joyce may have known how the phrase 'Bold Larry' originated, he may still have borrowed it from one or another of the Irish music-hall songs or other sources in which the phrase occurred. One such song not mentioned by Thornton, Gifford, SMT, Hodgart and Worthington, Zack Bowen, or Ruth Bauerle is 'The Wedding of Biddy McGrane' (Roud V30288)—written and sung by Harry Clifton (1832–1872) from the 1850s to the early 1870s, then taken up by Fred Coyne (c. 1845–1886)— which begins 'I'll sing you a song if you'll listen a while. | Of a damsel so pretty, so charming and witty, | Who lived from the city of Dublin a mile, | On the road to Clondalkin in the Emerald Isle'; and the third stanza of which reads:

> Now Larry was fond of a jig[,] the spalpeen[.]
> He went to the fair, and Biddy was there,
> And strolling up to the pretty Colleen,
> Soon led her out for a dance on the green;
> The blink of her eye was near driving him crazy.
> He asked her consent, but she looked with disdain[.]
> But when bold Larry he trampled the Daisy,
> It melted the heart [of] Biddy McGrane.

Another possible source, collected in *Thoughts in Rhyme* by Tom M'Lachlan (Glasgow, 1884), is the poem 'Bernard M'Shane', on pp. 76–77 of that volume. It begins: 'Bernard M'Shane was an Irishman bold | As any who went to the diggings for gold,' and its third stanza, which refers to Bernard and his fellow gold-digger Larry M'Quade, reads: 'But one autumn morn they were digging away, | When lo, "What can this be?" young Bernard did say; | "'Tis a nugget, a nugget ! bold Larry," he cried— | Ye'd thought that with joy the poor souls would have died.'

Uly 4.179: O please, Mr Policeman, I'm lost in the wood.

Thornton writes: 'Hodgart and Worthington list this as an allusion to a music hall song entitled "O Please, Mr. Policeman, I'm Lost in the Wood"', but he could not find a song so named, and it seems not to exist. Gifford writes: 'This apparently combines a music-hall song with the catch phrase "lost in the wood" (from the story "The Babes in the Wood")', adding that 'The song "Oh Please, Mr. P'liceman, Oh! Oh!

Oh!" was written by E. Andrews and popularized in the 1890s by the Tillie Sisters', and quoting its lyrics, which do not include 'I'm lost in the wood'. SMT and others also cite the title of 'O Please, Mr. P'liceman, Oh! Oh! Oh!' as a possible source.

Absent the discovery of a song perfectly matching the quoted phrase, it would appear that Joyce may also have had in mind a tale by the English writer of children's stories Mrs [Mary Louisa] Molesworth (1839–1921) entitled '"The Blue Dwarfs:" An Adventure in Thüringen', first published, in four parts, in *The Churchman* (London), vol. 45, nos. 8–11, from 25 February to 18 March 1882; then collected in *Aunt Judy's Annual Volume*, edited by H. K. F. Gatty (London, 1882), 195–213, with, on p. 212: '" Oh, please come and help me ! I'm lost in the wood !" she cried, thinking nothing of German or anything else but her sore distress.'

Uly 4.186: eager fire

This phrase, which passes unremarked by Thornton, Gifford, and SMT, precedes Bloom's hurried exit from Mr Dlugacz's butcher shop in hopes of catching a glimpse from behind of the vigorous hips of the next-door servant girl—who had been just ahead of him in line—as she walks home with the pound and a half of Denny's sausages she had just purchased.

Bloom's erotic interest in the servant girl and his frustration in failing to catch up with her are clear enough on the narrative level, but made clearer still by the presence of 'eager fire'. The phrase first occurred in early English translations of the Latin poet Catullus's (c. 84–c. 54 BCE) poem 45, which begins 'Acmen Septimius suos amores | tenens in gremio "mea" inquit | Acme' [Septimius, holding his lover Acme on his lap, said, my Acme], and which reads, in lines 17–21 of some lineations: 'sic, inquit, mea vita Septimille, | huic uni domino usque | serviamus, | ut multo mihi maior acriorque | ignis mollibus ardet in medullis' [So, she said, my life, my little Septimius, | let us be slaves to this one master always, | as a much more eager fire burns for me | in my soft marrow]. And 'eager fire' recurred as a similarly erotic metaphor in a handful of other poems, most notably, perhaps, in the opening lines of the English poet and Restoration courtier John Wilmot, Earl of Rochester's (1647–1680) pornographic poem 'The Imperfect Enjoyment' (before

1680), where the enjoyment in question is rendered imperfect by the poet-speaker's premature ejaculation (italics in the original):

> Naked she lay, claspt in my longing Arms,
> I fill'd with Love, and she all over Charms,
> Both equally inspir'd with eager fire,
> Melting through kindness, flaming in desire;
> With *Arms, Legs, Lips,* close clinging to embrace,
> She clips me to her *Breast,* and sucks me to her *Face.*
> The nimble *Tongue* (*Love*'s lesser Lightning) plaid
> Within my *Mouth,* and to my thoughts convey'd
> Swift Orders, that I should prepare to throw
> The *All dissolving Thunderbolt* below.
> My flutt'ring *Soul,* sprung with the pointed Kiss,
> Hangs hov'ring o're her *Balmy Lips* of Bliss.
> But whilst her busie hand, wou'd guide that part,
> Which shou'd convey my *Soul* up to her *Heart,*
> In Liquid *Raptures,* I dissolve all o're,
> Melt into Sperm, and spend at every Pore:
> A touch from any part of her had done 't;
> Her Hand, her Foot, her very Look's a *Cunt.*
> Smiling, she Chides in a kind murm'ring *Noise,*
> And from her *Body* wips the Clammy Joys;
> When with a Thousand Kisses, wand'ring o're
> My panting Breast, and is there then no more?
> She cries. All this to Love and Rapture's due[,]
> Must we not pay a Debt to Pleasure too?
> But I the most forlorn, lost Man alive,
> To shew my wisht Obedience vainly strive,
> I Sigh alas! and Kiss, but cannot *Swive.*
> Eager desire confound[s] my first intent,
> Succeeding shames does more success prevent,
> And Rage at last confirms me impotent[.][6]

It should be noted that the phrase 'eager fire' occurs many times elsewhere and generally without erotic import, as, for example, in the Anglo-Irish poet and clergyman Thomas Parnell's (1679–1718)

---

6 Text based, via Representative Poetry Online (https://rpo.library.utoronto.ca/content/imperfect-enjoyment), on *Poems on Several Occasions: By the Right Honourable, The E. of R—* (Antwerpen, 1680?), 14–19; as reprinted in John Wilmot, earl of Rochester, *Poems on Several Occasions* [1680?] (Scolar Press, 1971), 27–30. British Library X.989/13650. Bracketed edits are my own. After the portion quoted here, the poem continues for another forty-two lines.

translation from the Greek of the mock–heroic epic *Batrachomuomachia: or, The Battle of the Frogs and Mice* (London, 1717), with, in book 2 (of 3), 'How strong, how large, the num'rous heroes stride, | What length of lance they shake with warlike pride ! | What eager fire, their rapid march reveals ! | So the fierce Centaurs ravag'd o'er the dales'; and in chap. 11 ('A Picture and a Ring'), p. 174, of Dickens's unfinished novel *The Mystery of Edwin Drood* (Leipzig, 1870): 'Edwin took the easy chair in the corner; and the fog he had brought in with him, and the fog he took off with his great-coat and neck-shawl, was speedily licked up by the eager fire.'

Uly 4.256: his backward eye

Gifford calls Joyce's phrase '[a]n allusion to the one-eyed Malbecco, the cuckold husband of Hellenore in Edmund Spenser's [...] *The Faerie Queene*. While Hellenore lies with a group of satyrs, Malbecco is eternally unable to escape the presence of the past, "Still fled he forward, looking backward still" (Book 3, canto 10, stanza 56).' Joyce's phrase, however—part of the sentence in lines 256–57 reading 'Letting the blind up by gentle tugs halfway his backward eye saw her glance at the letter and tuck it under her pillow'—may itself look back to Wordsworth's long poem *Salisbury Plain*, begun in 1793, revised and renamed *Adventures on Salisbury Plain* between 1795 and 1799, and finally published under the title *Guilt and Sorrow: or, Incidents upon Salisbury Plain* in 1842. In the first, 1793 version of the poem, Joyce's phrase occurs in the fourth line of stanza 5, which begins at line 37:

> The troubled west was red with stormy fire,
> O'er Sarum's plain the traveller with a sigh
> Measured each painful step, the distant spire
> That fixed at every turn his backward eye
> Was lost, tho' still he turned, in the blank sky.

Another instance of the phrase that Joyce may have had in mind occurs in the English poet and artist Isaac Rosenberg's (1890–1918) *Moses: A Play*, first issued in a privately printed edition (London, 1916) and later collected, after his death in combat in 1918, in *Poems by Isaac Rosenberg* (London, 1922). The phrase as it occurs in scene one of both editions, spoken by Young Hebrew, reads: 'Help him not then, and push your safety away : | I for my part will be his backward eye, | His hands when they are shut.'

The phrase 'backward eye' minus the possessive pronoun also occurs in Hardy's 'The To-be-forgotten'—published on pp. 205–06 of his *Wessex Poems and Other Verses; Poems of the Past and the Present* (New York and London, 1898)—the first three of whose eight numbered stanzas read:

I
I heard a small sad sound,
And stood awhile among the tombs around :
" Wherefore, old friends," said I, " are ye distrest,
Now, screened from life's unrest ? "

II
—" O not at being here ;
But that our future second death is near ;
When, with the living, memory of us numbs,
And blank oblivion comes !

III
" Those who our grandsires be
Lie here embraced by deeper death than we ;
Nor shape nor thought of theirs can you descry
With keenest backward eye.["]

Uly 4.447–49: A soft qualm [...] the flowing qualm

Both phrases occur in a paragraph that finds Bloom feeling a sense of helplessness and inevitability about his just-turned-fifteen-years-old daughter Milly's emergent sexuality, particularly as it relates to her interest in Buck Mulligan's friend Alec Bannon and, at least potentially, his interest in her. 'A soft qualm, regret,' the paragraph reads, 'flowed down his backbone, increasing. Will happen, yes. Prevent. Useless: can't move. Girl's sweet light lips. Will happen too. He felt the flowing qualm spread over him. Useless to move now. Lips kissed, kissing, kissed. Full gluey woman's lips.'

What seems the only prior instance of 'soft qualm' occurs in Act 3 ('The Scene of the field continues') of *The History of Charles the Eighth of France; Or, The Invasion of Naples of the French* (London, 1671)—a tragedy by the British playwright John Crowne (1641–1712) collected in vol. 1

(of 4) of his *Dramatic Works* (Edinburgh and London, 1873)—in a speech by Julia to her sister Isabella recounting a dream she had of the dead King Charles and reading in part, on p. 171:

> In a soft qualm, I fell upon my knees,
> Fainting with love and dying by degrees,
> My sinking spirit ready to withdraw ;
> Which when, me thought, the royal shadow saw,
> With a soft voice he cried, see, see, she dies,
> And gently came, and kist my closing eyes.

As for 'flowing qualm', what appears to be the only pre-Joyce instance of that phrase occurs in vol. 1 (of 2) of a manual with the succinct title and verbose subtitle *The Self-Instructing Latin Classic: Whereby A Perfect Knowledge of the Latin Language may be readily acquired, without burdening the memory with the multifarious rules of syntactical grammar, the searching a dictionary for the interpretation of words, or even requiring the assistance of a classical tutor,* by W[illiam]. Jacobs (London, 1841), in which, on p. 187, the phrase in question occurs in the English translation of a Latin passage headed *Ad Mæcenatem* (To Mæcenas) and based on Horace's Epode 9 (italics in the original):

> More capacious bowls bring hither, boy, and the Chian wine or the Lesbian : or what might restrain *this* flowing qualm ; measure out, for us, the Cæcuban. The care and fear of Cæsar's affairs, it pleases *me*, with delicious wine to dissipate.

Uly 4.511: Life might be so.

This thought or fragment of a thought crosses Bloom's mind as he sits at stool, with the torn-out copy of the prize titbit 'Matcham's Masterstroke', by Mr Philip Beaufoy, Playgoers' Club, London, on his lap. 'Life might be so. It did not move or touch him', the episode's narrative voice reports, 'but it was something quick and neat. Print anything now. Silly season. He read on, seated calm above his own rising smell.' Joyce would have us believe that the quoted phrase came from Beaufoy's short story. It may, however, have been suggested by one or another of three antecedent texts.

First of the three: a short story, by one Redmond Darragh, called 'Ralph Brandon's Love', published in *The Shamrock*, vol. 18, no. 758 (23 Apr. 1881), 481–83, with, on the story's first page:

> Tom had been one day telling of a desperate fight with the natives in South Africa and of his own narrow escape from death, when Mildred exclaimed, with a shudder :
> " Oh, Tom, how can you care for such a life—how can you like to court death so when life might be so pleasant here ?"

Second, in a far more distinguished possible source: Tolstoy's novel *Anna Karenina* (1878) as translated by Constance Garnett (London, 1901), with, in vol. 1 (of 2), chap. 3, p. 8:

> The liberal party said, or rather allowed it to be understood, that religion is only a curb to keep in check the barbarous classes of the people ; and Stepan Arkadyevitch could not get through even a short service without his legs aching from standing up, and could never make out what was the object of all the terrible and high-flown language about another world when life might be so very amusing in this world.

And third: in *Twilight* (London, 1916), the final novel, written as she lay dying, of the Dublin-born British novelist Julia Frankau (1859–1916) as 'Frank Danby'—about a dying woman author whose final novel is about the death of a woman author. Chapter 4, letter number 7, of *Twilight*, dated 13 February 1902, from Gabriel Stanton to Mrs Capel, begins: 'I am breaking into the commonplace routine of a particularly tiresome business day, to give myself the pleasure of writing to you, and you will forgive me if I purposely avoid business—for indeed it seems to me today that life might be so pleasant without work.'

Uly 4.514: *laughing witch*

This phrase in what Joyce puts forward as the opening passage of Beaufoy's story—'*Matcham often thinks of the masterstroke by which he won the laughing witch who now*'—had previously occurred outside of children's literature a handful of times.

One such instance appeared in *The London Journal: and Weekly Record of Literature, Science, and Art* (London), vol. 69, no. 1783, for the week ending 12 April 1879, where the penultimate chapter ('How the News Was Received') of a serialized story called 'A Prize Worth Winning', by the English novelist Edith Stewart Drewry (1841–1925), ends with: '" Oh, dear, oh, dear !" said Madeline, shaking her head at the laughing witch who met her below ; "you will make a very wild Countess of Arancourt."'

Another could be found in chapter 2 of *The Anglomaniacs* (London, 1890), by the American novelist Constance Cary (Mrs Burton) Harrison (1843–1920). As first serialized in *The Century Magazine* (New York and London), vol. 40, no. 2 (June 1890), 269–82, the passage in which it occurs reads, on p. 279:

> Smoking a pipe to himself, as he strode up and down the deck at nightfall, Jencks was a prey to the most distracting reflections. If I were to write several pages in elaborating them for the benefit of my readers, it would be only to arrive at an inevitable and lame conclusion — the poor young man had fallen head over ears in love. His acceptance of this fact as definite had the disastrous result of infuriating him. Softer suggestions, imaginings sweeter than honey of Hymettus, were swept away in a torrent of self-contempt. This laughing witch with the bronze-red hair, the red-and-white complexion, the look of vigorous health, the outspoken fearlessness of character, whom at first he had looked on merely in the light of a pleasing variety upon the tedium of the voyage—how had she come to grapple his heart with cables stronger than those that beneath the Atlantic surge link two continents together ?

The phrase recurred in the anonymously published historical novel *High Treason: A Romance of the Days of George the Second* (London, 1902), where chap. 2 ('At Ranelagh'), p. 25, reads in part:

> Philip seemed to feel the solid earth of reality receding beneath his feet, but a sudden sturdiness saved him from giving to this laughing witch the spectacle of his confusion. He bowed calmly and replied, " I shall esteem it a privilege to recall myself to Lady Scarlett's remembrance."

Joyce may have had any one of these stories, or any of countless others, or no particular one in mind when he crafted, for Bloom's delectation, the opening sentence of 'Matcham's Masterstroke'. As he was looking to suggest not the literary distinction but the mediocrity and triteness of Beaufoy's tale—a style that Leopold Bloom could imagine himself one day aspiring to—any one of the three or any others of similar caliber would do.

5. 'Lotus-Eaters'

***Uly* 5.15–16: Bury him cheap in a whatyoumaycall.**

Joyce's 'Bury him cheap' may have been suggested by a similar phrase in Mary Elizabeth Braddon's debut novel, the murder mystery *Three Times Dead; or, The Secret of the Heath* (London, 1860), revised and reissued as *The Trail of the Serpent; or, The Secret of the Heath* (London, 1861), with, in book 4 ('Napoleon the Great'), chap. 5 ('The Cherokees take an Oath'), p. 213 of the 1861 edition: '" Who's dead?" muttered the domino-player. " I wish everybody was, and that I was contracted with to bury 'em cheap.["]'[7]

He may also have had in mind an anonymous tale called 'My Doctor' published in the humorous periodical *Pick-Me-Up* (London)—which ran from 1888 to 1897 as a competitor to *Punch*—vol. 11, no. 274, for 30 Dec. 1893, pp. 218–19, written in Cockney or pseudo-Cockney and semi-literate English, signed 'By our Office Boy' and with a second paragraph that reads:

> My life is valuerbel—at eny rate, it is to me ; so I determined to see Dockter Gallygull. Why I picked out Dockter Gallygull was becaws a man my farther knows is nevver tired of singin' his praises. It appeers this man had a son wot was run over, and he took him to Doctor Gallygull—who is also a surgeon—and he amperteted both his legs. The pore boy died, and why his farther—who is an orful miser—is never tired of singin' Dockter Gallygull's praises is because he cut

---

7   The 1861 text of Braddon's novel was also serialized from 1 Aug. to 28 Nov. 1864 as 'Three Times Dead: or, The Trail of the Serpent' in *The Halfpenny Journal: A Weekly Magazine for All Who Can Read* (London).

off his son's legs, so, of corse, he ownly required a littel koffin, and his farther was abel to bury him cheap.

Uly 5.36: Walk on roseleaves.

One of the earliest of several instances of Joyce's phrase occurred in a patronizing and glaringly sexist pamphlet by Henry Tyrrell, a mid-nineteenth-century teacher of elocution, historian, and Shakespeare scholar, entitled *Woman: And Her Failings* (London, 1857), the antepenultimate paragraph of which, on pp. 15–16, reads (italics in the original):

> In conclusion, I will briefly indicate what I consider to be the true position of woman in society. Her *true* position, because the one for which her form, mind, and affections best adapt her. It is pre-eminently a social one. Woman is most charming in the domestic circle ; most beautiful as daughter, wife, and mother. The fierce contests of the world and its stern struggles are not the fitting arena for her. They may harden her frame and strengthen her mind, but they rob her of the sweet graces which adorn her at the domestic hearth, and give her the power to throw pleasant things into that bitter cup which fate, sometime or other, forces to the lips of most of us. Woman is more appropriately employed in gathering garden flowers than in hewing down forest oaks. Sir E. B. Lytton calls an ambitious woman a ' moral contradiction.' Though I do not altogether coincide with this remark, yet I feel that assuredly the ambitious woman is one who does not walk in the path best fitted for her. The ambition of all but truly great women, also, is petulant and impatient ; they want the end, and try to leap over the slow and painful toil by which they must arrive at it. Their feet are better fitted to walk on rose leaves, than to trample down thorns. Home is woman's noblest temple, and its sacred altar is the fireside where no dark look ever comes, and to which the jaded toiler, man, is ever welcomed with a tender smile. It was finely said by a popular writer, ' We come to men for philosophy ; to women for consolation.'

The same phrase, but from a very different point of view, may be found in *Mohammed Ali und seine Haus* (Jena, 1871) by the German novelist Klara (or Clara) Mundt (1814–1873) as 'Luise Mühlbach'—based on the life of Muhammad Ali Pasha (1805–1849), progenitor of Egypt's (and Sudan's) ruling dynasty—translated from the German by Mrs Chapman Coleman as *Mohammed Ali and His House: An Historical*

Romance (New York, 1872). Chapter 5 ('The Story-Teller') of Coleman's translation reads, on p. 38:

> " What were Mother Khadra's words ? " he asked himself. " ' Only he who practises self-denial can enjoy.' Have I not always said to myself that I would accustom myself to want, and learn to enjoy by denying myself that which pleases me ? Have I not said that I would not walk on rose-leaves, but learn to tread on thorns, that my feet might become inured to pain ? And now, like a foolish child, I am delighted at the prospect of entering my cave, my throne-chamber ! 'Only he who practises self-denial can enjoy.' Remember that, Mohammed, and learn to practise self-denial ; I will learn it ! " he cried so loudly that his voice resounded throughout the entire cave.

For readers familiar with Mundt/Mühlbach's novel, Bloom's 'Walk on roseleaves' would have served to highlight, by contrast, the images of lassitude, forgetfulness, avoidance of pain, and self-indulgent pleasure that permeate this episode.

Uly 5.76–77: Talk: as if that would mend matters.

Minus the word 'talk', the phrase that passes through Bloom's mind as he strolls out of the post office and turns to the right, Martha Clifford's letter to him as 'Henry Flower Esq' in hand, occurs in several antecedent works.

One of these, by the Irish poet and author Julia M. O'Ryan (1823–1887), is 'John Richardson's Relatives', a story serialized in *The Irish Monthly: A Magazine of General Literature* (Dublin) between July 1874 and November 1875. In vol. 3 (1875), part 4, pp. 96–107, O'Ryan writes, on p. 105:

> " Strange ! " echoed his wife, interrupting him. " I declare I don't understand your family ! You spend your lives wide asunder and as if nothing to each other. But when Death shows his face, you must get together, all of you—as if that would mend matters."

Another instance occurs in George Gissing's first-published novel, *Workers in the Dawn* (London, 1880), in which Arthur Golding, born into poverty in London, manages to gain an education; becomes an artist; marries Helen Norman; when that marriage fails, weds a prostitute named Carrie Mitchell; and ultimately commits suicide by jumping over Niagara Falls. Joyce's phrase occurs in vol. 1 (of 3), chap. 8 ('A

Working-Man's Club'), pp. 204–05, in a speech by one of the club's members, reading in part:

> Friends, I have heard men speak in the cause of the poor who seemed as if their object was nothing more nor less than to take away all the wealth from the rich and give it to the poor, as if that would mend matters. Now, I'm not one of these men. I think I have seen very well, from my own experience and from the books I've read, that as long as this world is a world, there will be in it rich people and poor people. That I feel sure of, and I feel that it's no use grumbling about it.

And another occurs in *Fernley House* (Boston, 1901), a young-adult novel by the American writer Laura E. Richards (1850–1943), chap. 14 ('The Fire'), pp. 185–86, in which the house of Mrs Peyton, next door to the grand Long Island mansion of the title that is the ancestral family home of the extended Monfort clan, burns down:

> The side facing them was already wrapped in flames. Long wavering tongues shot through the open windows, and curled round the woodwork, lapping it ; they purred and chuckled like live creatures over their food ; they leaped up toward the roof, running along its edge, feeling their way higher and higher, while now and then one sprang aloft, tossing its scarlet crest over the rooftree itself. Evidently the fire had started in the upper story, for in the lower one, though the smoke poured dense and black through the open windows, there were no flames to be seen yet. Furniture, books, and knick-knacks of every description were scattered about the lawn in wild confusion, and two men, half stifled with smoke, were struggling frantically with a grand piano, one hacking at the window-frame with an axe to widen the opening, the other trying desperately to unscrew the legs, as if that would mend matters. Seven people out of ten, at a fire, will leave untouched pictures and books that can never be replaced, and spend their time and energies in trying to save the piano.

Uly 5.217: Too full for words.

Bloom playfully employs a familiar, usually sentimental, melodramatic, or maudlin expression commonly preceded by 'heart' or 'hearts'—as it is, for example, in the American novelist, short-story writer, and poet Louisa May Alcott's (1832–1888) *Little Women, or Meg, Jo, Beth and Amy* (Boston, 1869), part 1, chap. 18 ('Dark Days.'), p. 275: 'What they were to give, neither heard ; for both crept into the dark hall, and, sitting on the stairs, held each other close, rejoicing with hearts too full for words.'; and in the English journalist, novelist, poet, and short-story writer Rudyard Kipling's (1865–1936) novel *Kim* (London, 1901), chap. 10, p. 211: 'Kim turned about, pointed his toes, stretched, and felt mechanically for the moustache that was just beginning. Then he stooped toward Mahbub's feet to make proper acknowledgment with fluttering, quick-patting hands; his heart too full for words.'—but here in 'Lotus-Eaters' referring to carriage horses 'with their long noses stuck in nosebags' and their mouths too full to do anything but chew.

Uly 5.254: Then I will tell you all.

Passed over without comment by Thornton, Gifford, and SMT, this sentence from Martha Clifford's letter to Bloom—which Bloom recalls verbatim in lines 5.425–26—has, as one might expect, several antecedents in works of fiction, one of which is of particular interest. It occurs in 'The District Doctor,' one of the tales in the Russian novelist, short story writer, poet, playwright, and translator Ivan Turgenev's (1818–1883) first major publication, *A Sportsman's Sketches* (1852), as translated by Constance Garnett (London, 1895), pp. 56–71.[8] In the tale the narrator, having come down with a cold while passing through a remote district on a hunting trip, summons the district doctor for the customary medication and treatment. Having provided them, the doctor—identified only by his given and patronymic names, Trifon Ivanitch—befriends the narrator, shares with him, with extraordinary candor, an equally extraordinary story and, in effect, becomes the narrator himself.

The doctor relates how, years past, he was summoned one night to a far-off village where a beautiful young woman from a well-educated family of modest means had become seriously ill a day or two before

---

8 In *From the Old Waterford House* (London: Mellifont Press Limited, 1940), Joyce's friend the Irish artist and art critic Arthur Power (1891–1984) wrote, on pp. 64–65, that in response to his comment to Joyce that all great writers were international, Joyce replied: 'But they were national first ... and it was the intensity of their own nationalism which made them international in the end, as in the case of Turgenieff. You remember his "Tales of the Sportsman," how local they were – and yet out of that germ he became a great international writer.' 'Turgenieff' was an alternate, mostly early, English (and French) transliteration of Turgenev's Russian surname; 'Tales of the Sportsman' Joyce's approximation of one of the titles of English translations under which Turgenev's collection was first published.

and, by the time of the doctor's arrival, had lapsed into unconsciousness. Because or in spite of the doctor's best efforts, the young woman appears temporarily to rally, though her condition remains grave. After a few days with the doctor at her bedside but with no improvement in that condition, the young woman, identified only by her given name and patronym, Alexandra Andreevna, demands to know if she is dying. 'I sat there, you know, with my head bent,' the doctor relates to his patient-confidant as to a confessor on p. 66, 'I even dozed a little.'

> Suddenly it seemed as though someone touched me in the side ; I turned round. . . . Good God ! Alexandra Andreevna was gazing with intent eyes at me . . . her lips parted, her cheeks seemed burning. "What is it?" "Doctor, shall I die?" "Merciful Heavens!" "No, doctor, no ; please don't tell me I shall live . . . don't say so . . . If you knew. . . . Listen ! for God's sake don't conceal my real position," and her breath came so fast. "If I can know for certain that I must die . . . then I will tell you all—all !" (all ellipses in the original)

Convinced now—or perhaps convincing herself—that she will soon die, but seemingly exhilarated by that prospect, Alexandra Andreevna tells the doctor the 'all' she had withheld: that she desperately loves him and wants nothing more, and nothing less, than that before her death the doctor declare his love for her—which, despite his emotional and professional misgivings, he does. After another day or two, after lapsing back into unconsciousness and with her doctor-turned-fiancé maintaining his vigil by her bedside, the young woman dies.

Why might Joyce have knowingly and deliberately chosen to borrow this sentence, if that is what he did, from Turgenev's story, and from the mouth of the desperately ill and desperately infatuated Alexandra Andreevna? Perhaps because he wished to suggest—perhaps only half-seriously—that Martha Clifford's perceived need of, emotional attachment to, or love for 'Henry Flower'—whom she has never met, whom she only thinks she knows, and who does not even exist except as a fiction invented by Bloom—is, for her, as real and as intense as anything felt by the dying and delirious 'heroine' for the district doctor of Turgenev's tale.

Uly 5.365: Lourdes cure, waters of oblivion.

In their respective remarks on this five-word, verbless sentence, Thornton, Gifford, and SMT all note the purportedly miraculous curative powers of the waters of Lourdes, Thornton and SMT also mentioning the River Lethe in Hades and Thornton citing the English poet John Milton's (1608–1674) *Paradise Lost* (1674 version), Book 2, lines 583–85, with 'Lethe, the river of oblivion [...] whereof who drinks | Forthwith his former state and being forgets.' As for the phrase 'waters of oblivion' itself, none of the three names a specific and once well-known literary antecedent, though one such does exist.

In the first quarter of the eighteenth century (as noted above, see p. 64), the first English-language edition of *One Thousand and One Nights*, also known as *The Arabian Nights' Entertainment* or simply the *Arabian Nights*—based on a collection of Middle Eastern folk tales first published in Arabic during the Islamic Golden Age (from roughly the eighth to the thirteenth centuries)—was published in England. Half a century later, James Kenneth Ridley (1736–1765), an Oxford-educated English author and sometime chaplain to the British army in India—hoping perhaps to capitalize on the continuing popularity of the *Arabian Nights* and the more recent popularity of Macpherson's *Fingal*—published *Tales of the Genii* (London, 1764), a collection of short and novella-length stories 'faithfully translated from the Persian' (proclaimed its title page) by 'Sir Charles Morell, formerly ambassador from the British Settlements in India to the Great Mogul', of a work by 'Horam, the Son of Asmar'. Like Macpherson's Ossian and his *Fingal*, neither Morell, nor Horam, nor the tales themselves existed except as fictions crafted by Ridley himself. Nevertheless, Ridley's *Tales of the Genii*, first published in book form a year before his death, was itself a critical and commercial success— some comparing it to the English writer, lexicographer, and sage Samuel Johnson's (1709–1784) *History of Rasselas, Prince of Abissinia* (London, 1759)—with five editions of the two-volume work published by 1786, another four by 1814, and still others later in that century.

The phrase 'the Waters of Oblivion' features prominently in one of the longer tales of Ridley's collection, 'Sadak and Kalasrade', in which Kalasrade, beautiful wife of the retired military hero Sadak, is kidnapped by order of the evil sultan Amurath, who envies their domestic happiness and wants Kalasrade for himself. Kalasrade tells Amurath that she will submit to him only if she can first drink from the waters of oblivion and thereby forget her beloved husband. Amurath agrees but cynically sends Sadak himself in quest of the fabled waters, a quest from which, as he knows, no one has ever returned alive. Aided by the spirit Adiram, however, Sadak survives a storm at sea, a plague, evil genii, a whirlpool in a cave, and a harrowing climb up a volcanic mountain, reaches the waters of oblivion, and returns safely with his prize. Amurath, hoping to sooth his conscience and better enjoy Kalasrade's favors, insists on being the first to drink the magical waters—but, upon doing so, he instantly dies. Kalasrade is freed, she and Sadak are joyously reunited, and Sadak becomes the new sultan in Amurath's place.

As a further indication of how central it is to Ridley's tale, the phrase 'the Waters of Oblivion'—always so capitalized—occurs in it a total of two dozen times. And, as an indication of the story's familiarity and popularity, its climactic scene was the subject of an oil painting by the English painter, engraver, and illustrator John Martin (1789–1854) entitled 'Sadak in Search of the Waters of Oblivion' (1812) that has been called 'the most famous of the British Romantic works [of art]';[9] the English poet Percy Bysshe Shelley (1792–1822) versified the same scene in his eighty-line 'Sadak the Wanderer. A Fragment.', first published in the literary annual *The Keepsake* (London) for 1828; 'The Waters of Oblivion' was the title of a forgettable and now-forgotten poem by the Scottish renaissance-art collector and real-estate magnate John Malcolm of Poltalloch (1805–1893) collected in the 1830 edition of another literary annual, *Forget Me Not* (London); and the entire story was attempted in a now-forgotten grand opera, *Sadak and Kalasrade, Or, The Waters of Oblivion*, with music by Charles Packer (1810–1883) and libretto by the English author and dramatist Mary Russell Mitford (1787–1855), that debuted at the English Opera House (London) in April 1835, only to be withdrawn from production, after lukewarm reviews, a week later.

Did Joyce know the origin and history of the phrase 'waters of oblivion' before planting it in Bloom's mind in 'Lotus-Eaters'? Given its prominence in the once widely read tale of 'Sadak and Kalasrade' and its subsequent occurrences elsewhere, it seems likely that he did. As to why Joyce did so, it may have been because the phrase fit so well in an episode concerned with forgetfulness in all its manifestations. But its presence there may also owe something to the ironic contrast between the soon-to-be-cuckolded Bloom, the soon-to-be-unfaithful Molly, and the love and fidelity displayed by both Sadak and the Penelope-like Kalasrade in Ridley's romantic tale.

---

9   By Michael Jacobs and Paul Stirton in *The Knopf Traveler's Guides to Art: Great Britain and Ireland* (New York: Alfred A. Knopf, 1984), p. 27.

Uly 5.461–62: How goes the time?

Unremarked by Thornton, Gifford, and SMT, Bloom's question to himself—as he ponders whether he has time for a warm bath before Paddy Dignam's funeral—was anticipated verbatim in several prior works, at least some of which Joyce is likely to have read.

One of these is the English playwright, poet, and satirist John Marston's (1575?–1634) romantic comedy *The History of Antonio and Mellida* (London, 1602)—as collected in *The Works of John Marston*, ed. A. H. Bullen (London, 1887), vol. 1 (of 3), p. 48—III i 101–05, Andrugio and Lucio conversing:

> *Andrugio*   How goes the time?
> *Lucio.*   I saw no sun to-day.
> *Andrugio*   No sun will shine, where poor Andrugio breathes.
>   My soul grows heavy : boy, let's have a song :
>   We'll sing yet, faith, even in despite of fate.

Another, by the Scottish poet and dramatist Joanna Baillie (1762–1851), is her play *Rayner: A Tragedy* (London, 1805), with, in Act 5, sc. 2, Rayner speaking as he awaits his expected execution:

> Thank God for it ! Now to our task :
> What of it now remains we shall o'er-master.
> Pray thee how goes the time ? But pardon me !
> I have too oft inquired how goes the time :
> It is my weakness.

Another, in the opening lines of Tennyson's poem 'Will Waterproof's Lyrical Monologue', both as first published in 1842 and as revised in 1853:

> O plump head-waiter at The Cock,
>   To which I most resort,
> How goes the time ? 'Tis five o'clock.
>   Go fetch a pint of port :
> But let it not be such as that
>   You set before chance-comers,
> But such whose father-grape grew fat
>   On Lusitanian summers.

And again, in Dickens's *Dombey and Son* (London, 1848), chap. 55 ('Rob The Grinder Loses His Place'), p. 551, in which the fleeing Carker, who has just escaped from France, asks the waiter who is making preparations for his dinner "What day is this?":

> " Day, Sir ?"
> " Is it Wednesday ?"
> " Wednesday, Sir ! No, Sir. Thursday, Sir."
> " I forgot. How goes the time ? My watch is unwound."

Uly 5.563–64: the stream of life

Thornton and SMT claim that Bloom's phrase misquotes the ballad 'In Happy Moments Day by Day' from Act 2 of the Fitzball–Wallace light opera *Maritana* (1845), the first stanza of which begins: 'In happy moments day by day, | The sands of life may pass'. Perhaps so, but the phrase 'the stream of life', which Bloom recalls again in 8.176, occurs verbatim in, among other works, Byron's *The Giaour* (London, 1813), lines 761–64: 'There from thy daughter, sister, wife, | At midnight drain the stream of life ; | Yet loathe the banquet which perforce | Must feed thy livid living corse'; and Shelley's *The Revolt of Islam* (London, 1818), canto 6, stanza 29, p. 142: 'We know not where we go, or what sweet dream | May pilot us thro' caverns strange and fair | Of far and pathless passion, while the stream | Of life, our bark doth on its whirlpools bear, | Spreading swift wings as sails to the dim air'.

6. 'Hades'

Uly 6.67–68: I'll tickle his catastrophe

Thornton, Gifford, SMT, and others cite Shakespeare's *2 Henry IV*, II i 59–60, where Falstaff's boy, Page, attacking Hostess Quickly, cries: 'Away, you scullion ! you rampallian ! you fustilarian ! I'll tickle your catastrophe.' But Joyce's phrase also occurs, verbatim, in *The Merry Devill of Edmonton* (London, 1608)—a comedy of uncertain authorship about a Faust-like Cambridge magician, Peter Fabell, who has made a pact with the Devil—in Act 5, scene 2, of which Blague the Host, speaking to Sir Arthur Clare, says, in the play as edited by Hugh Walker, M.A. (London, 1897), p. 61:

> Body of Saint George, this is mine overthwart neighbour hath done this to seduce my blind customers. I'll tickle his catastrophe for this ; if I do not indict him at next assizes for burglary, let me die of the yellows ; for I see 'tis no boot in these days to serve the good Duke of Norfolk. The villanous world is turned manger ; one jade deceives another, and your ostler plays his part commonly for the fourth share. Have we comedies in hand, you whoreson, villanous male London lecher?

Uly 6.87–88: O jumping Jupiter!

Along with many other instances of the phrase in the late nineteenth and early twentieth centuries, most of them lacking the vocative 'O', most of them from America, and most of them in humor magazines, *Jumping Jupiter* was the title of a musical comedy with book and lyrics by, and starring, the American stage and (later) film actor, playwright, and stage director Richard Carle (1871–1941), with a score by the Bohemian-American composer and songwriter Karl Hoschna (1876–1911). As discussed by Charles Hamm in his *Irving Berlin: Songs from the Melting Pot: The Formative Years, 1907–1914* (Oxford University Press, 1997), p. 191:

> The show was popular in London and Chicago but less well received in New York. Percy Hammond wrote of the show in the *Chicago Tribune* for 5 August 1910: 'To the framework of an old time farce by Mr. Sydney Rosenfeld, Mr. Richard Carle, a dextrous adapter and tinkerer in plays with music, has added song and dance and color.' [...] After a well-received run of some months in Chicago, *Jumping Jupiter* was taken on the road and then brought to Broadway, where it ran for only a few weeks.

In fact, the show ran on New York City's Broadway only from 6 March to 25 March 1911. But Joyce may have seen, sung, or played the sheet music for some of its songs, which had been published by M. Witmark & Sons, of New York, Chicago, San Francisco, London, and Paris, in 1910.

Uly 6.88: Ye gods and little fishes!

This second of Milly Bloom's two 'tomboy oaths' seems to have originated in the early nineteenth century, possibly as part of a popular couplet of unknown date and origin: 'Ye gods and little fishes! | What is a man without his breeches?'

Among other early and subsequent instances, it occurred in *The Orientalist, or Electioneering in Ireland; a Tale, by Myself*—that is, by a Mrs Purcell—(London, 1820), vol. 1, pp. 83–84:

> When the driver of the piebalds first beheld the Earl's equipage advancing, he thus addressed his companion, " Do lay aside that paper, Vincent—here is something better worth looking at."
> " Ye gods and little fishes ! what roses and lilies—pink, satin, and sable."
> " You know the party?"
> " Not I ; they are strangers, perhaps the Clanroys : have we room enough to pass ?"
> " Scarcely—what a lovely girl !"

in *The Press, or Literary Chit-Chat. A Satire* (London, 1822), by the English poet, satirist, critic, and playwright John Hamilton Reynolds (1794–1852), part 2, section title 'Bas-Bleusia', pp. 71–72, lines 241–52:

> Men oft have fancies vague and wild,
> And love them as a fav'rite child ;
> Sir Thomas thus, in days of yore,
> Raved wisely of a fancied shore,
> Where laws and manners past a joke
> Ruled, he affirms, the docile folk.
> Now pray not at my fancy smile,
> If, like Sir Thomas, I've an isle ;
> Why should not Jocus as Sir Thomas
> Create a realm and people rum as ?
> Aid me, ye gods and little fishes,
> To versify up to my wishes !

in *Tom Cringle's Log* (see also the discussion below on *Uly* 6.252), by the Scottish author and autobiographer Michael Scott (1789–1835), chap. 15 ('The Cruise of the Firebrand'), as serialized in *Blackwood's*, vol. 32 (Nov. 1832), p. 752, and in the book version (Edinburgh and London, 1833) in vol. 2 (of 2), chap. 1, p. 3:

> I raised my eyes to hob and nob with the master, when—ye gods and little fishes—who should they light on, but the merry phiz—merry, alas ! no more—of Aaron Bang, Esquire, who, during the soup interlude, had slid into the vacant chair unperceived by me.

and, as a final example, in Louisa May Alcott's sequel to her *Little Women* (1868–69), the children's novel *Little Men, or Life at Plumfield with Jo's Boys* (Boston, 1871; London, 1872), chap. 2 ('The Boys'), p. 24 of the London edition:

> If he did not know his lessons, he always had some droll excuse to offer, and as he was usually clever at his books, and as bright as a button in composing answers when he did not know them, he got on pretty well at school. But out of school,—Ye gods and little fishes ! how Tommy did carouse !

Uly 6.124: Canvassing for death.

In the only pre-Joyce instance I have found, this phrase previously occurred in a similar context in the *Montreal (Canada) Herald and Daily Commercial Gazette* for Tuesday, 18 Dec. 1883, p. 4, suggesting that the phrase was or may have been 'out there' well before Joyce's use of it:

"Diphtheria" is among us canvassing for Death. It is a disease of this century, having been first noticed in France, where it raged as an epidemic in 1818. Beyond doubt it had also occurred centuries before medical science was able enough to diagnose it. It is one of the most fatal of diseases, and it seldom takes much longer than a week, after it has fairly started, to accomplish its purpose[,] viz.: —suffocation.

Uly 6.126–27: A dying scrawl.

Bloom's phrase, as he recalls his father's last letter—a suicide note that he wrote just before or while taking his own life—seems to have occurred, all but verbatim, only twice pre-Joyce, the first of the two instances in 'Augustus Law, S. J.[:] Notes in Remembrance', in *The Irish Monthly*, vol. 14, no. 158 (Aug. 1886), 430–39, in which the magazine's founder and editor, Rev. Matthew Russell (1834–1912), on pp. 434–35, describes Law's last months as a missionary priest before his death from a fever, at the age of 47, at Umzila Kraal, South Africa:

> " I have never yet suffered on the journey as much as I did when serving her Majesty in the Navy," [Law had written to his sister]. Yet a month later he was writing to his father his last letter, except one, the last of all. He was then on his way to Umzila's country under difficulties that we despair of describing in the space that now remains to us. The terrible tetze fly, fatal to oxen, no roads, no civilization—the three hundred odd miles between Gubuluwayo and Umzila's kraal was worse than thousands of miles in a fairly civilized country. " Goodbye for the present, dearest father. I hope that you have gone through this winter all right, and that you may live for many years to encourage and bless us all." Us ! But his only remaining letter to his father was his dying scrawl.

The second instance: in a novel (his only one) by the Islington-born sometime journalist Frederick Leal (1861–1897), *Wynter's Masterpiece*—whose title refers to the central character's first novel, the manuscript of which is stolen in the first chapter but ultimately recovered and published to great critical and commercial success—first serialized from 31 Oct. 1891 to 6 Feb. 1892 in the weekly *Leeds Times*, followed by publication in London, by Swan, Sonnenschein & Company, in 1892. The phrase in question occurs in the second of its two volumes, where the penultimate chapter, 36 ('What Friendship Is.'), reporting the death in India of Wynter's heroic best friend, reads on p. 526: 'The signature was incomplete, just as if the pencil—the dying scrawl was in black lead—had fallen from the writer's hand.'

Uly 6.136: the veiled sun

Among other pre-Joyce instances, this phrase occurred in 'The Voice of Nature', by the British poet and, from 1913 to 1930, Poet Laureate Robert Bridges (1844–1930), first collected in *The Shorter Poems of Robert Bridges* (London, 1890), pp. 49–50, the first stanza of which reads:

> I stand on the cliff and watch the veiled sun paling
>   A silver field afar in the mournful sea,
> The scourge of the surf, and plaintive gulls sailing
>   At ease on the gale that smites the shuddering lea :
>   Whose smile severe and chaste
> June never hath stirred to vanity, nor age defaced.
> In lofty thought strive, O spirit, for ever :
> In courage and strength pursue thine own endeavour.

And, though written first—the holograph manuscript is dated 27 February 1841—in a poem by the English novelist and poet Emily Brontë (1818–1848) first published as written in *The Complete Poems of Emily Brontë*, edited by Clement Shorter (London, 1910), pp. 261–62, reading in its entirety:

> And like myself lone, wholly lone,
>   It sees the day's long sunshine glow ;
> And like myself it makes its moan
>   In unexhausted woe.
>
> Give we the hills our equal prayer,
>   Earth's breezy hills and heaven's blue sea ;
> I ask for nothing further here
>   But my own heart and liberty.
>
> Ah ! could my hand unlock its chain,
>   How gladly would I with it soar ;
> And ne'er regret and ne'er complain
>   To see its shining eyes no more.
>
> But let me think, that if to-day
>   It pines in cold captivity,
> To-morrow both shall soar away,
>   Eternally, entirely free.

> Methinks this heart should rest awhile,
>   So stilly round the evening falls ;
> The veiled sun shone no parting smile,
>   Nor mirth, nor music wakes my halls.
>
> I have sat lonely all the day,
>   Watching the drizzly mist descend,
> And first conceal the hills in grey,
>   And then along the valleys wend.
>
> And I have sat and watched the trees,
>   And the sad flowers, how drear they blew ;
> Those flowers were formed to feel the breeze
>   Wave their light heads in summer's glow.
>
> Yet their lives passed in gloomy woe,
>   And hopeless comes its dark decline,
> And I lament because I know
>   That cold departure pictures mine.

Uly 6.149–50: *the retrospective arrangement*

As noted by SMT, this phrase, which first occurs here in a remark by Mr Power commenting on Ben Dollard's singing of 'The Croppy Boy', recurs six more times later in the novel: in 'Wandering Rocks' at 10.783 ('now in a kind of retrospective arrangement'); 'Sirens' at 11.798 ('harking back in a retrospective sort of arrangement'); 'Oxen of the Sun' at 14.1044 ('There, as in a retrospective arrangement'); 'Circe' at 15.442–43 ('harking back in a retrospective arrangement'); 'Eumaeus' at 16.1400–01 ('Looking back now in a retrospective kind of arrangement'); and 'Ithaca' at 17.1902–03 ('a retrospective arrangement of migrations and settlements').

But where did the phrase come from, what does it signify, and why does it occur repeatedly in *Ulysses*? Although isolated instances turn up two or three times in reports of British government official proceedings as early as 1809, the answer may lie on the title page of a book by one Thomas Smith, 'Preceptor of Youth, Greenwich, (formerly engaged in commerce.)', with a page-long title reading in part: *The Retrospective Tutors' Assistant; Being a Compendium of Practical Arithmetic, Both Mental and Scriptory: Containing An Entirely New Disposition of Matter to be Used in Inculcating a Knowledge of Computation Generally. Wherein the Principle of Deduction is Carried As Far As It is Available, Having Regard to Simplicity.* (London, 1839) and with, further down the title page, the following statement containing the phrase in question: 'One of the most perplexing difficulties attending the tuition of youth, is the habitual forgetfulness, on the part of the pupil, of that which has been apparently attained ; the object of the "retrospective arrangement" is to provide a remedy, by securing a frequent recurrence to similar principles, avoiding actual repetition as much as possible.'

It would seem that Joyce's repeated planting of the phrase 'retrospective arrangement' throughout his novel, always without obvious relevance to the passages in which it occurs, is a private joke—he could not have expected more than a handful of his readers to know of Smith's arithmetic primer with its pedantic title—in which he sets out not to avoid actual repetition as much as possible but to engage in actual repetition as much as possible—and to do so by playfully engaging in actual repetition of 'retrospective arrangement' itself.

Uly 6.228: unresisting knees

What appears to be the only pre-*Ulysses* instance of this phrase occurred in the English novelist and civil servant Anthony Trollope's (1815–1882) first novel—set in Ireland during the Great Famine—*The Macdermots of Ballycloran* (London, 1847), vol. 3 (of 3), chap. 2, p. 61. The phrase comes at the end of a long paragraph beginning on p. 59, also having to do with a ride in a crowded coach, and reading in its entirety:

> Indeed at the first glance any body would have said father John was in the right of it, for on the guard's seat there were two besides himself—both burley-looking men—not of the soft, compressible flabby genus, but large, strong, bony men ; you would sooner get an inch by pressing against a stone wall, than by squeezing against the sides of such rocky-looking individuals ; on the opposite seat there were also three people ; on the outside there was a dirty-looking traveller—a pig-jobber by trade—apparently as sullen and as obstinate as any of the swine whom it was his business to buy and sell ; then a goodnatured, fat gentleman, in a vast blue cloak ; from his face, you might have sworn he would have done anything to accommodate a fellow-traveller, he looked so soft—so yielding, and so modest ; but what could he do ? He was eighteen stone weight, and might have almost acted Falstaff without stuffing ; the third was a female, with a sharp, red nose, a cotton

umbrella, a basket-full of buns, and a child about five years old, who, for the sake of the free seat, she had converted into a baby, and purposed carrying in her lap, though between Boyle and Drumsna, she had contrived pretty nearly to wrap the boy in the goodnatured man's cloak, and to transfer at any rate half his weight, on his unresisting knees.

Regarding the phrase 'unresisting knees' as it functions in the 'Hades' episode: were there not instances in the episode of phrases and short passages with clear or apparent sexual import, construing this phrase as another such instance might seem unwarranted, even perverse. After all, with four grown men—Bloom, Mr Power, Martin Cunningham, and Simon Dedalus—sharing the limited space in a horse-drawn carriage for the ride to Glasnevin cemetery and Paddy Dignam's funeral, they would inevitably have found their knees bumping into those of their fellow passengers.

But the 'Hades' episode does have a number of sexually suggestive and sometimes sexually explicit recollections and remarks. They include Bloom's memory of Molly twelve years past 'watching the two dogs at it by the wall of the cease to do evil' (6.78–79) immediately followed by her summoning Bloom to couple with her—'Give us a touch, Poldy. God, I'm dying for it.'—the touch by which their son Rudy, who would die eleven days after his birth, was conceived. They also include the travellers noticing crustcrumbs under their thighs in the carriage, with Simon Dedalus and Martin Cunningham (in 6.103–04) further noticing (Dedalus: 'Unless I'm greatly mistaken ... What do you think, Martin?' 'It struck me too, Martin Cunningham said'.) signs of lovemaking—semen, perhaps—both the crumbs and the signs of such activity pointing proleptically to the crumbs and signs of lovemaking Bloom will find in his and Molly's bed when he returns to their home at 7 Eccles Street late that night.

The phrase 'unresisting knees' may thus reasonably be construed, along with its narrative-level sense in the context of the bumpy carriage-ride, as having another, sexual subtext, pointing both to a tryst that may have taken place in the carriage itself not long before the day of Dignam's funeral, and to the tryst Bloom expects to take place at 4 o'clock that afternoon in which his wife and her unresisting knees will yield to the touch of Blazes Boylan.

Uly 6.252: In all his pristine beauty

In employing this phrase, Mr Power refers sardonically to the presumptively Jewish Reuben J. Dodd, who is just then passing by. One of several, and possibly the earliest of, pre-Joyce instances of the phrase occurs in *Tom Cringle's Log* (cited in the discussion of *Uly* 6.88 on p. 132 above), in, once again, chap. 15 ('The Cruise of the Firebrand'), as serialized in *Blackwood's*, vol. 32 (Nov. 1832), p. 765, and in vol. 2, chap. 1, pp. 33–34 of the book:

> So down we all trundled into the cabin, masters and men. It was brilliantly lighted up—the table sparkling with crystal and wine, and glancing with silver plate ; and there on a sofa lay Aaron Bang in all his pristine beauty, and fresh from his toilet, for he had just got out of his cot after an eight-and-forty hours' sojourn therein—nice white neckcloth—white jean waistcoat and trowsers, and span-new blue coat.

Aaron Bang, Esquire, had been introduced in chap. 10 ('Vomito Prieto'), p. 308, as a 'fresh, nice-looking man [...] an incipient planting attorney in the neighbourhood, of great promise [...].' *Tom Cringle's Log*—the name was sometimes used by Scott as a pseudonym—tells the story of how Cringle rose from midshipman to lieutenant to a command of his own: the audacious little warship *Wasp*.

Another instance of the phrase occurs in *Not Wisely, But Too Well*, a novel first anonymously published in three volumes (London, 1867), then in a single volume (London, 1875) with its author identified as the Welsh novelist and short story writer Rhoda Broughton (1840–1920). In vol. 3, chap. 4, pp. 148–49 of the former, and chap. 30, p. 324, of the latter, the passage containing the phrase reads:

> "There are as good fish in the sea as ever came out of it," says the proverb ; and there were plenty better fish, better-looking fish, more valuable fish altogether, than George Chester at this very house ; but still silvery salmon, speckled trout, cod, and haddock might all swim finnily by ; they could not compare, in her blinded eyes, with the dull carp she was hankering after. When she had been away from home about three weeks, George made his appearance one day ; came walking over the grass, in all his pristine beauty and plumpness, as they were playing croquet. It was rather a fortunate moment for Margaret, she was looking

so undeniably pretty, flushed, excited, with eyes which, now that they were not seen beside Kate's, might pass for very bright ones.

A third instance, not very different in ironic tone from the previous two or from Joyce, occurs in *Youth On The Prow* (London, 1879), by the British novelist and artist Lady Emma Caroline Wood (1802–1879), vol. 2 (of 3), reading on p. 64:

> Lady Gower tried to think of Sir Atheline as he then was ; no doubt blear-eyed, red-nosed, bloated ; but her mind revolted from the image, and despite of reason, memory painted him in all his pristine beauty, with his delicate skin, tender blue eyes, mutable mouth, and faultless symmetry of figure.

Uly 6.351: Leading him the life of the damned.

Bloom is thinking here of the unfortunate Martin Cunningham, who must repeatedly set up the home he shares with his drunkard wife because she repeatedly pawns the family furniture to pay for drink. One nearly verbatim antecedent of the highlighted phrase occurs in the chapter on 'Lorenzo de' Medici (Considered as a Poet)' in Mary Wollstonecraft Shelley's (1797–1851) *Lives of the Most Eminent Literary and Scientific Men of Italy, Spain, and Portugal*, vol. 1 (London, 1835), p. 151, reading in part:

> Besides the philosophic and beautiful poem of Lucretius, we owe to [Emanuel Chrysoloras] the complete copies of Quintilian, Plautus, Statius, Silius Italicus, Columella, and many others. Several of these exist only from the copy found by him, and were thus rescued from certain destruction. " I did not find them in libraries," he says, " which their dignity demanded, but in a dark and obscure dungeon at the bottom of a tower, in which they were leading the life of the damned.["]

Another such instance, by the British journalist, author, dramatist, and autobiographer Edmund Hodgson Yates (1831–1894), occurs in his novel *A Waiting Race* (London, 1872), vol. 2 (of 3), chap. 8 ('Lady Osgood Has an Idea'), p. 245, in which Owen Cunliffe is speaking with Sybil Fleetwood, sister of the woman to whom he is engaged:

> ' I know nothing,' said Sybil calmly; ' I understand nothing. If you wish me to do so, you really must be more explicit.'

'Need I tell you,' he said, fixing his hungry eyes on hers, ' that I am leading the life of the damned, and that not Dives in his flame was more tortured and tormented than I am ? It is my own fault, and I have no one else to blame. A little more than three months ago I had the chance of winning you, the loveliest and dearest of women, whom I swear I love at this moment more madly, passionately, devotedly, than I ever thought I could love in my life. I threw aside that chance, like a fool that I was, and now where and what am I ?'

Uly 6.456: Left him weeping, I suppose?

As Gifford indicates in his note on the phrase, Tom Kernan has run up an increasingly large bill with the grocer Fogarty, and Kernan's failure to pay it down or off has left Fogarty weeping. As to any antecedent work or works containing the phrase that Joyce may have had in mind, Thornton, Gifford, and SMT are silent.

Among the several such works, one was George Macdonald's fantasy novel *Lilith: A Romance* (London, 1895), with, in chap. 42 ('I Sleep the Sleep'), an exchange on pp. 311–13 between a young and an old man that begins as follows:

> A little farther, I came where sat a grayheaded man on the sand, weeping.
> 'What ails you, sir ?' I asked. ' Are you forsaken ?'
> ' I weep,' he answered, ' because they will not let me die. I have been to the house of death, and its mistress, notwithstanding my years, refuses me. Intercede for me, sir, if you know her, I pray you.'
> ' Nay, sir,' I replied, ' that I cannot ; for she refuses none whom it is lawful for her to receive.'

The conversation between the two continues inconclusively, then ends on p. 313 with the speaker taking his leave: 'He fell to weeping afresh, and I left him weeping. What I said, I fear he did not heed. But Mara would find him !'

Another, by the Hellenized Syrian satirist, rhetorician, and pamphleteer Lucian of Samosata (c. 125 CE–after 180), was his 'Dialogues of the Gods,' collected in vol. 1 (of 4) of his complete works as translated by H. W. Fowler and F. G. Fowler (Oxford, 1905), in which, in section 6, p. 65, Hera tells her husband Zeus that the 'wretch' Ixion has for some time been making love to her—or attempting to do so—and that she has rebuffed his advances (italics in the original):

> 'For a long time I didn't like to say anything to you ; I thought his mad fit would pass. But when he actually dared to *speak* to me, I left him weeping and grovelling about, and stopped my ears, so that I might not hear his impertinences, and came to tell you. It is for you to consider what steps you will take.'

Uly 6.467: Gloomy gardens

Both Gifford and SMT cite 'the fields of mourning' (*lugentes campi*) in book 6 of Virgil's *Aeneid*. Another work, one of the several from which, and the most likely of which, Joyce could have derived the phrase 'gloomy gardens' itself, is the French novelist, poet, playwright, and politician Victor Hugo's (1802–1885) historical novel *Les Misérables* (Paris, 1862), in which, in vol. 1 (of 3), chap. 104 ('The Beginning of an Enigma'), p. 381, of Sir Lascelles Wraxall's (1828–1865) authorized English translation (London, 1862), the first sentence of the first paragraph reads: 'Jean Valjean found himself in a large garden of most singular appearance, one of those gloomy gardens that appear made to be looked at in winter, and by night.'

Uly 6.522–23: First the stiff: then the friends of the stiff.

Joyce and Bloom seem here to be recalling something one or both of them have read: a passage in Charles James Lever's (1806–1872)—as 'Harry Lorrequer'—much-reprinted novel *Charles O'Malley, The Irish Dragoon* (Dublin and London, 1841), vol. 2 (of 2), chap. 75 ('The Ghost'), p. 39:

> " I need say no more, only one thing, that it was principally among the farmers and the country people my father was liked so much. The great people and the quality—I ax your pardon : but sure isn't it true, Mister Charles, they don't fret so much after their fathers and brothers, and they care little who's driving them, whether it was a decent respectable man like my father, or a chap with a grin on him like a rat-trap ? And so it happened, that my father used to travel half the county ; going here and there wherever there was trade stirring ; and, faix, a man didn't think himself rightly buried if my father wasn't there : for ye see he knew all about it ; he could tell to a quart of spirits

what would be wanting for a wake ; he knew all the good cryers for miles round ; and I've heard it was a beautiful sight to see him standing on a hill, arranging the procession, as they walked into the churchyard, and giving the word like a captain.

"' Come on, the stiff,—now the friends of the stiff,—now de pop'lace.'

" That's what he used to say, and, troth, he was always repeating it, when he was a little gone in drink,—for that's the time his spirits would rise,—and he'd think he was burying half Munster.["]

Uly 6.533: dark thinking eyes

Unremarked by Thornton, Gifford, and SMT, Joyce's phrase, referring to Bloom's face as he rides behind Martin Cunningham and Mr Power on their way to Paddy Dignam's funeral, previously occurred verbatim in Dickens's novel *Hard Times. For These Times.* (London, 1854), book 2, chap. 6 ('Fading Away'), p. 182, where the working-class Stephen Blackpool, in conversation with the elderly Mrs Pegler while his friend Rachael looks on, refers to Louisa Gradgrind, now the wife of Josiah Bounderby, who unbeknownst to Stephen, Rachael, and Louisa is Mrs Pegler's son: "' Well, missus," said he, " I ha seen the lady, and she were yoong and hansom. Wi' fine dark thinkin eyes, and a still way, Rachael, as I ha never seen the like on."'

The same phrase occurred four years later in the novel *Eva Desmond: or, Mutation* (London, 1858), anonymous published but written (according to publisher Smith, Elder's accounts) by the otherwise unknown Mary Matilda Smith, in vol. 2 (of 3) of which, chap. 16 ('Farewell'), on pp. 199–200, she writes:

> Talk of Edward Phillips ! he was a spruce well-dressed man to Charles Stanhope, whose ill-made clothes hung on him as on a peg ; his long lank hair seemed never to have been asked to grow in any other way than it liked, his badly kept whiskers always looked untidy and uncurled. His face was not plain—no face could be plain with those large, dark, thinking eyes ; even when they gazed in vacancy, it seemed in intense thought, as if they could see nothing without because they were searching so deeply into something within : when he smiled (which was but seldom, the habitual expression of his face being rigidly grave) there was a mild kindness in his look that betokened a good and gentle disposition.

and occurred a third time in the English novelist Ellen Barlee's (1825-1893) *Helen Lindsay; or, The Trial of Faith* (London, 1859; second edn London, 1863), with, in chap. 16, p. 228, of the latter:

> His passion, eloquence, drew from Helen an avowal of her own feelings. Never, perhaps, had she felt such a moment of earthly happiness as when, his arm encircling her, he poured into her bruised heart his tale of love, as when, his dark thinking eyes bent pleadingly on her, he awaited her reply.

Uly 6.554–55: One must go first: alone under the ground: and lie no more in her warm bed.

Bloom is thinking here of himself predeceasing Molly, but he does so in terms that may also point to Ecclesiastes iv 11, reading, in the Douay version, 'And if two lie together, they shall warm one another: how shall one alone be warmed?'; and, in the King James, 'Again, if two lie together, then they have heat: but how can one be warm alone?'

Uly 6.673: with his toes to the daisies

As noted by John S. Farmer and W. E. Henley, compilers and editors of *Slang and Its Analogues Past and Present*, vol. 2 – C. TO Fizzle ([London], 1891), s.v. *Daisies*, the subsequently familiar expression 'to turn up one's toes to the daisies', meaning 'to die', first appeared in book form in *The Ingoldsby Legends; or, Mirth and Marvels* (London, 1840), by the English cleric, novelist, and humorous poet Richard Harris Barham (1788–1845) as 'Thomas Ingoldsby', from legends of his authorship first printed in 1837 in *Bentley's Miscellany* and later in *The New Monthly Magazine*. The specific legend in Barham's collection where the phrase originated was 'The Babes in the Wood; or, The Norfolk Tragedy', the fourth of whose twenty-four stanzas reads:

> " Now think, 'tis your Sister invokes
>   Your aid, and the last word she says is,
> Be kind to those dear little folks
>   When our toes are turned up to the daisies !—
> By the servants don't let them be snubb'd,—
>   —Let Jane have her fruit and her custard,—

> And mind Johnny's chilblains are rubb'd
> Well with Whitehead's best essence of mustard !"

Uly 6.759: Spice of pleasure.

One of several pre-Joyce instances of the phrase occurs in an essay by the English author George Walter Thornbury (1828–1876) entitled 'Fair and Foul Circassians,' published in *All the Year Round*, no. 36 (31 Dec. 1859), 218–23, and reading, on p. 220:

> I was seated under the broad brim of the roof of a fountain which, as usual in Mosque court-yards, filled the centre of the " quad." Twenty years ago, and I suppose the slice of a reaping-hook sabre would have been the first intimation that I should have had that I was in the sacred court of ablutions, and breaking the law of the Prophet. But things grow changed in twenty years ; no one disturbed me now ; and if there was just a spice of danger in the situation (for among Turks, when they are really fanatic, you are never safe), it gave a spice of pleasure to the situation, such as one feels in sitting on a sea-cliff, and hanging one's legs over among the fringing flowers, so that one may look France-ward, which is sea-ward, with more ease.

Another, far earlier instance: in the comedy *Amphitryon*, by the Roman playwright Plautus (d. 184 BCE), as translated from the Latin into 'familiar blank verse' by Bonnell Thornton, vol. 1, second edn, revised and corrected (London, 1769), Act 2, sc. 2, pp. 57–58, Alcmena, wife of Amphitryon, attended by Thessala:

> ALC. How scanty are the pleasures in life's course,
> If plac'd in opposition to it's [sic] troubles !
> For in the life of man to ev'ry one
> 'Tis thus allotted, thus it pleases heaven,
> That Sorrow, her companion, still should tread
> Upon the heels of Pleasure ; and if ought [sic]
> Of good befal us, forthwith there should follow
> Of ill a larger portion.—This I feel,
> And know it of myself now, unto whom
> A little spice of pleasure was imparted,
> In that it was permitted me to see
> My husband but one night : —he left me, and
> Departed on a sudden, ere 'twas day.—

Uly 6.772: Every man his price.

The more familiar version of Joyce's phrase—'Every man has his price'—was long attributed to British Prime Minister (Whig) Robert Walpole (1676–1745), who insisted he never said it and blamed the attribution on his political enemies. The phrase did, however, occur in a speech to the House of Commons delivered by the English Tory and Jacobite politician Sir William Wyndham (c. 1688–1740) on 13 March 1734; first published in *The Bee*, vol. 8, p. 97 (1734); and reading in part: 'It is an old maxim, That every man has his price, if you can but come up to it.' And both long before and long after Walpole's and Wyndham's day, it recurred widely elsewhere.

One of the many instances: in the British lawyer, folklorist, translator of folk tales from German and Norse mythology, and novelist George Webbe Dasent's (1817–1896) *Three To One, or, Some Passages Out of the Life of Amicia Lady Sweetapple* (London, 1872), after its serialization from October 1871 to September 1872 in *Belgravia: A London Magazine*. In vol. 1 (of 3), chap. 21 ('The Thunder-Storm and the Gipsy'), pp. 324–25 of that novel, Lady Sweetapple and her Romany friend Sinaminta, with Harry Fortescue looking on, are debating the validity of the proverbial phrase:

> " You think, then," said Lady Sweetapple, almost hissing like Lamia in the poem by Keats, " that every man has his price, and Mr. Fortescue is like all the rest ? "
>
> As she said this, she looked at Harry like the wolf in " Red Riding Hood ; " but, much to her surprise, Harry neither flinched nor blanched. For all their effect, her words might as well have been uttered to a deaf man.
>
> " What consummate hypocrisy !" was all that Amicia could murmur before the gipsy went on—
>
> " Yes, every man has his price, and every woman, too ; young men and husbands, maidens and wives and widows—they have all their price, as well as the Romany. When they're low, they put it low ; and when they're high they put it high. That's all the difference."

In Joyce's own time, the phrase recurred in, among other places, the Swedish playwright, novelist, poet, essayist, and painter August Strindberg's (1849–1912) autobiographical novel *The Inferno* (1897)—first written in French 'at the height of Strindberg's troubles with both censors and women', by one account; then translated into English by Claud Field (London, 1912); and then into Swedish by Eugène Fahlstedt in 1914, with, in chap. 6 ('Hell'), p. 98, of Field's translation: '" Every man has his price," says the proverb, but a large sum must have been necessary to bribe this strong character.'

Also in 1914, it recurred as the title of the Australia-born Max Rittenberg's (1880–1965) novel *Every Man His Price* (London, 1914)— perfectly matching Joyce's phrase—a tale, said a capsule review in *The Bookfellow* (Sydney) that November, in which 'the leading character invents and exploits a wireless telephone, marries the woman he loves, and is deserted by her because business occupies too much of his time.'

Uly 6.852–53: Last act of *Lucia. Shall I nevermore behold thee?* Bam! He expires.

Thornton and SMT both note (as does Bowen) that the phrase 'Shall I nevermore behold thee' seems not to have occurred in any English-language translation of Edgardo's well-known aria in Act 3 of Gaetano Donizetti's *Lucia di Lammermoor* (1835), an opera based on Sir Walter Scott's novel *The Bride of Lammermoor* (1819)—though Thornton adds that the phrase 'Shall we never more behold thee' is sometimes listed as an alternate title of the song—and both suggest that Bloom is or may be thinking of the refrain from Stephen Foster's popular song 'Gentle Annie,' which begins 'Shall we never more behold thee'. Another possible source: *The Marvellous History of King Arthur in Avalon and of The Lifting of Lyonnesse: A Chronicle of the Round Table Communicated by Geoffrey of Monmouth*, edited with an introduction and notes by William John Courthope (1842–1917) as 'Geoffrey Junior' (London, 1904), chap. 11 ('How Sir Cephalus Took Off His Crown of Forgetfulness, and Heard the Breathless Chant of the Bulls and Bears'), p. 70:

> These things, when he beheld, his hairs stood upright on his head, and he cried with a lamentable passion : " O Britain, O my country, whose image is always in my mind and heart, but the true soil whereof lieth so far away, shall I never behold thee more, but must I for ever, by my doom, abide amid the shows of things that I see in my soul to be false and fleeting ? "

Uly 6.917: by devious paths

The sentence in *Ulysses* in which this phrase occurs reads in its entirety: 'The mourners moved away slowly without aim, by devious paths, staying at whiles to read a name on a tomb.' One of the many theological and evangelical instances of the highlighted phrase reads, in Saint Augustine's commentary on Matthew vii 7 ('Ask, and it shall be given you; seek, and you shall find; knock, and it shall be opened unto you.'): 'Ask. But what advantage is it that he is now able to walk, or even run, if he should go astray by devious paths?'; one of the many secular instances, in Sir Walter Scott's *Guy Mannering; or, The Astrologer* (Edinburgh, 1815), vol. 2 (of 3), chap. 13, p. 211:

> Having thus dispersed his myrmidons in various directions, he himself hastened by devious paths through the Wood of Warroch, to his appointed interview with Hatteraick, from whom he hoped to learn at more leisure than last night's conference admitted, the circumstances attending the return of the heir of Ellangowan to his native country.

Uly 6.1033: How grand we are this morning!

'How grand we are' in this final sentence of the episode occurred several times in the nineteenth and early twentieth centuries in the highbrow, middlebrow, and lowbrow literature of the English-speaking world. Some of the more widely read instances, hence among those Joyce is most likely to have seen, include the following, arranged in chronological order:

First, in the English novelist, poet, playwright, and politician Edward Bulwer-Lytton's (1803–1873) novel *Rienzi: The Last of the Roman Tribunes* (London, 1835), book 4 ('The Triumph and the Pomp'), chap. 1 ('The Boy Angelo.—The dream of Nina fulfilled.'), p. 178: '" How grand we are to-day !" said he, clapping his hands with an eagerness which Ursula failed not to reprove.'

Second, in Dickens's novella *The Chimes: A Goblin Story of Some Bells that Rang an Old Year Out and a New Year In* (London, 1844), p. 22: '"Where will you dine, father ? On the Post, or on the Steps ? Dear, dear, how grand we are. Two places to choose from ! "'

Third, in Thackeray's novel *The History of Pendennis: His Fortunes and Misfortunes, His Friends and His Greatest Enemy* (London, 1850), chap. 68

('In Which the Major Neither Yields His Money Nor His Life'), p. 886: '" How does it concern me, indeed ? how grand we are ! How does it concern my nephew, I wonder ? How does it concern my nephew's seat in Parlyment : and to subornation of bigamy ? How does it concern that ?["]'

And fourth, in *Punch*, vol. 99 (22 Nov. 1890), p. 241, where an anonymous poem entitled 'Alice in Blunderland' and subtitled ('On the Ninth of November') was occasioned (a headnote quoting Lord Salisbury explains) by a trade war that had just broken out between America, England, and France because 'America has instituted a vast system of prohibitive tariffs, mainly, I believe, because...American pigs do not receive proper treatment at the hands of Europe.' Spoken by 'The Real Turtle [who] sang this, very slowly, and sadly', the first three of the poem's nine stanzas read (italics in the original):

> " We are getting quite important," said the Porker to the Seal,
> " For we're 'European Questions,' as a Premier seems to feel.
> See the 'unintelligent' Lobster, even he, makes an advance !
> Oh, we lead the Politicians of the earth a pretty dance.
>   Will you, won't you, Yankee Doodle, England, and gay France.
>   Will you, won't you, will you, won't you, let *us* lead the dance ?

> " You can really have no notion how delightful it will be,
> When they take *us* up as matters of the High Diplomacee."
> But the Seal replied, " They brain us ! " and he gave a look askance
> At the goggle-eyed mailed Lobster, who was loved (and boiled) by France.
>   " Would they, could they, would they, could they, give us half a chance ?
>   Lobsters, Pigs, and Seals all suffer, Commerce to advance ! "

> " What matters it how grand we are ! " his plated friend replied,
> If our destiny is Salad, or the Sausage boiled or fried ?
> Though we breed strife 'twixt England, and America, and France,
> If we're chopped up, or boiled, or brained where is *our* great advance ?
>   Will you, won't you, will you, won't you chuck away the chance
>   Of peace in pig-stye, or at sea, to play the game of France ? "

7. 'Aeolus'

Uly 7.47: All his brains are in the nape of his neck

Bloom is here recalling a remark of Simon Dedalus referring to, and directed against, the actual Anglo-Irish barrister and *Freeman's Journal* editor William John Henry Brayden, Esquire (1865–1933) 'of Oaklands, Sandymount', who in a stately manner has just entered the shared premises of the *Freeman's Journal* and *Weekly Freeman* and is now 'statelily' mounting the staircase leading to his office. As to the remark itself, it had occurred verbatim and apparently uniquely pre-*Ulysses* two centuries earlier, in the English poet William King's (1663–1712) satirical pamphlet *The Transactioneer, With some of his Philosophical Fancies in Two Dialogues* (London, 1700), mocking the editorial competence and professional reputation of the Anglo-Irish physician, naturalist, and collector Sir Hans Sloane (1660–1753), then-Secretary of The Royal Society and Editor of its journal *Philosophical Transactions*, while also mocking the scientific prose style of the journal's virtuoso contributors generally.

In *The Transactioneer*'s Dialogue II, 'Between a Gentleman [representing King] and a Transactioneer [Sloane]', two of the several studies slated for publication in *Philosophical Transactions*, as reported on p. 56, are: 'Numb. 226. [which] gives an Account of a Child born without a Brain, which had it lived long enough would have made an Excellent Publisher of *Philosophical Transactions*.'; and 'Numb. 228. [which] gives an Account of another, that had his Brains in the Nape of his Neck.'

It seems unlikely that Simon Dedalus would have known of and read a two-hundred-year-old satirical pamphlet mocking the editor of The Royal Society's official journal, and borrowed an eight-word phrase from that pamphlet to mock the editor of the *Freeman's Journal*. But Joyce himself might well have both read and remembered (or jotted down a note on) King's pamphlet, and have given the quoted phrase to Bloom as having come from Dedalus to mock the stately, plump Anglo-Irish barrister whose leadership of the *Freeman's Journal* and its now anti-Parnellite editorial stance Joyce himself would likely have abhorred.

Uly 7.215–16: Seems to see with his fingers.

This thought of Bloom's as he watches a worker busily setting type at the shared printing facilities of the *Freeman's Journal* and the *Evening Telegraph* may point to a passage in the often revised and reissued *Guesses at Truth by Two Brothers* (London, 1827)—the two being the English theological writer and Church of England clergyman Julius Charles Hare (1795–1855) and Augustus William Hare, also a writer and Church of England cleric (1792–1834)—vol. 1 (of 2), p. 138:

> There is something very odd in the disposition of an Englishman's senses. He sees with his fingers, and hears with his toes. If you enter a gallery of pictures, you find all the spectators longing to become handlers : if you go to hear an overture of Mozart's, your next neighbour keeps all the while kicking time, as if he could not kill it without.

Or perhaps to such a passage as this from 'The Sense of Touch', an article by the Rev. B. G. Johns, Chaplain of the Blind School, Southwark, in *The Quiver: An Illustrated Magazine for Sunday and General Reading* (London, Paris, and New York, 1873), vol. 8, p. 485:

> But it is only by dint of long experience, and after an infinite series of mistakes, of many of which he is unconscious—that the blind boy manages to see with his fingers, and now and then to do more than hear with his ears ; and a shrewd youth of his own age, with a good pair of eyes, will still give him twenty in every hundred yards, and yet win the race.

Uly 7.232: A sudden screech of laughter

While 'screech of laughter' occurs countless times in pre-Joyce writings, the phrase 'sudden screech of laughter', with or without the indefinite article, seems first to have occurred in the English parodist and caricaturist Max Beerbohm's (1872–1956) essay 'Whistler's Writing' in *The Pall Mall Magazine*, vol. 33, no. 133 (May 1904), 137–41[10]—reviewing the American painter and printmaker James Abbot McNeill Whistler's (1834–1903) *The Gentle Art of Making Enemies* (London, 1890; second edn, revised and enlarged, 1892)—with, on p. 140, a passage that may have inspired Joyce's, and Bloom's, phrase:

> It matters not that you never knew Whistler, never even set eyes on him. You see him and know him here. The voice drawls slowly, quickening to a kind of snap at the end of every sentence, and sometimes rising to a sudden screech of laughter ; and, all the while, the fine fierce eyes of the talker are flashing out at you, and his long nervous fingers are tracing quick [*extravagant* replaces *quick* in *Yet Again*, p. 116] arabesques in the air.

The phrase's next and possibly only other pre-Joyce instance occurred in the prominent and prolific English journalist (a frequent contributor to *Blackwood's*, *The Cornhill*, *Macmillan's* and a dozen other magazines), editor (of *The Theatre*), and author Bernard Capes's (1854–1918) novel *The Great Skene Mystery* (London, 1907), chap. 30 ('Hard Pressed'), p. 286: 'He wiped his white face with a ball of handkerchief. Inspector Jannaway's appeared the only composed countenance amongst us. But even his answered with a momentary pallor to the shock of a sudden screech of laughter uttered hard by.'

Since Joyce did not begin work on the 'Aeolus' episode before 1912, either or both Beerbohm's essay as first published in 1904 or as reprinted in 1909, and Capes's novel as first published in 1907, could have brought the highlighted phrase to his attention.

Uly 7.315: inflated windbag

Professor MacHugh's interjected demand that Ned Lambert cease his recitation of the Dublin merchant and politician Dan Dawson's flowery speech of the night before as printed in the *Freeman's Journal*—'Bombast! [...] Enough of the inflated windbag!'—borrows a phrase that seems first to have appeared in the Scottish essayist, historian, and philosopher

---

10   Later reprinted in Beerbohm's *Yet Again* (London, 1909), pp. 105–19.

Thomas Carlyle's (1795–1881) *On Heroes, Hero-worship and the Heroic in History* (London, 1841), lecture 5 (of 6), 'The Hero as a Man of Letters. Johnson, Rousseau, Burns.' Praising the poise and equanimity with which Burns received the adulation of high society on his first visit to Edinburgh, Carlyle wrote, on p. 228 (italics in the original):

> I admire much the way in which Burns met all this. Perhaps no man one could point out, was ever so sorely tried, and so little forgot himself. Tranquil, unastonished ; not abashed, not inflated, neither awkwardness nor affectation : he feels that *he* there is the man Robert Burns ; that the ' rank is but the guinea-stamp ;' that the celebrity is but the candle-light, which will show *what* man, not in the least make him a better or other man ! Alas, it may readily, unless he look to it, make him a *worse* man ; a wretched inflated wind-bag,—inflated till he *burst*, and become a *dead* lion ; for whom, as some one has said, ' there is no resurrection of the body ;' worse than a living dog !—Burns is admirable here.

Of the phrase's many subsequent occurrences in print, Joyce seems most likely to have seen and recalled an essay by the Irish socialist, journalist, trade union leader, and republican rebel James Connolly (1868–1916), later executed by the British for his leading role in the 1916 Easter Rising, published in the 'Home Thrusts' column for 20 August 1898, of *The Workers' Republic* (Dublin)—the official organ of the Socialist Party of Ireland, of which he was editor—where he refers contemptuously to Dublin Lord Mayor Daniel Tallon's prominent role in the Wolfe Tone Demonstration held on 15 August: 'Poor Wolfe Tone. Lived, fought, and suffered for Ireland in order that a purse-proud, inflated windbag should exploit your memory to his own aggrandisement.'

Uly 7.448: O, my rib risible!

A rare pre-*Ulysses* instance of the phrase 'rib risible'[11] occurs in the American art, book, music, and theater critic James Huneker's (1857–1921) *Ivory Apes and Peacocks: Joseph Conrad, Walt Whitman, Jules Laforgue, Dostoïevsky and Tolstoy, Schoenberg, Wedekind, Moussorgsky, Cézanne, Vermeer, Matisse, Van Gogh, Gauguin, Italian Futurists, Various*

---

11 The only other instance I am aware of occurs in Huneker's *Painted Veils* (New York, 1920).

Latter-Day Poets, Painters, Composers and Dramatists (New York and London, 1915), where, in the chapter on Schoenberg and its subsection on 'Music of To-Day and To-Morrow'—the latter of which also appeared in mid-1914 in *The Century Magazine* and *Scribner's*—Huneker writes, on p. 110:

> It is hardly necessary to consider here the fantastic fashionings of Erik Satie, the "newest" French composer. He seems to have out-Schoenberged Schoenberg in his little piano pieces bearing the alluring titles of Embryons desséchés, preludes and pastorales. Apart from the extravagant titles, the music itself is ludicrous qua music, but not without subtle irony. That trio of Chopin's Funeral March played in C and declared as a citation from the celebrated mazurka of Schubert does touch the rib risible.[12]

That Joyce had this passage from Huneker's chapter in mind is further suggested when, two lines later, Lenehan 'began to mazurka in swift caricature across the floor on sliding feet past the fireplace to J. J. O'Molloy'.

Uly 7.508–09: Youth led by Experience visits Notoriety.

Likely suggested by 'The National Monument to the Forefathers' in Boston, Massachusetts, which—quoting here and below from A[lfred]. S[tevens]. Burbank's *Guide to Historic Plymouth: Localities and Objects of Interest* (Plymouth, 1895), pp. 4 and 6—was 'completed in October 1888 and dedicated with appropriate ceremonies August 1st, 1889. [...] On the third of its four buttresses or wing pedestals is a seated figure [...] emblematic of the principles upon which the Pilgrims proposed to found their commonwealth.' Along with the figures of Morality, Law, and Freedom, 'the third figure is Education: on one side Wisdom, ripe with years ; on the other Youth led by Experience.'

---

12 Huneker's essay mentioning Chopin's Funeral March and containing the same phrase had previously appeared as 'Music of To-Day and To-Morrow' in *The Century Magazine*, vol. 8, no. 1 (May, 1914), 33–37.

Uly 7.553: We were always loyal to lost causes, the professor said.

While, as SMT note, references to 'lost causes' have long been common in Ireland, 'professor' MacHugh's 'loyal to lost causes' appears to reflect Joyce's familiarity with either or both of two antecedent texts.

The first of these, written by the Scottish philosopher David George Ritchie (1853–1903), Professor of Logic and Metaphysics in the University of St. Andrews, is his *Natural Rights: A Criticism of Some Political and Ethical Conceptions* (London and New York, 1903), in which chapter 6 ('The Right of Life') reads, at p. 124:

> Where societies are in a process of transition, it may indeed be very difficult for individuals to decide where their strongest duty of allegiance lies ; and in our historical judgments we are frequently compelled to give our warmest praise to some of those who from unselfish motives have been loyal to lost causes or to causes successful at the time, which we have come to consider mistaken.

The second, written by the American philosopher Josiah Royce (1855–1916), a professor of the history of philosophy at Harvard University, was *The Philosophy of Loyalty* (New York, 1908), reading, on p. 280:

> Loyalty to lost causes is, then, not only a possible thing, but one of the most potent influences of human history. In such cases, the cause comes to be idealized through its very failure to win temporary and visible success. The result for loyalty may be vast. I need not remind you that the early Christian church itself was at first founded directly upon a loyalty to its own lost cause,—a cause which it viewed as heavenly just because here on earth the enemies seemed to have triumphed, and because the Master had departed from human vision.

Uly 7.560: A smile of light

Joyce's phrase had verbatim antecedents in several mostly nineteenth-century works, three of which he seems more likely than the others to have known: in the English poet Bryan Waller Procter's (1787–1874), as 'Barry Cornwall', much-reprinted 'The Nights', from his *English Songs, and Other Small Poems* (London, 1832), pp. 29–30, beginning: 'Oh! The

Summer Night | Has a smile of light, | And she sits on a sapphire throne ; | Whilst the sweet Winds load her | With garlands of odour, | From the bud to the rose o'er-blown !'; in the Scottish poet and journalist Charles Mackay's (1814–1889) 'The Wood-Nymph', from his *Songs and Poems* (London, 1834), p. 123, with 'Poor she is in things of earth, | Poor in worldly treasure, | But she hath a smile of light, | And an eye of hazel bright, | Beaming love and pleasure.'; and in the American poet Henry Wadsworth Longfellow's (1807–1882) 'The Two Angels' from *The Courtship of Miles Standish, and Other Poems* (London, 1858) 151–54, with, in stanza 10, on p. 90: 'All is of God ! If He but wave his hand, | The mists collect, the rain falls thick and loud, | Till, with a smile of light on sea and land, | Lo ! He looks back from the departing cloud.'

Uly 7.578: ponderous pundit

This phrase in the first line of Lenehan's limerick—and repeated in 11.267—had previously occurred a handful of times, all but two, it appears, non-literary. One of the latter occurs in a footnote in vol. 3 (of 3), p. 577, of the Scottish lawyer, biographer, and historian Mark Napier's (1798–1879) *Memorials and Letters Illustrative of Life and Times of John Graham of Claverhouse, Viscount Dundee* (Edinburgh and London, 1862), where it refers to David Irving, author of *The History of Scotish* [sic] *Poetry* (Edinburgh, 1861), including that of the poet and soldier William Cleland (1661–1689) (italics in the original):

> The pious and ponderous Pundit who edits this precious poetry, and *history*, adds the following note of his own, which is, in every respect[,] worthy of that which he edits. Of course, he is speaking of Dundee:—"This atrocious murderer of the pious and unarmed peasantry of his native country, has, with some peculiarity of taste, been described as a *gallant General.*"

The other occurs on p. 15 of the Introduction to Charles Mackay's *New Light on Some Obscure Words and Phrases in the Works of Shakspeare* [sic] *and His Contemporaries* (London, 1884), where it refers to Samuel Johnson: 'It was this which puzzled the learned Dr. Johnson, and which has puzzled his successors in the industry of compiling Dictionaries, from the days of that ponderous pundit to our own.'

Uly 7.599: Paris, past and present

Two works so-titled were published in the years before this episode was first serialized in October 1918: the first, *Paris Past & Present*, by the American author and foreign correspondent James Henry Haynie (1841–1912), in two volumes (New York: Frederick A. Stokes, 1902); and the second, *Paris Past and Present*, with illustrations, edited by Charles Holme, with text by E[rnest]. A[rchibald]. Taylor (London, Paris, and New York, 1915).

Uly 7.602: You look as though you had done the deed. General Bobrikoff.

J. J. O'Molloy's remark to Stephen Dedalus and the journalist Mr O'Madden Burke—referring to an actual shooting that morning, by a Finnish nationalist, of the Russian Governor General of Finland (who died the next day)—echoes a phrase in *Macbeth*, II ii 14, where Macbeth, who has just murdered Duncan with a weapon provided by his wife, tells her: 'I have done the deed.' Among the several other pre-*Ulysses* works echoing the same phrase, two of the better known are Shelley's verse drama *The Cenci. A Tragedy, in Five Acts* (London, 1819) and Dickens's last completed novel, *Our Mutual Friend* (London, 1864–65).

In the former, the phrase occurs in Act 4, scene 4, in which Beatrice, the daughter of Count Francesco Cenci, informs Lucretia, the Count's wife and thus her stepmother, that at her instigation though without her direct involvement, the lawless and bloodthirsty count has been murdered. 'The deed is done', she proclaims in lines 46–47, 'And what may follow now regards not me.'

In the latter, the phrase occurs in vol. 2 (of 2), chap. 12 ('The Sweat of an Honest Man's Brow'), p. 115, where Roger 'Rogue' Riderhood, under questioning by lawyer Mortimer Lightwood, is falsely claiming, for his own ends, that his now-estranged associate Jesse 'Gaffer' Hexam has confessed to the murder of John Harmon:

> " Take care what you say, my friend," returned Mortimer.
> " Lawyer Lightwood, take care, you, what I say ; for I judge you'll be answerable for follering it up !" Then, slowly and emphatically beating it all out with his open right hand on the palm of his left ; " I,

Roger Riderhood, Lime'us Hole, Waterside character, tell you, Lawyer Lightwood, that the man Jesse Hexam, commonly called upon the river and along-shore Gaffer, told me that he done the deed. What's more, he told me with his own lips that he done the deed. What's more, he said that he done the deed. And I'll swear it !"

Uly 7.608: The gentle art of advertisement.

MacHugh's tossed-off remark, referring to a topic of Bloom's professional interest and expertise, may also point to the title of James McNeill Whistler's *The Gentle Art of Making Enemies* (see entry above on line 7.232).

Uly 7.623: mental pabulum

This phrase, which occurs in O'Madden Burke's remark after *Freeman's Journal* editor Myles Crawford invites Stephen Dedalus to become a contributor—'We can all supply mental pabulum'—predates the action of *Ulysses* by more than half a century. In one early instance—albeit clearly not one Joyce is likely to have seen—an unsigned article entitled 'Obligations of Literary Men' published in the Cincinnati, Ohio-based *Quarterly Journal and Review for 1846* reads in part (italics in the original):

> There is a small minority who attach a higher importance to education, and, occasionally, read beyond the partizan, sectarian and commercial news of the day. But what is the kind of mental food their tastes select ? Why, as a body, they demand, and get in overwhelming tides, the light, fictitious, boyish *trash*, that does more to enervate the stronger faculties, and induce mental indolence, than all the inebriating drugs taken for the indulgence of acquired habits. Such is the taste to which many, yea most, whose efforts are rewarded, pander, regardless of the public good. To see the extent of this greediness for *trash* look at all our newspapers, whose name is legion. What is the character of the intellectual feast they weekly spread before their readers ? A little political news, and a fictitious account of some lover's freaks. Why is this ? Because the reading public do not relish more invigorating mental pabulum, and editors must make their papers please or they cannot live.

Twenty years later, the phrase recurs in a journal closer to home, *Meliora: A Quarterly Review of Social Science in its Ethical, Economical,*

Political, and Ameliorative Aspect (London), vol. 9, no. 35 (1866), 193–204— in an unsigned article reviewing five books on 'Self-Culture' including the British author Samuel Smiles's (1812–1904) widely read and much reprinted *Self–Help* (London, 1859 et seq)—reading in part, on p. 200:

> There are many books which one may take up with no expectation of finding in them real originality of sentiment, or even that which happens to be new to oneself. They are taken up simply for the sake of removing into a healthful mental or moral atmosphere. Our physical frames do not exist upon fresh air, but they could not exist without it. And so, in reading a book, though we may not derive therefrom any large amount of mental pabulum, we may just as certainly have contributed to our mental and moral development, as, by a walk in the open air, we should contribute to our physical health and strength.

It is hardly surprising, if this is the sort of mental pabulum Myles Crawford wants Stephen Dedalus to produce for publication in the *Freeman's Journal*, that Stephen, poor though he is, would have no interest in doing so.

Uly 7.682: a shape of air

An early—perhaps the earliest—instance of this phrase occurs in Byron's long and enormously popular poem *The Corsair, A Tale* (London, 1814), where canto 2, section 13, begins:

> She gazed in wonder, " can he calmly sleep,
> " While other eyes his fall or ravage weep ?
> " And mine in restlessness are wandering here—
> " What sudden spell hath made this man so dear ?
> " True—'tis to him my life, and more, I owe,
> " And me and mine he spared from worse than woe :
> " 'Tis late to think—but soft—his slumber breaks—
> " How heavily he sighs !—he starts—awakes !"
>
> He rais'd his head—and dazzled with the light,
> His eye seem'd dubious if it saw aright :
> He moved his hand—the grating of his chain
> Too harshly told him that he liv'd again.
> " What is that form ? if not a shape of air,
> " Methinks, my jailor's face shows wond'rous fair !"

It next occurs in *The Literary Gazette and Journal of Belles Lettres, Science, and Art* (London) for 19 January 1822, in 'Sketch Second'—one of several 'Poetic Sketches' and other poems by the English poet and novelist Letitia Elizabeth Landon (1802–1838), as 'L.E.L.', published in the same journal over the course of that year—on pp. 44–45, and begins (after a two-line verse epigraph from Barry Cornwall's 'Marcian Colonna, An Italian Tale' (1820):

> It lay mid trees, a little quiet nest
> Like to the stock dove's, and the honeysuckle
> Spread o'er the cottage roof, while the red rose
> Grew round the casement, where the thick-leaved vine
> Wove a luxuriant curtain, with a wreath,
> A bridal wreath of silver jessamine ;—
> A soft turf lay before the door, o'erhung
> With a huge walnut-tree's green canopy,
> Encircled round with flowers ; and, like a queen
> Of the young roses, stood a bright-cheeked Girl,
> With smile of Summer and with lips of Spring,
> A shape of air, and footsteps of the wind.

And occurs a third time in the Irish poet and barrister Sir Samuel Ferguson's (1810–1886) 'The Abdication of Fergus Mac Roy'—collected on pp. 27–35 of his *Lays of the Western Gael, and Other Poems* (London, 1865)—which begins: 'Once, ere God was crucified, | I was King o'er Uladh wide : | King, by law of choice and birth, | O'er the fairest realm of Earth.'; and stanza 20 (of 42) of which, on p. 31, reads: 'I am but a shape of air, | Far removed from love's repair ; | Yet, were mine a living frame | Once again I'd say the same.'

Uly 7.776: Stephen, his blood wooed by grace of language and gesture, blushed.

Stephen's visceral response, as J. J. O'Molloy recites from memory a portion of Seymour Bushe's speech to the jury in defense of Samuel Childs in the Childs murder case, echoes a phrase that had previously occurred in the Anglican cleric and author Rev. R[obert]. W[ilson]. Evans's (1789–1866) *Parochial Sermons, Preached in the Parish Church of Heversham, Westmoreland* (London, 1855), vol. 3, sermon 27 ('The Conversion of Manaen'), reading, at p. 269:

> Manaen had to shake off the acquaintance of princely youths, with Herod, a sovereign, at their head. Had that son that afterwards mocked Christ no mockery for him that quitted his company for Christ's, and that too more keen and intolerable for the grace of language and gesture which accompanied it ?

This sermon takes as its text Acts xiii 1, reading: 'Now there were in the church that was at Antioch certain prophets and teachers; as Barnabas, and Simeon that was called Niger, and Lucius of Cyrene, and Manaen, which had been brought up with Herod the tetrarch, and Saul.'

Uly 7.804–05: full of courteous haughtiness

This phrase, from a remark by MacHugh commenting on a celebrated speech by the patriotic barrister and journalist John F[rancis]. Taylor (c. 1850–1902), may have been suggested by a passage in the Anglican cleric and author Rev. John Hobart Caunter's (1792–1851) *Sermons on The Lord's Prayer and the Eight Beatitudes* (London, 1849), where sermon 19, on Matthew v 9 ('Blessed are the peace-makers; for they shall be called the children of God.'), reads in part on pp. 267–68:

> Look again at official men. How seldom do they bear their honours meekly. How much more commonly are they haughty than courteous. Haughtiness is the official infirmity of public functionaries. It has passed into a proverb. There are bright exceptions, but the general fact is notorious. It is among petty retainers that discourtesy is the most offensively conspicuous. Glorying in their little brief authority, they are proud to exercise it. This is, I believe, a cause of complaint throughout the civilized world. Such are not "peace-makers."

The phrase 'courteous haughtiness' itself, however, occurs a number of times later in that century. In a multi-part story called 'The Caged Lion' by the English novelist and friend of the Oxford Movement Charlotte Mary Yonge (1823–1901)—published in *The Monthly Packet of Evening Readings for Members of the English Church* (London), new series, vol. 7—part 40 (Apr. 1869), chap. 10 ('The Whitsuntide Festival'), 336–50, reads, on p. 344:

The hot blood rushed into James's cheek at this tone of condescension ; but he answered, with courteous haughtiness, ' Of myself, Sir Duke, there is no question. My ransom waits England's willingness to accept it ; and my hand is not free, even for the prize you have the goodness to offer. I came not to speak of myself.'

' Not to make suit for my sister, nor my intercession !' exclaimed Philippe.

In 'The Crafty Fox', a story by the American illustrator, painter, and children's author Howard Pyle (1853–1911) published in *St. Nicholas: Scribner's Illustrated Magazine for Girls and Boys* (New York), vol. 4, no. 4 (Feb. 1877), 261–63, the fox says to the cock, on p. 262 (italics in the original):

" Did I not know your extreme patience under correction, I should hesitate to tell them, or rather *it*, for I have only noticed one in my acquaintance with you. You are, sir, I grieve to say it, but you are, sir, extremely haughty and exclusive in your manners. Your blood, your aristocratic breeding, your culture, and your refinement all tend to cause you to look upon your more vulgar yet still honest fellow-creatures with a courteous haughtiness, if I may so express it. It is a fault to which your superior station may plead some extenuation ; still it is a fault. Let me beg you, honored sir, to correct this one failing, and so render yourself the model of perfection you would then be. Recollect, sir, that though humbler, we are still your fellow-creatures."

And a year later, the phrase recurs in the English journalist and diplomat Eustace Clare Grenville Murray's (1824–1881) *The Russians of To-Day* (London, 1878), chap. 6 ('The Briskatstartine Hussars'), p. 47, describing the efforts of a half-German commoner and cavalry major, his identity masked by the pseudonym Strengmann, to present his reports to the Russian noblemen who are his superior officers:

Strengmann was never on familiar terms with these gentlemen, who lived in high state in houses of their own at Odessa and who treated him with courteous haughtiness. They never invited him to dinner, and he did not expect they should. Strengmann has never sat at an aristocratic table in his life. When he went to make his reports to Topoff or Tripoff he usually found them in bed, sleepy after an agreeable night's baccarat at the Club of Nobles. They would keep him standing while he told his business, then sign his reports without a word, and dismiss him with a nod.

Uly 7.874–75: A sudden-at-the-moment-though-from-lingering-illness-often-previously-expectorated-demise

An entry in the British lexicographer and author E[benezer]. Cobham Brewer's (1810–1897) *Dictionary of Phrase and Fable, New Edition, Revised, Corrected, and Enlarged* (London, 1895), reads in part, on p. 771: 'Miss Burney has furnished the longest compound in the English tongue: [namely] "the sudden-at-the-moment-though-from-lingering-illness-often-previously-expected death of Mr. Burney's wife." De Vere.' That name denotes the play *Hubert de Vere* (written c. 1790–1793), one of four tragedies by the English satirical novelist, diarist, and playwright Frances ('Fanny') Burney (1752–1840), only one of which, *Edwy and Elgiva*, has ever been staged.[13] Brewer's *Dictionary* misattributes this purported 'compound' to Frances Burney herself. It is, however, based on a passage in *Memoirs of Doctor Burney, Arranged From His Own Manuscripts, From Family Papers, and From Personal Recollections. By His Daughter, Madame d'Arblay* [i.e., Frances Burney] (London, 1832), vol. 3 (of 3), section title 'Mrs. Phillips', p. 223:

> But not here ended the sharp reverse of this altered year ; scarcely had this harrowing filial separation taken place, ere an assault was made upon his conjugal feelings, by the sudden, at the moment, though from lingering illnesses often previously expected, death of Mrs. Burney, his second wife.

Since this passage, in the original, awkwardly written though it is, is hyphen-free, Joyce's source for Lenehan's hyphen-laden compound must have been the entry in Brewer's *Dictionary* and not the *Memoirs of Doctor Burney* on which that entry was based.

Uly 7.875–76: And with a great future behind him.

Lenehan's tossed-off witticism, which has little or no relevance to Moses, is generally supposed to have originated in a remark by the German poet, writer, and literary critic Christian Johann Heinrich Heine (1797–1856)

---

13   Eleanor Crouch, 'Hubert de Vere'. *The Literary Encyclopedia*. First published 24 Jan. 2011 at https://www.litencyc.com/php/sworks.php?rec=true&UID=23811

directed against his near-contemporary the French dramatist, poet, and novelist Alfred de Musset (1810–1857). In the revised edition of vol. 1 of his three-volume biography *Franz Liszt: The Virtuoso Years, 1811–1847* (Ithaca: Cornell University Press, 1987), Alan Walker writes, on p. 163: 'Poets, playwrights, and painters all feared Heine's banter. Alfred de Musset never forgave Heine for calling him "a young man with a great future behind him."'

An instance of the anecdote, and of the phrase, that may have brought both to Joyce's attention appeared in the 13 February 1892 issue of *Punch*, vol. 102, p. 84, in an item entitled 'Essence of Parliament. Extracted from the Diary of Toby, M.P.': '" You remember TOBY, what HEINE said of DE MUSSET ? ' A young man with a great future — behind him.' There he goes."'

Uly 7.915: I have much, much to learn.

Stephen's remark to himself, which to my ear seems both out of character and out of the blue, previously occurred in *The Survival of Man: A Study in Unrecognized Human Faculty* (London, 1909), by the British physicist, inventor, and spiritualist Sir Oliver Joseph Lodge, FRS (1851–1940). In chap. 12 ('Personal Identity') of that book—in which book he expresses his belief, as a Christian Spiritualist and the father of a son lost in the Great War, that life after death has been demonstrated by mediumship—he records a purported transcription of automatic or spirit writing produced by a deceased person named Blanche Abercromby. It reads, on p. 188:

> A spirit who has before communicated will write for you herself[.]
> She will then leave you, having given the evidence that is required.
> " I should much like to speak more with you, but it is not permitted. You have sacred truth. I know but little yet. I have much, much to learn. — BLANCHE ABERCROMBY.
> " It is like my writing as evidence to you."
>
> The statement that the writing of this particular message is like that of the lady's was long afterwards verified with some care and trouble by Mr. Myers, and is correct. The *amende*, and the sentence, " I have much, much to learn," are characteristic[.]

Uly 7.917: I have a vision too

Stephen's assertion, which he directs at 'professor' MacHugh, previously occurred in a page-long, four-part story, entitled '"SHE–THAT–OUGHT–NOT–TO–BE–PLAYED!" A Story of Gloomy Gaiety', in the 15 September 1888 issue of *Punch*, vol. 95, p. 132. Part 4 of the story, the paragraph-long 'Caught on the Cheek', begins:

> Then came several hours in the land of Kor. I have a recollection of a lady wearing white muslin and a serpent, who wandered about always, always, in the limelight. I fancy she must have spoken for a very long while. And the ancient and portly Greek in the horsey clothes and tattooed arms, he, too, seems to have had a great deal to say. And I recall to mind an old man who got a laugh by calling the person in the puce-coloured and black-striped trousers "a baboon." And I have a vision too of some mild dancing by a small and select *corps de ballet*.

There is Stephen's 'I have a vision too', in what seems to be the only pre-*Ulysses* instance of the phrase. The paragraph continues for another thirty-two lines.

8. 'Lestrygonians'

***Uly* 8.17–18: His wife will put the stopper on that.**

Joyce's 'put the stopper on that' may have been inspired by the same phrase in *Mrs. Brown on the Royal Russian Marriage* (London, 1874), one of the thirty-two 'Mrs. Brown' novels—described by one critic as 'the slightly dotty ravings and rantings of an illiterate little old British lady of the lower middle-class who gossips about all the topics-of-the-day'—by the English dramatist, novelist, and entertainer George Rose (1817–1882), as 'Arthur Sketchley'. The passage of the novel in which the phrase occurs reads, on pp. 129–30:

> So I was glad when Brown got back agin, and told me all as he'd 'eard about this 'ere Rooshun marridge, as were werry different from Miss Pilkinton's rubbish, as said as she'd 'ave dimon's the size of a nubley coal, and as her pa wouldn't never give 'is consent unless it were promised as she should come back whenever she pleased, and stop as long as she liked ; as aint the way to make 'er a good wife, cos, in course, the best of friends will 'ave their little tiffs, and if a wife can always 'ave 'er mother and father to fly to with their complaints, why, she aint likely to square it with 'er 'usban' not so soon ; and I do 'ope as Queen Wictorier will put the stopper on that, as I'm sure aint the one to incourage 'er own dorters to come 'ome a-complainin', tho' they do live both close to 'er, when she's at Win'sor or in the 'Ighlands, and might be a-poppin' in for everlastin' with a somethink, such as, "Oh ! ma ! he've been in that passion cos his tea was smoked," or "cos he didn't like 'is dinner," and all manner like that.

Uly 8.39: All for number one.

SMT write, in two notes on this phrase, that it 'plays on the slogan for Bass beer' and specifically on the red triangle logo for Bass Pale Ale, 'which is called "number one" because it was the first trademark registered in the United Kingdom', in 1876. Here and in lines 8.714 and 12.1761, however, where the four-word phrase recurs, it may also point to the title of the English writer Henry Johnson's (c. 1848–1922) *All for Number One, or, Charlie Russell's Ups and Downs: A Story for Boys and Girls* (London, 1888), published, as were most of his novels, by the Religious Tract Society. A review of this and other 'New Books for Young People' in *The Literary World* (London), new series, vol. 38, no. 999 (21 Dec. 1888), p. 531, summarized its content:

> *All For Number One*, by Henry Johnson, is the story of Charlie Russell's ups and downs in life. It opens with Reuben Smith's unexpected inheritance of a hundred thousand pounds, which removes him from an East-end grocer's shop to a mansion at Bayswater, but does not change his naturally grasping, selfish character for a better. Mr. Smith commands his daughter to give up the young carpenter she is about to marry, but Ellen considers it dishonourable, and carries out her pledge. Little Charlie Russell is her only son, and the poor child loses his loving mother when five years old. John Russell becomes insane through grief, and the boy is placed with a kindly woman by some friends who take an interest in him. Reuben Smith resolves to have the boy and bring him up in accordance with his own views, and the rest of the story is occupied with details of the conflict between two wills. Charlie escapes from his grandfather, and, years after, has the satisfaction of returning good for evil in rescuing the old man who has been 'all for number one,' from poverty and sin.

Uly 8.40: mum's the word

A now-familiar cliché ultimately traceable to Shakespeare's *2 Henry VI*, I ii 89–90, where the priest John Hume says to himself: 'Seal up your lips, and give no words but mum; | The business asketh silent secrecy.' In one extreme case among countless other instances—most often found in musical comedies and comic stories and novels—chap. 12 of the anonymous, serialized story 'Nights At Mess', published in *Blackwood's*, vol. 37, no. 236 (June 1835), 929–36, the phrase 'mum's the word' occurs a total of nine times.

Uly 8.61: Live by their wits.

Another now-common phrase, an early, perhaps the earliest, instance of which occurs in the English playwright and poet Ben Jonson's (1572–1637) *The Alchemist* (London, 1612), III ii, Face to Kastril: 'Spend you ? It will repair you when you are spent. | How do they live by their Wits there, that have vented | Six Times your Fortunes ?'

Uly 8.62–63: *The hungry famished gull | Flaps o'er the waters dull.*

Citing a note by Fritz Senn published in a 1975 issue of the *James Joyce Quarterly*, SMT write: 'Bloom's "poem" recalls elements from one of Lord Byron's better known lyrics: "Adieu, adieu! My native shore | Fades o'er the waters blue" (*Childe Harold's Pilgrimage*, canto 1, after stanza XIII, ll. 118–19).' The lines Bloom invents or recalls, however, more strongly suggest those found in stanza 4 of the poem 'An English Girl (Seen on Lac Leman)' by Mark Hyam (1895–1918)—who died while serving with the British army in France—published on pp. 28–29 of his *Moods & Memories: A Volume of Verse* (London, 1916): 'Other maidens there also be— | Dainty, or quaint, or dull, | Watching the foam as it races home, | Or feeding the famished gull'.

Uly 8.77–78: greed and cunning

The passage in which this phrase occurs, beginning in line 76, reads: 'The gulls swooped silently, two, then all from their heights, pouncing on prey. Gone. Every morsel. Aware of their greed and cunning he shook the powdery crumb from his hands.' Along with the literary antecedents of the passage as a whole cited to date, including the Lestrygonians' attack upon Odysseus's landlocked ships in the *Odyssey*, book 10; and (by Richard Ellmann, in *The Consciousness of Joyce*, pp. 8–9, 133) *The Common Objects of the Sea Shore* (London, 1866) by J. G. Wood—a book, Ellmann notes, that was in Joyce's Trieste library—the phrase 'greed and cunning' recurs with considerable frequency in nineteenth-century fiction, nonfiction, sermons, and elsewhere. The most widely read and memorable instance, however—hence the instance Joyce seems most likely to have had in mind—occurs in Dickens's *The Personal History of David Copperfield* (London, 1850), chap. 52 ('I assist at an explosion'), p. 538, David speaking to Uriah Heep, where the phrase in question occurs twice:

> " As I think I told you once before," said I, "it is you who have been, in your greed and cunning, against all the world. It may be profitable to you to reflect, in future, that there never were greed and cunning in the world yet, that did not do too much, and over-reach themselves. It is as certain as death."

Uly 8.269: The unfair sex.

Unremarked by Thornton, Gifford, and SMT—other than Thornton's note that it is 'Bloom's variation on the common description of woman as "the fair sex"'—the highlighted phrase occurred multiple times over the course of the nineteenth and early twentieth centuries, in essays, stories, novels, poems, polemics, and other genres. Two of the many instances that Joyce may have encountered and found of interest were written by, respectively, the Anglo-Irish British Army senior officer Sir Garnet Joseph Wolseley (1833–1913) and the Irish novelist Mrs [Margaret Wolfe] Hungerford (1855?–1897)—best known as the author of *Molly Bawn* (London, 1878), which Joyce's Molly mentions in the final episode of *Ulysses* and whose work Joyce himself is known to have read.[14]

Viscount Wolseley's *Corrafin* (London, 1878), published a year after his first and only other novel, *Marley's Castle* (London, 1877), reads, in vol. 1 (of 2), chap. 8, pp. 111–12 (italics in the original):

> " Well, now that I have seen you, I must see what I can do for you. But what in the world have you done with your face ?"
> " Faith, sir, as quare a thing as you ever knew. I was going down the street one evening lately, and I heerd sich screechin' in a house I was passin', that I put me head in to see what was the row, and there was a nasty big baste of a man bating his unfortinate wife like anything. Av

---

14   Lines 656–58 of the 'Penelope' episode read: '[…] Molly bawn she gave me by Mrs Hungerford on account of the name I don't like books with a Molly in them like that one he brought me about the one from Flanders a whore […]'.

coorse I wint between them, but the moment I got the poor woman, who scarcely had a breath left in her, out of his rache, the big bully attacked me. So I had to defend meself, to be sure, and give him as good as I got. But the very first blow I gev him, the wife darted over to me and hit me a box in the face that blackened both my eyes, and nearly sent me into the middle of next week. ' Take that !' says she ; 'and that, and that ! you miserable spalpeen ! And I hope it will tache you better manners than to strek a dacent boy like *my* husband again ! And now the sooner you take your ugly mug and your long nose out of me sight, the better for you !' 'Oh thin, for the matter of that,' ses I, 'I don't think ayther of us has much beauty to boast of ; and as to me nose, if there was a taste of it tacked on to your own, it might be an improvement to that fayture !' You see, sir, I wanted to hit her hard wid me tongue when I couldn't wid me hands ; and that was doing it wid a vingeance, for you never seed sich a scrubby, rudimintary little apology for a nose as she had on her face, in yer life. But, yer honor, isn't it a mistake, after sich ungratitude as that, to call women the fair sex ? In my opinion the *un*fair sex would be a much more shootable name for thim."

Mrs Hungerford's novel *An Unsatisfactory Lover* (London, 1894), chap. 16, reads, on p. 146:

" I'm so sorry, dear fellow," says Mr. Kitts, who, I regret to say, is convulsed with laughter, " but as I thought you were really going to kneel, I gave up that comfortable chair to—er—one of the unfair sex. By Jove !" in a low, sympathetic tone, " she has been unfair, you know. I hope," sweetly, " she hasn't hurt you."

Uly 8.322: Be a feast for the gods.

SMT cite *Julius Caesar*, II i 173: 'Let's carve him, as a dish fit for the gods'. But the phrase 'a feast for the gods' occurs nearly verbatim in Scott's *Ivanhoe*, second edn (Edinburgh, 1820), vol. 2 (of 3), chap. 10, p. 178: '" Say not so, maiden," answered the Templar; " revenge is a feast for the gods ! And if they have reserved it, as priests tell us, to themselves, it is because they hold it an enjoyment too precious for the possession of mere mortals.["]' And this early, perhaps earliest, instance recurs often over the following century, in novels, stories, essays, and elsewhere, making it difficult or impossible to determine which if any of its many appearances Joyce may have had in mind.

Uly 8.329: Tell me who made the world.

The typographical error of Bloom's erotic pen pal echoes a line in scene 6 of the 1604 quarto (the A text), also known in the B text of 1616 as Act 2, scene 2, of the English playwright, poet, and translator Christopher Marlowe's (1564–1593) *The Tragical History of the Life and Death of Doctor Faustus* (1592)—a line that seems to be the only verbatim pre-Joyce instance of the phrase:

Faustus to Mephistophilis.	Well, I am answered. Tell me who made the world.
Mephistophilis.	I will not.
Faustus.	Sweet Mephistophilis, tell me.
Mephistophilis.	Move me not, for I will not tell thee.
Faustus.	Villain, have I not bound thee to tell me any thing?
Mephistophilis.	Aye, that is not against our kingdom ; but this is. Think thou on hell, Faustus, for thou art damned.
Good Angel.	Think, Faustus, upon God that made the world.

Uly 8.333: drinking sloppy tea

Having just run into and briefly conversed with Josie Breen—an old friend of his and Molly's whose husband Denis has sunk into madness—Bloom resumes his walk thinking about Martha Clifford and the other forty-three women who have answered his (as Henry Flower) help-wanted ad reading 'Wanted, smart lady typist to aid gentleman in literary work.' One such respondent comes particularly to his mind: 'And the other one Lizzie Twigg. My literary efforts have had the good fortune to meet with the approval of the eminent poet A. E. (Mr Geo. Russell). No time to do her hair drinking sloppy tea with a book of poetry.'

The phrase 'sloppy tea' makes at least four pre-Joyce literary appearances. The first of these occurs in the English novelist and playwright Wilkie Collins's (1824–1889) sensation novel *Man and Wife* (London, 1870), vol. 2 (of 3), chap. 22 ('Scared'), p. 24:

> Oh, bother the women ! one of them is the same as another. They all waddle when they run ; and they all fill their stomachs before dinner with sloppy tea. That's the only difference between women and men— the rest is nothing but a weak imitation of Us.

the second: in another sensation novel, *Joshua Haggard's Daughter* (London, 1876), by Mary Elizabeth Braddon, vol. 2 (of 3), chap. 1 ('" O, Let My Joys Have Some Abiding !"'), p. 8:

> These filled Miss Webling's parlour to overflowing, and taxed the resources of the household in the way of teapots. If Cynthia had been less handy, things could not have gone off so genteelly ; and the sisters might have been lowered in the esteem of Mrs. Pamble, who really condescended somewhat in visiting them, by sloppy tea ; but Cynthia contrived to have a fresh brew in the every-day crockery teapot ready to replenish that silver vessel which adorned the tray. She brought in the rock-cakes hot, and nestling in a clean napkin, and she was never behind-hand with bread-and-butter of the genteelest thinness.

the third: in the English actress and writer Gertrude Warden's (1859–1925) novel *Her Fairy Prince*—first serialized from July to October 1895 in *The Family Herald; or, Useful Information and Amusement for the Million* (London), then published in book form in Philadelphia (1895) and London (1896)— and reading, in chap. 20, p. 201, of the Philadelphia edition:

> I can't sit hour after hour tied to a desk quill-driving ; I can't pretend to interest myself in tomes and ledgers and bills-of-exchange any more than I can talk twaddle in a drawing-room over sloppy tea, or play lawn-tennis with a lot of prim bread-and-butter misses without a word to say for themselves.

and the fourth: in what seems to be the sole verbatim pre-Joyce instance of the phrase '*drinking* sloppy tea' (emphasis added): in the novel *Left Alone; or, The Fortunes of Phillis Maitland. A Story.* (London, 1879), by the Northumberland businessman and writer Francis Carr (1834–1894), the first chapter of which ('Phillis') reads, on p. 4 (italics in the original):

> At half-past seven the bell rang again, and Phillis went into the dining-room to sit down to her lonely dinner. There was a second place laid at the other end of the table, but she did not think of waiting for the occupant of it. Evening after evening she went through the empty ceremony of a solitary late dinner, because on one rare occasion *he* had come home at this hour, and finding her, as he described it, '*drinking sloppy tea,*' he had angrily asked her how she could expect a man to come home in the evening when there wasn't a decent meal for him to sit down to, and had then departed in a rage. Since that day she had substituted dinner for the late tea she liked so much better, but the empty place was seldom or never filled.

Uly 8.344–45: in at the death

Gifford writes: 'Or in at the kill: present when the hounds overtake and kill the fox. It usually means that one has ridden extraordinarily well, courageously, if not recklessly.' To this may be added that Joyce's phrase frequently occurs verbatim in nineteenth- and early twentieth-century fiction, usually but not always in reference to fox (or buck) hunting.

It occurs, for example, in the title of an illustration opposite p. 193 in an early (1852) London edition of the American author Harriet Beecher Stowe's (1811–1896) *Uncle Tom's Cabin; or, Life Among the Lowly*, which title reads 'FIELD SPORTS "DOWN SOUTH." COMING IN AT THE DEATH'; the illustration itself showing a fleeing, enslaved African man on the ground beset by, and battling, a pack of hunting dogs; and the text of which, below the illustration, from chap. 19, p. 198, of the novel, reading:

> *St. Clare.* [the speaker]—" He ran and bounded like a buck, and kept us well in the rear for some time ; but at last he got caught in an impenetrable thicket of cane ; then he turned to bay, and I tell you he fought the dogs right gallantly. He dashed them to right and left, and actually killed three of them with only his naked fists, when a shot from a gun brought him down, and he fell, wounded and bleeding, almost at my feet."

It occurs, to take another example, in Barry Cornwall's tale 'The Portrait on My Uncle's Snuff-Box. An Anecdote', first published in *The Keepsake for 1828* (London), vol. 1 of that literary annual, 56–76, reading, on p. 66: ' But, when the news actually *did* come to his ears, nothing could surpass his indignation. A rebel ! a Jacobite ! He resolved to make one in the chase, and if possible to be in at the death.[']

It also occurs, in a third example, as the main title of the English barrister, journalist, and novelist George F[rederick]. Underhill's (1864–1903) *In At The Death: A Tale of Society* (London, 1888), in which the author's preface begins:

> Before the following pages were sent to the Press, a critic, who had been kind enough to read the manuscript, told me that under the disguise of a novel I had written, what he was pleased to term, an elaborate sneer at humanity. He also said that none of the characters had any sense of right or wrong, and that I suggested that nobody cared for such things now-a-days. This criticism astounded me. It was not my intention either to be satirical, or to hold up for the admiration

of my readers the worse side of human nature. On the contrary, it had rather been my endeavour to show the great power of maternal affection as portrayed in the character of Geramis, and also to point out how all good qualities, not even excepting honour, are capable of being destroyed by jealousy. Beyond this, I was not vain enough to attempt to teach any lesson.

Uly 8.495: Feel as if I had been eaten and spewed.

While 'eaten and spewed' occurs pre-*Ulysses* from time to time elsewhere, the antecedent coming closest to Bloom's entire phrase may be found in *The Book of Nettercaps, being Poutery, Poetry, and Prose* (Dundee, 1875), by the Scottish musician, choirmaster, dancing instructor, and author Alexander Burgess (1808–1886) as 'Poute of the Leven Saat Pans', with, on p. 80, in an essay in Scottish dialect called 'Kirsty Klatterhorn on the Absurdities of Fashion': 'The fact is, that the feck o' oor young men now-a-days look as if they had been eaten and spewed again—they hae neither gut nor gaw, as the sayin' is.'

The phrase may point ultimately to the story of Jonah and the whale in the Book of Jonah chapters 1 and 2, including Jonah i 17: 'Now the LORD had prepared a great fish to swallow up Jonah. And Jonah was in the belly of the fish three days and three nights.' Jonah ii 10 continues: 'And the LORD spake unto the fish, and it vomited out Jonah upon the dry land.'

Uly 8.543: Those literary etherial people they are all.

Joyce's 'etherial people' could hardly be more literary: the phrase occurs in Milton's *Paradise Lost*, book 10, in the second, revised, twelve-book edition of 1674, reading, in lines 17–28:

> Up into Heav'n from Paradise in haste
> Th' Angelic Guards ascended, mute and sad
> For Man, for of his state by this they knew,
> Much wondring how the suttle Fiend had stoln
> Entrance unseen . Soon as th' unwelcome news
> From Earth arriv'd at Heaven Gate, displeas'd
> All were who heard, dim sadness did not spare
> That time Celestial visages, yet mixt

> With pitie, violated not thir bliss.
> About the new-arriv'd, in multitudes
> Th' ethereal People ran, to hear and know
> How all befell: [...]

The same phrase also occurs in Dryden's 'opera, written in heroique verse' *The State of Innocence, and Fall of Man* (London, 1677), his rhymed adaptation of Milton's epic, where it appears in a speech by the Archangel Gabriel in Act 5, scene 1, p. 37—and where, unlike Milton's, Dryden's spelling of 'etherial' matches that of Joyce:

> *Gabriel.* I saw th'Angelic guards, from earth ascend ,
>   (Griev'd they must now no longer man attend :)
>   The beams about their Temples dimly shone ;
>   One would have thought the crime had been their own.
>   Th'Etherial people flock'd for news in hast ,
>   Whom they, with down cast lookes, and scarce saluting past :
>   While each did, in his pensive brest, prepare
>   A sad accompt of their successless care.

Perhaps with its prior use by Milton and Dryden in mind, the early Shakespeare biographer Charles Symmons, D.D. (1749–1826) employed the same phrase in his much-reprinted 'Life of the Poet', a long essay at the beginning of his edition of Shakespeare's dramatic works (Chiswick, 1826 *et seq*). Referring to the 'little beings' that, like England's elves and fairies, 'flutter in his scenes, from an idea of his own', Symmons continued: 'To this little etherial people, our bard has assigned manners and occupations in perfect consistency with their nature ; and has sent them forth in the richest array of fancy, to gambol before us, to astonish and delight us.'

Uly 8.549–50: The dreamy [...] waters dull.

See entry on *Uly* 8.62–63.

Uly 8.638: hungered flesh

From the much-worked-over sentence 'With hungered flesh obscurely, he mutely craved to adore.'—Joyce told Frank Budgen he had spent an entire day arranging the constituent words of that and the previous sentence 'Perfume of embraces all him assailed.¹⁵—the rare phrase 'hungered flesh' previously occurred in Edward Bulwer-Lytton's unfinished but published play *Eugene Aram, a Tragedy* (London, 1833), a play based on the actual case of the philologist-turned-murderer of its title (1704–1759), on the English poet and author Thomas Hood's (1799–1945) narrative poem *The Dream of Eugene Aram, the Murderer* (London, 1831), and on Bulwer-Lytton's own melodramatic novel *Eugene Aram. A Tale.* (London, 1832). In Bulwer-Lytton's verse drama as first published in *The New Monthly Magazine*, vol. 38, no. 152 (Aug. 1833), Aram is talking with his friend Boteler late in Act 1, scene 3, pp. 405–06 (italics in the original):

> *Aram.* Lo !
> How many deathful, dread, and ghastly snares
> Encompass him whom the stark Hunger gnaws,
> And the grim demon Penury shuts from out
> The golden Eden of his bright desires !
> To-day, I thought to slay myself, and die,
> No single hope once won !—and now I hear
> Dark words of blood, and quail not, nor recoil.—
> 'Tis but a death in either case ;—or mine
> Or that poor dotard's !—And the guilt—the guilt,—
> Why, *what* is guilt ?—A word ! We are the tools,
> From birth to death, of destiny ; and shaped,
> For sin or virtue, by the iron force
> Of the unseen, but unresisted, hands
> Of Fate, the august compeller of the world.
> *Boteler.* It works. Behold the devil at all hearts !
> I am a soldier, and enured to blood ;
> But *he* hath lived with moralists forsooth.
> And yet one word to tempt him, and one sting
> Of the food-craving clay, and the meek sage
> Grasps at the crime he marvelled at before.
> *Aram (abruptly).* Thou has broke thy fast this morning ?
> *Boteler.* Ay, in truth.

---

15 See Budgen, *James Joyce and the Making of 'Ulysses'* (1972 edn), p. 20.

> *Aram.* But *I* have not, since *yester*morn, and asked
> In the belief that certain thoughts unwont
> To blacken the still mirror of my mind
> Might be the phantoms of the hungered flesh
> And the faint nature. I was wrong ; since you
> Share the same thoughts, nor suffer the same ills.

The phrase subsequently occurred in a volume called *Songs of Sleepy Hollow and Other Poems* (New York and London, 1886) by the American banker, author, poet, and literary editor Stephen Henry Thayer (1839–1919), where, in the poem '"The Dead Year"' on pp. 164–66, stanza 6 reads:

> Sure, every day is a divine presaging ;
> Nor art, nor life is lost to human good ;
> Even our daily food
> Decrees some ransom than the sheer assuaging
> Of the hungered flesh, as sap to flower
> Yields an ethereal dower.

Uly 8.684–85: Born with a silver knife in his mouth.

After this phrase has crossed Bloom's mind, his interior monologue continues: 'That's witty, I think. Or no. Silver means born rich. Born with a knife. But then the allusion is lost.' The phrase 'Born with a silver knife in his mouth" is, however, indeed allusive, on Joyce's part if not knowingly on Bloom's, pointing not only to the proverbial expression 'Born with a silver spoon in his mouth' (as noted by Thornton, Gifford, SMT, and others) but to the one prior instance (the other two published abroad) that Joyce is likely to have known.

That one instance: in the English writer, philosopher, Christian apologist, and critic G[ilbert]. K[eith]. Chesterton's (1874–1936) not-yet-published (as of 1904) *What's Wrong With The World* (London, 1910), Part I. The Homelessness of Man, Section 5. The Unfinished Temple, p. 41:

> Some of our political houses are parvenu by pedigree ; they hand on vulgarity like a coat-of-arms. In the case of many a modern statesman to say that he is born with a silver spoon in his mouth is at once inadequate and excessive. He is born with a silver knife in his mouth. But all this only illustrates the English theory that poverty is perilous for a politician.

Uly 8.730: Famished ghosts.

Both Gifford and SMT cite book 11 of the *Odyssey*, in which the souls Odysseus encounters in Hades are desperate to drink the sacrificial blood he has spilled so as to attract Tiresias. But Joyce could have crossed paths with the phrase itself in a considerable number of antecedent texts, including but not limited to the three below.

First and earliest of the three: *The Queenes Exchange, A Comedy* (London, 1657), 'Acted [its title page declares] with generall applause at the *Black-Friers* BY *His* MAJESTIES *Servants*', written by the English dramatist Richard Brome (1590–1652) and reprinted, along with fourteen of his other comedies, in *The Dramatic Works of Richard Brome* published by John Pearson (London, 1873). In Act 5, scene 1, of the play—in vol. 3 (of 3), p. 540, of Pearson's edition—Offa, a son of the banished lord Segebert, has a speech reading in part:

> So, so, so, Holla, holla, gentle earth.
> Open not here, not near that part of thee
> That has but now disgorg'd those famish'd ghosts,
> That with the Furies would have beckned me
> Along to hell with 'em ; so, let me down,
> I must not follow yet, but sleep and think upon't.

Second, the English poet and journalist Sir Edwin Arnold's (1832–1904) *Indian Idylls: from the Sanskrit of the Mahâbharâta* (London, 1883), 'The Entry Into Heaven', pp. 270–71:

> A burning forest shut the roadside in
> On either hand, and 'mid its crackling boughs
> Perched ghastly birds, or flapped amongst the flames,—
> Vultures and kites and crows,—with brazen plumes
> And beaks of iron ; and these grisly fowl
> Screamed to the shrieks of Prets,—lean, famished ghosts,
> Featureless, eyeless, having pin-point mouths,
> Hungering, but hard to fill,—all swooping down
> To gorge upon the meat of wicked ones ;
> Whereof the limbs disparted, trunks and heads,
> Offal and marrow, littered all the way.

And third, the Greek-Japanese writer, translator, and teacher Lafcadio Hearn's (1850–1904) *Glimpses of Unfamiliar Japan, First Series* (London,

1894), in which a note for chap. 8 ('Kitzuki: The Most Ancient Shrine in Japan'), on p. 177, reads: 'The gaki are the famished ghosts of that Circle of Torment in hell whereof the penance is hunger ; and the mouths of some are "smaller than the points of needles."'

9. 'Scylla and Charybdis'

Uly 9.2–3: A great poet on a great brother poet.

This sentence and the one immediately preceding it, 'And we have, have we not, those priceless pages of *Wilhelm Meister*.'—both spoken by the 'quaker librarian' Lyster—may together point to the long essay by the American physician, poet, essayist, and educator Oliver Wendell Holmes (1809–1894) on Sir Edwin Arnold's *The Light of Asia; or, The Great Renunciation* (London, 1879), a book-length narrative poem on the life and times of the Indian Prince Gautama Buddha, who, after attaining enlightenment, was recognized as the Buddha. Holmes's essay, in *The International Review* (New York), vol. 7 (Oct. 1879), 345–72, reads, on p. 348 (italics in the original):

> One fear the reader may be assured is groundless, — that of finding the poem before him dull. Dulness is apt to be an infirmity of religious poems. One would have hardly thought Dante could be reproached for such a failing by a great brother-poet, but Goethe is said to have told a young Italian that he thought the " Inferno " abominable, the " Purgatorio " doubtful, and the " Paradiso " *tiresome*.

Wilhelm Meister's Apprenticeship, the second novel, after *The Sorrows of Young Werther* (1774), by the German poet, playwright, and polymath Johann Wolfgang von Goethe (1749–1832), was published in 1795–96.

Uly 9.245: no truant memory

Thornton: 'This phrase may echo Horatio's statement to Hamlet that he is away from the university at Wittenberg because of his "truant disposition" (*Hamlet*, I ii 169).' But Stephen's phrase occurs verbatim and apparently uniquely pre-*Ulysses* in the English poet John Fitchett's (1776–1838) 131,000-word Romantic epic *King Alfred: A Poem* (London, 1841 and 1842)—edited and completed after Fitchett's death by his friend Robert Roscoe—vol. 3 (of 5), book 18, p. 45, lines 90–91, Asser addressing the Queen of Mercia: '" Oh ! my fair Queen, no truant memory | Fails to record such bounty, but confirms.["]' Pre-Joyce variants of the phrase also occur from time to time, among them the three below.

In *Manuel; A Tragedy, in Five Acts* (London, 1817), by the Dublin-born Protestant (Church of Ireland) cleric and author of Gothic plays and novels Charles Robert Maturin (1780–1824)—best known for his four-volume novel *Melmoth the Wanderer* (Edinburgh and London, 1820)—Mendizabel, a noble of Cordova, declares to De Zelos, a kinsman of Manuel, Count Valdi, in Act 3, scene 3: 'My noble lord, | A word with you :—A trifle, but a strange one, | Had well nigh made my memory a truant'.

In the American clergyman and hymn writer Samuel Longfellow's (1819–1892) poem 'The Homestead' (1839)—referring to the Longfellow family's (including Samuel's older brother Henry Wadsworth Longfellow) home and estate in Gorham, Maine—the last stanza reads:

> And one there was — now distant far —
>   Who shared my childish plays,
> With whom I roamed in deeper joy
>   In boyhood's thoughtful days.
> Dear cousin, round thine early home
>   When truant memory
> Lingers in dreams of fond regret,
>   Dost thou e'er think of me ?

And in *Ephemera* (London, 1865), a volume of poems by Lady Emma Caroline Wood (1802–1879) and her daughter Anna Caroline Steele (1841–1920), writing under the names of, respectively, Helen and Gabrielle Carr, a sonnet numbered 25, dated February 1846 and printed on p. 109 of a section called 'Sonnets and Versicles', reads:

> Sleep comes not through the dreary hours of night,
>   But in its stead a dull and heavy pain
>   Weighs on my eyelids and my burning brain ;
> Patient, although perplexed, I watch the light
> Dance on the chequered ceiling, until sight
>   Reels at the useless rack ; and hear the rain
>   Pour its full volume on the rattling pane.
> Then memory, potent in my own despite,
> Brings back the thought, subdued in sunshine bright,
>   And busy occupation ; once again
>   (Whilst vainly I my truant memory rein)
> That sense of ill returns with added might,
> Then, hopeless e'er to guide my mind aright,
>   I for the morn's pure breezes sigh in vain.

Uly 9.345–46: warm and brooding air

Thornton and Gifford pass over the phrase without comment; SMT declare it to be 'After *Hamlet*: "a nipping and an eager air" (I ii 4).' But one verbatim and a handful of near-verbatim instances seem far more likely to have inspired Joyce's phrase.

The verbatim instance: in a long story or short novel published anonymously in the January 1902 issue of the penny dreadful *Happy Hour Stories* (London), no. 109, pp. 1–46, under the title 'A Weak Woman' and written 'By the Author of "A Great Mistake," "Little Slyboots," "Yes or No?" &c.'—that author identifiable as the prolific, usually anonymous or pseudonymous, English romance novelist Charlotte Mary Brame (1836–1884), here as 'Bertha M. Clay'. The phrase in question occurs on the penultimate page of Brame's story in a paragraph reading in its entirety (italics in the original):

> The scent of ripening fruit was in the air, the windows were all wide open to the sunshine. Now and then one of the kind gray sisters passed across the leafy *cour* to the chapel ; a bee was diving deep into the honeysuckle on a wall and humming busily in the warm and brooding air.

As for the two near-verbatim instances, the first of these, commonly found among the evening prayers of many Anglican, Presbyterian, and other Protestant churches, reads (italics in the original): 'O God, for your love for us, *warm and brooding*, which has brought us to birth and opened our eyes to the wonder and beauty of creation, *We give you thanks'*. The second, a secular instance, occurs in *Venetia's Lovers: An Uneventful Story* (London, 1884), by the Scottish novelist Grace Leslie Keith Johnson (1843–1929), as 'Leslie Keith', with, in vol. 3 (of 3), chap. 4, p. 94:

> Dick passed Venetia's chair without looking at her. When they had left the room she rose swiftly and made her escape by the open window on to the terrace. The warm, brooding air hung like a veil over the valley ; she could hardly draw a free breath ; it was intensely, alarmingly still, and to the west there was piled a mass of red-edged cloud that held in it a dark threat of coming storm.

Uly 9.352: coffined thoughts

From a sentence reading 'Coffined thoughts around me, in mummycases, embalmed in spice of words', Stephen's phrase previously occurred in stanza 3 of the Irish historian William Edward Hartpole Lecky's (1838–1903) 'On An Old Song', first published in *Macmillan's Magazine*, vol. 51, no. 304 (Feb. 1885), 257–58, later collected in his *Poems* (London, 1891), on p. 27:

> There were mighty scholars then,
> With the slow, laborious pen,
> Piling up their works of learning,
> Men of solid, deep discerning,
> Widely famous as they taught
> Systems of connected thought,
> Destined for all future ages ;
> Now the cobweb binds their pages ;
> All unread their volumes lie
> Mouldering so peaceably,
> Coffined thoughts of coffined men,
> Never more to stir again
> In the passion and the strife,
> In the fleeting forms of life,
> All their force and meaning gone,
> As the stream of thought flows on.

Uly 9.356: Once quick in the brains of men.

Unremarked by Thornton, Gifford, and SMT, the last five words of the quoted phrase had previously occurred verbatim in *Julius Caesar*, II i 229–33, Brutus speaking:

> Boy! Lucius! Fast asleep? It is no matter,
> Enjoy the honey-heavy dew of slumber.
> Thou hast no figures nor no fantasies,
> Which busy care draws in the brains of men;
> Therefore thou sleep'st so sound.

In *The Spirit of the Age: or Contemporary Portraits*, second edn (London, 1825), the English essayist, drama and literary critic, painter, social commentator, and philosopher William Hazlitt (1778–1830), echoing Shakespeare's lines but substituting an italicized passion for Shakespeare's care, writes on p. 189, of 'Mr. Wordsworth' (italics in the original): 'He has " no figures nor no fantasies, which busy *passion* draws in the brains of men :" neither the gorgeous machinery of mythologic lore, nor the splendid colours of poetic diction.'

Uly 9.374–75: I thank thee for the word

SMT declare this phrase to be 'From Gratiano's taunting of Shylock at the end of the trial scene in *Merchant of Venice*: "A Daniel still say I, a second Daniel, / I thank thee, Jew, for teaching me that word" (IV i 335–36).' Joyce's phrase occurs verbatim, however, not there but, to take one of several pre-*Ulysses* instances, in *Literary Fables, From the Spanish of Yriarte*—that is, of the Spanish neoclassical poet Tomás de Iriarte or Yriarte (1750–1791)—as translated by Robert Rockliff and first published in *Blackwood's*, vol. 46, no. 286 (Aug. 1839), 202–11, where Fable 6, 'The Parrots and the Monkey', reads in part, on pp. 206–07 (italics in the original):

> One day, instead of *olla*, he
> Called for *un gratin de bouillie*,
> When, with a face of much amazement,
> A monkey, from a neighbouring casement,
> Politely asked him what the phrase meant ;
> And, being told, discharged a volley
> Of laughter at the pedant's folly.
> Surprised and vex'd at this rebuff,
> The parrot answer'd, in a huff :
> " Thou art a *Purist*, I suspect,
> And I despise thy sober sect."
> The monkey, bowing to the bird,
> Replied, " I thank thee for the word :

> Though parrots may despise the same,
> It is an honourable name."[16]

And, to take another example, in George MacDonald's poem cycle *A Book of Strife, in the Form of the Diary of an Old Soul* (privately printed, 1880; new edition London, 1909), with, in the latter, section title 'March', stanza 19, p. 39:

> " I am but as a beast before thee, Lord."—
> Great poet-king, I thank thee for the word.—
> Leave not thy son half-made in beastly guise—
> Less than a man, with more than human cries—
> An unshaped thing in which thyself cries out !
> Finish me, Father ; now I am but a doubt ;
> Oh ! make thy moaning thing for joy to leap and shout.

Uly 9.376–78: weave and unweave

This phrase occurs twice in the cited lines, which read: '—As we, or mother Dana, weave and unweave our bodies, Stephen said, from day to day, their molecules shuttled to and fro, so does the artist weave and unweave his image.' Thornton cites, by the writer, editor, critic, poet, painter, Theosophist, and Irish nationalist George William Russell (1867–1935)—also known as Æ, AE, or A.E.—his play *Deirdre* (1902) and, citing an article by J. Prescott (in *Modern Language Quarterly*, XIII, 154), the Conclusion of the English essayist, art and literary critic, and fiction writer Walter Pater's (1839–1894) *Studies in the History of the Renaissance* (London, 1873); Gifford and SMT, Russell's poem 'Dana', to which SMT add the funeral garment woven and unwoven by Penelope in the *Odyssey*. To these may be added, among several other verbatim instances, Swinburne's *Atalanta in Calydon. A Tragedy.* (London, 1865; new, revised edition, London, 1892), the earlier of which has, on p. 15:

> But whatsoever intolerable or glad
> The swift hours weave and unweave, I go hence
> Full of mine own soul, perfect of myself,
> Toward mine and me sufficient ; and what chance
> The gods cast lots for and shake out on us,

---

16 Rockliff's translation of Yriarte's *Literary Fables* was subsequently issued in book form by the publisher Longmans (London) in editions of 1851, 1854, and 1866.

That shall we take, and that much bear withal.[17]

Uly 9.415–17: *How many miles to Dublin? [...] by candlelight?*

Commenting on Joyce's lines, which read in their entirety (italics in the original) *'How many miles to Dublin? | Three score and ten, sir. | Will we be there by candlelight?'*, Thornton, Gifford, SMT, and others declare them to be a version of the nursery rhyme 'How many miles to Babylon?', SMT adding that '[t]here are numerous versions, many of which substitute other cities for Babylon' and citing the *Oxford Dictionary of Nursery Rhymes*, pp. 63–64. But Joyce's lines echo nearly verbatim the nursery rhyme as it appears in a number of pre-*Ulysses* publications, one of which, *Cassell's Little Folks: The Magazine for Boys and Girls* (London), vol. 82 (1915), reads on p. 153: 'How many miles to Dublin town ? | Three score and ten, sir ! | Shall I get there by candle light ? | Yes, and back again, sir !'

Uly 9.539: Take her for me.

The paragraph in 'Scylla and Charybdis' where the highlighted phrase occurs reads in its entirety: 'There be many mo. Take her for me. In pairing time. Jove, a cool ruttime send them. Yea, turtledove her.' For the phrase itself, see Judges xiv 3 as it appears in the Douay-Rheims Bible: 'And his father and mother said to him: Is there no woman among the daughters of thy brethren, or among all my people, that thou wilt take a wife of the Philistines, who are uncircumcised? And Samson said to his father: Take this woman for me, for she hath pleased my eyes.' The corresponding verse in the King James Version reads: 'Then his father and his mother said unto him, *Is there* never a woman among the daughters of thy brethren, or among all my people, that thou goest to take a wife of the uncircumcised Philistines? And Samson said unto his father, Get her for me; for she pleaseth me well.'

---

17 In *Uly* 9.616–17, as noted by SMT, Mulligan quotes a line from the chorus of this verse drama.

Uly 9.539: In pairing time.

Joyce's use of this phrase, while it commonly occurs in natural history, ornithological, and other such texts as a synonym for mating season, may have been suggested by its presence in two literary works. The first of these: Robert Louis Stevenson's *Virginibus Puerisque and Other Papers* (London, 1881), chap. 11 ('Pan's Pipes'), pp. 281–82: 'For it is a shaggy world, and yet studded with gardens ; where the salt and tumbling sea receives clear rivers running from among reeds and lilies ; fruitful and austere ; a rustic world ; sunshiny, lewd, and cruel. What is it the birds sing among the trees in pairing-time ?'

The second, from *Sister Songs: An Offering to Two Sisters* (London, 1895), by the English poet and Catholic mystic Francis Thompson (1859–1907): 'Poet and Anchorite', reading in part on p. 28:

>   And I deem well why life unshared
>   Was ordainèd me of yore.
>   In pairing-time, we know, the bird
>   Kindles to its deepmost splendour,
>   And the tender
>   Voice is tenderest in its throat :
>   Were its love, for ever nigh it,
>   Never by it,
>   It might keep a vernal note,
>   The crocean and amethystine
>   In their pristine
>   Lustre linger on its coat.
>   Therefore must my song-bower lone be,
>   That my tone be
>   Fresh with dewy pain alway ;
>   She, who scorns my dearest care ta'en,
>   An uncertain
>   Shadow of the sprite of May.

Uly 9.934: and from her arms

As Thornton notes, Hodgart and Worthington list this phrase—which recurs in line 9.937—as an allusion to 'The Moon Hath Raised Her Lamp Above' from Julius Benedict's three-act opera *The Lily of Killarney* (1862), but, Thornton adds, 'no copies of the song which I have seen have such a line.' He continues: 'Context makes an allusion to "Goodbye, Sweetheart, Goodbye" [a song by H. L. Hatton, also cited by SMT] more likely [...] the lover who is departing remarks on the fading of the stars and says, "time doth tear me from thine arms."'

Verbatim antecedents of Joyce's phrase do, however, exist. One such occurs in the English poet and physician Sir Richard Blackmore's (1654–1729) *Prince Arthur. An Heroick Poem. In Ten Books.* (London, 1695), with, in book 4, p. 100:

> The savage Foes, that did her Anger dread,
> And from her Arms, to Wilds and Mountains fled,
> Now leave the Coverts, where they sculking staid,
> And roaring out, th' unguarded Land invade.

Another: in MacPherson's *The Poems Of Ossian, &c.* (Edinburgh, 1805), where the purported Ossianic poem 'The Hunter', canto 10, lines 115–16, reads: 'Blow, Boreas, blow the rough cerulean main, | And from her arms the lovely youth detain'.

Uly 9.938: Wait to be wooed and won.

Thornton, Gifford, SMT, and others cite Shakespeare's *1 Henry VI*, Suffolk to Regnier: 'Thy daughter shall be wedded to my king, | Whom I with pain have wooed and won thereto' (V iii 137–38). But the quoted phrase occurs verbatim in at least two pre-*Ulysses* works: first, in an essay by the American literary critic, Unitarian minister, abolitionist, and politician Thomas Wentworth Higginson (1823–1911) entitled 'The Disappearance of Ennui', collected in his *Book and Heart: Essays on Literature and Life* (New York, 1897), and reading, on p. 215: 'The great success of *Little Women* in England was largely due, no doubt, to the novelty of the situation there rendered—the family of maidens, all poor, all busy, all happy, and all content to wait to be wooed and won as it might please Providence.'

And second—in *The Arabian Nights' Entertainments: Stories from The Thousand and One Nights Told for Young People* (Boston, New York, and London, 1915), by the American children's author Martha A. L. Lane (1862–1948)—the tale of 'Prince Ahmed and Peribanou', p. 184: '" I did not bring thee here," she answered, " to be my slave, but to be my husband. Among us fairy folk it is the maiden's right to choose the one who pleases her best, nor need we wait to be wooed and won before we speak of our affection."'

Uly 9.950: fantastical humour

The passage in which this phrase occurs (9.949–50), directed at Stephen Dedalus by John Eglinton, reads: 'Your own name is strange enough. I suppose it explains your fantastical humour.' Among the earliest instances of the phrase, one occurred in the much-reprinted *Seneca's Morals by Way of Abstract: to Which is Added, a Discourse Under the Title of An After-thought* (1685 et seq.), by the English pamphleteer, author, courtier, and press censor Sir Roger L'Estrange (1616–1704), in chap. 8 ('Of Anger') of the eleventh edition (London, 1718), with, on p. 331: 'It is a Phantastical Humour, that the same Jest in private, should make us Merry, and yet Enrage us in Publick ; nay, we will not allow the Liberty that we take.'

Another early instance: in Richard Steele's *The Tatler*, no. 77 (5 Oct. 1709), as reprinted in *Steele: Selections from the Tatler, Spectator and Guardian*, edited by Austin Dobson (Oxford, 1885), an essay 'On the Affectation of Faults and Imperfections' reading in part:

> As bad as the world is, I find by very strict observation upon virtue and vice, that if men appeared no worse than they really are, I should have less work than at present I am obliged to undertake for their reformation. They have generally taken up a kind of inverted ambition, and affect even faults and imperfections of which they are innocent. The other day in a coffee-house I stood by a young heir, with a fresh, sanguine, and healthy look, who entertained us with an account of his diet-drink ; though, to my knowledge, he is as sound as any of his tenants.
>
> This worthy youth put me into reflections upon that subject ; and I observed the fantastical humour to be so general, that there is hardly a man who is not more or less tainted with it.

It later recurred in a much-reprinted observation on novelty usually attributed to William Makepeace Thackeray but in fact based on a passage—translated from the French and published, without attribution, on p. 19 of T. Nixon's *Maxims, Observations & Reflections on Morality and Religion; Selected from Various Authors* (London, Nottingham, and Sheffield, 1806)—in the soldier, hedonist, essayist, and literary critic Charles de Saint-Evremond's (1613–1703) *Quelques Observations sur le Goût et le Discernement des François* [Some observations on the taste and discernment of the French] (Paris, 1683):

> Novelty has charms, that our minds can hardly withstand. The most valuable things, if they have for a long time appeared among us, do not make any impression as they are good, but give us distaste as they are old. But when this fantastical humour is over, the same men or things will come to be admired again, by a happy return of our good taste.

Uly 9.1036: bewept by all frail tender hearts

Thornton and SMT have no comment on the highlighted phrase; Gifford only 'Source unknown'. But "frail, tender hearts" did occur pre-*Ulysses* in the penultimate line of the sonnet 'Grief' by the Jamaican poet and schoolteacher Matthew Josephs (1831–1901), collected on pp. 216–17 of his *The Wonders of Creation and Other Poems* (London, 1876), and reading in its entirety:

> Handmaid of Sorrow, ever pining Grief,
> Why thus forlorn, so silent and alone ?
> Laden with weight of cares to all unknown,
> Hast thou no one to bring thee sweet relief ?
> But as the blushing leaf, the lovely flower
> Protects from piercing heat and chilling blast,
> So doth each of thy lone and crystal shower
> The heart relieve, when stormy clouds o'ercast
> Her horizon serene. Thy tenderness
> And anxious care to those who are distrest
> Are known. This world would be a wilderness
> Had not thy gracious smiles oft soothed to rest
> Frail, tender hearts that waves of sorrow know,
> And breasts that feel the depth of human woe.

Uly 9.1040: where the bad niggers go

Thornton, Gifford, SMT, Bowen, and others cite the chorus of the American composer Stephen Foster's (1826–1864) song 'Old Uncle Ned' (1848), ending 'He's gone whar de good niggers go.' But the highlighted phrase previously occurred, in Foster-like pseudo-African-American dialect but otherwise verbatim, in the Irish-American soldier, adventurer, and author 'Captain' Mayne Reid's (1818–1883) *The Pierced Heart and Other Stories* (London, 1885), the eleventh of which, 'Among the Palmettoes, An Adventure in the Swamps of Louisiana', has the following passage on pp. 277–78 (italics in the original):

> Chagrined at my ill-luck, late looking so good, I was about to turn back, when an object caught my eye, causing me to keep my place. It was on the opposite side of the *bayou*, something which glanced amid the green leaves of the palmettoes. Shading off the sun with my spread palm, I soon made it out to be the barrel of a gun, at the same time seeing that the weapon was in the hands of a man. No ordinary individual either, nor stranger to me ; but one with whose history, or at least some antecedents of his life, I was already acquainted. That very morning over the breakfast-table my uncle had been talking about one of his slaves ; a mulatto who had absconded, and, as supposed, taken to the swamps—" de place whar de bad niggers go," as one of my male cousins facetiously informed me. I had once or twice seen this runaway—" Yellow Jerry " he was called—about the plantation, and heard much talk of him ; that he was a daring, desperate fellow, who scorned staying within the negro-quarter at night, instead stealing out and ranging the neighbourhood around, a terror to the timid. His tawny face, with a tint of saffron, moustached and bearded, once seen could not be easily forgotten ; and soon as that now amid the palmettoes, as it were, set in a *chevaux-de-frise* frame, came under my eyes, I was satisfied of its being his.

Uly 9.1087: honeying malice

Joyce's phrase may be traced proximately to the English author of novels, short stories, and nonfiction Evelyn May Clowes (1872–1942) including, as 'Elinor Mordaunt', the novel *The Processionals* (London, 1918) with, in chap. 21, on p. 184: 'He had served as a peg for those garlands of filial affection and self-sacrifice which it had been his delight to weave. Now, however, under the snick of her sister-in-law's honeyed malice, she began to think of him with real affection.'

And traced ultimately to the Genevan philosopher, writer, and composer Jean-Jacques Rousseau's (1712–1778) autobiographical, unfinished, posthumously published *Les Rêveries du Promeneur Solitaire*

(Geneva, 1782) or *The Reveries of the Solitary Walker*—written between 1776 and 1778; reminiscent of the English poet Edward Young's (1683–1765) *The Complaint: or Night-Thoughts on Life, Death, & Immortality* (London, 1742–1745) and of Goethe's *The Sorrows of Young Werther* (Leipzig, 1774; first English edition 1779) not to mention Joyce's own *A Portrait of the Artist as a Young Man*—the Eighth Walk of which reads in part in the French original:

> Il n'en est pas ainsi des tristes momens que je passe encore au milieu des hommes, jouet de leurs caresses traîtresses, de leurs complimens ampoulés & dérisoires, de leur mielleuse malignité. De quelque façon que je m'y suis pu prendre, l'amour-propre alors fait son jeu. La haine & l'animosité que je vois dans leurs cœurs à travers cette grossiere enveloppe, déchirent le mien de douleur, & l'idée d'être ainsi sottement pris pour dupe ajoute encore à cette douleur un dépit très-puéril, fruit d'un sot amour-propre dont je sens toute la bêtise, mais que je ne puis subjuguer.

That is, in one early, anonymous translation, in *The Confessions of J. J. Rousseau, Citizen of Geneva. Part The First. To which are added, The Reveries of a Solitary Walker. Translated from the French*, vol. 2 (of 2), third edn (London, 1796), p. 347:

> It is not thus in those melancholy moments which I yet sometimes pass among men, the dupe of their treacherous caresses, their false deceitful compliments, and honied malignity : however I endeavour to suppress it, self pride then prevails, and the hatred and animosity I perceive in their hearts, through every weak concealment, tears mine with keenest sorrow ; while the idea of being taken for so gross a dupe, adds to my grief a childish vexation, the fruit of this foolish pride, which, though I feel the ridiculousness of, I cannot conquer.

Joyce's substitution of 'honeying' for Rousseau's (and Mordaunt's) 'honied' (mielleuse) in the highlighted phrase serves to make clear that he is referring to Stephen's feelings in response to Mulligan gibes, and not to the feelings of Mulligan himself.

Uly 9.1094–95: orts and offals

This phrase—from a passage Stephen thinks to himself (though in Mulligan's voice and presence) reading 'Come, Kinch. You have eaten all we left. Ay. I will serve you your orts and offals.'—may be traced ultimately to the English dramatist Thomas Otway's (1652–1685) Restoration comedy *The Soldier's Fortune* (London, 1681), where Captain Beaugard says to Sir Jolly Jumble in Act 1, scene 1 of the 1717 edition: 'I am sorry for that with all my Heart ; do you know, say you, Sir, and would you put off your mumbled Orts, your Offal upon me—'.

But Joyce's phrase occurs more nearly verbatim in another, later work, the English pamphleteer and journalist William Cobbett's (1763–1835) *Advice to Young Men, and (incidentally) to Young Women, in the Middle and Higher Ranks of Life.* (London, 1829), Letter 5 ('Advice to a Father'), unpaged:

> In HERON's collection of God's judgments on wicked acts, it is related of an unnatural son, who fed his aged father upon orts and offal, lodged him in a filthy and crazy garret, and clothed him in sackcloth, while he and his wife and children lived in luxury[.]

and perfectly verbatim in an anonymously published autobiographical work entitled *Self-Formation; or, the History of an Individual Mind: Intended as a Guide for the Intellect Through Difficulties to Success. By a Fellow of a College* (London, 1837) later revealed to be the English lawyer, political figure, miscellaneous writer, and amateur astronomer Capel Lofft (1751–1824). The passage in vol. 2 (of 2) of Lofft's book where the phrase 'orts and offals' occurs, in chap. 8, on pp. 37–38, reads:

> It is the odds and ends of our time, its orts and offals, laid up, as they usually are, in corners, to rot and stink there, instead of being used out as they should be—these, I say, are the occasions of our moral unsoundness and corruption ; a dead fly, little thing as it is, will spoil a whole box of the most precious ointment ; and idleness, if it be once suffered, though but for a brief while, is sure, by the communication of its listless quality, to clog and cumber the clockwork of the whole day. It is the ancient enemy—the old man of the Arabian Tales. Once take him upon your shoulders, and he is not to be shaken off so easily.

The portion of Lofft's book of which this passage is an excerpt was widely reprinted, usually if not always without attribution and often under the title 'It Will Never Do To Be Idle', in essay collections for general readers and in student reading, spelling, writing, and conduct manuals, throughout the nineteenth century.

Uly 9.1170: sweetly varying voices

An early instance of this phrase occurred in *The Poetical Works of Philip Late Duke of Wharton; And Others of the Wharton Family, and of the Duke's Intimate Acquaintance. Particularly Lord Bolinbroke, Dean Swift* [and others]. *Together with some Original Letters of Wit, Gallantry, &c.* (London, [1731]), which, in a long 'Description of JAMAICA', unidentified as to its sender or recipient (though it begins with the salutation 'Sir') and dated 'Port Royal, Jamaica, 5 July 1726, reads in part, on pp. 14–15:

> Your Ears are ravished with a thousand *Nightingales*, and other sweetly varying Voices and shriller Notes of the Song-kind, by Intervals busy in shewing the Pride and Lustre of their Wings, and perching, place aright the gold and silver Colours on their Plumage[.]

The peer referred to in the book's title was Philip Wharton, 1st Duke of Wharton (1698–1731). The Governor of Jamaica from 1728 until his death in March 1734 was the British army officer, playwright, and colonial administrator Robert Hunter, who may have written the letter from which this excerpt is quoted.

The highlighted phrase also occurs in a Postscriptum to the Scottish author, hymnist, and tractarian cleric Rev. James Skinner's (1818–1881) *Cœlestia. The Manual of St Augustine: The Latin Text Side by Side with an English Interpretation. In Thirty-Six Odes.* (London, 1881)—the Postscriptum being Skinner's translation of 'Oratio pro Amore Dei' (as 'A Prayer for God's Love') from *Paradisus Precum* (1589 et seq.) by the Dominican friar, theologian, writer, and preacher Luis de Granada (1504–1588). Stanza 13 of the Prayer, on p. 133, reads:

> More sweetly varying voices sound,
>   In tuneful harmony combined,
> When by exact proportion bound,
>   Than when their equal strength they find
> In unison ; so too in thee,
> My soul, this inequality
> With God, in Glory throned Above,
> Is cause of more abounding Love.

Uly 9.1202: Seas between.

Joyce's phrase occurs in a considerable number of antecedent literary texts, most of them poems. Among the earliest and most familiar of these—and, as such, the one Joyce seems most likely to have had in mind—was the Scottish poet and lyricist Robert Burns's (1759–1796) 'Auld Lang Syne' (1788), whose fourth stanza reads: 'We twa hae paidlet i' the burn, | Frae mornin' sun till dine: | But seas between us braid hae roar'd | Sin auld lang syne.'

The phrase recurs in a poem by English novelist and poet Dinah Maria Craik (1826–1887)—best known for her novel *John Halifax, Gentleman* (London, 1856)—in which poem, 'My Christian Name', first published in the 1 June 1850 issue of *Chambers's Edinburgh Journal* and later collected in her *Poems* (London, 1866), the third of its five stanzas reads:

> Brothers and sisters, mockers oft
>   Of the quaint name I bore,
> Would I could leap back years, to hear
>   Ye shout it out once more !
> One speaks it still, in written lines,
>   The last fraternal claim :
> But the wide seas between us drown
>   Its sound—my Christian name.

Another text, first published in his *Indian Leisure. Petrarch. On the Character of Othello. Agamemnon. The Henriad. Anthology.* By Captain [later Major] Robert Guthrie MacGregor (1805–1869) of the Bengal Retired List. (London, 1854)—and later reprinted in several editions of Petrarch's poems—was Major Macgregor's translation of the Italian poet, scholar, and humanist Francesco Petrarca's, or Petrarch's (1304–1374) 'Canzone IV.', subtitled, in Macgregor's translation, 'He grieves that he is so far from her.' (that is, from Laura), and reading in a passage on p. 31:

> What rivers and what heights,
> What shores and seas between
> Me rise and those twin lights,
> Which made the storm and blackness of my days
> One beautiful serene,
> To which tormented Memory still strays:
> Free as my life then past fro ev'ry care,
> So hard and heavy seems my present lot to bear.

The phrase also occurs in the English poet and herpetologist Arthur W. E. O'Shaughnessy's (1844–1881) *Lays of France* (*Founded on the Lays of Marie*) (London, 1872), with a passage in the long poem 'Chaitivel; or, the Lay of Love's Unfortunate' reading, on pp. 104–05:

> The intense flower
> Of waving strange-leaved trees that sang
> His dirge with voices wild and soft,
> Wafted her perfume that had power
> To shake her heart ; warm air, that rang
> With ends of unknown singing, oft
> Broke in upon her, as though space
> Of cold climes and cold seas between
> Were dwindling, and she should have seen
> That fair unconsecrated place,
> Golden in sunlight, green in shade
> Of many a palm and might blade
> Of monstrous herb.

And, as a final (though not the only remaining) example, it recurs once again in the American poet and critic Ezra Pound's poem 'In Durance', written in 1907 and first published in his *Personae* (London, 1909), with an eight-line section on pp. 41–42 reading:

> Oh ye, my fellows : with the seas between us some be,
> Purple and sapphire for the silver shafts
> Of sun and spray all shattered at the bows
> Of such a " Veltro " of the vasty deep
> As bore my tortoise house scant years agone :
> And some the hills hold off,
> The little hills to east us, though here we
> Have damp and plain to be our shutting in.

Uly 9.1221–22: Cease to strive.

As Thornton notes, although the passage in which Joyce's phrase occurs reads in part 'Cease to strive. Peace of the druid priests of Cymbeline, hierophantic', the phrase highlighted above does not occur in *Cymbeline* or anywhere else in Shakespeare; nor—although Hodgart and Worthington list it as an allusion to Yeat's 'Who Goes with Fergus'— does it occur in that poem. Robert Kellogg, on p. 178 of his essay on

'Scylla and Charybdis' in *James Joyce's 'Ulysses': Critical Essays* (1974), cites a line from the last stanza of 'My Lady's Tears' in the English composer, lutenist, and singer John Dowland's (1563–1626) *Third and Last Book of Songs and Airs*, 'O strive not to be excellent in woe'. It does not occur in Blake's lyric beginning 'And did those feet in ancient time' in the preface to his *Milton: a Poem in 2 Books* (London, 1810), though that is cited by Gifford. And, although SMT write 'Possibly in reference to the motto of Tennyson's version of *Ulysses*: "To strive, to seek, to find, and not to yield" ('Ulysses', l. 70),' that seems no more likely than the other candidates previously suggested.

The phrase 'cease to strive' does, however, occur verbatim in several antecedent literary (as distinct from evangelical or theological) works. Among the earliest of these: the English poet, courtier, scholar, and soldier Sir Philip Sidney's (1554–1586) mainly prose pastoral romance *The Countess of Pembroke's Arcadia* (London, 1590), with, in Book 1, a sonnet ostensibly by that lady that begins (as edited in one modern edition):

> Transform'd in shew, but more transform'd in mind,
> I cease to strive with double conquest foil'd :
> For, woe is me, my powers all I find
> With outward force, and inward treason, spoil'd.

A second instance: in Dryden's verse translation of Virgil's *Georgics* (London, 1697), where book 1, lines 290–93—translating Virgil's 'non aliter quam qui adverso vix flumine lembum | remigiis subigit, si bracchia forte remisit, | atque illum in praeceps prono rapit alveus amni.' (book I, lines 201–03, of the Loeb Classics edition)—read: 'So the Boats brawny Crew the Current stem, | And, slow advancing, struggle with the Stream : | But if they slack their hands, or cease to strive, | Then down the Flood with headlong haste they drive.'

A third instance: in a poem by Goethe called, as translated by Edgar Alfred Bowring (1826–1911), 'The Doubters and the Lovers' and as published in *The Poems of Goethe, Translated in the Original Metres* (London, 1853):

> THE DOUBTERS.
> Ye love, and sonnets write ! Fate's strange behest
> The heart, its hidden meaning to declare,
> Must seek for rhymes, uniting pair with pair ;
> Learn, children, that the will is weak, at best.

Scarcely with freedom the o'erflowing breast
    As yet can speak, and well may it beware ;
    Tempestuous passions sweep each chord that's there,
Then once more sink to night and gentle rest.

Why vex yourselves and us, the heavy stone
    Up the steep path but step by step to roll ?
        It falls again, and ye ne'er cease to strive.

        THE LOVERS.
But we are on the proper road alone !
    If gladly is to thaw the frozen soul,
        The fire of love must aye be kept alive.

And, as a fourth instance, the Scottish poet, playwright, and novelist John Davidson's (1857–1909) 156-line poem 'A Ballad of a Nun', as first published in *The Yellow Book: An Illustrated Quarterly* (London), vol. 3 (Oct. 1894), 273–79—revised and republished, as 'The Ballad of a Nun', in Davidson's *Ballads and Songs* (London, 1894), pp. 52–61—with, in lines 121–24 of the *Yellow Book* version: 'She said between her chattering jaws, | " Deep peace is mine, I cease to strive ; | Oh, comfortable convent laws, | That bury foolish nuns alive !"'

10. 'Wandering Rocks'

Uly 10.94: two unlabouring men

Joyce's phrase seems to have occurred previously only once: in *The Lazy Tour of Two Idle Apprentices*, a humorous narrative co-authored by the English novelist and playwright Wilkie Collins (1824–1889) and his friend and mentor Charles Dickens, based on their walking tour of Cumberland in September 1857, first published from 3 Oct. to 31 Oct. 1857 in Dickens's weekly magazine *Household Words* and from 31 Oct. to 28 Nov. 1857 in *Harper's Weekly, A Journal of Civilization* (New York); first issued in book form three decades later in *The Lazy Tour of Two Idle Apprentices and Other Stories* (London, 1890).

In the narrative, Collins is represented by Thomas Idle, a bornand-bred idler; and Dickens by Francis Goodchild, whose character is laboriously idle. A passage in the third chapter (of four), containing one of the apparently only three pre-Joyce instances of the word 'unlabouring'—the other two both occurring in Yeats's poem 'Aedh Tells of the Perfect Beauty' (1899), with 'the unlabouring brood of the skies' and 'the unlabouring stars'—reads:

> Never did Thomas move more harmoniously in concert with his elders and betters than when he was qualifying himself for admission among the barristers of his native country. Never did he feel more deeply what real laziness was in all the serene majesty of its nature, than on the memorable day when he was called to the Bar, after having carefully abstained from opening his law-books during his period of probation, except to fall asleep over them. How he could ever again have become industrious, even for the shortest period, after that great reward conferred upon his idleness, quite passes his comprehension. The kind

Benchers did everything they could to show him the folly of exerting himself. They wrote out his probationary exercise for him, and never expected him even to take the trouble of reading it through when it was written. They invited him, with seven other choice spirits as lazy as himself, to come and be called to the Bar, while they were sitting over their wine and fruit after dinner. They put his oaths of allegiance, and his dreadful official denunciations of the Pope and the Pretender, so gently into his mouth, that he hardly knew how the words got there. They wheeled all their chairs softly round from the table, and sat surveying the young barristers with their backs to their bottles, rather than stand up, or adjourn to hear the exercises read. And when Mr. Idle and the seven unlabouring neophytes, ranged in order, as a class, with their backs considerately placed against a screen, had begun, in rotation, to read the exercises which they had not written, even then, each Bencher, true to the great lazy principle of the whole proceeding, stopped each neophyte before he had stammered through his first line, and bowed to him, and told him politely that he was a barrister from that moment.

Uly 10.121: Father Conmee liked cheerful decorum.

Among the several instances of 'cheerful decorum' in nineteenth-century British and Irish publications—most often in books and articles advising middle-class English readers on how to conduct themselves when travelling at home or abroad—two instances occur in books Joyce seems likely to have read.

The first of the two is the historical novel *Arthur Arundel, A Tale of the English Revolution* (London, 1844) by the English poet, novelist, friend of Percy Bysshe Shelley, and stockbroker Horace Smith (1779–1849), in vol. 1 (of 3), chap. 6 of which Arundel's childhood friend Wardour, now a courtier and confidant of *le Roi Soleil*, Louis XIV, is preparing Arthur for his imminent presentation to the king. The passage in question, on pp. 162–63 of that chapter, reads (italics in the original):

" Even his fondness for the heroic romances of Scuderi and Culprenade, turgid and inflated as they are, tended to elevate his aspirations, and to inspire him with a portion of that magnanimity upon which he still piques himself, and which he has endeavoured, by his example, to communicate to others. But these military sports, and the lotteries where every number was a costly prize, and the rural

masqueradings and banquets at which the King waited on the ladies, and
the games of chance, where so many thousand *louis d'ors* were lost and
won have all disappeared, and the literary or religious occupations which
Madame de Maintenon has rendered fashionable, and has managed
to combine with a cheerful decorum, present a marked contrast to the
vaunted politeness and gaiety of the Court of Charles the Second."

The second of the two: *A Full and True Account of the Wonderful Mission
of Earl Lavender, Which Lasted One Night and One Day: With a History of
the Pursuit of Earl Lavender and Lord Brumm by Mrs Scamler and Maud
Emblem* (London, 1895), by John Davidson—the same John Davidson
whose poem 'A Ballad of a Nun', as discussed above, may have inspired
Joyce's use of the phrase 'cease to strive' in *Ulysses* 9.1221–22—a comical
send-up of Darwin's Theory of Evolution, in which the long, single-
paragraph 'Note' at the beginning of the novel ends as follows:

What seems to deserve some commendation in these modern
Flagellants, who are now introduced to the public for the first time in an
episode in this veracious history, is the cheerful decorum of their whole
procedure : they are not bigots—only unfortunate people with no vital
interest in life, ignorant of what to do with their health and strength.

Uly 10.172: man's race on earth

A rare phrase, one pre-Joyce instance of which occurs in *The Paradise of
the Christian Soul, Delightful for Its Choicest Pleasures of Piety of Every Kind*
(London, 1850), by the Dutch-German Roman Catholic theologian Jacob
(or James) Merlo Horstius (1597–1644)—an authorized translation
of his *Paradisus Animae Christianae: lectissimis omnigenae pietatis delitiis
amoenus* (1670)—in which Joy 6 (from 'The Seven Joys of the Blessed
Virgin Mary') reads, on pp. 588–89:

> Joy to thee ! the Paraclete,
> From thy Son's majestic seat,
>   Forms anew man's race on earth,
>   With heav'nly birth.
> Let his fire our hearts inflame,
> Which unlit were dull and tame ;
>   So shall we unwearied prove
>   In toils of love !
>   *Hail Mary.*

Uly 10.174: walked and moved

From a sentence reading 'Don John Conmee walked and moved in times of yore', the highlighted phrase was rare pre-Joyce but not unique. One prior instance: in remarks said to have been made by the German priest and theologian Martin Luther (1483–1546) at the dinner table of his Wittenberg home, Lutherhaus, on 4 June 1539 (or possibly 1542), published in 1566 along with other of his off-the-cuff remarks as recorded by his former students in the *Tischreden* (*Table Talk*). In his remarks, Luther refers to, and disparages, the then-revolutionary heliocentric theory developed by the Polish mathematician, astronomer, and Catholic canon Nicolaus Copernicus (1473–1543) and previewed in his widely circulated (though not printed) and discussed *Commentariolus* [little commentary] well in advance of the publication, in 1543, of his magnum opus *De Revolutionibus orbium cœlestium* (On the revolutions of the heavenly spheres), which declared that the earth moved around the sun and not the other way round:

> There is talk of a new astrologer who wants to prove that the earth moves and goes around instead of the sky, the sun, the moon, just as if somebody were moving in a carriage or ship might hold that he was sitting still and at rest while the earth and the trees walked and moved. But that is how things are nowadays : when a man wishes to be clever he must needs invent something special, and the way he does it must needs be the best ! The fool wants to turn the whole art of astronomy upside-down. However, as Holy Scripture tells us, so did Joshua bid the sun to stand still and not the earth.[18]

Another instance: in chap. 27 ('This Is The Last Of Earth') of Stowe's *Uncle Tom's Cabin*, describing the scene after the frail, saintly Little Eva's

---

18   The German original on which this English translation is based may be found in the *Tischreden*, Weimar edition, vol. 1 (1912), p. 467, no. 419, and reads: 'Es ward gedacht eines neuen Astrologi, der wollte beweisen, dass die Erde bewegt würde und umginge, nicht der Himmel oder das Firmament, Sonne und Mond, gleich als wenn einer in einem Wagen oder in einem Schiff sitzt und bewegt wird meynete, er sässe still und ruhete, das Erdreich aber und die Bäume gingen und bewegten sich. Aber es gehet jetzt also: wer da will klug sein, der muss ihm etwas Eigenes machen, das muss das Allerbeste sein, wie er's machet. Der Narr will die ganze Kunst Astronomiae umkehren. Aber wie die heilige Schrift anzeigt, so hiess Josua die Sonne still stehen und nicht das Erdreich.' The phrase 'die Bäume gingen und bewegten sich' means, literally translated, 'the trees walked and moved'.

death, including the response to that death from her slave-holding father Augustine St. Clare, with, in vol. 2 (of 2), p. 117, of the first English edition (London, 1852): 'and St. Clare lived, and walked, and moved, as one who has shed every tear'.

Uly 10.181–82: a flock of small white clouds

Joyce may have borrowed and slightly modified a metaphor that had appeared in the first line of the poem 'Evening Clouds' by the Irish nationalist, laborer, miner, soldier, and poet Francis Ledwidge (1887–1917)—a poem written in memory of Rupert Brooke (1887–1915) and published posthumously in Ledwidge's *Songs of Peace* (London, 1917) shortly after his own death at the Battle of Passchendaele on 31 July 1917. The first eight of the poem's sixteen lines, on p. 98, read:

> A little flock of clouds go down to rest
> In some blue corner off the moon's highway,
> With shepherd winds that shook them in the West
> To borrowed shapes of earth, in bright array,
> Perhaps to weave a rainbow's gay festoons
> Around the lonesome isle which Brooke has made
> A little England full of lovely noons,
> Or dot it with his country's mountain shade.

But he could also have borrowed the phrase verbatim from either of two other works in which it had previously appeared. One of these was *Jan of the Windmill: A Story of the Plains* (London, 1896), by the English writer of children's novels Juliana Horatia Ewing (1841–1885), first serialized in *Aunt Judy's Magazine* (London) under the title 'The Miller's Thumb' from November 1872 to October 1873, then published by the Society for Promoting Christian Knowledge under the new title, in which a passage in chap. 11 ('Scarecrows and Men—Jan Refuses to "Make Gearge"—Uncanny—"Jan's Off"—The Moon and the Clouds'), p. 114, reads: 'The air was chill and fresh, but not bitterly cold. The moon rode high in the dark heavens, and a flock of small white clouds passed slowly before its face and spread over the sky.'

The other work was the German socialist philosopher, Marxist, and journalist Josef Dietzgen's (1828–1888) final book, *The Positive Outcome* of *Philosophy* (1887), as translated by Ernest Untermann (Chicago, 1906), with, in chap. 5 ('The Understanding as a Part of the Human Soul'), p. 361:

> Just as my soul of today has something analogous to my soul of yesterday, so it has also with the soul of my brother, and finally with the souls of animals, plants, stones, etc., proving that everything is more or less analogous. A herd of sheep is analogous to yonder flock of small, white clouds in the sky, and a poet has the license to call those small clouds little sheep.

Uly 10.183: A just and homely word.

While the phrase is Father Conmee's as he thinks about the French verb *moutonner*, the phrase 'just and homely' seems to have occurred pre-Joyce only once: in the prolific biblical commentator and prominent Irish member of the Plymouth Brethren—a low church and Nonconformist Christian movement, with roots in Anglicanism, founded in Dublin in the mid to late 1820s—William Kelly's (1821–1906) commentary on 2 Thessalonians iii 10–15, first published in *The Bible Treasury: A Monthly Magazine of Papers on Scriptural Subjects*, edited by Kelly, vol. 14, no. 330 (Nov. 1883), 360–62, and reading in part, on p. 361:

> None who looks to Christ could be a drone : if inclined to it, let him not forget the apostolic charge that whoever does not choose to work, neither let him eat. This would be an effectual cure, if faithfully carried out ; and are not the saints bound to do so ? It is a just and homely way of dealing, no doubt but the [C]hristian is surely equal to the occasion, not less than a Jew or a Gentile. If anything be contrary to Christ, it is the selfishness that would take advantage of grace ; and we are called not to humour but to reprove and repress what is so unworthy of the Christian, because it misrepresents Christ.[19]

If Joyce expected some of his readers to recognize the echo of this passage in Father Conmee's interior monologue, he may have intended it as another subtle brushstroke in his portrayal of Conmee's worldliness and spiritual complacency.

---

19 Transcribed from a scanned copy of Kelly's article kindly provided to me by Tereza Ward, curator of the Christian Brethren Archive, The University of Manchester.

Uly 10.188: his reign was mild

Referring to Father Conmee's role as rector at Clongowes Wood College, Joyce may have borrowed the phrase from the German Protestant theologian Emil Schürer's (1844–1910) *A History of the Jewish People in the Time of Jesus Christ* as translated by Rev. John Macpherson (Edinburgh, 1890), division 1, vol. 2, section 17 ('The Sons of Herod'), pp. 13–14: 'Philip himself was certainly a real exception among the sons and grandsons of Herod. While all the others, copying fathers and grandfathers, were ambitious, imperious, harsh, and tyrannical toward their subjects, nothing but what is honourable is told of Philip. His reign was mild, just, and peaceful.'

Among other publications in which Joyce could have encountered, and from which he could have borrowed, the phrase, one was an unsigned memorial essay in *The Freemasons' Quarterly Review* of 30 September 1837, following the death of 'His Royal Highness, the Grand Master' William the Fourth, reading on p. 61: 'His reign was mild ; and although war might be said to have shunned it, yet events were important, and required great discrimination to steer between the difficulties of public opinion.'

Uly 10.486: Tell him I'm Boylan with impatience.

The first of the novel's five instances or versions of 'Boylan with impatience'—the others occurring in lines 11.289, 11.426, 11.526, and 11.766. Joyce puns both here and there on an idiomatic expression well-established as such by the time he wrote *Ulysses*. What seems to have been the earliest recorded instance of the phrase occurs in *The Expedition of Humphry Clinker* (London, 1771), by the Scottish novelist, surgeon, critic, and playwright Tobias Smollett (1721–1771) with, on pp. 34–35 of the one-volume London 1835 edition, in a letter from Jeremy Melford to his friend Sir Watkin Phillips dated Bath, April 24, Melford writes:

> All this time, uncle sat boiling with impatience, biting his fingers, throwing up his eyes, and muttering ejaculations : at length he burst into a kind of convulsive laugh ; after which he hummed a song ; and, when the hurricane was over, exclaimed — ' Blessed be God for all things !'

Another early instance, in a work by the Anglo-Irish author Maria Edgeworth (1768–1849) that was a sequel to her first and better-known novel *Castle Rackrent, An Hibernian Tale* (London, 1800), occurred in *The Absentee*, occupying vols. 5 and 6 of her *Tales of Fashionable Life* (London, 1812), with, in chap. 16 of the latter volume, p. 388 (italics in the original):

> This speech lord Colambre and the count tacitly agreed to consider as another *apart*, which they were not to hear, or seem to hear. The count began again on the business of their visit, as he saw that lord Colambre was boiling with impatience, and feared that he should *boil over* and spoil all.

Subsequent instances of the phrase occurred in works by, among others, Frederick Marryat, Eugène Sue, Alexandre Dumas, W. M. Thackeray, Margaret Oliphant, and George Ohnet.

Uly 10.548: Fast and furious it was.

Unremarked by Thornton, Gifford, and SMT, the apparently earliest of many instances of the phrase 'fast and furious' occurred in Robert Burns's poem 'Tam O' Shanter' (1791), lines 143–44 of which read (italics in the original): 'As *Tammie* glowr'd, amaz'd, and curious, | The mirth and fun grew fast and furious'.

Uly 10.559: Hell's delights!

Lenehan's ejaculation, in his conversation with M'Coy as he recalls a bumpy late-night carriage ride in close proximity to and occasional physical contact with Molly Bloom and her 'fine pair', previously occurred in the first of his eighteen Dartmoor novels, *Children of the Mist* (London, 1898), by the India-born English author, poet, and dramatist Eden Phillpotts (1862–1960). In chap. 8 ('Mr. Blee Forgets Himself'), p. 241, Billy Blee vents his rage that Mrs Coomstock, whom he has long courted, has told him that she plans to marry someone else:

> 'She 'm gwaine to marry t' other, arter all ! From her awn lips I 've heard it ! That 's what I get for being a church member from the womb ! That 's my reward ! God, indeed ! Be them the ways o' a plain-dealin' God, who knaws what 's doin' in human hearts ? No fay ! Bunkum an' rot ! I 'll never lift my voice in hymn nor psalm no more, nor pray a line o' prayer again. Who be I to be treated like

that? Drunken auld cat! I cussed her—I cussed her! Would n't marry her now if she axed wi' her mouth in the dirt. Wheer 's justice to? Tell me that. Me in church, keepin' order 'mong the damn boys generation arter generation, and him never inside the door since he buried his wife. An' parson siding wi' un, I 'll wager. Mother Coomstock 'll give un hell's delights, that 's wan gude thought. A precious pair of 'em! Tchut! Gar!'

Joyce's 'She has a fine pair, God bless her' (10.559–60) may also owe something to Phillpotts's 'A precious pair of 'em!' in the same passage— referring to Mrs Coomstock and her fiancé.

Philpotts's novel was not, however, the first instance of Lenehan's phrase. Two other early ones (their ultimate sources not identified) occur in the entry for 'Hell' in *Slang. A Dictionary of the Turf, the Ring, the Chase, the Pit, of Bon-Ton, and the Varieties of Life*, by Jon Bee [pen name of John Badcock], Esq. (London, 1823), reading in part on p. 95 (italics in the original):

> *Hell's delights*—much mental pain. 'I had *hell's delights* all the vhile I vas in quod, a-thinking about my old mother; as for I know'd sh'd be in a b——— taking about my liberty.' 'Kicking up *hell's delights*,' a scolding, a quarrel, or domestic battle; capsizing the crockery and upsetting the sticks.

Uly 10.601–02: *Fair Tyrants* by James Lovebirch.

As Thornton, Gifford, SMT, and others note, there was an author of sado-masochistic novels going by the name James Lovebirch whose work was published in French, then English, in the early twentieth century, but none of these were called *Fair Tyrants*. The title phrase did, however, occur often pre-*Ulysses*.

One early instance: in *New Poems, Songs, Prologues and Epilogues. Never before Printed. Written by Thomas Duffett, And Set by The most Eminent Musicians about the Town.* (London, 1676), p. 27, the poem 'Gratitude to Fidelia', which begins:

> The Frantick Zealot who to Bliss aspires,
> On Racks of care and mortifi'd desires,
> Mistakes the way, by blind devotion driv'n;
> Your favours lead me to a sweeter Heav'n.
> As Souls of Lovers murther'd with despair,
> Do hover still where their fair Tyrants are.

Another early instance: in *LETTERS from the Marchioness de M***, to the Count de R***. Translated from the Original French By Mr. HUMPHREYS*. (London, 1735)—that is, Samuel Humphreys (1698?–1738)—with, on p. 37:

> I am as little satisfied with your Aversion to Life, and should be in some Apprehension for you, did we live in an Age, which made it fashionable for Lovers to destroy themselves, that they may have the Happiness of being lamented by their fair Tyrants ; but you are a Gentleman of Understanding, and know, as well as my self, that Death is the most ridiculous Proof of Love that can possibly be given.

And a third, in a poem called 'On FEMALE POWER' signed by R. Beatson—possibly Robert Beatson (1741–1818), a Scottish compiler and miscellaneous writer—published in *The Lady's Magazine, or Entertaining Companion for the Fair Sex* (London), vol. 13 (Oct. 1782), p. 551, reprinted, unsigned, in the January 1784 issue on p. 47, and reading in both in its entirety:

> In Britain's isle, where female beauty reigns,
> Where looks are darts, and smiles are massy chains ;
> Where beauteous tyrants claim despotic sway,
> 'Tis woman rules, and man who must obey.
> Poor captive man ! how vain thy boasted fame,
> Who fight for freedom, yet but know the name ;
> Who stake your lives in liberty's defence,
> But still have slav'ry for your recompense.
>   Ye hero's [sic] brave, who vanquish Bourbon's arms,
> Confess your weakness 'gainst one female's charms.
> Say how enfeeble [sic] human efforts are,
> To crush the victor of the god of war ;
> For ev'ry beauty will her birthright have,
> And ev'ry man is born to be a slave—
> Ah cruel fate ! and yet the chain is sweet,
> Which binds the captive at an angel's feet.
> Cease ye fair tyrants ! act a nobler part,
> Let ev'ry charmer wed her captive heart.

Uly 10.734–35: *America [...] What is it? The sweepings of every country including our own.*

Mr Kernan here recalls his recent conversation with Mr Crimmins, a client, to whom he had expressed the quoted view. As Joyce probably knew but Mr Kernan probably did not, a similar view had been expressed nearly verbatim in a passage in *Miscellanies in Prose and Verse ; including Remarks on English Plays, Operas, and Farces, And on a Variety of other Modern Publications, by the Honourable Lord Gardenstone*—that is, by the lawyer and judge Francis Garden, Lord Gardenstone (1721–1793)—second edition, corrected and enlarged (Edinburgh, 1792), p. 148, a passage subsequently reprinted in *The Reveries of a Recluse; or, Sketches of Characters, Parties, Events, Writings, Opinions, &c.* (Edinburgh, 1824), and reading, on p. 302 of the latter:

> I beg, once for all, that the English traveller, who may chance to cast his eye on these motley remarks [concerning the English Drama], will believe, that when I express contempt of a London audience, which I most heartily feel, I mean no reflection on the nation in general, nor that audience in particular, but the bulk of them, who are not Englishmen, but the sweepings of every country in Europe.

Uly 10.807: Muddy swine-snouts, hands, root and root, gripe and wrest them.

Joyce may have found *swine-snouts* in Archer's translation of Ibsen's *When We Dead Awaken* (see the full citation on p. 79 above in the discussion of *Portrait* 5.2729)—more specifically, in Act 1, p. 14, where Professor Rubek says of the wealthy patrons to whose portrait busts he now entirely devotes his energies:

> On the surface I give them the " striking likeness," as they call it, that they all stand and gape at in astonishment—[*Lowers his voice*]—but at bottom they are all respectable, pompous horse-faces, and self-opinionated donkey-muzzles, and lop-eared, low-browed dog-skulls, and fatted swine-snouts—and sometimes dull, brutal bull-fronts as well. [...] And it is these double-faced works of art [he continues on p. 15] that our excellent plutocrats come and order of me. And pay for in all good faith—and in good round figures too—almost their weight in gold, as the saying goes.[20]

Archer's 'fatted swine-snouts'—his version of Ibsen's Dano-Norwegian 'mæskede svinehoder', literally 'overstuffed pigheads'—and the passage of his translation in which it occurs are cited and quoted in

---

20 Thornton, Gifford, and SMT all note and discuss the allusion to Ibsen's *When We Dead Awaken* in the 'Eumaeus' episode at lines 16.52–54.

Sir James A. H. Murray, C. T. Onions, et al., *A New English Dictionary on Historical Principles* (London, 1919), vol. 9, part 2, SU–TH., s.v. *swine.*, def. 4. 'Obvious Combination'.

Note also that 'swine-snout' had previously occurred from time to time elsewhere, including in the Elizabethan playwright, poet, satirist, and pamphleteer Thomas Nashe's (1567–1601) satirical pamphlet *Pierce Penilesse his Supplication to the Divell* (London, 1592), where, speaking of a second-rate sonneteer, Nashe writes (italics in the original):

> Sometimes (because love commonly wears the livery of wit) he will be an *inamorato poeta*, & sonnet a whole quire of paper in praise of Lady Swine-snout, his yellow-faced mistress, & wear a feather of her rain-beaten fan for a favour, like a fore-horse.

and also including the Anglican cleric John Chetwind or Chetwynd's (1623–1692) *Anthologia Historica, Containing fourteen CENTURIES OF Memorable Passages AND Remarkable Occurrents, Collected out of the English, Spanish, Imperial, and Jewish Histories, and several other Authors and Writers* (London, 1674), with, on p. 52, quoting a passage from Popedom. Imp[erial]. Hist[ory], p. 538 (italics in the original):

> A *Cardinal* named *Swine-snout, Os porci*, in the daies of *Ludovicus Pius Emperor* was chosen *Pope*, and because it was a very unseemly *name* for so High a *dignity*, by a general consent it was *changed*, and he was called *Sergius* the second. Hence arose the *custom* of the *Popes* altering their *names* after their election to the *Popedom*.

Uly 10.822: Beingless beings.

In *Biblical Commentary on the Prophecies of Isaiah*, vol. 2 (Edinburgh, 1874), by the German Lutheran theologian and Hebraist Franz Delitzsch (1813–1890) as translated by the Rev. James Martin, Delitzsch—referring on p. 232 to the Seventh Prophecy in Isaiah xlvi ('Fall of the Gods of Babel')—writes:

> The gods of Babylon have all stooped at once, have sunken down, and have been unable to save their images which were packed upon the cattle, out of the hands of the conquerors. In ver[se]. 2*b* he destroys this delusion : they are going into captivity [...], even " their ownself"

(*naphshâm*), since the self or personality of the beingless beings consists of nothing more than the wood and metal of which their images are composed.

Uly 10.866: Shadow of my mind.

What seems to be the only pre-*Ulysses* instance of this phrase occurred in the dedicatory poem at the beginning of *Sonnets By Lord Alfred Douglas* (London, 1909), their author (1870–1945) an English poet and journalist principally remembered as the beloved of Oscar Wilde. The poem's sestet (which poem begins 'What shall I say, what word, what cry recalls') reads:

> This is my book, and there as in a glass,
> Darkly beheld, the shadow of my mind
> Wavers and flickers like a flame of fire.
> So through your eyes, it may be, it will pass,
> And I shall hold my wild shy bird confined
> In the gold cage of shadowless desire.

Uly 10.1074–75: The joy of creation ....

Although 'the joy of creation' is a commonplace in evangelical literature, this truncated phrase (ellipsis in the original) in Buck Mulligan's remarks to Haines critical of Stephen Dedalus may point to an essay, 'The Divine Sacrifice', by the British writer and poet Emma Marie Caillard (1852–1927), published in *The Contemporary Review* (New York and London), vol. 67 (Feb. 1895), 265–77, and reading on p. 270: 'And thus we are led to enter into the joy of creation, so strikingly expressed in the familiar words [from Job xxxviii 7], " When the morning stars sang together, and all the sons of God shouted for joy," and to regard it as more than a poetic fiction, a mere figment of the imagination.'

It may also point, more directly, to an essay by William Archer (1856–1924), the Scottish author, theater critic, and early champion and translator into English of the plays of Henrik Ibsen, entitled 'The Drama in the Doldrums', published in *The Fortnightly Review*, vol. 52 (n.s.), no. 308 (1 Aug. 1892), 146–67, and reading, on p. 158:

"Master Cotton," the burlesque Englishman who makes a brief appearance in Ibsen's *Peer Gynt*, has one saying which is truly characteristic of his nationality. Demanding to know what profit Peer Gynt proposes to reap from his yachting cruise, he lays it down as an axiom that

" No one hoists
His sails for nothing but the sailing."

It appears that to the English mind the joy of creation, of artistic production in and for itself, is a thing unknown. " No one hoists his sails for nothing but the sailing." How different is the case in France ! Around the Théâtre Libre, there has risen up a whole school of playwrights [...] who deliberately reject popularity in order to devote themselves to an artistic ideal. It may be a mistaken, a deplorable ideal, but they pursue it with a singleness of purpose which compels the respect even of their opponents. They produce play after play which lives its little hour on the boards of the Théâtre Libre, and then is heard no more. Now and then, perhaps, they make a trifle out of the publication of their writings, but practically their sole reward is the inward joy of production and the appreciation of a very narrow public—a clique if you choose to call it so. They may hope ultimately to gain the ear of a wider public (the " great public " they neither hope nor desire to conquer), but compromise they scorn and reject. And observe that their talent is uncontested even by their severest critics. No one doubts that they could, an if they would, produce the melodrama and vaudeville of commerce, and earn praise and pudding of the bourgeois public. Or rather let us admit that they could not even if they would ; but the impossibility arises, not from defect of talent, but from excess of artistic impulse and conviction. The born artist cannot *will* to be a tradesman. His genius stands or falls with the joy of creation. When he loses that, he loses his cunning of hand.

A passage that would resonate not just with Mulligan, as a frenemy of Stephen Dedalus all too willing to mock the brilliant but blighted artist in Stephen for his failure to experience the joy of creation, but resonate, in very different ways, for Stephen and for Joyce themselves.

Uly 10.1082–83: amid the cheerful cups

Joyce's phrase is ultimately traceable to the opening lines of Martial's (Marcus Valerius Martialis, 40 CE–c. 104) Epigram 11.104: 'Uxor, vade foras aut moribus utere nostris: | non sum ego nec Curius nec Numa nec

Tatius. | Me iucunda iuvant tractae per pocula noctes: | tu properas pota surgere tristis aqua.'; that is, in a prose translation by Walter A. C. Ker accompanying the poem in vol. 2 (of 2) of *Martial, Epigrams* (Cambridge, Mass., 1920), p. 311—published a year after 'Wandering Rocks' was first serialized—'Wife, out of my house, or conform to my ways; no Curius am I, or Numa, or Tatius. Nights drawn out by cheerful cups are my pleasure: you with a sad air haste to get up after drinking water.' The allusion, if it is such, is apt: Haines and Mulligan have just ordered, and just received, two mélanges, which, as SMT note, is a mixed drink containing 'coffee, milk, water, whipped cream, and castor sugar (*OED*)'—but no alcohol.

Joyce's 'cheerful cups' may also point to a passage in the 'Winter' section (first published in 1726) of the Scottish poet and playwright James Thomson's (1700–1748) poem cycle *The Seasons* (London, 1730), with, in lines 851–53: 'These their tents, | Their robes, their beds, and all their homely wealth | Supply, their wholesome fare and cheerful cups.'

Or, far less likely, to a third poem, signed only 'Pelham,' published on p. 73 of the short-lived periodical *The Meteor* (London), a collection of miscellaneous pieces edited by one E. Yewens (1840), which—like the quoted lines in Thomson's 'Winter' and the quoted phrase in 'Wandering Rocks'—owes a clear debt to Martial's epigram (italics in the original):

> Where friends are met for cheerful mirth,
> A *Kettle* decks the social hearth,
> With polished face and lulling song
> Recall our childhood's days now gone ;
> When full of frolic, fun, and glee,
> We hail'd the words, " go out to tea,"
> And though perchance more sober grown,
> Yet still we love its well-known tone ;
> And as the cheerful cups go round,
> In which no alcohol is found,
> May we enjoy a friendly cup,
> But let not scandal be mixed up.
> *Kettles!!* teetotallers sing thy fame,
> (A title which we cannot claim)
> For though of social boards the graces,
> We love them only in their places.

11. 'Sirens'

Uly 11.79: Aren't men frighful idiots?

What seems to have been the only pre-*Ulysses* instance of 'frightful idiots' plural occurred in a story by the American author and illustrator Mary Hallock Foote (1847–1938) entitled 'The Eleventh Hour', published in *The Century Magazine*, vol. 71, no. 3 (Jan. 1906), 485–93, with, on its final page—referring to a horse named Sweet Peggy that one of the story's principal characters, Cameron Hilliard, had rescued from a fire—'"She had n't sense enough to live. Horses are frightful idiots," said Cameron between his teeth.'

But 'frightful idiot' singular did occur pre-Joyce from time to time, most notably in Victor Hugo's novel *L'Homme qui rit* (Paris and Brussels, 1869)—set in England during the reigns of James II and Queen Anne—as translated from the French by William Young (1809–1888) under the title *The Man Who Laughs* (New York, 1869); reissued as *By the King's Command* (London, 1875) by Chatto & Windus; and again under that title by Ward, Lock and Tyler (London, 1876). Part 2, book 2 ('Gwynplaine and Dea'), chap. 11 ('Gwynplaine has Justice on his Side; Ursus has Truth'), p. 255 of the 1876 edition, reads (Ursus speaking): '" Do you know that I was once domestic physician in the establishment of a lord who was named Marmaduke, and who had nine hundred thousand French francs for his yearly revenue ? Get yourself out of that, you frightful idiot !["]'

Uly 11.144–45: like a snout in quest

SMT, following Gifford, write: 'That is, like a hunting hound's nose on the trail of prey.' But see also the entry on 'Porpoise' in *The Treasury of Natural History; or, A Popular Dictionary of Animated Nature* (London, 1848; revised edition, 1870)—by the English writer and composer Samuel Maunder (1785–1849)—p. 543 of both editions, reading in part: 'they root about the shores with their snout in quest of food, like hogs, and are believed to act in concert when in pursuit of their prey'. Maunder's entry—which seems clearly based on the entry on 'Porpesse' in the English cleric, naturalist, and writer William Bingley's (1774–1823) *Animal Biography; or, Authentic Anecdotes of the Lives, Manners, and Economy, of the Animal Creation, Arranged According to the System of Linnaeus* (London, 1805), vol. 2, pp. 147–48—concludes: 'The term *Porpoise*, *Porpesse*, or *Porpus*, is said to be derived from the Italian *Porcopesce*, or hog-fish, from the supposed resemblance of its projecting snout to that of the Hog.'

Interestingly, Joyce's phrase also occurs verbatim in section 2 ('Rats and Mice') of an article entitled 'Rus in Urbe', and signed 'Ruricola', in *The Month, a Catholic Magazine and Review* (London and Dublin), vol. 83 (Jan. 1895), 99–106, whose penultimate paragraph, on p. 106, reads in part:

> The water-rat, with body immersed, or nearly so, shows only his head above water, but the water-shrew, floating like a cork, with scarcely any portion beneath the surface, darts about on top like the skating insects with which all are doubtless familiar. Sometimes it rushes on to the surface of a stone, sometimes a little way on to the bank, always rooting and feeling with its long flexible snout, in quest of food.

Uly 11.149–50: Why do I always think Figather? Gathering figs, I think.

The gathering of figs is referred to twice in familiar New Testament parables: first, in Matthew vii 16, reading: 'Ye shall know them by their fruits. Do men gather grapes of thorns, or figs of thistles?'; and again in Luke vi 44, with 'For every tree is known by its own fruit. For of thorns men do not gather figs, nor of a bramble bush gather they grapes.'

The phrase 'fig gathering' itself occurs in *"Gather up the Fragments.": Notes of Bible Classes.* (London, 1869), by the English hymnodist, evangelist, home mission worker, magazine editor, and author C[atherine]. P[ennefather]. (1818–1893), p. 36, commenting on Psalm i 3 ('And he shall be like a tree planted by the rivers of water, that bringeth forth his fruit in his season; his leaf also shall not wither; and all whatsoever he doeth shall prosper.'):

> The barren fig-tree was just the opposite of this ! The Lord sought figs on it, and they should have been there, for the time of the fig gathering was not past ; but He looked among those broad leaves and found none. They would have been there if it had been bringing forth fruit in its season.

Uly 11.154: comely virgins.

Possibly pointing to book 1 ('The Legend of the Knight of the Red Crosse') in the English poet Edmund Spenser's (1552–1599) *The Faerie Queene* (London, 1590, 1596), in which canto 12, stanza 7, lines 50–54, read: 'Soone after them all dauncing on a row | The comely virgins came, with girlands dight, | As fresh as flowres in medow greene do grow, | When morning deaw vpon their leaues doth light: | And in their hands sweet Timbrels all vpheld on hight.'

Among many other instances, the phrase also occurs in the English theologian, historian, scientist, and mathematician William Whiston's (1667–1752) translation from the Latin of *The Genuine Works of Flavius Josephus, The Jewish Historian* (London, 1737), 'Antiquities of the Jews', book 11, chap. 6 ('Concerning Esther, and Mordecai, and Haman [...]'), p. 195, speaking of Cyrus and his late wife Vashti:

> But when his friends saw him so uneasy, they advised him to cast the memory of his wife, and his love for her, out of his mind, but to send abroad over all the habitable earth, and to search out for comely virgins, and to take her whom he should best like for his wife, because his passion for his former wife would be quenched by the introduction of another, and the kindness he had for Vashti would be withdrawn from her, and be placed on her that was with him.

Uly 11.166: pinnacles of hair

Joyce's phrase—which is repeated in line 11.547—may have been suggested by a similar one in *Pointed Roofs* (London, 1915), vol. 1 of the English author and journalist Dorothy M[iller]. Richardson's (1873–1957) modernist, thirteen-volume, semi-autobiographical novel sequence *Pilgrimage*. In *Pointed Roofs*, chap. 20, p. 89, central character Miriam Henderson—at seventeen lately arrived in Germany from England to teach English at a finishing school in Hanover—pushes back when two of her student-friends urge her to join them in doing up their hair in a classical manner:

> " We've all got to do our hair in clash . . . clashishsher Knoten, Hendy, all of us," said Jimmie judicially, sitting forward with her plump hands clasped on the table. Her pinnacle of hair looked exactly as usual.
> " Oh, really." Miriam tried to make a picture of a classic knot in her mind.
> " If one have classic head one can have classic knot," scolded Clara.

Uly 11.213: With the greatest alacrity

Miss Douce's highfalutin phrase, in response to Simon Dedalus's request for some fresh water and a half glass of whisky, may reflect Joyce's wish to suggest that she had picked it up by reading such portrayals of middle-class life, diction, and manners as might be found in the English writer and magistrate Henry Fielding's (1707–1754) sentimental novel *The History of Amelia* (London, 1752), book 9, chap. 9 ('A Scene of modern Wit and Humour'): 'The doctor was proceeding thus, when the servant returned, saying, the coaches were ready ; and the whole company with the greatest alacrity, attended the doctor to St. James's church.'; in the English novelist Jane Austen's (1775–1817) *Mansfield Park* (London, 1814), where the phrase occurs in vol. 1 (of 3), chap. 14, p. 276: 'To storm through Baron Wildenhaim was the height of his theatrical ambition, and with the advantage of knowing half the scenes by heart already, he did now with the greatest alacrity offer his services for the part.'; and in Thackeray's *Vanity Fair: A Novel Without a Hero* (London, 1848), where it occurs in chap. 25 ('In Which All the Principal Personages Think Fit to Leave Brighton'), p. 216:

> This matter arranged, George, and Jos, and Dobbin, held a council of war over their cigars, and agreed that a general move should be made for London in Jos's open carriage the next day. Jos, I think, would have

preferred staying until Rawdon Crawley quitted Brighton, but Dobbin and George overruled him, and he agreed to carry the party to town, and ordered four horses, as became his dignity. With these they set off in state, after breakfast, the next day. Amelia had risen very early in the morning, and packed her little trunks with the greatest alacrity, while Osborne lay in bed deploring that she had not a maid to help her.

Uly 11.312: drowsy silence

Among other instances of the phrase, 'drowsy silence' occurs in at least three works that Joyce likely knew well: first, in the nineteen-year-old Lord Byron's first-published book *Hours of Idleness* (London, 1807), the 'Episode of Nisus and Euryalus. A Paraphrase from the Æneid, Lib. 9.', lines 27–28: 'Where confidence and ease the watch disdain, | And drowsy Silence holds her sable reign ?'; in the English poet Elizabeth Barrett Browning's (1806–1861) verse novel *Aurora Leigh* (London, 1856), book 8, lines 5–7: 'While Marian, in the garden down below, | Knelt by the fountain I could just hear thrill | The drowsy silence of the exhausted day'; and Ouida's novel *Folle-Farine* (London, 1871), vol. 1 (of 2), book 2, chap. 3, pp. 142–43:

> The town became quite still, the market-place quite empty ; the drowsy silence of a burning, cloudless afternoon was over all the quiet places about the cathedral walls, where of old the bishops and the canons dwelt ; grey shady courts ; dim open cloisters ; houses covered with oaken carvings, and shadowed with the spreading branches of chestnuts and of lime-trees that were as aged as themselves.

Uly 11.418: the essence of vulgarity

Thornton and Gifford have no comment on this phrase; SMT declare it to be 'From Ralph Waldo Emerson's *The Conduct of Life*: "What is vulgar, and the essence of all vulgarity, but the avarice of reward?"' While Joyce may have had in mind Emerson's phrase as it appears on p. 143 of the essay 'Worship' in that book—which was published simultaneously in Boston and London in December 1860—the phrase had also occurred verbatim in the English writer, philosopher, art critic, and polymath John Ruskin's (1819–1900) lecture-based essay 'Sir Joshua [Reynolds] and [Hans] Holbein' published in *The Cornhill*, vol. 1, no. 3 (Mar. 1860),

322–28, nine months before Emerson's book was published. The passage in Ruskin's essay in which the phrase occurs—in a footnote on p. 323—reads in its entirety:

> The reader must observe that I use the word [gentlemanliness] here in a limited sense, as meaning only the effect of careful education, good society, and refined habits of life, on average temper and character. Of deep and true gentlemanliness—based as it is on intense sensibility and sincerity, perfected by courage, and other qualities of race ; as well as of that union of insensibility with cunning, which is the essence of vulgarity, I shall have to speak at length in another place.

That 'other place' appears to have been Ruskin's lecture-based essay 'Water Colour Societies', collected in *The Works of John Ruskin*, edited by E[dward]. T[yas]. Cook and A[lexander]. Wedderburn (London, 1904), vol. 14 ('Academy Notes: Notes on Prout and Hunt and Other Art Criticisms 1855–1888'), subsection 'Academy Notes, 1859', 241–50, with, in a note on p. 243, the following comment annotating Ruskin's reference in the essay's main text to vulgarity as 'the habit of mind and act resulting from the prolonged combination of insensibility with insincerity':

> It would be more accurate to say, " constitutional insensibility " ; for people are born vulgar, or not vulgar, irrevocably. An apparent insensibility may often be caused by one strong feeling quenching or conquering another ; and this to the extent of involving the person in all kinds of cruelty and crime : yet, Borgia or Ezzelin, lady and knight still ; while the born clown is dead in all sensation and capacity of thought, whatever his acts or life may be.
> Cloten, in *Cymbeline*, is the most perfect study of pure vulgarity which I know in literature ; Perdita, in *Winter's Tale*, the most perfect study of its opposite (irrespective of such higher virtue or intellect as we have in Desdemona or Portia). Perdita's exquisite openness, joined with as exquisite sensitiveness, constitute the precise opposite of the apathetic insincerity which, I believe, is the essence of vulgarity.

Subsequent pre-*Ulysses* instances of the phrase include, among others, this from *The Art of Elocution*, third edition (London, 1862), by the English actor and elocutionist George Vandenhoff (1820–1885), reading on pp. 251–52:

> The essence of vulgarity, I imagine, consists in taking manners, actions, words, opinions on trust from others, without examining

one's own feelings, or weighing the merits of the case. It is coarseness and shallowness of taste, arising from want of individual refinement, together with the confidence and presumption inspired by example and numbers. To affect a gesture, an opinion, a phrase, because it is the rage with a large number of persons, or to hold it in abhorrence, because another set of persons, very little, if at all better informed, cry it down to distinguish themselves from the former, is in either case equal vulgarity and absurdity.

Uly 11.461: smitten by sunlight

From a sentence reading 'Miss Douce's brave eyes, unregarded, turned from the crossblind, smitten by sunlight', the highlighted phrase may have been suggested to Joyce by a reading of the Glasgow-born Baptist minister Alexander Maclaren's (1826–1910) *St. Paul's Epistle to the Ephesians* (London, 1909), where the section entitled 'The Resurrection of Dead Souls', commenting on Ephesians ii 4–5 ('God, who is rich in mercy, for His great love wherewith He loved us, even when we were dead in sins, hath quickened us together with Christ.'), begins, on p. 81, with the following passage: 'Scripture paints man as he is, in darker tints, and man as he may become, in brighter ones, than are elsewhere found. The range of this portrait painter's palette is from pitchiest black to most dazzling white, as of snow smitten by sunlight.'

Uly 11.601: touched the obedient keys

Joyce's phrase 'the obedient keys' previously occurred in poems and prose from time to time. One of the former that he is likely to have known, by the Scottish poet and Jacobite army officer William Hamilton of Bangour (1704–1754), was 'To Lady Mary Montgomery', first published in the third (Edinburgh, 1760) edition of his *Poems on Several Occasions* and much reprinted thereafter. The passage in which the phrase occurs, on p. 241, in lines 119–22 of Hamilton's 228-line poem, reads: 'How do we gaze with vast delight | Her fingers' swift harmonious flight, | When o'er th' obedient keys they fly, | To waken sleeping harmony ?'

One of the latter was *Franz Liszt, Artist and Man. 1811–1840*—by Liszt's authorized biographer the writer and teacher L[ina]. Ramann (1833–1912), as translated from the German by Miss E. Cowdery, vol.

2 (London, 1882), pp. 150–51—where the phrase occurs in line 9 of a thirty-three-line poem, translated from the French original entitled 'Liszt au Piano', signed 'T. W.', first published in the Geneva-based periodical *Le Fédéral* on 15 April 1836, and called, as translated, 'Liszt at the Piano', the opening lines of which read (ellipsis in the original):

> He sits ; behold ! on that pale brow
> Precocious genius hath its seal impressed ;
> And lights the fire in that all-powerful eye
> Where sits the artist's soul.
> His sweet and pensive smile
> Spreads o'er his face a charm unspeakable,
> Bright as a rainbow in a stormy sky . . .
> He preludes ; listen, friends ! be nought but ear.
> Under his hands inspired the obedient keys
> Grow living, and send forth a language eloquent[.][21]

Uly 11.698: Keep a trot for the avenue.

Gifford notes that the phrase means 'retain the ability to make a good appearance on occasion even though one is in decline, after the aging horse that can still show in competitive moments.' It may be added that the phrase occurs verbatim, in an entry dated 14 April 1828, in *The Journal of Sir Walter Scott, from the original manuscript at Abbotsford* (Edinburgh, 1890), vol. 2 (of 2), p. 158: 'Always politic to keep a trot for the avenue, like the Irish postillions'; and again, in an unsigned essay under the title '"International Vanities" no. VIII. – Glory', in *Blackwood's*, vol. 116, no. 710 (Dec. 1874), which begins, on p. 723: 'As Irish postboys used, in former times, to " keep a trot for the avenue," so, on the same principle of reserving a flourish for the finish, has Glory been held back for the final chapter of this series.'

---

21 In the original: 'Sous ses doigts inspirés, la touche obéissante | S'anime et fait entendre une langue éloquente'. The Hungarian composer and pianist Franz Liszt (1811–1886) is directly referred to in line 11.983 ('Like those rhapsodies of Liszt's, Hungarian, gipsyeyed'), tending to confirm that Joyce is indirectly referring to him in line 11.601.

Uly 11.906: Wisdom while you wait.

Unremarked by Thornton, Gifford, and SMT, Joyce's phrase previously occurred verbatim as the title of a booklet or long pamphlet subtitled *Being a foretaste of the glories of the 'Insidecompletuar Britanniaware.'*—co-created by the English humorist and author E[dward]. V[errall]. Lucas (1868–1938) and the Irish journalist and travel writer C[harles]. L[arcom]. Graves (1856–1944)—privately printed in 1902 as a mock prospectus of a purportedly forthcoming edition of the *Encyclopaedia Britannica*. The fifty-six-page booklet was subsequently published in a limited, ninety-five-page edition by Isbister & Co. (London, 1903).

Uly 11.973: Tongue when she talks like the clapper of a bellows.

Bloom is referring here to the wife of C. P. M'Coy, on whose behalf her husband repeatedly 'borrows' valises for her purported out-of-town singing engagements that they always fail to return—and presumably sell or pawn for their own gain. It may be no coincidence that the quoted phrase previously occurred nearly verbatim and in an apposite context in the 'Author's Edition' (apparently the only one published) of a book by the former New York City detective Philip Farley (1826–1882), *Criminals of America; or, Tales of the Lives of Thieves. Enabling Every One To Be His Own Detective. With Portraits, Making a Complete Rogues' Gallery* (New York, 1876), in chap. 34 of which Farley describes the criminal career of the once middle-class Elizabeth Thompson, born in London in 1835, who, he writes on p. 501, came to be known—before plying her trade in America—as 'the queen of English pickpockets'. The passage of the chapter, on p. 505, in which the quoted phrase occurs describes Eliza's (as she was known) initial resistance to her thief-lover Johnny Martin's demand that 'she should go out into the streets and steal':

> Seeing that it would be dangerous to push her too far just at that time, Martin left her alone for a few days, and might probably have given her a longer respite but for the importunities of an old receiver, who kept constantly urging him on to push the girl out to work.

"Send her at it, my dear," this hag would say to him. "That pretty, innocent face would clear her anywhere, and those little hands of hers were made for the business."

"Don't be in a hurry, ' Mother Klapp.' " She received this name from a peculiar noise she made with her tongue when speaking, that sounded like the clapper of a bellows, " all in good time."

"Never too soon to begin, my dear," urged " Mother Klapp. "

Uly 11.1104: a fence of lashes

The highlighted phrase, from a sentence in 'Sirens' reading 'A liquid womb of woman eyeball gazed under a fence of lashes, calmly, hearing.', seems to have occurred only once pre-*Ulysses*, in an English translation from the Latin of Cicero's *De Natura Deorum* (On the nature of the gods), by Francis Brooks, M.A. (London, 1896), reading in section 57, on pp. 147–48:

And what artificer besides Nature, whose cunning nothing can surpass, would have been able to carry out in the senses so much detailed ingenuity ? In the first place she clothed and encased the eyes with the finest membranes, which she made, first of all, transparent, so that they might be able to be seen through, and at the same time firm, that the eye might be held together ; to the eyes themselves she gave the power of moving and turning, that they might both avert themselves from anything hurtful, and easily direct their gaze where they wished. The actual point of the eye, by means of which we see, and which is called the pupil, is so small as to easily avoid what might harm it ; the eyelids, which are the coverings of the eyes, and extremely soft to the touch, so as not to injure the point of the eyes, were most conveniently constructed both for shutting the pupils, that nothing might strike against them, and for opening them, and Nature took means to enable this to be done continually and with the greatest rapidity. The eyelids were protected by a kind of fence of lashes, by which anything falling in the eyes when open might be stopped, and which might, as it were, muffle the eyes when they rested closed in sleep, and we did not need them for seeing.

12. 'Cyclops'

***Uly* 12.31–32:** *He drink me my teas. He eat me my sugars. Because he no pay me my moneys?*

Unremarked by Thornton, Gifford, and SMT, the passage highlighted above may point to Shakespeare's *The Merchant of Venice*, I iii 106–10, Shylock to Antonio:

> Signior Antonio, many a time and oft
> In the Rialto you have rated me
> About my moneys and my usances.
> Still have I borne it with a patient shrug
> (For suff'rance is the badge of all our tribe).

But a more proximate source—itself clearly influenced by Shakespeare's portrayal of Shylock—may be Trollope's *Sir Harry Hotspur of Humblethwaite* (London, 1871), part 5, chap. 15 ('Cousin George Is Hard Pressed'), reading, on p. 68:

> " What is Mr. Boltby to me ?"
> " He is a great deal to me, because he vill pay me my moneys, and he vill pay Captain Stubber, and vill pay everybody. He vill pay you too, Captain 'Oshspur — only you must pay poor Valker his moneys. I have promised Valker he shall have back his moneys, or Sir Harry shall know that too. You must just give up the young woman : eh, Captain 'Oshspur ?"
> " I'm not going to be dictated to, Mr. Hart."

Uly 12.59: Anything strange or wonderful, Joe?

The phrase 'anything strange or wonderful' seems to have occurred only once pre-*Ulysses*, in *The House of Souls* (London, 1906) by the Welsh author and mystic Arthur Llewelyn Jones (1863–1947) as 'Arthur Machen', and specifically in the story therein called 'A Fragment of Life,' p. 49: '["]It was such nonsense, you know ; as if there could be anything strange or wonderful in London."'[22]

Minus 'anything', the phrase 'strange or wonderful' also occurred in the Russian playwright and short-story writer Anton Chekhov's (1860–1904) 'Gusev', a tale written and first published in Russia in 1890, then first published in English in *The Witch and Other Stories* (London, 1918) as translated by Constance Garnett. Early in the tale, on p. 148, Gusev, a discharged soldier, is homeward bound from the Far East in the sick bay of a military ship, along with his fellow soldier Pavel Ivanitch and several others suffering, like them, from illness or injury, the ship's rocking, the waves' pounding, and the intense heat.

> Pavel Ivanitch was subject to sea-sickness. When the sea was rough he was usually ill-humoured, and the merest trifle would make him irritable. And in Gusev's opinion there was absolutely nothing to be vexed about. What was there strange or wonderful, for instance, in the fish or in the wind's breaking loose from its chain ? Suppose the fish were as big as a mountain and its back were as hard as a sturgeon : and in the same way, supposing that away yonder at the end of the world there stood great stone walls and the fierce winds were chained up to the walls . . . if they had not broken loose, why did they tear about all over the sea like maniacs, and struggle to escape like dogs ? If they were not chained up, what did become of them when it was calm ?

By story end, Pavel Ivanitch has died and so has Gusev himself, his shroud-wrapped body cast overboard and, as we watch, sinking down through the depths of the shark-infested sea.

---

22 Before its appearance in book form, Machen's tale was serialized in the first four issues of *Horlick's Magazine. And Home Journal for Australia, India and the Colonies.* (London, 1904), edited by the Brooklyn-born British poet and scholarly mystic Arthur Edward Waite (1857–1942), a friend of Machen's, and published by Horlick's Malted Milk, of which Waite was manager for much of the new century's first decade, as a promotional tool for the company's products throughout the (then) British Empire.

Uly 12.69: There sleep the mighty dead

Thornton, Gifford, SMT, and others note the remarkably well-preserved condition of some ancient bodies buried in the crypt of St Michan's Church of Ireland, Dublin. As to the phrase itself, it occurs nearly verbatim in the English poet and cleric Robert Montgomery's (1807–1855) book-length poem *The Age Reviewed: A Satire: In Two Parts* (London, 1827), with, in part 2, on pp. 252–53:

> For thoughts sublime, aloft the Abbey rears
> Its towers, in all the majesty of years ;
> Unawed, no British patriots here can tread,
> The dim cold fane where sleep the mighty dead ;—
> But, while each dome and ancient fane conspire,
> To rouse the poet, and attune his lyre ;
> Compel'd, we mark, where London scenes entice,
> This queen of cities in the sink of vice !

Other instances of 'the mighty dead' occur in several works of poetry and prose, among them Thomson's *The Seasons*, 'Winter', lines 431–32: 'There studious let me sit, | And hold high converse with the mighty dead'; and the English Romantic poet John Keats's (1795–1821) *Endymion: A Poetic Romance* (London, 1818), book 1, lines 20–21: 'And such too is the grandeur of the dooms | We have imagined for the mighty dead'.

Uly 12.70–71: A pleasant land it is [...] of murmuring waters, fishful streams

For 'murmuring waters' see Milton's *Paradise Lost*, book 4 (1674 version), lines 257–63:

> Another side, umbrageous Grots and Caves
> Of coole recess, o're which the mantling vine
> Layes forth her purple Grape, and gently creeps
> Luxuriant; mean while murmuring waters fall
> Down the slope hills, disperst, or in a Lake
> That to the fringed Bank with Myrtle crownd,
> Her chrystal mirror holds, unite thir streams.

and, from his *Poems* (Boston, 1847), the American essayist and poet Ralph Waldo Emerson's (1803–1882) 'To Rhea', which begins:

> Thee, dear friend, a brother soothes,
> Not with flatteries, but truths,
> Which tarnish not, but purify
> To light which dims the morning's eye.
> I have come from the spring-woods,
> From the fragrant solitudes ;—
> Listen what the poplar-tree
> And murmuring waters counselled me.

See also the Italian composer Claudio Monteverde's (1567–1643) *Ecco Mormorar L'Onde* [Hear the Murmuring Waters], for five unaccompanied voices, with text by the Italian poet Torquato Tasso (1544–1595), in *Il Secondo Libro de' Madrigali* [The Second Book of Madrigals] (1590). *The Cambridge Companion to Monteverdi* (2007), edited by John Whenham and Richard Wistreich, calls *Ecco Mormorar L'Onde* 'deservedly the best-known madrigal of Monteverdi's Second Book.'

For 'fishful streams', see the lyric 'Páistín Fionn' from *The Four Winds of Eirinn* (Dublin, 1902) by the Irish journalist, writer, and poet Anna Johnston MacManus (1866–1902), as 'Ethna Carbery', stanza 4: 'So you left our glens, and our fishful streams, | To follow the lure of your boyish dreams : | Through the lonely cities you wander long, | Far from the moors and the blackbird's song.'

Uly 12.74: denizens of the aqueous kingdom

Joyce's phrase seems to have originated in an item on p. 231 of the journal *Nature*, vol. 35, no. 897, for 6 January 1887, reading in its entirety:

> In lecturing upon the " Denizens of the Aqueous Kingdom" on Friday last at the Royal Aquarium, Mr. August Carter referred to deformities that exist among fish. In 1885 and 1886 he had examined many thousands of trout and salmon fry at South Kensington on their emerging from the ova, and found one case of deformity in every thousand, and one case of monstrosity, such as twin and dual-headed fish, in every four thousand. From observations he had made at the South Kensington Aquarium and elsewhere, the lecturer concluded that certain fish, such as the carp and perch, have the power of communicating with one another.

Though Mr. Carter may have done so in his lecture, the item in *Nature* does not indicate either the connection, if any, between the deformities in fish to which he refers and the power of fish to communicate with one another, or the nature of the communication he has in mind.

Uly 12.161–62: The eyes in which a tear and a smile strove ever for the mastery

For 'a tear and a smile' Thornton, SMT, and others cite Thomas Moore's song 'Erin, the Tear and the Smile in Thine Eyes', which begins 'Erin, the tear and the smile in thine eyes | Blend like the rainbow that hangs in the skies!' It would seem, however, that Joyce's sentence—which continues and concludes 'were of the dimensions of a goodsized cauliflower.'— points more directly to another possible source: *Clavering Tower. A Novel. In Four Volumes* (London, 1822) by Rosalia St. Clair, pen name of the Scottish novelist, non-fiction author, and translator Agnes C. (Scott) Hall (1777–1846), with, in vol. 3 (of 4), chap. 7, p. 105:

> The gentlemen very soon joined the ladies after they retired to the drawing-room ; and while drinking their coffee, a whispering kind of conversation was carried on between lady Emmeline and her father-in-law. A tear and a smile strove for mastery in the good merchant's features, as he pressed the hand of his darling to his lips, who, giving him a look of unutterable affection, turned to the circle, and inquired who would join her and papa to Covent-garden ?

In a revised version of her tetralogy published under the title *The First and Last Years of Wedded Life* (London, 1827), the corresponding passage, in vol. 3, p. 170, reads:

> A smile and a tear strove for mastery in the face of the stranger, as he gazed on the animated girl.—" May no dark cloud intervene to obscure the happiness of your future days, sweet maid !" he mentally ejaculated. " Yet how unstable are all sublunary joys !—how vain for even the most virtuous to expect permanent felicity in this vale of tears ! else had no unkindly blight nipped the blossoms of thy domestic peace, my earliest, my dearest friend !"

In *The Devoted* (London, 1836), with Hall's phrase seemingly in mind, the English novelist Lady Charlotte Campbell Bury (1775–1861) wrote, in chap. 6, p. 110: 'And the ghastly smile and the heart-wrung tear strove together for mastery.' Over the balance of the century, many other authors showed a wide range of conflicting emotions also 'striving for mastery'.

Uly 12.174: his portentous frame

Joyce's mock-heroic description of the otherwise nameless Citizen reads in part, at lines 173–74, 'From his girdle hung a row of seastones which jangled at every movement of his portentous frame'. The highlighted phrase may have been suggested by the Scottish author John Sterling's (1806–1844) story 'The Last of the Giants', first published anonymously in the London-based *Athenæum: Literary and Critical Journal*—which Sterling co-edited with the English theologian F[rederick]. D[enison]. Maurice—issue no. 32 (4 June 1828), 503–04, and posthumously collected in *Essays and Tales by John Sterling* (London, 1848), edited by Julius Charles Hare. The story as reprinted in vol. 2 (of 2), 207–19, of the latter reads, on p. 213: 'Roderick gazed upon the Giant and his labour with breathless awe. As he moved round the pile, his portentous frame was perpetually displayed in some new attitude, that called forth new astonishment, by exhibiting afresh the miracles of his size and power.'

Uly 12.202: sunk in uneasy slumber

The apparently sole pre-Joyce instance of this phrase occurs in the Anglican cleric and Literary Superintendent of the British and Foreign Bible Society T[homas]. H[erbert]. Darlow's (1858–1927) 'The Implicit Promise of Perfection,' in *The Expositor* (London), edited by the Rev. W. Robertson Nicoll, fourth series, vol. 9 (1894), 319–20, which begins:

> The chapel of San Lorenzo at Florence contains the monuments which Michael Angelo executed in memory of his princely patrons. On one of these marvellous tombs the sculptor has carved two reclining figures, to represent respectively the Night and the Day. Night is personified as a woman sunk in uneasy slumber. Day is portrayed in the shape of a man, who lifts himself in disturbed awakening. But this latter figure has never been finished.

Uly 12.215: bedight in sable armour

What appear to be the only two pre-*Ulysses* instances of the phrase both occur in the British romance novelist Jeffery Farnol's (1878–1952) *Beltane the Smith* (London, 1915), chap. 68 ('Friar Martin's Dying Prophecy'), the first of the two on p. 537: 'I see one that rideth from the north—and this I give thee for a sign—he is tall, this man, bedight in sable armour and mounted upon a great white horse.'; and the second in a passage on p. 540:

> Now behind this herald two knights advanced, the one in glittering armour whose shield was resplendent with many quarterings, but beholding his companion, Beltane stared in wondering awe ; for lo ! he saw a tall man bedight in sable armour who bore a naked sword that flashed in the sun and who bestrode a great, white charger. And because of Friar Martin's dying words, Beltane stood awed and full of amaze.

Uly 12.332: they took the liberty of burying him

The exchange about Paddy Dignam's death, involving Bob Doran, Alf Bergan, and Joe Hynes, reads in part, in lines 12.330–33 (ellipsis in the original):

> —What about Dignam! says Bob Doran. Who's talking about....?
> —Dead! says Alf. He's no more dead than you are.
> —Maybe so, says Joe. They took the liberty of burying him this morning anyhow.

Thornton, Gifford, and SMT all note that a similar, and similarly witty, exchange takes place in Jonathan Swift's *A Complete COLLECTION Of Genteel and Ingenious CONVERSATION, According to the Most Polite Mode and Method Now Used At COURT, and in the BEST COMPANIES of England. In THREE DIALOGUES. By Simon Wagstaff, Esq.* (London, 1738)—commonly referred to as Swift's *Polite Conversation*. But one post-Swift, pre-Joyce antecedent came considerably closer to the dialogue in 'Cyclops'. It occurred—after the book's serialization from June 1844 to June 1846 in *The New Monthly Magazine*—in *Captain O'Sullivan; or, Adventures, Civil, Military, and Matrimonial, of a Gentleman on Half Pay*

(London, 1846) by the Irish novelist and military historian William Hamilton Maxwell (1792–1850), reading, in vol. 1 (of 3), chap. 3 ('Legal Revelations—The Painter's Wife'), p. 88:

> " [...] Do you know a Frederick Lewisham ?"
> " My cousin !" replied the painter's wife. " What of him ?"
> " He's dead, that's all," replied Mr. Egan.
> " Dead ! Impossible."
> " They have taken the liberty of burying him, at all events," continued the sheriff.

In a later, single-volume edition of Maxwell's novel, published under the title *Adventures of Captain O'Sullivan* (London, 1858), the quoted passage appears on p. 34.

Further suggesting that Joyce was aware of Maxwell's published works, SMT write in a note on 'smashall sweeney's moustaches' in *Uly* 12.1066 that Smashall Sweeney is the name of a Connemara bumpkin in Maxwell's *Wild Sports of the West* (London, 1832).

Uly 12.335: He paid the debt of nature

SMT cite Archibald McDonald's *Some of Ossian's Lesser Poems Rendered into Verse* (Liverpool, 1805), with 'Thou must at length the debt of nature pay.' The phrase 'paid the debt of nature' occurs verbatim, however, in several instances predating McDonald by up to three centuries.

The earliest such instance cited in the *OED* occurred in the London draper, sheriff, alderman, and author Robert Fabyan's (1470–c. 1512) *New Chronicles of England and France, in Two Parts* (London, 1515), part 2, chap. 41, p. 28, referring to the second-century Gallic king Archigallo: 'But fynally he payde the dette of nature whan he had reygned now lastly after most wryters x. yeres, & was buryed as sayth the sayd olde Cronycle, at Caerbrank or Yorke'; with further instances to be found in, among other works, Marlowe's *The Troublesome Raigne and Lamentable Death of Edward the Second, King of England* (London, 1594) with, in Act 4, 'Pay natures debt with cheerefull countenance', and the English poet Francis Quarles's (1592–1644) *Emblemes* (London, 1634), book 2, p. 113, with 'The slender debt to Nature's quickly paid, | Discharg'd perchance with greater ease then made'.

Uly 12.448–49: for I will on nowise suffer it even so saith the Lord

Thornton writes: 'Though this has a distinctly biblical ring, I have found no direct source for it in either the King James or the Douay Bible.' The phrase 'on no wise [or nowise] suffer it' does, however, occur verbatim four times in the English poet and translator John Payne's (1842–1916) *The Decameron of Giovanni Boccaccio* (London, 1886), vol. 1 (of 3): first, in the fifth story on the second day, p. 139: 'but she would on no wise suffer it and making a show of being sore vexed, embraced him and said, " Ah, woe is me ! I see but too clearly how little dear I am to thee !["]' ; again, in the same story, p. 40: 'Then, when they rose from the table and Andreuccio would have taken his leave, she declared that she would on no wise suffer this, for that Naples was no place to go about in by night, especially for a stranger'; again in the seventh story on the second day, p. 190: 'Antigonus, hearing this, incontinent knew her for the Soldan's daughter Alatiel, who was thought to have perished at sea, and would fain have paid her the homage due to her quality; but she would on no wise suffer it and besought him to sit with her awhile.'; and next in the eighth story on the second day, p. 216:

> Then, after they had all three discoursed awhile of each one's various adventures and wept and rejoiced together amain, Perrot and Jamy would have re-clad the count, who would on nowise suffer it, but willed that Jamy, having first assured himself of the promised guerdon, should, the more to shame the king, present him to the latter in that his then plight and in his groom's habit.

And variations of the phrase, with 'on no wise suffer' followed by *him, her, them,* and the like occur widely in both secular and spiritual literature.

Uly 12.525: The last farewell was affecting in the extreme.

While 'affecting in the extreme', often in proximity to the word 'farewell', was a well-worn cliché long before Joyce first put pen to paper, the highlighted sentence seems to have occurred all but verbatim only once pre-*Ulysses*, in

The Examiner (London) for 26 June 1825, where an item under 'Accidents, Offences, &c.' on the 'Execution of Probert, &c.' reads in part:

> Mrs. Probert and Miss Noyes were with the unhappy man till a late hour. Their last farewell was affecting in the extreme. Mrs. P. hung upon her wretched husband's neck, and bathed their faces in each other's tears, whilst Miss Noyes sunk into a deep apathy, out of which she was with difficulty aroused. On leaving her husband, Mrs. Probert hysterically but faintly exclaimed, " God bless you, William ; God forgive you ; I hope we shall soon meet again."

Uly 12.544: inimitable drolls

The phrase 'inimitable drolls' occurs in two or three antecedent works, but the similarities of tone and content between Joyce's language and one of those antecedent works—the English theatrical impresario, journalist, and writer John Hollingshead's (1827–1904) *My Lifetime* (London, 1895), vol. 1 (of 2), chap. 12, p. 121—suggest that may have been the work which inspired Joyce's use of the phrase. Lines 12.541–46 of *Ulysses* read:

> Considerable amusement was caused by the favourite Dublin streetsingers L-n-h-n and M-ll-g-n who sang *The Night before Larry was Stretched* in their usual mirthprovoking fashion. Our two inimitable drolls did a roaring trade with their broadsheets among lovers of the comedy element and nobody who has a corner in his heart for real Irish fun without vulgarity will grudge them their hardearned pennies.

The corresponding passage in Hollingshead reads:

> I cannot honestly pass over this period without a word about the coarseness and vulgarity of farce-acting by the leading comedians in the leading theatres. The two greatest offenders were Buckstone and Wright, both inimitable drolls—natural and irrepressible, juicy, low comedians, and not dry, though artistic, character actors.

Uly 12.650–51: That monster audience simply rocked with delight.

SMT write: 'Recalls Daniel O'Connell's "monster meetings"'—held, as Catherine Flynn notes on p. 220 of her edition, in connection with his campaign for Repeal of the Act of Union. As for 'monster audience' itself, an early assemblage of that and similarly hyperbolic phrases—but not so early as to prevent the vogue for 'monster' as a modifier from becoming something of a joke—occurred in the weekly newsletter *The Musical World* (London), 'A record [its masthead proclaimed] of the theatres, music, literature, fine arts, foreign intelligence, &c.', vol. 22, no. 7, for Saturday, 13 February 1847, in which an unsigned item headlined 'Concerts' on p. 103 begins (italics in the original):

> MR. ALLCROFTS' MONSTER ANNUAL CONCERT took place on Tuesday evening in the Lyceum theatre, and was in every respect indeed a monster concert. There was a monster bill which contained a monster programme, in which no less than fifty (a monster number) *morceaux* were announced to be sung or played by artists of monster reputation. Then there was a monster orchestra, which performed monster overtures of monster composers, and to conclude, there was a monster audience, who enjoyed themselves with monster delight. In fact, every thing was *monsterous*, not *monstrous*.

Another 'monster audience' was reported a year later by *The New Monthly Belle Assemblée; A Magazine of Literature and Fashion, Under the Immediate Patronage of Her Royal Highness the Duchess of Kent* (London), vol. 28, the January 1848 issue of which had, on pp. 55–56, in the 'Amusements of the Month' section, an item on 'The Shakespeare Night' held at Covent Garden on 7 December 1847, reading in part: 'The monster audience did not settle itself into quietude for some time, and consequently much of the effect of the first scene—" Death of Henry the Fourth"—was lost.'

Monster audiences were also reported several times in the eighteen eighties and nineties in publications of The Theosophical Society to indicate, and perhaps exaggerate, the turnout at the Society's public meetings. It may have been the purportedly monster audiences at these meetings, as much as any other factor, that accounted for Joyce's use of the phrase in *Ulysses*.

Uly 12.738–39: suppressed rancour

Among the many pre-*Ulysses* instances of this phrase, one of those more likely to have come to Joyce's attention occurred in the English poet, linguist, and diplomat Joseph Charles Mellish's (1768–1823) translation, as *Mary Stuart, A Tragedy* (London, 1801), of the German physician, playwright, poet, and philosopher Friedrich Schiller's (1759–1805) five-act tragedy *Maria Stuart* (Tübingen, 1801). In Act 3, scene 4, on p. 129 of the Mellish translation, the Roman Catholic Mary—realizing after nineteen years of house arrest that her cousin and rival the Protestant Queen Elizabeth will never set her free—employs the phrase in rejecting Shrewsbury's call for moderation and patience:

> Moderation ! I've supported
> What human nature can support : farewell,
> Lamb-hearted resignation, passive patience
> Fly to thy native heaven ; burst at length
> Thy bonds, come forward from thy dreary cave,
> In all thy fury, long-suppressed rancour !—
> And thou, who to the anger'd basilisk
> Impart'st the murd'rous glance, O ! arm my tongue
> With poison'd darts !

Another such instance occurred in the anonymous English translation of the Italian poet, novelist, and philosopher Alessandro Manzoni's (1785–1873) historical novel *I promessi sposi* (1827) as *The Betrothed* (London, Edinburgh, and Dublin, 1834), chap. 21, p. 251 (italics in the original):

> " Who is he ? Do you wish me to tell you ? you must wait awhile first. You are proud, because he protects you ; provided you are satisfied, no matter what becomes of me. Ask *him* his name. If I should tell you, he would not speak to me so gently as he did to you. I am an old woman, I am an old woman," continued she, grumbling : but hearing the sobs of Lucy, she remembered the threat of her master ; and addressing her in a less bitter tone, " Well ! I have said no harm. Be cheerful. Do not ask me what I cannot tell you, but have courage. How satisfied most people would be, should he speak to them as he has spoken to you ! Be cheerful ! Directly, you shall have something to eat ; and from what he said, I know it will be something good. And then, you must lie down, and you will leave a little room for me," added she, with an accent of suppressed rancour.

A third occurred in the English journalist and author Ernest Alfred Vizetelly's (1853–1922) translation from the French of Émile Zola's novel *Au Bonheur des Dames* (Paris, 1883) as *The Ladies' Paradise* (London, 1886), with, in chap. 1, pp. 29–30:

> Then, turning round, Denise again found the Baudus behind her. Though they thought Bourras so stupid, they also, despite themselves, ever and ever returned to the contemplation of that spectacle which rent their hearts. It was, so to say, a rageful desire to suffer. Geneviève, very pale, had noticed that Colomban was watching the shadows of the saleswomen pass to and fro on the first floor opposite ; and, whilst Baudu almost choked with suppressed rancour, Madame Baudu began silently weeping.

Uly 12.1351: On which the sun never rises

In a conversation among the Citizen, John Wyse, and Joe Hynes, the Citizen's contemptuous remarks about the British navy and, more broadly, the British empire include (at 12.1349–50): 'That's the great empire they boast about of drudges and whipped serfs', to which Hynes replies: 'On which the sun never rises'. Hynes's remark, a play (as Thornton, Gifford, and SMT note) on a phrase previously applied to one or another of the Persian, British and other empires, including that of the Habsburgs under the leadership of emperor Charles V, 1500–1558), as a dominion on which 'the sun never sets', occurred several times in the nineteenth century, among these in the fourth of Charles Dickens's five Christmas books, *The Battle of Life: A Love Story* (1846). The passage in which the phrase occurs reads:

> " It's a world full of hearts," said the Doctor, hugging his younger daughter, and bending across her to hug Grace—for he couldn't separate the sisters ; " and a serious world with all its folly—even with mine, which was enough to have swamped the whole globe ; and a world on which the sun never rises, but it looks upon a thousand bloodless battles that are some set-off against the miseries and wickedness of Battle-Fields ; and a world we need be careful how we libel, Heaven forgive us, for it is a world of sacred mysteries, and its Creator only knows what lies beneath the surface of His lightest image !"

Another instance of the phrase occurred a half-century later in the inaugural issue, dated April 1899, of *Die Fackel* (The Torch), founded and edited by the Austrian journalist, critic, playwright, and poet Karl Kraus (1874–1936). Kraus's introductory essay ends, on p. 3: 'So möge denn die Fackel einem Lande leuchten, in welchem—anders als in jenem Reiche Karls V.—die Sonne niemals aufgeht.' [So may the Torch shine on a land in which—unlike the empire of Charles V—the sun never rises.]

Joyce may also have had in mind the American biographer, essayist, poet, and magazine publisher Horace Traubel's (1858–1919) review—in the March 1915 issue of his Philadelphia-based literary magazine *The Conservator*—of *German World Policies* (New York, 1915), the English translation of the German writer Paul Rohrbach's *Der Deutsche Gedanke in der Welt* (Düsseldorf and Leipzig, 1912), which review reads in part, on p. 12:

> That thing which produced the British may produce the German empire. Rohrbach is calm. He shows no temper. I find him finely self critical. But these arguments for empire : what do they come to ? I want something different. I want arguments for people. I care nothing for these monstrous overgrown tyrannies. I don't care for any empire on which the sun never sets. For the empire on which the sun never sets is the empire on which the sun never rises. One of them's enough.

Uly 12.1552–53: never backed a horse in anger in his life

The Citizen's scornful remark directed at Bloom plays on a phrase first recorded in the anonymous 'Personal Recollections of Thomas Campbell, Esq.' published in *The Dublin University Magazine*, vol. 25, no. 149 (May 1845), 557–63, in which the then-late Scottish poet (1777–1844) is quoted on p. 560 as saying, among other comments scornful of Lord Byron, that unlike Dante in this as in other respects, Byron 'like a carpet warrior, hid himself in a barrack at Missolonghi, and never fired a shot or brandished a sword in anger in his life.'

Uly 12.1596: Saucy knave!

An early instance of the phrase, synonymous with 'impudent fellow', occurs in the first quarto edition (1597) of Shakespeare's *Romeo and Juliet*, where Capulet says to Tybalt, at I v 60: 'Go to, you are a saucy knave.'

Another early instance: in a poem collected in *Epigrams, Both Pleasant and Serious, Written by that All-Worthy Knight, Sir John Harrington*—also spelled *Harington*—published three years after the death of the English courtier, author, translator, and inventor of the flush toilet (1560–1612), under the title 'On the games that have been in request at the court', and reading in its entirety (italics in the original):

> I heard one make a pretty observation
> How games have in the court turn'd with the fashion.
> The first game was the best, when free from crime,
> The courtly gamesters all were in their *Prime*.
> The second game was *Post*, untill with posting
> They paid so fast, 'twas time to leave their bosting.
> Then thirdly follow'd *heaving of the maw*,
> A game without civility or law,
> An odious play, and yet in court oft seene,
> A sawcy knave to trump both king and queen,
> Then follow'd *Lodam*.—
> Now *Nody* follow'd next.
> The last game now in use is *Bankerout*,
> Which will be plaid at still, I stand in doubt,
> Untill *Lavolta* turne the wheele of time,
> And make it come about againe to Prime.

By the time Joyce wrote *Ulysses*, the phrase 'saucy knave' had long since become a pseudo-Elizabethan cliché.

Uly 12.1820: the most affecting cordiality

The earliest of what appear to be only three or four pre-*Ulysses* instances of this phrase occurs in an anonymous, loosely historical narrative called *The Captive of Valence; or The Last Moments of Pius VI* (London, 1804), which begins after the title page with a publisher's note 'To The Reader' (italicized in the original) reading: 'The Author from whom the following sheets are translated, asserts the various incidents contained in the succeeding narrative to be founded in fact, though clad in the guise of a novel. It is hoped, therefore, that the sigh of commiseration will not be denied to the unhappy fate of the virtuous though unfortunate Pius VI.'

As for the highlighted phrase itself, it occurs in vol. 1 (of 2), p. 214, at the end of a passage describing the cessation of hostilities, at least for the present, between Pius VI—who served as Pope from 1775 until his death in 1799—and the King of Naples: 'Thus terminated these vexatious disputes, which lasted 'till the beginning of 1789. The reconciliation was sincere. The King and Queen of Naples visited Rome in a short time after, and were received by his holiness with the most affecting cordiality.'

Another of the four pre-*Ulysses* instances—the other two are of little interest[23]—is of the lot the most noteworthy. It occurs in *Personal Adventures during The Late War of Independence in Hungary*, by an author identified on its title page as the Baroness von Beck (London, 1850), vol. 1 (of 2), p. 332:

> The reader will suppose that I did not meanwhile forget our own poor fellows. Every day I came to them, accompanied by my servant, who carried a large basket laden with little delicacies and luxuries which I shared amongst them ; and never were children more delighted at having the choice of a confectioner's shop, than were the invalids when I made my appearance. Every one of them who could walk hastened to meet me, and welcome me with the most affecting cordiality.

Filled, according to one later description, 'with dangerous spy-missions, hair-raising escapades, romantic entanglements, and bloody encounters', the book was well-written, well-reviewed, partially serialized in one newspaper, reprinted in a second edition, and widely read—sufficiently so for its publisher, Richard Bentley, to invite its purported author to produce a sequel. But such was not to be. It was subsequently reported, based on information supplied by (among others) one or two of the people maligned in the book, that the 'Baroness' was no noblewoman but a Hungarian commoner and impostor named Vilma or Wilhelmine Racidula who, as a sometime agent for the Hungarian nationalist cause, had carried out several low-level intelligence assignments in England and elsewhere, whose book had been ghost-written by a journalist familiar with Hungarian history and politics and fluent in English, and whose

---

23 One of these appears in an anonymous, locally produced pamphlet entitled *The Speeches and Public Addresses of The Right Hon. George Canning, during The Election in Liverpool, which commenced On Friday the 7th and Terminated on Wednesday the 12th of June, 1816*; the other in *The Autobiography of a Blind Minister*, by Timothy Woodbridge, D. D. (Boston, 1856).

personal history and purported relationships and activities as a spy were largely or entirely invented.

On the night of 29 August 1851, while on tour to sell subscriptions for the second edition of her book, the 'Baroness' was arrested at a private home outside Birmingham, England, and charged with obtaining money under false pretenses. The next morning, while being conducted from a jail cell in Birmingham to a hearing before the local Bench of Magistrates, she suffered an apparent heart attack—suicide seems not to have been suspected—and, at fifty-four, died. But *Personal Adventures*, good read that it was, continued to sell. Seven decades later, Joyce may have picked up a copy of the first or second edition, borrowed from it the phrase 'the most affecting cordiality', and mined from it other details of Hungarian history, politics, and culture for use in his novel.[24]

Uly 12.1858: The catastrophe was terrific and instantaneous in its effect.

Joyce's phrase echoes a similar one in an account of a lopsided naval engagement, which occurred on 7 January 1841, between the iron steamship *Nemesis*, owned and operated by the British East India Company, and Chinese warships attempting to resist a British assault against the Chinese government's forts at Chuenpee during the First Opium War, fought between China and Britain from 1839 to 1842. The account, as published in *The Nautical Magazine and Naval Chronicle for 1841: A Journal of Papers on Subjects Connected With Maritime Affairs* (London), reads in part on p. 334 (italics added):

> [The *Nemesis*] then pushed on to attack the " war junks " strongly moored at the mouth of a small and shallow river, at the bottom of

---

24 For further details on the Beck/Racidula affair, see the pamphlet entitled *The Facts of the Case as to the Pretended "Baroness Von Beck" Stated, and Illustrated with Documentary Evidence* (London, [1852]), by the British political theorist, lawyer, and Birmingham historian J[oshua]. Toulmin Smith (1816–1869); and, similarly brief, *The Persecution and Death of the Baroness von Beck, at Birmingham, in August, 1851. Refutation of Mr. Toulmin Smith's Defence of the Disgraceful Proceedings Against that Defenceless Exile* (London, 1852)—published by Richard Bentley, New Burlington Street, publisher of Beck/Racidula's *Personal Adventures*. See also the *Vasváry Collection Newsletter* (2008), at http://vasvary.sk-szeged.hu/newsletter/08dec/musicians.html, from which the quoted passage describing the book's content and some other details are derived.

Ansons Bay, and when within 500 yards commenced a heavy fire of shot and shell on the four largest, which was returned by them. The first Congreve rocket fired by her took terrific and instantaneous effect, blowing up one of the largest with all her crew. The others being soon silenced, she then despatched her boats, in company with those of her Majesty's ship *Sulphur*, and one or two others from the *Larne*, *Calliope*, and *Hyacinth*—junk after junk was boarded and set fire to. The whole, eleven in number, blew up as the fire reached their magazines, and thus were completely destroyed.

13. 'Nausicaa'

In the headnote to their section on 'Nausicaa,' SMT write: 'The first half of the episode owes much to the sentimental tone of Maria Cummins's immensely popular 1854 novel *The Lamplighter*.' But as the notes below indicate, verbatim and nearly verbatim echoes of antecedent works span and permeate the entire episode, playing a major role in shaping its tone and content.

Uly 13.1–2: The summer evening had begun to fold the world in its mysterious embrace.

This first sentence of this episode may point to a short passage in one or the other of two antecedent works, and to a phrase in one or the other of two more.

As for 'The summer evening had begun to fold the world', see Oliphant's *Madonna Mary* (London, 1867), with, in vol. 1 (of 3), chap. 12, pp. 206–07: 'The summer evening had begun to decline, and it was at this meditative moment that the master of Earlston liked to sit and contemplate his Psyche and his Venus, and call a stranger's attention to their beauties, and tell pleasant anecdotes about how he picked them up.'

See also 'Christ's Invitation', a poem by the English poet, journalist, and biographer (of Florence Nightingale) Annie Matheson (1853–1924)—published, after its initial appearance c. 1870, in her *Selected Poems: Old and New* (London, 1899)—the fourth (final) stanza of which, on p. 136, reads: 'My heart is yearning with a strong desire | To fold the world in tender, close embrace ; | Come to me through the sanctifying fire | That hides my face.'

As for 'mysterious embrace', one of the handful of pre-Joyce, and secular, instances of that phrase—most other instances having to do with Christian or otherwise spiritual mysteries—occurs in the historical novel *The Red Shirt. Episodes.* (London, 1865) by Alberto Mario (1825–1883), an Italian politician, journalist, and supporter of Giuseppe Garibaldi, in a lyrical passage on page 64 during a brief lull in the violent struggle, led by Garibaldi, for the unification of Italy:

> The Ionian and the Tyrrhenian Sea kissed the Sicilian shores with their purple waves ; the island, veiled in a mist of golden light, seemed to tremble in that mysterious embrace ; the murmur of the pine forests which clothed the distant mountain slopes, echoing across the plain, gave tone and colour to the idyll. Meanwhile, the horseman drew near, and we rushed towards him with questions and glad welcome.

Another such instance occurs in George MacDonald's *Rampolli: Growths From a Long-Planted Root, Being Translations, New and Old, Chiefly From the German; along with A Year's Diary of an Old Soul* (London, 1897), with, on p. 11, MacDonald's prose translation of a passage from 'Hymns to the Night' by the German aristocrat and polymath Georg Philipp Friedrich Freiherr von Hardenberg (1772–1801), better known as 'Novalis':

> Among the people which, untimely ripe, was become of all the most scornful and insolently hostile to the blessed innocence of youth, appeared the New World, in guise never seen before, in the song-favouring hut of poverty, a son of the first maid and mother, the eternal fruit of mysterious embrace.

Uly 13.2: Far away in the west

Among other instances, this phrase previously occurred as the title of a song with lyrics by the Scottish poet Meta Orred (c. 1845–1925) and music by the English singer and composer Virginia Gabriel (1825–1877), published by Duff & Stewart (London, c. 1870), in which song the phrase was repeated a dozen times beginning with its first four lines: 'Far away in the west | The dews are falling ; | Far away in the west | The birds are calling [.]' The lyrics first appeared under the title 'Rest'— and the subtitle 'Suggested by Goethe's fugitive stanza, beginning "Auf allen Gipfeln ist Ruh."' [There is peace on all peaks]—on pp. 127–28 of Orred's first verse collection, *Poems* (London, 1874).

Uly 13.2–3: all too fleeting day

The apparently only prior instance of this phrase occurred in an unsigned poem called 'Her "Day of Rest." (The Song of the Shop-Girl.)', published in *Punch*, vol. 104, for 8 Apr. 1893, on pp. 158–59—where, on the first of the two pages, it is accompanied by a large pen-and-ink drawing of a young woman who has collapsed in exhaustion face down on her sofa with a magazine spread open and also face down on the floor beside her. The highlighted phrase occurs in the second line of the poem's final stanza, which reads (italics in the original):

> Out to the green fields ? Nay,
> This all too fleeting day
> To rest is dedicate. But not the rest
> Of brightened spirit, and of lightened breast.
> The dull, dead, half-inanimate leaden crouch
> Of sheer exhaustion on this shabby couch
> Is all my week's repose.
> Read ? But the tired eyes close,
> The book from nerveless fingers drops ;
> Almost the slow heart stops.
> But the clock halts not on its restless round,
> Weariness shudders at the whirring sound,
> As the sharp strike declares
> Swift to its closing wears
> One more of those brief interludes from toil
> Which leave us still the labour-despot's spoil,
> Slaves of long hours and unrelaxing strain,
> Unstrengthened and unsolaced, soon again
> To tread the round, and lift the lengthening chain ;
> *Stand*—till hysteria lays its hideous clutch
> On our girl-hearts, or epilepsy's touch
> Thrills through tired nerves and palsied brain.
> Again—again—again !
> *How long ?* Till Death, upon its kindly quest,
> Gives a true Day of Rest !

Uly 13.3: lingered lovingly

Continuing the pattern of back-to-back echoes—usually of well-worn and often trite phrases—marking the opening and many subsequent lines of the episode, this phrase occurred often over the course of the nineteenth century. One of the several works in which it appears: in a story called 'Christmas Eve at Warwingie' by the Australian novelist and writer Mary Eliza Bakewell Gaunt (1861–1942), first published in *The English Illustrated Magazine* (London), vol. 8, no. 88 (Jan. 1891), 299–307, subsequently collected in Gaunt's *The Moving Finger* (London, 1895), 47–80, and reading on p. 48 of the latter:

> Her rosy lips were just parted in a smile ; the long, level beams of the setting sun, falling on her through the passion vine, lingered lovingly in her golden hair, and made a delicate tracery as of fine lace work, on her pink gingham gown. Such a pretty picture she made, rocking slowly backwards and forwards, thought her companion, but he dared not say so.

In addition to 'lingered lovingly', the quoted passage echoes the setting sun of the episode's opening lines, and may point forward to the pretty picture Gerty MacDowell will make later in the episode as she rocks slowly backward and forward, for Bloom's and her own sexual arousal, on Sandymount strand.

Uly 13.3–4: proud promontory

Another phrase with several textual antecedents. One instance occurs in *Armata: A Fragment*, a fanciful, proto-science-fiction tale in which a man sails to the moon on a highway of ocean, anonymously published but known to have been written after his retirement by the Scottish advocate and, later, British Chancellor of the Exchequer Thomas Erskine (1750–1823). Part 1, second edn (London, 1817), chap. 5 ('In which Morven continues his account of the Island of Armata'), begins on p. 46: 'This highly favoured island now sat without a rival on this proud promontory in the centre of all the waters of this earth, with her mighty wings outspread to such a distance, that with your limited ideas of its numerous nations, it is impossible you should comprehend.'

Another, later instance of the phrase occurs in *The Sketch: A Journal of Art and Actuality* (London), vol. 27, no. 343 (23 Aug. 1899), p. 202, where paragraph 10 of the unsigned article 'Eastbourne, Queen of Watering-Places' reads: 'And so you bathe (but not on the sands). After your bath, if you are wise, you take a walk. If you are very wise, you walk along the Duke's Drive to Beachy Head, proud promontory rearing its grass-green head six hundred feet above the grass-green sea, where the winds are let loose and sing the litany of the dead men lying down below.'

Uly 13.4–5: weedgrown rocks

Another phrase with several antecedents. Joyce may have encountered the phrase—which also occurs in *Portrait*, chap. 2, line 121—in the Yorkshire poet John King's (fl. 1863–1874) *Rustic Pictures and Broken Rhymes* (London, 1874), pp. 59–60, in which each of the three stanzas of the poem 'The Siren' ends with an identical refrain: 'Then listen to her singing, | The weed-grown rocks among ; | With Neptune's caverns ringing, | Ringing, with her song.'

Or perhaps he crossed paths with it in Dorothy M. Richardson's *Backwater* (London, 1916), vol. 2 of her thirteen-volume novel sequence *Pilgrimage* (see note above on *Ulysses* 11.166), where the second paragraph in chap. 5, on p. 230, begins: 'At the end of half an hour's thoughtless wandering over the weed-grown rocks she found herself sitting on a little patch of dry silt at the end of a promontory of sea-smoothed hummocks with the pools of bright blue-green fringed water all about her watching the gentle rippling of the retreating waves over the weedy lower levels.'

Uly 13.6–7: the quiet church whence there streamed forth at times [...] the voice of prayer

The phrase 'streamed forth at times' previously and, it seems, uniquely occurred pre-Joyce in a similarly devout context: in *Doctrine and Practice: Lectures Preached in Portman Chapel, London* (London, 1861), by Rev. J[ohn]. W[illiam]. Reeve, M.A., Minister of the Chapel and Chaplain in Ordinary to Her Majesty the Queen (1807–1882), with, on p. 79: '"Him hath God exalted with His own right hand." Gleams of this glory and power and authority as King streamed forth at times while He was here on earth.'

Uly 13.7: in her pure radiance

The earlier of two pre-Joyce instances of this phrase may be found in *Harry Dangerfield, the Poacher* (Edinburgh and London, 1860), a novel by Charlotte Maria Tucker, as 'A.L.O.E.', with, in chap. 5 ('The Examination'), p. 34:

> Presently the full moon arose, and shone calmly into his little cell, throwing the dark shadow of his window-bars upon the bare opposite wall. There was something peaceful and tranquillising in her pure radiance which was not without its effect upon the prisoner. He opened the book, where the leaf had been turned down by Faith, at the parable of the prodigal son—that beautiful parable which has brought healing to so many broken hearts, over which so many contrite tears have been shed.

The later of the two occurred four decades later in *London Society, A Monthly Magazine of Light and Amusing Literature for the Hours of Relaxation* (London), edited by James Hogg and Florence Marryat, vol. 74, no. 6 (Dec. 1898), p. 656, in line 8 of a sonnet called 'My Mistress' by one Ellis Reid (italic in the original):

> She longed for beauty, though her eyes
>   Were heaven's own colour, warm with love.
> She minded me of some soft dove
>   That toward some sheltering bosom flies.
> Her lovely hair was dusky gold,
> And her self-mastery so serene,
> She must have seemed to souls terrene
> In her pure radiance almost cold.
> She longed for beauty, and I thought
>   One instant of a shy coquette.
> Forgive me, sweet, the pain I wrought,
> Though *I* forgive not, nor forget ;
> I know thee now for what thou art,
> And bless thee for thy childlike heart !

Uly 13.8: stormtossed heart

An early instance of this now-familiar phrase occurs in *Euryanthe*, a grand opera in the heroic manner with music by the German Romantic composer Karl Maria von Weber (1786–1826) and libretto by the German journalist and poet Helmina von Chézy (1783–1856). First performed in Germany in 1823, it was staged in London—in German—at the Theatre Royal Drury Lane in 1842 with a literal-translation, English-language libretto printed alongside the German original produced, published, and sold at the theatre and elsewhere by the London firm of A[lfred]. Schloss. In that booklet, Schloss's translation of the air sung by Lysiart, Count of Forest and Beaujolais near the beginning of Act 2 reads:

> Thus I devote myself to Revenge's powers,
> They allure me to the dark deed !
> Sown is the seed of mischief,
> The germ of death it must disclose.
> Fall in pieces, lovely image !
> Hence, last and sweetest pain !
> Revenge alone, revenge can fill
> This storm-tossed heart.

Although the opera itself received mixed reviews—with its music highly praised but its libretto widely deemed inferior and absurd—it was not long before the phrases 'storm-tossed heart' and 'the storm-tossed heart of man' had become clichés, turning up repeatedly in sermons, short stories, novels, and other genres in England, America, and elsewhere in the English-speaking world, from any one of which Joyce could have borrowed it for use in this cliché-packed episode.

Uly 13.11: that favourite nook

One instance of this rare phrase occurs pre-*Ulysses* in the British-American novelist and playwright Frances Hodgson Burnett's (1849–1924) *The Fortunes of Philippa Fairfax* (London, 1888), reading, in chap. 11, pp. 62–63:

> But notwithstanding her private resolutions, there were times when she felt that she melted ignominiously—times when Wilfred was more

than usually bright and lovable, or when certain Fates worked with him. Times when they had wandered up the hillside to that favourite nook of theirs, when Wilfred stretched himself upon the grass to be charming, when sun and wind, blue sky and blue water, seemed to combine to entrap her into being subdued and overruled.

Another instance occurs in 'The Isles of Destiny', a tale by the India-born English novelist Helen Halyburton Ross (1873–1936), serialized from 20 Aug. to 8 Oct. 1904 across eight issues of *Chambers's Journal*, sixth series, including in vol. 7, no. 358 (8 Oct. 1904), chap. 11, where the phrase occurs on p. 711: '" It's too high up ; it makes her giddy," replied Eric. " And I must say, looking down from that favourite nook of yours, one feels as if Providence had hardly acted fair in not bestowing wings upon one."'

Uly 13.12: beside the sparkling waves

Although the phrase occurs elsewhere from time to time, Joyce's 'sparkling waves' may have been inspired by Wordsworth's familiar lyric 'I Wandered Lonely as a Cloud', stanza 2 of which, as it appears in his *Poems In Two Volumes* (London, 1807), reads in vol. 2, p. 49:

> The waves beside them danced, but they
> Outdid the sparkling waves in glee : —
> A Poet could not but be gay
> In such a laughing company :
> I gaz'd—and gaz'd—but little thought
> What wealth the shew to me had brought :

Joyce's echo of a phrase from Wordsworth's stanza may also point proleptically to the scene later in 'Nausicaa' in which Bloom gazes, and masturbates, at the erotic show Gerty MacDowell puts on for him before they leave the Sandymount shore and go their separate ways.

Uly 13.15–17: Tommy and Jacky Caffrey were twins [...] darling little fellows

See *Selections from 'The Girl's Own Paper', 1880–1907*, edited by Terri Doughty (Peterborough, Ontario: Broadview Press, 2004), where, on

p. 122, the winning essay for a third prize of £1 1s, which is to say, one guinea—entitled 'My Professional Work,' signed 'Pimpernel,' from Plumstead, and dated 5 January 1897—reads in part: 'On Saturday mornings I begin at nine o'clock with a girl who teaches in a school all the week. She takes both pianoforte and singing lessons, and is now preparing for the Trinity College Senior Local. At the end of her hour, two little boys arrive, twins of nine years old. They are darling little fellows : both learn pianoforte, and they are also being trained for a church choir.'[25]

The Girl's Own Paper, a British story paper aimed at girls and young women—like its male-focused counterpart *The Boy's Own Paper*—was published by the London-based Religious Tract Society, sold for a penny per copy, and issued weekly from 3 January 1880 to and well beyond 1907.

Uly 13.17–18: but for all that [...] endearing ways about them

After noting (in 13.16–17) that the four-year-olds Tommy and Jacky Caffrey were 'very noisy and spoiled twins sometimes'—traits they will demonstrate over the course of the episode—the narrator adds that nevertheless the boys had 'endearing ways about them'. One early instance of the phrase 'endearing ways' alone occurs in Defoe's *The Fortunate Mistress: or, A History of the Life and Vast Variety of Fortunes of Mademoiselle de Beleau, Afterwards Call'd The Countess de Wintselsheim* etc (London, 1724)—better known today as, simply, *Roxana*. But two instances closer to Joyce's own time and, though less than verbatim, closer to his language in the highlighted phrase may be worth noting.

The earlier of the two occurred in a moralistic tale by the English aristocrat, traveller, and author Georgiana, Lady Chatterton (1805–1876), called *Lost Happiness; or, The Effects of a Lie* (London, 1845), and reading, in chap. 1, pp. 5–6:

> "Mrs. Langdale was very particular about her rooms, and had a number of ornamental things in them. As poor Edward [Langdale] was more lively and high-spirited than any of the other children, he was

---

25 This prize-essay was first published in *The Girl's Own Paper*, vol. 18, no. 900 (27 Mar. 1897), pp. 413–14; the quoted passage in the middle column on the latter page.

constantly doing some mischief; but then he appeared so amiable, and had so many little endearing ways, that his parents could not help being fonder of him than of the others, and therefore more ready to believe what he said.["]

The later of the two occurred in the Scottish novelist James Grant's (1822–1887) *The King's Own Borderers. A Military Romance.* (London, 1865), vol. 1 (of 3), chap. 7 ('Our Story Progresses'), p. 69, which begins (after a slightly misquoted epigraph from Tennyson's 'The Lord of Burleigh'):

> Kind old Rohallion was deeply interested in and attracted by the little boy, who had many winning and endearing ways about him ; and he particularly excelled in a bright and captivating smile, that was joyous in its perfect innocence.

Uly 13.21–22: the chubby baby [...] fairly chuckled with delight

One of the several pre-*Ulysses* instances of the latter phrase occurs in *Bootles' Baby. A Story of the Scarlet Lancers* (London, 1891)—first published under the title *Bootles' Baby: A Novelette* in four issues between January and June 1885 of *The Graphic: An Illustrated Weekly Newspaper* (London)—by the British novelist Henrietta Eliza Vaughan Stannard (1856–1911) as 'J[ohn]. S[trange]. Winter', chap. 4, p. 58:

> " Well, you little rogue," said the Colonel, reaching a nectarine for her. " What do you want ? "
> " I wanted Bootles, sir," said Miss Mignon, confidentially. " And nurse fell asleep, so I tooked French leave." Almost the only peculiarity in her speech was the habit of making all verbs regular.
> " And who are you, my little maid?" the General asked in extreme amusement.
> " Oh ! I'm Miss Mignon," with dignity.
> The old General fairly chuckled with delight, and as he had put his arm round the child, Bootles, who was standing behind, could not very well take her away.

Uly 13.24–25: the dainty dimple in his chin

This phrase, passed over without comment by Thornton, Gifford, and SMT, may have been suggested to Joyce by one or another of three antecedent texts.

First of the three: by the Irish journalist, novelist, dramatist, and poet Frank Frankfort Moore (1855–1931)—a Belfast Protestant and unionist—his novel *A Gray Eye or So* (London, 1893), vol. 2 (of 3), chap. 21 ('On the Elements of Party Politics'), with, on pp. 19–20:

> Before the hour of brandy-and-sodas and resplendent smoking-jackets had come, the fact of his having kept Beatrice Avon so long entertained had attracted some attention.
> It had attracted the attention of Miss Craven, who commented upon it with a confidential smile at Harold. It attracted the attention of Harold's father, who commented upon it with a leer and a sneer. It attracted the attention of Lady Innisfail, who commented upon it with a smile that caused the dainty dimple in her chin to assume the shape of the dot in a well-made note of interrogation.

Second of the three: by the Scottish author, journalist, and historian Alexander Allardyce (1846–1896), *Earlscourt, A Novel of Provincial Life* (Edinburgh, 1894), serialized in *Blackwood's*, vols. 153 and 154, Jan. 1893–Jan. 1894, with, in the January 1893 issue, chap. 4 ('Cloete Sparshott'), p. 14:

> It had never occurred to the doctor that his daughter was beautiful, else he would doubtless have sought for some scientific explanation of the fact. But beautiful Cloete Sparshott was, although her beauty was not of the kind that painters generally seek for in their models, or poets delight in assigning to their subjective mistresses. The broad arched brow, with thick masses of dark-brown hair parted evenly and delicately to each side, and a slightly aquiline nose such as we see on Julian coins and medals, if they were too strong for a face of feminine softness, were balanced by the beautiful moulding of the cheeks and mouth, the sweet arch of her lips, the dainty dimple of her chin, the poise and perfection of her neck flowing downwards in gentle lines to her shapely shoulders.

Third of the three: in a two-act musical comedy called *A Chinese Honeymoon*—about a Chinese emperor in search of a bride, and an English couple honeymooning in China who inadvertently violate its kissing laws—with book and lyrics by the English lyricist and librettist George Dance (1857–1932), additional lyrics by the English writer and dramatist Harry Greenbank (b. 1865), and music by Howard Talbot (1865–1928) and the Belgian–born composer Félix Marie Henri Tilkin (1861–1921), known professionally as Ivan Caryll. The quoted phrase occurs in a song from Act 2 of the musical, composed by Caryll and sung by Princess Soo-Soo and Chorus, the first verse of which reads:

> Dolly was a baby
> Just as others may be,
> With a pair of eyes of blue ;
> Looking like her father,
> Like her mother, rather,
> Just as other babies do.
> She'd her aunty's tint of rose
> And her uncle's classic nose,
> But her special merit
> She did not inherit,
> It was, what do you suppose ?
> She'd a dainty darling dimple on her chin.

The phrase 'a dainty darling dimple on her chin' and variations thereof recur fifteen more times over the course of the song.

Are this song, its lyrics, and the sheet music based on them likely to have been familiar to Joyce and/or to Gerty MacDowell and her friends? More than likely. *A Chinese Honeymoon* opened at the Theatre Royal in Hanley, England, on 16 October 1899, toured extensively in England and America (though not, it seems, in Ireland), then returned to London in October 1901 and ran at that city's Strand Theatre a total of 1,075 times—becoming the first musical production to break the one-thousand mark in consecutive performances at a single location. Joyce might not have seen the musical in person during its long run in London, but he would likely have known, played, or sung the sheet music based on it.

Uly 13.80: gazing far away into the distance

The phrase with which, immediately following 'lost in thought', Joyce introduces Gerty MacDowell occurred pre-Joyce several times, including, perhaps most notably, in chap. 25 of Turgenev's novel *Smoke* (Moscow, 1867)—partly a story of frustrated love, partly a satirical portrait of the social, economic, and political divisions of mid-nineteenth-century Russian society—as translated from the Russian by Constance Garnett (London, 1906), with, on pp. 284–85 (ellipsis in the original):

> Till night-time Litvinov did not leave his room ; God knows whether he was expecting anything. About seven o'clock in the evening a lady in a black mantle with a veil on her face twice approached the steps of his hotel. Moving a little aside and gazing far away into the

distance, she suddenly made a resolute gesture with her hand, and for the third time went towards the steps. . . .

Uly 13.83–84: Her figure was slight and graceful, inclining even to fragility

The first six words of the highlighted phrase echo verbatim, and the next four very nearly so, a sentence in the English-language version of Balzac's story 'La Bourse' (1832), first published as one of the *Scènes de la vie privée* (Scenes of private life) in *La Comédie humaine*, translated by Clara Bell, published as 'The Purse', collected in Balzac's *At the Sign of the Cat and Racket* (London, 1895), and occurring there on p. 145: 'Her figure was slight and graceful, and frail in form.'

In Balzac's tale, the young woman to whom the quoted passage refers is Adélaïde Leseigneur, who with her mother Madame de Rouville comes to the aid of the young painter Hippolyte Schinner when he falls off a ladder while working on a large canvas in his studio above their apartment. In the weeks that follow Hippolyte falls in love with Adélaïde; after various plot complications, the lovers are engaged to be married.

Uly 13.87–88: almost spiritual in its ivorylike purity

One of the few pre-*Ulysses* instances of the latter phrase, with 'ivorylike' hyphenated or not, occurs in *Shadowed to Europe: A Chicago Detective on Two Continents* (Chicago and New York, 1885; repr. 1887), by the American author Symmes M[ajor]. Jelley (1855–1925), as 'Le Jemlys', chap. 11 ('A Beautiful Adventuress – An Exquisite Bed – Lora and Felix – "How She Teases To-Night" – "You Would Be a Dead Man" – An Appointment to Meet a Stranger – A Yellow Rose – Another Shadow.'), pp. 118–19 (italics in the original):

> Lora Lambert was a beauty.
> Her hair was of that peculiar shade of brown which livens into gold in the sunlight, and at night assumes such somber shades as to appear black ; it was heavy, long, and silken. A broad, low forehead, large gray eyes, heavily shadowed by long, pensive lashes, lent an air of melancholy to her face. Her cheeks were round, dimpled and pretty ; an exquisitely cut nose, a voluptuous mouth, and a finely

turned chin, with a complexion of ivory-like purity, completed the *tout ensemble* of her features.

Another occurs in *Digger Dick's Darling, and Other Tales* (London, New York, and Melbourne, 1888), by the Australian writer Julia Blitz (1846–1923)—also known as Mrs. A[ntonio]. Blitz and sometimes as Modicum—in the novella of the title, chap. 3 ('The Cat and Kittens Entertain the Lion'), pp. 41–42:

> Carrie reddened. Clara flushed, too, slightly. But these sisters were animated by contrary emotions, inasmuch as one was irritated, and the other strangely elated. Clara scanned it for a few seconds in silence. It represented truthfully his handsome face and head and bust. There were the same dreamy brown eyes, the waving forest of hair, the long, silky, drooping moustache, the fresh lips, the square jaw. But the complexion in ivory-like purity (as photography always fails in this one particular) was not the same. Whether it was her staunch love of the truth, or mischief, it is hard to tell ; but she was audacious enough to return it to him, saying, " It is a good picture, but flattering."

Uly 13.104: the love that might have been

Along with the echo, noted by Gifford and SMT, of the American poet John Greenleaf Whittier's (1807–1892) 'Maud Muller' (1856)—with 'For of all sad words of tongue or pen, | The saddest are these : " It might have been ! "'—see, among the several instances in which the phrase occurs, the American poet Edwin Markham's (1852–1940) 'A Lyric of the Dawn', published in his best-known collection, *The Man with the Hoe and Other Poems* (New York, 1899; London, 1900), and reading, in lines 68 to 85:

> But hark again,
> From the secret glen,
> That voice of rapture and ethereal youth
> Now laden with despair.
> Forbear, O bird, forbear :
> Is life not terrible enough forsooth ?
> Cease, cease the mystic song—
> No more, no more, the passion and the pain :
> It wakes my life to fret against the chain ;
> It makes me think of all the agèd wrong—
> Of joy and the end of joy and the end of all—
> Of souls on Earth, and souls beyond recall.

> Ah, ah, that voice again!
> It makes me think of all these restless men,
> Called into time—their progress and their goal;
> And now, oh now, it sends into my soul
> Dreams of a love that might have been for me—
> That might have been—and now can never be.

Uly 13.105: tense with suppressed meaning

SMT cite the British novelist, feminist, and suffragette Beatrice Harraden's (1864–1936) novel *The Guiding Thread* (New York and London, 1916) as the source of line 13.128's 'all the freshness of a young May morning', as well as of phrases in lines 13.368–70 and 13.518. The phrase highlighted above occurs, perhaps uniquely pre-Joyce, in the same novel, chap. 4, pp. 26–27:

> " I think it is remarkable the way you have got hold of the mind and meaning of Savonarola," he said. " Nothing could be better. I shall leave him entirely to you to work out. Those notes and passages of yours are invaluable. All of them. I should like to go carefully through them with you some day soon. But meanwhile I wish you'd read me again now what you read last night, will you ? "
> Joan got up and faced him.
> " I can't, Horace," she said in a low voice, tense with suppressed meaning.
> " You can't ? " he repeated in a wondering tone. " And why not ? What's the difficulty ? "
> " Because I've burnt them," she said. " Burnt them — every one of them."

Uly 13.106: a strange yearning tendency

A rare pre-Joyce instance of the phrase 'yearning tendency' occurs in Eustace Clare Grenville Murray's novel *That Artful Vicar: The Story of What a Clergyman Tried to Do for Others and Did for Himself* (London, 1879), vol. 2 (of 2), chap. 44 ('Mendelssohn's Wedding March'), p. 293:

> It was an indirect courtship, the yearning tendency of which was all summed up in the closing words which he emitted with a sigh:—
> ' Oh, Miss Amy, you could make life such a paradise to the man who loved you !'

' Not unless I loved him too,' said she, shaking her head, and drying her eyes.

The phrase recurred twenty years later in the British periodical *Truth* (London), vol. 45, no. 1157 (2 Mar. 1899), p. 516, reprinting an anonymous poem that was a 'bitter cry...uttered by a Scotch minister in his parish magazine', entitled 'Why People Cough At Church: By a Candid Friend of the Clergy', and reading, in the fifth of its eight stanzas:

> The cause is clear—when interest holds
>   The house's ear with grip sustained,
> The yearning tendency to cough
>   Is automatic'lly restrained ;
> When hearts are thrilled and tears are trickling,
> Throats cease instinctively from tickling.

Uly 13.116: wealth of wonderful hair

This phrase previously occurred verbatim in 'The End of an Escapade'— 'By the Author of "Betty's Husband",' the pseudonymous Amy Savage— in the *English Illustrated Magazine*, vol. 28 (Mar. 1903), 500–07, with, on p. 502: '" Do you mind taking off your sun-bonnet ? I think I will make a sketch of your head instead of the hands today." He noted with approval the slightly irregular features and the wealth of wonderful hair turned for his inspection.'

It also occurred—two years before the 'Nausicaa' episode was first serialized in *The Little Review* in mid-1920—in the English novelist E[dward]. Phillips Oppenheim's (1866–1946) *Mr. Lessingham Goes Home* (London, 1918), published in America as *The Zeppelin's Passenger* (Boston, 1918), chap. 31, p. 291, of both editions: 'Her head pressed upon his arm. She nodded. It was just that convulsive movement of her head, with its wealth of wonderful hair and its plain black motoring hat, which dealt the death-blow to his hopes. She was just a child once more — and she trusted him.'

Uly 13.118–19: a profusion of luxuriant clusters

One of the earliest of many pre-Joyce instances of 'luxuriant clusters'— and one of the few not referring to flowers, foliage, or fruit—may be found in Mayne Reid's *The Wood-Rangers: or, The Trappers of Sonora* (London, 1860)—set in Mexico in the 1830s, and adapted from the French of the adventure novel *Le coureur des bois, ou Les chercheurs d'or* (Paris, 1856) by Louis de Bellemare *père* (1809–1852) as 'Gabriel Ferry'. Volume 3 (of 3), chap. 11 ('The Stranger's Story') of Reid's version begins, on pp. 225–26:

> Her head veiled by a silk scarf, which partly concealed the luxuriant tresses of her dark hair, as they fell in luxuriant clusters upon her bosom, Doña Rosarita's countenance gave evidence of long and secret suffering.
>
> As she seated herself, a look of deep disquietude increased her paleness. It seemed as though the young girl feared the approach of a moment in which she might be required to renounce those sweet dreams of the past, for the reality of a future she dared not contemplate.

Another such instance of 'luxuriant clusters' occurs in the American lawyer, politician, author, and translator (including of Jules Verne's *Around the World in Eighty Days*) George M[akepeace]. Towle's (1841–1893) *The Story of Magellan or the First Voyage Round the World* (London, 1896), with, in chap. 12 ('The Barbarians Converted'), p. 121:

> One day, the Queen of Sebu came to hear mass in all her state. She was attired in black and white, and wore a long silk veil with gold stripes, flowing down gracefully over her shoulders. Before her went three young girls, each carrying one of the queen's palm-leaf hats. Following the queen flocked a great number of women of rank, wearing smaller veils, and hats above them. Otherwise, they only wore a palm-leaf apron about their waists, while their long black hair fell in luxuriant clusters over their shoulders to their knees.

Uly 13.136–37: dull aching void in her heart

The phrase 'dull aching void' recurs often in the popular literature of nineteenth-century Britain and America. It appears, however, that the sole verbatim instance of 'dull aching void in her heart' occurred in *The Railway Signal, or Lights Along The Line: A Journal of Evangelistic and Temperance Work on all Railways* (London), vol. 7, no. 3 (Mar. 1889), on p. 57 of a story by one Rosa A. Rice of Stow Bedon, Norfolk, called '"Why Not To-Night?"':

> Bessie's visits became more frequent. One day she asked her friend the secret of her happy home, and Mrs. Fisher told her that the reason

of their happiness was that they had admitted Christ to dwell with them. Bessie thought that sounded very strange, so she tried not to think of it ; but there was a dull aching void in her heart that would not be satisfied. At length she resolved she would see what religion would do for her ; but, alas ! she was so sadly ignorant upon such subjects, she did not know how to make a beginning, so she resolved to tell Mrs. Fisher her difficulties.

Uly 13.154–55: a navy threequarter skirt [...] showed off her slim graceful figure to perfection

In *The Pall Mall Magazine*, vol. 31, no. 125 (Sept. 1903), 41–48, see 'The Town Twin', a story by the English author and London society columnist Mrs Hugh Adams (*née* Evelyn Wills), with, on p. 45: 'Arthur resented them ; they were as offensive to him as her high-heeled shoes with soles of the consistency of brown paper, her beautifully-dressed hair, and her slim, graceful figure clad in trailing gowns which he felt belonged to the town and had no part in the country.'

See also, published the following year, the Anglo-French journalist, writer, diplomat, and traveller William Le Queux's (1864–1927) *The Closed Book: Concerning the Secret of the Borgias* (London, 1904), with, in chap. 27 ('If You Knew The Truth'), p. 231: 'At last the door opened, and there appeared my pale-faced love, neatly dressed in black, with a small toque that suited her admirably, and a bodice that showed off her figure to perfection.'

Uly 13.162: the lovely reflection which the mirror gave back to her

Here and in 13.192–93, Thornton sees a probable allusion to the German fairy tale 'Snowwhite'—from the Low German *Sneewittchen* (modern spelling *Schneewittchen*), later and better known as 'Snow White'— collected and published in 1812 by the brothers Jacob and Wilhelm Grimm. But the highlighted text also echoes nearly verbatim passages in a considerable number of antecedent novels and tales.

One of the former: *Margaret's Engagement* (London, 1867), by the English writer Catherine Simpson Wynne (1817–1905), vol. 1 (of 3), chap. 4 ('Our Heroine') of which reads, on pp. 63–64:

> If the old lady [her grandmother, Lady Tolmaine] had been bodily present in Margaret's room this evening, she would hardly have approved of the maiden's prolonged contemplation of herself in the cheval-glass, before which she was yet standing when her maid had quitted her, and the first dinner-bell was about to sound. To do her justice, she was not greatly addicted to this feminine (is it *exclusively* feminine?) recreation ; but she seemed profoundly interested in it to-day, as she stood, arrayed in pure white, without a single ornament of flower or gem, gazing with a grave air of quite dispassionate criticism on the reflection her mirror gave back to her. It was a reflection that could bear criticism well, too. Margaret was not, strictly speaking, beautiful ; but the glance that once dwelt upon her would seek her again and again, when it had wearied of more faultless beauty than hers.

One of the latter: 'The Jewel Princess', by Frances Freeling Broderip, in her story collection *The Daisy and Her Friends: Simple Tales and Stories for Children* (London, 1869), 26–43, with, on p. 32:

> Next morning, after her perfumed bath, [Princess Brilliantine] seated herself languidly before her vast mirror, and commanded her women to attire her as usual. The great shining mirror gave faithfully back a lovely reflection of her fair face and her graceful figure, and the beautiful vain Princess smiled gaily back at her mimic image.

Uly 13.172: the fluttering hopes and fears of sweet seventeen

An early, perhaps the earliest, instance of 'fluttering hopes and fears' occurs in the much-reprinted story collection *Passages from the Diary of a Late Physician*, by the British barrister, novelist, and Member of Parliament Samuel Warren (1807–1877), serialized Aug. 1830 to Aug. 1837 in *Blackwood's*, also issued in a three-volume collection (London, 1832). Chapter 1 as excerpted in *Blackwood's* vol. 28, no. 170 (Aug. 1830), 322–38, reads, on p. 324:

> For several months I was up early and late, at a work on Diseases of the Lungs. [...] When at length it was completed, having been read and revised twenty times, so that there was not a comma wanted, I hurried, full of fluttering hopes and fears, to a well-known medical bookseller, expecting he would at once purchase the copyright.

Another, later instance of the phrase occurred in *Rita: An Autobiography* (London, 1858), a novel, its title notwithstanding, by the Greek-British writer of novels, poems, songs (which he also sang), and plays (in which he sometimes privately acted) Charles Hamilton Aïde (1826–1906), vol. 2 (of 2), chap. 1 of which begins, on pp. 3–4:

> In spite of my mother's assumption that I was fully prepared for the intelligence her letter contained, it was a great surprise,—I had almost written *shock*. I was glad ; I was very glad, of course. But what a child she was ! At least I had been accustomed to consider and treat her as such, until quite lately : and even then, was so completely and selfishly engrossed, that whenever the image of my sister crossed my thoughts, it was only as a gleam of sunshine in the home-picture—a morning gleam, as yet far removed from the glare and heat of mid-day passions. She had not made a confidante of me—she had never poured into my ear the secret tale of fluttering hopes and fears ; and I had no right to expect it.

A third instance occurred in a tale by 'H.O.' called 'The Two Widows', published in *The National Magazine* (London), vol. 4 (1863), 159–64, with, on p. 162: 'Who can measure or calculate all the fluttering hopes and fears, the flattering whispers, and agitating anticipations, that, while those weeks were passing, trembled and fermented in the full heart and busy little brain of the expectant and love-sick Louisa !'

Uly 13.188–89: a gnawing sorrow

One of the several pre-*Ulysses* instances of this phrase, with or without the indefinite article, occurs in Trollope's *Barchester Towers* (London, 1857; new, one-volume edn, London, 1858)—the second of six novels in his Chronicles of Barsetshire series—in which chap. 30 ('Another Love Scene') of both editions begins with the following paragraph:

> But there was another visitor at the rectory whose feelings in this unfortunate matter must be somewhat strictly analysed. Mr. Arabin had heard from his friend of the probability of Eleanor's marriage with Mr. Slope with amazement, but not with incredulity. It has been said that he was not in love with Eleanor, and up to this period this certainly had been true. But as soon as he heard that she loved some one else, he began to be very fond of her himself. He did not make up his mind that he wished to have her for his wife ; he had never thought of her, and did not now think of her, in connection with himself ; but

he experienced an inward indefinable feeling of deep regret, a gnawing sorrow, and unconquerable depression of spirits, and also a species of self-abasement that he—he Mr. Arabin—had not done something to prevent that other he, that vile he, whom he so thoroughly despised, from carrying off this sweet prize.

The phrase recurs in Ibsen's play *Little Eyolf* (1894) as translated by William Archer (London, 1895), Act 2, p. 89, where Alfred Allmers speaking to his half-sister Asta says: 'Yes, for me it's impossible. Before you came to me, here I sat, torturing myself unspeakably with this crushing, gnawing sorrow———'.

Among other instances, the phrase also occurs in the American novelist, short story writer, and poet Herman Melville's (1819–1891) *White-Jacket; or, The World in a Man-of-War* (London, 1850), chap. 61 ('The Surgeon of the Fleet'), p. 292: 'Chief among these was a cast, often to be met with in the Anatomical Museums of Europe, and no doubt an unexaggerated copy of a genuine original ; it was the head of an elderly woman, with an aspect singularly gentle and meek, but at the same time wonderfully expressive of a gnawing sorrow, never to be relieved.'; and in the English poet Christina Rossetti's (1830–1894) 'Songs in a Cornfield' (1866), lines 27–30: 'To-day she must weep | For gnawing sorrow, | To-night she may sleep | And not wake to-morrow.'

Uly 13.193–94: infinitely sad and wistful

Joyce's phrase previously occurred verbatim in *Léonie; or, Light Out of Darkness. And, Within Iron Walls: A Tale of the Siege of Paris. Twin-Stories of the Franco-German War.* (London, 1875) by the English author Annie Lucas (fl. 1870–1890), with, in the first of its two tales, chap. 3 ('My Mother's Death'), p. 30:

> I said something about her being better when the warm spring weather came. She did not answer ; but, oh, the look in those bright, mournful eyes, so infinitely sad and wistful ! I tried again to cheer her, but she said, in her low, gasping voice :—
>
> " No, mademoiselle—I am dying. I know it—I feel it. And I do not know where I am going ;—it is all so dark,—so dark ;" [*sic*] and she shuddered.

The phrase also occurs, minus *infinitely*, in *A Soldier of the Legion* (London, 1914), by the British writers C[harles]. N[orris]. Williamson (1859–1920) and his wife A[lice]. M[uriel]. Williamson (1869–1933), chap. 14 ('Two on the Roof'), p. 140: 'No sinister thing looked out from the eyes of Ourïeda, but something very sad and wistful kept repeating, "Can I trust you? Oh, I think so, I believe so, more and more. But it is so desperately important to be certain. I must wait a little while yet."'

Uly 13.209–10: a rare and wondrous love

One of two pre-*Ulysses* instances of 'rare and wondrous love' occurred in a much-reprinted sermon—entitled 'The Name Above Every Name' and reflecting his theological emphasis on God's love—by the prominent American Congregational minister, abolitionist, and social reformer Henry Ward Beecher (1813–1887), delivered in Plymouth Church, Brooklyn, New York, on 7 November 1869, collected in *The Sermons of Henry Ward Beecher*, third series (New York, 1872), 149–60, and reading on pp. 156–57:

> Have you pity ? Find me pity that stands out among men remarkable, and I will place by the side of it the pity of Christ, and say, "Here is a name which is above every name in that." Show me mercy—that mercy which suffers rather than make suffering—and over against the most saintly and notable instance that you can find, I will lift up a name that is above every other name in that. Show me a love that longs to die rather than that another should die—yea, that is willing to live through tribulation and sorrow to do good to those that are beloved—and over against this rare and wondrous love, I will lift up a name of love that is above every name—the name of Jesus, that rebukes our want of faith, and our want of an elevated conception, in fashioning him to ourselves.

the other, in an 1869 edition (Oxford and London) of Horstius's *Paradise of the Christian Soul* (see entry above for *Uly* 10.172), with, on p. 108, 'O rare and wondrous love ! O that we, who profess the Name of CHRIST, may imitate it!'

Uly 13.213: his deep passionate nature

One of the several pre-Joyce instances of this phrase occurs in *Heriot's Choice: A Tale* (London, 1879), by the English children's writer and popular novelist Rosa Nouchette Carey (1840–1909), vol. 2 (of 3), chap.

21 ('Under Stenkrith Bridge'), p. 213: 'Would his hearth be always warm and bright when she bloomed so sweetly beside it ; would her innocent affection content this man, with his deep, passionate nature, and yearning heart ; would there be no void that her girlish intellect could not fill ?'

Heriot's Choice—one of the thirty-three triple-decker novels Carey wrote and published—was serialized in M. Yonge's *The Monthly Packet* from July 1877 to October 1879. Carey was herself on the staff of the *Girl's Own Paper*, for which she wrote eight serials.

Uly 13.241–42: he would give his dear little wifey a good hearty hug

Most of the several pre-*Ulysses* instances of 'his dear little wifey' originated in America, but at least two of the lot appeared in humorous items in the London-based *Punch*. The earlier of the two: in *Punch*, vol. 23 (17 July 1852), p. 43, in a piece called 'Matrimonial Biology' that reads in part: 'Again, he hates dancing :—No, he won't dance, not even to please his dear little wifey—but it is in vain his holding out—He *must* dance—No, he won't : when he feels several smart shocks down his elbow—and, strangely enough, he dances for a whole hour against his will.' The later of the two: in *Punch*, vol. 29 (13 Oct. 1855), p. 146, in a piece called 'If Women Bet, What Do They Bet?', which begins:

> Some men, when they lose wagers, pay in hats. We do not know whether ladies ever wager together, or what the nature of their wagers may be, but you may be sure they are not bonnets, simply because ladies would derive no pleasure whatever in winning bonnets from one another. A wager, so won, would destroy the amusement a lady always has in getting a new bonnet out of her husband, and would take away most materially from the enjoyment of that husband's society whenever he had been persuaded to leave the City a trifle earlier, "just to take a stroll before dinner with his dear little wifey."

Uly 13.242: and gaze for a moment deep down into her eyes

One of the many all-but-verbatim instances of Joyce's phrase—which turned up more often than not in nineteenth-century sentimental-evangelical fiction—occurred in *Alone in London* (London, 1869), written by the evangelical English author Sarah Smith (1832–1911), as 'Hesba Stretton', published by the Religious Tract Society, and reading in chap. 18 ('No Room For Dolly'), pp. 123–24:

> They reached home at last, after a weary and heart-broken journey, and carried Dolly in and laid her upon old Oliver's bed. She was wide awake now, and looked very peaceful, smiling quietly into both their faces as they bent over her. Tony gazed deep down into her eyes, and met a glance from them which sent a strange tremor through him. He crept silently away, and stole into his dark bed under the counter, where he stretched himself upon his face, and buried his mouth in the chaff pillow to choke his sobs. What was going to happen to Dolly ? What could it be that made him afraid of looking again into her patient and tranquil little face ?

Another such instance occurred in Dinah Maria Craik's *Young Mrs. Jardine* (London, 1879), vol. 2 (of 3), chap. 4 ('Betrothed'), pp. 74–75:

> Roderick felt that he had found it. When, for the first time in his life, thank God ! he clasped a woman to his breast, the one beloved woman who to him was all the world ; when, gazing deep down into her eyes, he saw reflected there a heaven of pure love—the love that seemed to look beyond himself and into heaven—there came to him a great calmness. He was satisfied.

Craik's novel was also serialized in the monthly evangelical illustrated magazine *Good Words* (Edinburgh and London) from January to December 1879.

Uly 13.286–87: the storms of this weary world

While the phrase 'this weary world' or versions of it were a common feature of many nineteenth-century sermons, songs, and poems, a rare verbatim, and secular, pre-*Ulysses* instance of Joyce's entire phrase occurs in a long unsigned article in *The Dublin University Magazine*, vol. 27, no. 160 (Apr. 1846), 440–52, entitled 'Recollections of the Burschenschaft of Germany', and chap. 2 of which ('The Castle of Heidelberg by Moonlight—The Pistol Duel—The Student's Funeral'), reads, on p. 451:

> At the distance of little more than a mile from the town lies the new burial-place of Heidelberg. It is a quiet spot, embosomed by trees, upon a sunny slope on the mountain's side. We have seldom seen a place in which the spirit, shattered by the disappointments and torn by the storms of this weary world, could find a calmer repose.

Another verbatim, also secular, instance of the same phrase occurs in the India-born British novelist Janet Maughan's (1828–1926) *The Co-Heiress* (London, 1866), vol. 3 (of 3), chap. 6 ('The Convent of Santa Lucia'), p. 79 (italics in the original):

> No hard lines of condemnatory harshness were there, but worn furrows that spoke of bygone sufferings, and dewy eyes that looked as though they had shed many a heavy and bitter tear. *Had* shed ; for consolation seemed to have reached her now ; and her air of pensive serenity gave convincing proof that for her the storms of this weary world were over—a haven of peace and security had been reached at last.

Uly 13.368–70: the face that met her gaze [...] wan and strangely drawn, seemed to her the saddest she had ever seen

SMT write: 'After Beatrice Harraden's [...] novel *The Guiding Thread* (1916): "she saw that his face was strangely drawn and tired."' But see also the 20 May 1893 issue of *All the Year Round* (after Dickens's death in 1870, owned and edited by his son Charles Dickens Jr.), in which the final lines of chap. 11 of the anonymous serialized story 'Outlawed', on p. 480, contain a passage—'and it seemed to the girl that they were the saddest [eyes] she had ever seen'—matching nearly verbatim the passage from 'Nausicaa' highlighted above:

> Even now, while she shrank from his sins, in her simple faith in the truth of repentance and divine forgiveness, she thought most of the possibility within him of higher things. As she looked at him, hurt, shrinking, sorry, a sudden inspiration of the divine truth shone into her perplexed soul.
> " Tell me," she said. " Have you found it more worth living from your point of view ? "

For a second he looked back at her. Then one of his slow, sweet smiles crossed his lips. But it did not touch his eyes, and it seemed to the girl that they were the saddest she had ever seen.

" I have chosen," he said.

Uly 13.375–76: and many who had erred and wandered

SMT write that 'erred and strayed' is 'a familiar phrase in the General Confession in the Anglican/Episcopal Church; for example, from a morning prayer: "Almighty and most merciful Father; We have erred and strayed from Thy ways like lost sheep" (*The Book of Common Prayer*, p. 4).' But the phrase 'erred and wandered' has itself occurred both verbatim and widely in Western religious, secular, and popular literature, including in the English Puritan clergyman, theologian, historian, and martyrologist John Foxe's (1516–1587) *Actes and Monuments of these Latter and Perillous Days, Touching Matters of the Church* (London, 1563)— later more commonly known as *Foxe's Book of Martyrs*—with, in vol. 4, part 2, book 8, p. 634, of the London 1857 edition, 'my flock hath erred and wandered in every mountain, and upon every high hill, and is dispersed throughout all the earth'; in *Meditations of Marcus Aurelius* (London, 1634) as translated from the Greek by the French-English classical scholar Meric Casaubon, D.D. (1599–1671), with, in book 8, 'Thou hast already had sufficient experience, that of those many things that hitherto thou hast erred and wandered about, thou couldst not find happiness in any of them'; and in 'Two Kinds of Service', a story by the American author and publisher J[ames]. Edson White (1849–1928) published anonymously along with other of his evangelical tales in *The King's Daughter and Other Stories for Girls* (n.p., 1910), with, on p. 202:

> " How terribly I have erred and wandered from the way," she said aloud. " This dream has opened my eyes, and I see what I have been doing. What must have papa thought of me? No wonder that he is not a Christian. I have wondered, too, that the children have been so indifferent to religious teaching, but the influence of my life has spoiled everything. But, thank God! the present is mine, my dear ones are spared to me, and henceforth I will strive to have my life count for Christ."

Uly 13.396: his infant majesty

This phrase, fancifully applied to Baby Boardman, may have been suggested by the historical situation in England and Scotland in July 1567, when, after the forced abdication of Queen Mary, her son, at the age of about thirteen months, was crowned James VI. As the Scottish historian Charles Mackie wrote in *The Castles of Mary Queen of Scots*, third edition (London, 1835), p. 57: 'After [the coronation], the Earls of Morton and Home gave a promissory oath, in the name of his infant Majesty, that he should profess and maintain the Reformed religion, and govern the kingdom accordingly. On their return to the Castle, Atholl carried the crown, Morton the sceptre, Glencairn the sword of state, and Mar the young king.'

Uly 13.412–13: His eyes burned into her as though they would [...] read her very soul.

A survey of popular and pulp fiction published in England and America in the second half of the nineteenth century finds few motifs and phrases as common as male eyes burning into a female's eyes or face and thereby 'read[ing] her very soul'. Among the many instances of this motif and versions of this phrase that Joyce may have come across in his search for material usable in *Ulysses* generally, and 'Nausicaa' in particular, are those in the following examples.

Thomas Hardy's first novel, *Desperate Remedies*, as published anonymously by Tinsley Brothers (London, 1871), reading in vol. 3 (of 3), chap. 5 ('The Events of Three Days'), pp. 114–15:

> All this feigning was most distasteful to Graye. The riddle having been solved, he unconsciously assumed his natural look before she had withdrawn her face. She found him to be peering at her as if he would read her very soul—expressing with his eyes the notification of which, apart from emotion, the eyes are more capable than any other—inquiry.

Mrs Molesworth's *Hathercourt Rectory* (London, 1878), reading, in vol. 3 (of 3), chap. 2 ('Arthur's Cousin'), p. 40:

> A pair of dark eyes were gazing down upon her—gazing as if they would read her very soul, so earnest, so *true* in their expression that

> Mary could not but own to herself that it was difficult to realise that they belonged to an unprincipled and dishonourable man.

Mrs Hungerford's *Doris*, new one-volume edn (London, 1885), reading in chap. 11, p. 129:

> ' No ! ' says Burke, frowningly ; then his mood changes, and the most grievous dejection takes the place of his short-lived anger. 'If they did, it would not be true, would it ? ' he says, closing his fingers over hers, and gazing at her as if he would read her very soul.

And the American editor, author, and translator Nathan Haskell Dole's (1852–1935) translation of Tolstoy's *Anna Karenina*, first published in New York in 1886, revised and republished in London in 1889, and reading in vol. 1 (of 2), part 2, chap. 2, p. 132 of the London edition:

> The old prince smoothed Kitty's hair with his hand : she raised her head, and with an effort smiled as she looked at him ; she felt that her father alone, though he did not say much, understood her. She was the youngest, and therefore her father's favorite daughter, and his love made him clairvoyant, as she imagined. When her eyes met his, it seemed to her that he read her very soul, and saw all the evil that was working there.

Uly 13.415–16: She could see at once by his dark eyes and his pale intellectual face

An early—though not quite the earliest[26]—pre-Joyce instance of 'pale, intellectual face' occurs in the American novelist and short-story writer Nathaniel Hawthorne's (1804–1864) tale 'The Birth-Mark', first published in the March 1843 issue of *The Pioneer. A Literary and Critical Magazine* (Boston), edited by James Russell Lowell, and later collected in part 1 of Hawthorne's *Mosses from an Old Manse* (London, 1846):

---

26 That distinction appears to belong to the anonymous author of a story called 'A Soiree at Monsieur Guizot's', published in *The New Monthly Magazine*, vol. 60, no. 24 (Dec. 1840), 441–47, with, on p. 442: 'His was no vulgar grief ; but the long, pale, intellectual face of the Christian philosopher—resembling a cast of sorrowing marble, yet with an eye full of subdued but living disappointment—can never be forgotten by those who, like myself, witnessed the scene.' The story also ran in the Boston-based edition of that magazine, where Hawthorne could have encountered the phrase 'pale, intellectual face'.

> With his vast strength, his shaggy hair, his smoky aspect, and the indescribable earthiness that incrusted him, [Aminadab] seemed to represent man's physical nature ; while Aylmer's slender figure, and pale, intellectual face, were no less apt a type of the spiritual element.

But seven decades and many pale, intellectual faces later, Joyce appears to have read and echoed a more recent instance of the phrase in the prolific and popular British writer of sensational fiction Edgar Wallace's (1875–1932) novel *The Man Who Knew* (London and Boston, 1918)—whose central character is a detective investigating the death in London of a South African diamond magnate—with, in chap. 6 ('The Man Who Knew'), on p. 122 of the Boston edition, the following passage:

> The girl's mind was in a ferment. An ordinary meeting had developed so tumultuously that she had lost her command of the situation. A hundred thoughts ran riot through her mind. She felt as though she were an arbitrator deciding between two men, of both of whom she was fond, and, even at that moment, there intruded into her mental vision a picture of Jasper Cole, with his pale, intellectual face and his grave, dark, eyes.

Uly 13.421–22: a haunting sorrow

Pointing, perhaps, to an early instance of the phrase in Whittier's poem 'The Prophecy of Samuel Sewall' (1859), lines 21–32:

> Touching and sad, a tale is told,
> Like a penitent hymn of the Psalmist old,
> Of the fast which the good man lifelong kept
> With a haunting sorrow that never slept,
> As the circling year brought round the time
> Of an error that left the sting of crime,
> When he sat on the bench of the witchcraft courts,
> With the laws of Moses and Hale's Reports,
> And spake, in the name of both, the word
> That gave the witch's neck to the cord,
> And piled the oaken planks that pressed
> The feeble life from the warlock's breast !

But 'a haunting sorrow' also occurs from time to time in Victorian fiction, including in novels by, respectively, Edward Bulwer Lytton and the English novelist Mary Elizabeth Carter (1853–1935).

In the former, *Kenelm Chillingly: His Adventures and Opinions* (London, 1875), Bulwer Lytton writes, midway through the first paragraph of book 8, chap. 9, pp. 446–47:

> They were friends who had chanced to meet abroad—unexpectedly—joined company, and travelled together for many months, chiefly in the East. They had been but a few days in Naples. The elder of the two had important affairs in England which ought to have summoned him back long since. But he did not let his friend know this ; his affairs seemed to him less important than the duties he owed to one for whom he entertained that deep and noble love which is something stronger than brotherly, for with brotherly affection it combines gratitude and reverence. He knew, too, that his friend was oppressed by a haunting sorrow, of which the cause was divined by one, not revealed by the other.

In the latter, *Mrs. Severn. A Novel.* (London, 1889), the phrase occurs in vol. 1 (of 3), chap. 8 ('Sin the Traveller'), p. 155, reading in part: 'Years ago sunbeams had been in her limpid blue eyes too. But now they were sad, a haunting sorrow and a furtive fear brooded there.'

Uly 13.422–23: She would have given worlds to know what it was.

One pre-*Ulysses* instance of the phrase 'She would have given worlds to know'—here referring to Gerty MacDowell's wish to know the source of what seems to her the haunting sorrow on Bloom's face—which proliferated in popular literature on both sides of the pond in the second half of the nineteenth century and beyond, occurs in the English novelist Annette Marie Maillard's (1812–1890) *Miles Tremenhere* (London, 1853), vol. 1 (of 2), chap. 22, p. 295: 'There was a calm dignity about him which she had never before seen. She would have given worlds to know what he alluded to—what he had heard.'

Another such instance: in the American novelist Henry Sydnor Harrison's (1880–1930) *Queed* (Boston, New York, and London, 1911)—by some accounts the fourth-best-selling book in America in that year—chap. 13, p. 158, of the London edition:

> Sharlee made no reply. She had no idea that the young man's dismissal from the *Post* had been a crucifixion to him, an unendurable

infamy upon his virginal pride of intellect. She had no conception of his powers of self-control, which happened to be far greater than her own, and she would have given worlds to know what he was thinking at that moment.

Uly 13.439–41: Then mayhap he would [...] love her, his ownest girlie, for herself alone.

An early and rare instance of the phrase 'ownest girlie' occurred in a humorous poem called 'What Bliss!' by the American novelist, poet, and short-story writer Lurana W. Sheldon (1862–1945), printed in a handful of American and Canadian periodicals in late 1907 and early 1908, whose third stanza reads: 'And then—oh, well, | If I must tell! | Your own-y ownest girlie | In coat and hood, | All tucked in good, | And warned to "come home early."'

But a second such instance that Joyce is far more likely to have seen occurs in the first stanza of a song by the Dublin-born American composer and conductor Victor Herbert (1859–1924), written in 1908, included in his operetta *The Rose of Algeria* (1909) with book and lyrics by Glen Mac Donough (1870–1924), and called 'Ask Her While the Band is Playing':

> If you adore a frosty maid
> And are afraid
> Your love to speak
>
> If when you meet your ownest girl
> Your senses whirl
> Your knees grow weak
>
> This is, I think, the thing for you
> At once to do
> To end your doubt
> Try at a ball
> To tell her all
> And let the music help you out.

Uly 13.511: a radiant little vision

An early, possibly the earliest, instance of this phrase—other than the work's initial publication in 1889 in the extra Christmas number of

The Quiver—occurred in *Frances Kane's Fortune* (London, 1890), by the Anglo-Irish writer of girls' stories Elizabeth Thomasina Meade Smith, as 'L. T. Meade' (1844–1914). In the book version of Kane's novel, the phrase occurs twice, first in chap. 14 ("I Hate the Squire."), reading, on p. 70: 'The lawyer was at home, and the pretty, excitable little girl was quickly admitted into his presence. Mr. Spens thought he had seldom seen a more radiant little vision than this white-robed, eager, childish creature—childish and yet womanly just then, with both purpose and desire in her face.'; and again in chap. 16 ("Sweetly Romantic"), p. 80: '" Sit down, my dear, sit down. You really are a radiant little vision. It is really most entertaining to me to see anything so fresh and pretty. I must congratulate you on the damask roses you wear in your cheeks, my pretty one."'

Uly 13.548–49: he spoke in measured accents

While the highlighted phrase or versions of it occur several times elsewhere, Joyce seems most likely to have encountered it in, and perhaps borrowed it from, Hawthorne's widely read tale 'Dr. Heidegger's Experiment'—first published anonymously as 'The Fountain of Youth' in the January 1837 issue of *The Knickerbocker Magazine* (New York), then collected in vol. 1 (of 2) of his *Twice-Told Tales* (Boston, 1837), with, on p. 328:

> Now he rattled forth full-throated sentences about patriotism, national glory, and the people's right ; now he muttered some perilous stuff or other, in a sly and doubtful whisper, so cautiously that even his own conscience could scarcely catch the secret ; and now, again, he spoke in measured accents, and a deeply deferential tone, as if a royal ear were listening to his well-turned periods.

A subsequent instance of 'in measured accents' minus 'he spoke' occurred in Mayne Reid's *The Wood-Rangers; or, The Trappers of Sonora* (see the entry above on *Uly* 13.118–19), chap. 50 ('Lynch Law'), p. 392:

> " Blood for blood," continued Fabian ; " a death for a death !"
> Then he rose, and addressing Don Antonio in measured accents, said : " You have shed blood and committed murder. It shall therefore be done to you as you have done to others. God commanded it to be so."

Uly 13.549: there was a suspicion of a quiver in the mellow tones

Instances of 'a suspicion of a quiver' occur pre-Joyce several times, most notably in novels by Margaret Oliphant; by the English author of historical novels, moral tales, and other pieces Grace Stebbing (1840–1936); and, in one translation, by Ivan Turgenev.

In Oliphant's *The Son Of His Father* (London, editions of 1886 and 1887), the phrase occurs on p. 290 of the one-volume 1886 edition and in vol. 3 (of 3), p. 150, of the 1887, reading in chap. 10 ('Mother and Son') of both:

> Now it was different. Her fine nostrils moved, dilating and trembling, with a sensitiveness which was a revelation to her son ; her eyes shone ; her mouth, which was so much more delicate than he had been aware, closed with an impassioned force, in which, however, there was the same suspicion of a quiver.

In Grace Stebbing's *That Bother of a Boy* (London, 1888), the phrase occurs in chap. 5 ('Table-Cloth Maps, Done in Brown'), p. 72:

> Ted raised his head with a sudden jerk.
> " But I'll never abuse you, Uncle Edward," he blurted out, hastily.
> " You're a brick. I thought you'd box my ears and—and—" —and there was just the suspicion of a quiver in the sturdy young voice—" I almost wish you had. That's a horrid mess on the clean cloth. If I knew a bit how to wash, I'd try to get it out for you."
> " Pray don't then," said his uncle with a rather husky laugh.

In Turgenev's novel *Smoke* (1868), as translated by the American Isabel F. Hapgood (New York, 1903; London, 1905)—but not as translated by Constance Garnett (London, 1896)—the phrase occurs in a long paragraph on p. 124 (ellipses in the original):

> Irína extended both her hands to him. Litvínoff pressed them warmly, and did not immediately release them. . . . A mysterious something which had long ceased to exist began to stir in his heart at that soft contact. Again Irína looked him straight on the face; but this time he smiled. . . And for the first time he gazed directly and intently at her. . . Again he recognised the features, once so dear, and those deep eyes with their unusual lashes, and the little mole on the cheek, and the peculiar sweep of the hair above the brow, and her habit of curling

her lips in a certain gracious and amusing way, and of imparting to her eyebrows the suspicion of a quiver, he recognised all, all. . . But how much more beautiful she had grown ! What charm and power in the young feminine body ! And there was neither red paint, nor white, nor blackening for the eyebrows, nor powder, nor any sort of artificiality on the fresh, pure face. . . Yes, she was a real beauty !

Uly 13.564: literally worshipping at her shrine

Minus the initial intensifier, this phrase occurs, along with other appearances in various English translations of Greek and Roman myths and occasionally elsewhere, in *Heliondé; or, Adventures in the Sun* (London, 1855), a visionary, learned, science-fiction romance—published anonymously but known to have been written by the English barrister, poet, and author Sydney Whiting (1820–1875)—whose unnamed hero, vaporized by the heat of an illness, is transported to the Sun, finds it inhabited by beautiful ethereal people in a paradisal realm, falls in love with one of them, but must ultimately return to Earth. Chapter 7 ('Last But Not Least') reads on p. 322:

> When I arose in the morning, after fully determining to abandon the worship of my beautiful idol, I grieve to confess I felt more than ever disposed to begin the day by worshipping at her shrine, and I found myself plucking flowers to grace the pedestal on which the beloved image rested, while this little act of weakness was soon followed by a flood of enthusiasm overwhelming my soul, the more impetuous from the embargo I had resolved to lay upon my feelings.

A later and more down-to-earth instance of the same phrase, again minus 'literally', occurred in William Le Queux's *A Secret Service: Being Strange Tales of a Nihilist* (London, 1896), with, in chap. 5 ('Sophie Zagarovna's Secret'), p. 102:

> In more than one instance a young man, madly in love with her and enthusiastic in the cause of freedom, had journeyed to the land of his birth determined to strike a blow against Tzardom in order to secure her favour, yet, alas ! the result has been fatal—either death, or the mines. Vain, and fond of admiration, she had numbers worshipping at her shrine, yet through all the breath of scandal had never touched her. Indeed, so intensely bent was she upon her purpose, that her heart appeared steeled against love, and she treated those who paid

her court with queenly reserve. Of her parentage or real name nothing was known except that she took the oath in Petersburg and afterwards went to Switzerland, where she speedily developed into one of the most fearless of Terrorists.

Uly 13.576: scathing politeness

What seems to have been the earliest of a handful of instances of this phrase occurs in the Canadian novelist May Agnes Fleming's (1840–1880) dime-novel romance *One Night's Mystery* (New York and London, 1876), part 2, chap. 24 ('Into Marvellous Light'), p. 441 (italics in the original):

> " Well," cries the owner of the vinegar face, in a most vinegary voice, to " You Pete," who reappears : " *is* Mr. Vaughan coming or is he not ? Does he mean to keep me here all day, or—— Oh ! really, Mr. Vaughan, here you are at last ! " (this in accents of scathing politeness.) " How very good of you to condescend to come at all ! "

The phrase recurs in the English author, antiquarian, and swordsman Egerton Castle's (1858–1920) novel *Consequences* (London, 1891), vol. 2 (of 3), chap. 14 ('Dea Ex Machinâ'), p. 263:

> ' There,' said the visitor, leaning back in her chair, ' and so you are Mr. Kerr. I am glad I have found you in at last. You've just come back from Indja, haven't you ? Is that where you got that gash on your face ?'
> ' No,' returned Lewis shortly, ' it is not ; and now that you are quite at home,' with scathing politeness, ' I presume I may ask what I owe the honour of your visit to ? You appear to know a good deal about me ; but I have yet to learn whom I have the privilege to address.'

And occurs again in *Captain Desmond, V.C.* (Edinburgh and London, 1910; extensively revised as reissued, New York and London, 1914), by the English author Maud Diver (1867–1945), whose novels, short stories, biographies, and journalistic essays mostly concerned British India, where she was born. The relevant passage of chap. 29, pp. 309–10, of the 1910 edition reads:

> [Evelyn] took the cup and plate from him, still smiling, and passed on into the study. Desmond lifted his head, as she bent above the table, in a vain effort to get a glimpse of her face.

" Thank you—thank you—how good of you ! " he said, his constraint softened by a certain repressed eagerness, which gave her courage to speak her thought.

" Why am I suddenly to be discomfited by such elaborate thanks, such scathing politeness ? " she asked in a tone of valiant good-humour.

" I didn't intend it to be scathing."

Uly 13.578–79: A brief cold blaze [...] from her eyes [...] spoke volumes of scorn immeasurable

For 'scorn immeasurable' see *Japhet in Search of a Father* (London, 1836) by the English novelist, Royal Navy officer, and friend of Charles Dickens Captain [Frederick] Marryat, R. N. C. B. (1792–1848), vol. 1 (of 3), chap. 6 ("My prescriptions very effective and palatable, but I lose my patient—the feud equal to that of the Montagues and the Capulets [...]"), p. 70: 'All I can say is, that the feuds of the rival houses were most bitter — the hate intense — the mutual scorn unmeasurable.'

The phrase also occurs in the English poet F[rederick]. B[rickdale]. Doveton's (1802–1882) *Snatches of Song* (London, 1880), in the last stanza, on p. 34, of the poem 'Scorned' (italics in the original): '*One glance of scorn immeasurable, shot | From those resistless eyes— | The world grows dark—e'en Heaven is forgot— | And rapture slowly dies ! | Let me dream on—dreams do not paint her scorn, | But mock me sweetly till I wake at morn.*'; in Egerton Castle's *The Light of Scarthey: A Romance* (London, 1895), chap. 29 ('The Light Goes Out'), p. 425: 'It was with undisguised hatred and with scorn immeasurable that he now surveyed the woman who had degraded him in his own eyes.'; and in the American novelist and historian Owen Wister's (1860–1938) romantic but racist novel of the post-Civil War South *Lady Baltimore* (New York and London, 1906), chap. 10 ('High Walk and the Ladies'), p. 144 (italics in the original): '" Are such subjects as — as *stocks* " (she softly cloaked this word in scorn immeasurable) — " are such subjects mentioned in your good society at the North ? "'

Uly 13.597: one look of measured scorn

The phrase 'unmeasured scorn' occurred often pre-*Ulysses*; far less often, the phrase 'measured scorn'. One early instance of the latter: in

The Duke of Mercia, an historical drama (London, 1823), by the Anglo-Irish nobleman and poet Sir Aubrey de Vere Hunt (1788–1846)—the 'Hunt' was dropped after 1831—with, in Part the Third, at p. 126, in a soliloquy by Edric Streon, Duke of Mercia, after his political, military, and romantic rival Canute, King of the Danes, exits: 'With what a look | Of measured scorn he leaves me !—Out upon 't ! | I have borne this shame too far.'

Another instance, a decade later: near the end of the title poem of the Scottish poet and schoolmaster D[avid]. M[oncrieff]. Ferguson's (1796–1875) *Evan Bane; A Highland Legend: and Other Poems* (London, 1832), with, on p. 31: 'Again she wakes the smile—the tear— | The look of terror—glance of fear— | The measured scorn—the rising bile, | Which schoolboy's eye and lip beguile'.

But the instance of the phrase Joyce seems most likely to have known occurred in Kipling's *Kim*, chap. 12, p. 310:

> ' Yes,' said Kim, with measured scorn. ' Their stock-in-trade is a little coloured water and a very great shamelessness. Their prey are broken-down kings and overfed Bengalis. Their profit is in children — who are not born.'

Uly 13.600: a towering rage

SMT write that Joyce's phrase is 'From Clarence E[dward]. Mulford's (American writer, 1883–1956) novel *Bar–20 Days* [Chicago, 1911]: "'Ahoy, men!' roared the captain in a towering rage."' Wherever the phrase is or may be 'from', it also occurs elsewhere and widely pre-Joyce, including in the three examples cited below.

First of the three, in Dickens's *David Copperfield*, chap. 42 ('Mischief'), p. 578, midway through a quarrel between David and Uriah Heep:

> There was another long pause. His eyes, as he looked at me, seemed to take every shade of colour that could make eyes ugly.
>
> " Copperfield," he said, removing his hand from his cheek, " you have always gone against me. I know you always used to be against me at Mr. Wickfield's."
>
> " You may think what you like," said I, still in a towering rage. " If it is not true, so much the worthier you."
>
> " And yet I always liked you, Copperfield ! " he rejoined.

Second of the three: in the American novelist F[rancis]. Marion Crawford's (1854–1909) *Saracinesca* (Edinburgh and London, 1887)—which was also serialized in *Blackwood's* from May 1886 to April 1887—vol. 3 (of 3), chap. 34, pp. 303–04:

> On the following evening, without any warning, old Saracinesca arrived, and was warmly greeted. After dinner Giovanni told him the story of Del Ferice's escape. Thereupon the old gentleman flew into a towering rage, swearing and cursing in a most characteristic manner, but finally declaring that to arrest spies was the work of spies, and that Giovanni had behaved like a gentleman, as of course he could not help doing, seeing that he was his own son.

And last of the three, in Henrietta Eliza Vaughan Stannard's, as 'John Strange Winter' (see note on lines 13.21–22) novel *A Born Soldier* (London, 1894)—published in America as *Every Inch A Soldier* (Philadelphia, 1894)—chap. 30 ('A Bright Idea'), p. 246, in which Jill asks Jervis if he was not angry with Katey:

> " Yes, I did feel rather angry with her this morning," said Jervis, " because I thought—really I don't want to speak against her, I am awfully in love with her—but I felt that she had made me suffer enough, and that she might try to look at the matter from my side a little. I was rather angry with her this morning."
> " In fact, you were in a towering rage," said Jill, who wanted to get at the rights of things.
> " I never get into towering rages," said Jervis. " I wasn't in a towering rage when that ill-conditioned young lout, Sylvester, started abusing me. Sometimes, I wish I could get into a rage. That sort of thing lets the steam off, you know."

Uly 13.616: Gerty stifled a smothered exclamation

Pre-Joyce instances of 'a smothered exclamation' proliferated in the mid- to late-nineteenth century, occurring in novels and tales by, among dozens of others, Mrs. Oliphant, Mrs. Molesworth, Marie Corelli, and John Strange Winter. One of the earliest instances of the phrase could be found in the English novelist and poet Charlotte Brontë's (1816–1855) second novel—after *Jane Eyre. An Autobiography.* (London, 1847)—*Shirley* (London, 1849), vol. 2 (of 3), chap. 6 ('The School-Feast'), pp. 145–46:

> Caroline's ears yet rung with that thrilling whisper, " I expect Mr. Moore," her heart yet beat and her cheek yet glowed with it, when a note from the organ pealed above the confused hum of the place. Dr. Boultby, Mr. Helstone, and Mr. Hall rose, so did all present, and grace was sung to the accompaniment of the music ; and then tea began. She was kept too busy with her office for a while to have leisure for looking round, but the last cup being filled, she threw a restless glance over the room. There were some ladies and several gentlemen standing about yet unaccommodated with seats : amidst a group she recognised her spinster friend, Miss Mann, whom the fine weather had tempted, or some urgent friend had persuaded, to leave her drear solitude for one hour of social enjoyment. Miss Mann looked tired of standing : a lady in a yellow bonnet brought her a chair. Caroline knew well that " chapeau en satin jaune ;" she knew the black hair, and the kindly, though rather opinionated and froward-looking face under it ; she knew that " robe de soie noire ;" she knew even that " schal gris de lin ;" she knew, in short, Hortense Moore, and she wanted to jump up and run to her and kiss her—to give her one embrace for her own sake, and two for her brother's. She half rose, indeed, with a smothered exclamation, and perhaps—for the impulse was very strong—she would have run across the room, and actually saluted her, but a hand replaced her in her seat, and a voice behind her whispered :—
> " Wait till after tea, Lina, and then I'll bring her to you."

One of the later instances: in an anonymous, revised translation from the French of Alexandre Dumas's 1844 classic *The Count of Monte-Cristo* (New York, 1894), vol. 1, chap. 6 ('The Deputy Procureur du Roi'), p. 50, where the villainous public prosecutor Villefort is speaking to a group that includes his doomed wife Renée:

> "[...]Besides, one requires the excitement of being hateful in the eyes of the accused, in order to lash one's self into a state of sufficient vehemence and power. I would not choose to see the man against whom I pleaded smile, as though in mockery of my words. No ; my pride is to see the accused pale, agitated, and as though beaten out of all composure by the fire of my eloquence." Renée uttered a smothered exclamation.

Uly 13.624: the gathering twilight

See, in the English Anglican priest and poet John Keble's (1792–1866) *The Christian Year: Thoughts in Verse for the Sundays and Holidays Throughout the Year* (London, 1827), the poem under the heading 'Twenty-First Sunday After Trinity'—beginning 'The morning mist is clear'd away'—where stanza 6, on p. 264, reads: 'That is the heart for watchman true | Waiting to see what God will do, | As o'er the Church the gathering twilight falls : | No more he strains his wistful eye, | If chance the golden hours be nigh, | By youthful Hope seen beaming round her walls.'

The phrase occurs twice in George MacDonald's novel *Donal Grant* (London, 1883), where, on pp. 269–70, section 3 of his poem 'The Old Garden' reads:

> I stood in the gathering twilight,
>   In a gently blowing wind ;
> And the house looked half uneasy,
>   Like one that was left behind.
>
> The roses had lost their redness,
>   And cold the grass had grown ;
> At roost were the pigeons and peacock,
>   And the dial was dead gray stone.
>
> The world by the gathering twilight
>   In a gauzy dusk was clad ;
> It went in through my eyes to my spirit,
>   And made me a little sad.
>
> Grew and gathered the twilight,
>   And filled my heart and brain ;
> The sadness grew more than sadness,
>   And turned to a gentle pain.
>
> Browned and brooded the twilight,
>   And sank down through the calm,
> Till it seemed for some human sorrows
>   There could not be any balm.

And recurs in Constance Garnett's translation (London, 1914) of the Russian novelist Fyodor Dostoevsky's (1821–1881) *Crime and Punishment* (1867), part 2, chap. 6, with, on pp. 155–56:

> Raskolnikov walked straight to X—— Bridge, stood in the middle, and leaning both elbows on the rail stared into the distance. On parting with Razumihin, he felt so much weaker that he could scarcely reach this place. He longed to sit or lie down somewhere in the street. Bending over the water, he gazed mechanically at the last pink

flush of the sunset, at the row of houses growing dark in the gathering twilight, at one distant attic window on the left bank, flashing as though on fire in the last rays of the setting sun, at the darkening water of the canal, and the water seemed to catch his attention.

Uly 13.637–38: it did not err on the side of luxury

An early instance of the phrase occurs in *The Christian Lady's Magazine* (London)—edited by the English writer and novelist Charlotte Elizabeth Tonna (1790–1846) as 'Charlotte Elizabeth'—vol. 13 (June 1840), p. 524, in the second paragraph of a letter to the editor 'On Feasting,' signed 'A.T.N.':

> I am aware that this is open to much argument, and far be it from me to take an ascetic or one-sided view of this question ; but do we not all vastly err on the side of luxury, and are not our feasts prepared as though no such words as these [referring to Luke xiii 12–14] existed in that book which we profess to be our rule of life ?

Other instances of the phrase occur in *The Wide World Magazine: An Illustrated Monthly of True Narrative: Adventure[,] Travel[,] Customs and Sport* (London), vol. 1, no. 4 (July 1898), in an essay by the U.S.-born, later British subject, journalist, and engineer Thomas Gaskell Allen Jr. (1868–c. 1955) entitled 'From St. Paul's to Pekin by Rail' reading, on p. 387: 'It is not often that employers err on the side of luxury in providing for their workmen.'; and in Frederic Martyn's *A Holiday in Gaol* (London, 1903), chap. 11 ('Remand Diet'), p. 90: 'This diet does not err on the side of luxury, and few people get used to it during their stay at Brixton if they happen to be making their first acquaintance with it'.

Uly 13.655: and gild his days with happiness

The lineage of this phrase may be traced at least as far back as 1663, to the lyrics for a song—collected and published by one Sergeant-Major P[ayne]. Fisher (1616–1693) in his *Poems On Several Choice and Various Subjects. Occasionally Composed By An Eminent Author* (London, 1663)—called 'An HYMENÆUM, Or Bridal-Sonet', written by Mr Will Webb, and with a first chorus, printed on pp. 42–43, that reads (italics in the original): 'May all felicity betide | This Princely Bridegroom and his Bride. | May those Delights this Morn shall bring | Be *endless*, as their

Nuptial *Ring*. ‖ May they be constant, and exceed | Each others Wishes, Hopes and Creed. | May the three Regions of the Air | Pour showres of Blessings on this Pair, | May *Sol* and *Cynthia* with their Rays | *Silver* their Nights, and *Gild* their Days.'

Another early instance occurs in *The Rose, a Comic Opera in Two Acts, as it is performed at the Theatre-Royal, in Drury-Lane, the Words by a Gentleman Commoner of Oxford. The Music by Doctor* [*Thomas Augustine*] *Arne* (London, 1773), with, in Act 2, sc. 3, p. 19, Mrs Violet to her daughter Miss Serina: 'Sweet girl, I am your convert.—But how will your wounded sensibility bear up against the affecting loss of the only man who has the power to gild your future days with happiness ?'

The phrase occurs once again, again nearly verbatim, in the English novelist Lady Charlotte Campbell Bury's (1775–1861) *The History of a Flirt. Related by Herself.* (London, 1840), vol. 3 (of 3), chap. 5, p. 150:

> Mrs. Fortescue's gay address and lively conversation had amused
> Captain Bates till he loved as fervently as seventy years of age
> could love ; and even if the admiration he felt might not bear that
> designation, still his mind was filled by her image, and he had flattered
> himself her attentions spoke interest, and might possibly extend to a
> friendship and union which would gild his days with long-resigned
> happiness[.]

And, as a final example, in Ernest Alfred Vizetelly's preface to his translation of Emile Zola's novel *Travail* (Paris, 1901), as *Work* (London, 1901) which preface concludes, on p. vii (italics in the original):

> But then it is M. Zola's desire that man should *labour* no more ; he does
> not wish him to groan beneath excessive toil—he simply desires that he
> should *work*, in health and in gaiety, with the help of science to lighten
> his task, and a just apportionment of wealth and happiness to gild his
> days until he takes his rest.

Uly 13.690–91: a light broke in upon her

SMT write that, like 'a towering rage' in *Uly* 13.600, this phrase is 'from' Clarence E. Mulford's *Bar–20 Days* (1911): 'A light broke in on him then and he wondered how soon it would be his turn to pay tribute to Neptune'. But 'a light broke in upon her' occurred verbatim at least twice before Joyce had occasion to use it.

The first of these two instances: in the short story 'An Episode in High Life' by Grant Allen as 'J. Arbuthnot Wilson', published in *Belgravia*, vol. 48, Holiday Number for 1882, 59–76, with, on p. 72: '" What nonsense, Surrey ! " cried Gladys, colouring up to her eyebrows in a second : " how dare you say such a thing about mamma ? " But a light broke in upon her suddenly all the same, and a number of little unnoticed circumstances flashed back at once upon her memory with a fresh flood of meaning.'

And the second: in the novel *Daggryning* (Stockholm, 1902) by Mathilda Malling (1864–1942), translated from the Swedish as *Daybreak* and published in *Tales, A Magazine of the World's Best Fiction* (New York), vol. 32, no. 1 (June 1906), 1–75, with, on p. 43: '"Only for that reason," Sarah muttered slowly, doubting. And yet a light broke in upon her. The whole question suddenly seemed much simpler and clearer than she could ever have thought with all her conjecturing hither and thither.'

An early version of the phrase, and perhaps its origin, occurred in Byron's poem 'The Prisoner of Chillon' first collected in *The Prisoner of Chillon and Other Poems* (London, 1816), line 251 of which reads 'A light broke in upon my brain'. Many versions of the phrase followed over the next century, making it difficult or impossible to determine which of them, if any—verbatim or not—was the one that Joyce had in mind.

Uly 13.691: silent as the grave

One notable pre-*Ulysses* instance of this phrase occurs in Schiller's five-act tragedy *Don Karlos, Infant von Spanien* (Leipzig, 1787) as translated from the German by R. Dillon Boylan. In Boylan's *Don Carlos* (London, 1872), Act 1, sc. 2, p. 10, Carlos says to Roderigo:

> 'Tis now eight months,
> Eight maddening months, since the King summoned me
> Home from my studies,—since I have been doom'd
> To look on her,—adore her, day by day,
> And all the while be silent as the grave !

Another such instance: in the English poet and playwright Robert Browning's (1812–1889) historical drama *King Victor and King Charles* (London, 1842)—based on events in the Kingdom of Sardinia in 1730–32 involving the aged King Victor Amadeus II, who has abdicated, and his son King Charles Emmanuel III—in the section called 'Second Year, 1731—King Charles. Part I', lines 188–90, Victor speaking:

> Rather shake it off at Turin,
> King Victor ! Say : to Turin—yes, or no ?
> 'T is this relentless noonday-lighted chamber,
> Lighted like life but silent as the grave,
> That disconcerts me.

And a third: in the Irish writer and botanical illustrator Mrs [Edith Osborne] Blake's (1846–1926) *The Realities of Freemasonry* (London, 1879), with, in chap. 9, on p. 198, a portion of her account of the order's initiation rite: 'The canvas is rolled over the novice, the three ruffians retire, the lodge is darkened, and all remains as silent as the grave, till at length the Master strikes twelve times on a triangle or bell.'

Uly 13.733–34: She would fain have cried to him chokingly

Lacking only the word 'chokingly', an early, otherwise verbatim instance of Joyce's phrase occurred in *Edith Heron, or, The Earl and the Countess* (London, 1862), a novel by the British author of penny dreadful fiction James Malcolm Rymer (1814–1884). In vol. 2, chap. 209 ('Captain Heron Revisits His Old Haunt at Epping Forest, and Meets with a Surprise') reads, on p. 95:

> " Nay, Edith, look not scared at a visit to those green old haunts where we have passed some happy days. The owl, the bat, and the timid hare alone inhabit the darksome recesses of our beautiful and sylvan home."
> Edith sighed.
> A feeling of unknown peril took possession of her, and she would fain have cried to him, " Go not forth to night."
> She saw, however, that he was bent upon the enterprise, and she would rather he went with her prayers to accompany him, than detain him until perhaps some more unpropitious time.

Another early pre-*Ulysses* instance of the same phrase, lacking only the same word but also otherwise verbatim, occurs in the English lawyer and novelist Sir Henry Stewart Cunningham's (1832–1920) *Late Laurels* (London, 1864), vol. 2 (of 2), chap. 14 ('Fire!'), pp. 276–77:

> A plank was within her reach, smooth, yielding, and hard to grasp, she clutched it with the agony of a death convulsion ; it slipped from her hand, and again she was sinking into some infinite depth—black, mysterious, stifling ; wave upon wave pressing her mercilessly down, more and more utterly shutting out light and air : and Erle stood over her and held a hand, as if to help, which, as she struggled towards it, ever just escaped her. She would fain have cried to him, but strength, voice, breath, had failed ; she was choking, fainting, dying—mercy ! mercy !

From April 1863 to February 1864, Cunningham's novel was also serialized in *Fraser's Magazine for Town and Country* (London), where, in vol. 69, the chapter—renumbered 27—appeared in the February 1864 issue.

Uly 13.734–35: to feel his lips laid on her white brow

Prior versions of the phrase occur in, among other works, 'The French Peasant Girl,' signed by 'E.Y.', in *The Young Lady's Magazine of Theology, History, Philosophy and General Knowledge, embracing Literature, Science, and Art* (London), vol. 1 (1838), pp. 269–70:

> With a full heart the young girl knelt down to receive her father's blessing, a blessing not of the lips, but of the heart. André was moved against his feelings and better judgment to consent, and pressing his lips on her white brow with passionate tenderness, he said in a scarcely audible whisper—
> " Pauline, no other kiss must efface this first, this pure pledge of our mutual affection, until we meet again."
> The blushing girl wept her vows and promises upon his bosom.

And, with its authorship attributed to the otherwise anonymous 'B...... and A......'—though clearly based on Fanny Burney's verse tragedy of the same name (1790)—*Edwy and Elgiva: A Romance of the Olden Time* (London, 1868), chap. 16 ('The Queen's Decision'), p. 95: 'Edwy clasped Elgiva's hand in his, and threw his arm around her. He gazed fondly at her beautiful face, and pressed his lips on her white brow, and the long dishevelled curls, which had been blown about so rudely by the night wind.'

Uly 13.735: a little strangled cry

One of the many prior instances of the cry to which Joyce refers—'the cry of a young girl's love, a little strangled cry, wrung from her, that cry that has rung through the ages'—occurs in the English novelist Angelica Selby's (1858–1917) *In the Sunlight: A Tale of Mentone* (London, 1892) with, in chap. 7, on p. 81 (italics and ellipsis in the original):

> " Ivy !"—how the words hiss between her clenched teeth—" Ivy, do you live to say it ? Stand up and say it is not true ! Say it *shall* not be ! Say, I will tear my heart in all its living passion from my being. I will trample it down. I will conquer it ; it *shall not* conquer me. I can force it under the iron keeping of my own will. I will bury the existence of this love—*love*, ah !" with a little strangled cry, and covering her burning cheeks with the poor little trembling hands, " I have said it, and it is true, O God ! it is *true* ! . . .["]

Another instance: in the short story 'Lucretia', by the English novelist K[atharine]. Douglas King (1869–1901), first published in *The Yellow Book*, vol. 10 (July 1896), 223–44, with, on p. 237: 'He called her Lucy, and Mrs. Burnett leaped to her feet, and with a little, strangled cry, threw herself upon his breast. His arms met tightly round her, and he held her thus pressed to him, for a minute, without speaking.'

And a third: in *Esther's Charge: A Story for Girls* (Edinburgh, 1899), one of the three hundred and fifty-odd titles produced, under her own and various other names, by the English novelist E[velyn]. Everett-Green (1856–1932), with, in chap. 1 ('A Little Manager'), p. 20: '" Hallo, madam ! and whither away so very fast ? " cried a great deep voice from somewhere out of the heart of the earth ; and Esther stopped short, with a little strangled cry of terror, for it was Mr. Trelawny's voice, and yet he was nowhere to be seen.'

Uly 13.742–43: a pathetic little glance of piteous protest

Joyce may have borrowed 'a pathetic little glance' from Mrs Hungerford's novel *Doris* (London, 1885), chap. 6, p. 82:

Just at this moment she is standing in the empty hall, with Brabazon's arm around her. Something had lain heavily upon her mind all the way home, that she feels now must be got off it before she goes to bed, or sleep will refuse to visit her eyelids. She had cast a pathetic little glance at her lover, as they all went towards the library, a while since, that had made him execute several deep manœvres, the result of which may be seen in the fact, that they two are standing out here now, together, and—alone!

Or perhaps from the British novelist and science writer Agnes Giberne's (1845–1939) *Enid's Silver Bond* (London, 1898) with, in chap. 2 ('By The Roadside'), p. 16: 'He cast a pathetic little glance at Enid from under his long black lashes, to see whether her pity were moved. Apparently not.'

As for 'piteous protest', Joyce may have crossed paths with that phrase in (among other mostly nineteenth-century fiction) Ouida's previously cited *Folle-Farine*, vol. 2, book 4, chap. 4, p. 230:

> Hence, pity entered very little into his thoughts at any time ; the perpetual torture of life did indeed perplex him, as it perplexes every thinking creature, with wonder at the universal bitterness that taints all creation, at the universal death whereby all forms of life are nurtured, at the universal anguish of all existence which daily and nightly assails the unknown God in piteous protest at the inexorable laws of inexplicable miseries and mysteries.

in the English actress and author Florence Warden's (1857–1929) novel *A Witch of the Hills* (London, 1888), vol. 1 (of 2), chap. 6, pp. 123–24:

> I kept a small whip to separate the combatants on these occasions, but I only dared use it very sparingly ; as, though its effect upon To-to's coarser nature was salutary in the extreme in reducing him to instant love and obedience, as the boot of the costermonger does his wife, the gentler Ta-ta would look up at me with such piteous protest in her dark eyes that I felt a brute for the next half hour.

or in the British author of romantic fiction Muriel Hine's (1874–1949) first novel *Half In Earnest* (London, 1910), part 1 ('Love in the Sunshine'), chap. 11, p. 106: 'They had dined together in a moody silence, and afterwards she had gone early to bed, pleading fatigue, with a last look of piteous protest at the man she loved.'

Uly 13.745: young guileless eyes

Among the multitude of guileless eyes found in pre-Joyce, English-language fiction, the phrase *young* guileless eyes seems to have occurred only once: in 'At the Stuffed-Animal House', the last of six stories collected—after its initial publication in the May 1903 issue of *Harper's Magazine* (New York)—in the American author and poet Margaret Wade Campbell Deland's (1857–1945) *Dr. Lavendar's People* (New York and London, 1903), with, on p. 327:

> " Don't come into my shop," Miss Harriet used to say, laughing and impatient, when Miss Annie would follow her into the room in the barn where she did her work—" don't come in here, and then you won't see things that hurt your feelings."
>
> But Annie, smoothing her hair back from her temples with a curious, girlish gesture, would only shake her head and sidle closer to her sister, the young, guileless eyes in the withered face full of protest and appeal.

The same phrase seems also to have occurred pre-Joyce only once in a work of non-fiction: the personal memoir *Tyne Folk: Masks, Faces, and Shadows* (London, 1896) by the prominent English Congregational preacher, theologian, and author Joseph Parker (1830–1902), whose portrait of his long-time friend the sheep farmer and Latinist Ralph Culver explains, on p. 199, what had led a handsome local youth named Darley Fairbank to elope with his daughter Kitty:

> He had a "fetching" smile, and he could use his eyes significantly, and could sometimes turn round to watch departing [female] figures. I know it. And Darley knew it. And feminine Linstead was aware of it. Yet all the time Darley's heart was at Fishbrook, one pair of young guileless eyes perpetually arresting the vision of his heart.

Uly 13.746: A fair unsullied soul

Joyce's 'fair unsullied soul' seems to have previously occurred verbatim only twice, the first instance in the twenty-one-stanza 'Address to His Majesty King George the Fourth, for the Repeal of the Insurrection Act in Ireland,' by the weaver-poet Joseph Carson (fl. 1830)—known in his time as 'the Bard of Kilpike', from Seapatrick, near Banbridge, in County

Down—published in his *Poems, Odes, Songs, and Satires* (Newry, 1831). Its twelfth stanza, on p. 65, reads: '(Poor, hapless, injured Caroline ! | Thy fair unsullied soul divine, | In bright etherial rays will shine, | When all thy foes | In dark abyss will growl and whine, | Absorb'd in woes.)'

The second instance: in *Alice, or The Wages of Sin* (New York, 1883), a short novel by the American editor and writer Frederic Werden Pangborn (1855–1934), with, in chap. 13 ('"Be sure your sin will find you out."'), p. 114:

> So let them rest: she the fair, unsullied soul, so fit to live, so fit to die, prepared for either state; he the noble and the ignoble, who thought that repentance alone without reparation could atone for wilful sin, and of whom it is best to say [quoting lines 125–128 of Gray's 'Elegy Written in a Country Churchyard']: '" No further seek his merits to disclose, | Or draw his frailties from their dread abode | (There they alike in trembling hope repose), | The bosom of his Father and his God."'

Uly 13.764: her sweet flowerlike face

One of the several pre-Joyce instances of 'sweet flowerlike face' occurs in *The Glorious Return: A Story of the Vaudois* (London, 1889), by the England-born, Ireland-raised author Clara Lavinia Corfield (1846–1916) as 'Crona Temple', published by the Religious Tract Society (London, 1880), and commemorating the return from exile, in 1689, of the Waldensian Church. The phrase occurs near the beginning of chap. 13, in a passage reading:

> As the notes of Madeleine's evening psalm died down on the hill-side, a figure raised itself from behind a jutting crag and crept stealthily off in the darkness. The two women, well used to the desolate mountains, slept serene and safe in the hut. Renée's head rested on her foster-mother's arm, and over the sweet flower-like face there was spread the reflection of the peace that passeth understanding.

Another instance—or rather, three instances—may be found in a single novel, *A Woman's Temptation*, by Charlotte M. Brame as 'Bertha M. Clay' (see the entry above on *Uly* 9.345–46), serialized in *The Family Reader* (London), 12 June to 16 Sept. 1875; then issued widely in book form. The first of the three instances: in chap. 8 ('"What Can It Be?"'), p. 58, with 'If she would only look away. But the lovely gray eyes and the sweet flower-like face were turned to him.'; the second: in chap. 11 ('The Passing Cloud'), p. 80, with 'He contented himself by kissing the sweet, flower-like face, and spending the rest of the sunshiny morning in talking about love.'; and the third: in chap. 14 ('"I Shall Die If I Lose You."'), p. 93, with '"Do I please you ?" she asked, quietly, looking so winning as she spoke, he could not help clasping his arms round her, and kissing the sweet, flower-like face.'

The phrase also occurs in the Irish poet and songwriter Marie Hedderwick Browne's (1857–c. 1892) *A Spray of Lilac, and Other Poems and Songs* (London, 1892), in the first line of the penultimate stanza of the poem 'A Mother's Grief', on pp. 6–8:

> Whenever a child's sweet flowerlike face
>   Met mine, a sickness would o'er me creep,
> And I'd turn wild eyes to the lonely place
>   Where she was lying alone—asleep.
> At strife was I with the world, and God
>   Had drawn around Him an angry cloud ;
> Earth held no green but the churchyard sod,
>   And the daisies wore the gleam of a shroud.

Uly 13.805: on the track of the secret

Based on its title, Thornton, Gifford, SMT, and others cite Frederick Diodati Thompson's *In the Track of the Sun: Diary of a Globe Trotter* (London, 1893), and note that Bloom is said in the novel to own a copy. Joyce's phrase, however, occurs verbatim elsewhere: in chap. 1 ('A Mission is Proposed') of the Scottish novelist, historian, and unionist politician John Buchan's (1875–1940) wartime espionage thriller *Greenmantle* (London and Boston, 1916), with, on p. 19:

> " I can't tell you where you'll get on the track of the secret, but I can put a limit to the quest. You won't find it east of the Bosporus—not yet. It is still in Europe. It may be in Constantinople, or in Thrace. It may be farther west. But it is moving eastwards. If you are in time you may cut into its march to Constantinople. That much I can tell you. The secret is known in Germany, too, to those whom it concerns. It is in Europe that the seeker must search—at present."

Uly 13.851–52: that little limping devil

Joyce is here referring to Gerty MacDowell, who Bloom, after their erotic encounter at a distance on Sandymount strand, has just discovered is lame. But the highlighted phrase may owe something to one or another of four antecedent works.

The earliest of the four: the prolific and much admired (by Cervantes and Lope de Vega, among others) Spanish playwright Luis Vélez de Guevara's (1579–1644) only novel, *El Diablo Cojuelo* (the lame or limping devil), first published in Madrid in 1641, a novel known for its fantastic plot and complex wordplay; the second, partly inspired by Guevara's novel, the French novelist and playwright Alain René Lesage's (1668–1747) novel *Le Diable Boiteux* (the lame devil), first published in Paris in 1707, then in London and in English in 1708 as *Le Diable Boiteux: or, the Devil Upon Two Sticks*, later dramatized for the London stage by Henry Fielding (1768); the third, the comic opera *Der krumme Teufel* (The crooked devil) inspired in turn by Lesage's novel, the Austrian composer Joseph Haydn's (1732–1809) first opera (1751–52), in Singspiel style, commissioned by its librettist, the prominent comic actor Joseph Felix von Kurz; and the fourth, Goethe's *Faust: A Tragedy* (1880), which in Act 3, sc. 2 of the play as translated from German into English verse by John Stuart Blackie of the University of Edinburgh, second edition (London, 1880), has Siebel say to Faust—'*Softly, eyeing* MEPHISTOPHELES *from the one side*'—'What! does the fellow limp upon one foot?'

Uly 13.858–59: Little sweetheart come and kiss me

Unremarked by Thornton, Gifford, and SMT, as well as by Hodgart and Worthington, Bowen, and Bauerle, Joyce's phrase matches verbatim the title of the popular song 'Little Sweetheart Come and Kiss Me', written by the American journalist and songwriter Arthur W[ells]. French with music by the American composer W. H. Brockway, published by White & Goullaud, Boston, in 1872, the lyrics of which were widely reprinted elsewhere, including in *The Irish National Songster, containing A Choice Selection of Sentimental, Patriotic, and Comic Songs* (New York, 1882), p. 160; and *The Aquarium Songster, containing the newest and most popular songs now being sung with great success* (London, c. 1890), unpaged. The song's lyrics as they appear in its sheet music as published in 1873 read:

> Little sweetheart, come and kiss me,
>   Just once more before I go ;
> Tell me truly, will you miss me,
>   As I wander to and fro ?
>
> Let me feel the tender pressing
>   Of your ruby lips to mine,
> With your dimple hands caressing,
>   And your snowy arms entwine.
>
>   *Chorus*
> Little sweetheart, come and kiss me,
>   Come and whisper sweet and low !
> That your heart will sadly miss me,
>   As I wander to and fro.
>
> Little sweetheart, come and kiss me,
>   We may never meet again !
> We may never roam together
>   Down the dear old shady lane !
>
> Future years may bring us sorrow,
>   That our hearts but little know,
> Still of care we should not borrow ;
>   Come and kiss me ere I go.

Uly 13.943–44: Then I will tell you all.

See my comments on *Uly* 5.254, where the same phrase occurs.

Uly 13.976: As God made them he matched them.

Of the highlighted phrase Thornton writes: 'Though this statement seems to me proverbial, it is not listed in the [*Oxford Dictionary of English Proverbs*, second edn (Oxford, 1948), aka the *ODEP*] or in [G. L. Apperson's *English Proverbs and Proverbial Phrases: A Historical Dictionary* (London, 1929)]. Compare Mrs Poyser's statement in George Eliot's *Adam Bede*, "I'm not denyin' the women are foolish: God almighty made 'em to match the men" (chap. LIII)'. Gifford writes: 'A variant of

Robert Burton's (1577–1640) proverb [in *Anatomy of Melancholy* (1621)], "Marriage and hanging go by destiny; matches are made in heaven"'; SMT write: 'Presumably a variation of the proverb "Marriages are made in heaven," from 1580 (*ODEP*); a common expression in Ireland.' To these comments may be added that Joyce's phrase occurs verbatim in the Irish poet and novelist Frances Marcella 'Attie' O'Brien's (1840–1883) *Won by Worth*, probably written in the 1870s and posthumously serialized in vols. 19 and 20 of *The Irish Monthly*, from December 1891 to July 1892. In the latter volume, no. 224 (Feb. 1892), chap. 28 ('The Election'), p. 90, O'Brien writes:

> " So much the worse for the object," said Huntingdon. " She hasn't come off better, I should fancy. I think it is White Melville who speculates in one of his novels whether any man is worth the love of a woman."
> " Oh, dear, no, why should he?" answered the Doctor. " The love of such a seraphic being ! Indeed, then, I'd tell White Melville, or black Melville either, to make his mind easy, for as God made them He matched them. There are plenty of them bad and good on both sides. "

Uly 13.977: Twice nought makes one.

Bloom's arithmetical misstatement, unremarked by Thornton, Gifford, and SMT, is reminiscent of another such misstatement, 'Once one is two,' in the anonymous story 'The Maniac, Or Once One Is Two' possibly first printed in *The Rochester Gem*, a local newspaper in upstate New York; subsequently reprinted in vol. 2, no. 7 (14 June 1834) of *The People's Magazine*—a fortnightly published by the Society for Promoting Christian Knowledge, London—and repeatedly reprinted for decades thereafter in several editions of McGuffey's Readers. As it appears in *The People's Magazine*, the story reads in its entirety (italics in the original):

> A writer in the Rochester Gem, relates that during his travels in Europe, he one day visited the Hospital of Berlin, where he saw a man whose exterior was very striking. His figure, tall and commanding, was bending with age, but more with sorrow ; the few scattered hairs which remained on his temples were white, almost as the driven snow, and the deepest melancholy was depicted in his countenance. On inquiring who he was, and what brought him there, he startled, as if from sleep, and after looking round him, began with slow and measured steps to stride

the hall, repeating in a low but audible voice, " Once one is two ; once one is two." Now and then he would stop and remain with his arms folded on his breast, as if in contemplation, for some minutes, then again resuming his walk, he continued to repeat, "Once one is two ; once one is two." His story, as our traveller understood it, was as follows.

Conrad Lange, collector of the revenues of the city of Berlin, had long been known as a man whom nothing could divert from the paths of honesty. Scrupulously exact in all his dealings, and assiduous in the discharge of his official duties, he had acquired the good will and esteem of all who knew him, and the confidence of the minister of finance, whose duty it is to inspect the accounts of all officers connected with the revenue. On casting up his accounts at the close of a particlar year, he found a *deficit* of 10,000 ducats. Alarmed at this discovery, he went to the minister, presented his accounts, and informed him that he did not know how it had arisen, and that he had been robbed by some person bent on his ruin. The minister received his accounts, but thinking it a duty to secure a person who might probably be a defaulter, he caused him to be arrested, and put his accounts into the hands of one of his secretaries for inspection, who returned them the day after, with the information that the deficiency arose from a miscalculation ; that in multiplying, Mr. Lange had said, *once one is two*, instead of once one is *one*. The poor man was immediately released from confinement, his accounts returned, and the mistake pointed out. During his imprisonment, which lasted but two days, he had neither eaten, drank, nor taken any repose—and when he appeared his countenance was as pale as death. On receiving his accounts, he was a long time silent, then suddenly awaking as if from a trance, he repeated " once one is two."

He appeared to be entirely insensible of his situation ; would neither eat nor drink, unless solicited ; and took notice of nothing that passed around him. Whilst repeating his accustomed phrase, if any one corrected him by saying, " once one is *one*," he was recalled for a moment, and said, " ah, right; once one *is* one;" and then again resuming his walk, he continued to repeat, " once one is two." He died shortly after the traveller left Berlin.

This affecting story, whether true or untrue, obviously abounds with lessons of instruction. Alas ! how easily is the human mind thrown off its " balance, " especially when it is stayed on *this world* only ;—and has no experimental knowledge of the meaning of the injunction of Scripture, to cast all our cares upon Him who careth for us, and who heareth even the young ravens cry.

Uly 13.1110: Think you're escaping and run into yourself.

A phrase perhaps derived from a passage in the German-Dutch canon regular Thomas à Kempis's (1380–1471) devotional work *De Imitatione Christi* (c. 1418–1427) as translated from Medieval Latin by (among others) the Rev. W. H. Hutchings (London, 1876) as *The Imitation of Christ*, book 2, chap. 12 ('Of the Royal Way of the Holy Cross'), p. 82:

> No one is so touched with a heartfelt sense of the Passion of Christ, as the man whose lot has been to suffer like things.
> The cross, then, is always at hand, and everywhere awaits you.
> You cannot escape it, run where you will; for wherever you go, you take yourself with you, and you will always find yourself.

Uly 13.1110–11: Longest way round is the shortest way home.

A proverbial expression, among the earliest verbatim or nearly verbatim instances of which occurs in the English dramatist George Colman the Elder's (1732–1794) *The Spleen, or, Islington Spa; A Comick Piece, of Two Acts* (Dublin, 1776), Act 2, p. 16, Jack Rubrick to Merton: 'Well! Ay, very well. There is no going always in a direct line, Tom. A Curve sometimes answers the purpose better. The longest way about is the shortest way home, you know.'; and among later pre-*Ulysses* instances, in the Scottish Baptist minister Alexander Maclaren's (1826–1910) *The Wearied Christ and Other Sermons* (London, 1893), sermon 8 ('How to Work the Work of God'), p. 77:

> And so, dear friends, we are going by the direct road to enrich lives with all the beauties of possible human perfection when we say, " Begin at the beginning. The longest way round is the shortest way home ; trust Him with all your hearts first, and that will effloresce into whatsoever things are lovely, and whatsoever things are of good report."

14. 'Oxen of the Sun'

Uly 14.8–9: by mortals with sapience endowed

A phrase perhaps inspired by the British poet and cleric H[enry]. F[rancis]. Cary's (1772–1844) blank-verse translation of Dante's *Divina Commedia* (1321) as *The Vision: or, Hell, Purgatory, and Paradise* (London, 1814), with, in *Paradise*, canto 10, p. 277, lines 105–11:

>   The fifth light,
> Goodliest of all, is by such love inspir'd,
> That all your world craves tidings of its doom :
> Within, there is the lofty light, endow'd
> With sapience so profound, if truth be truth,
> That with a ken of such wide amplitude
> No second hath arisen.

or by Pollok's *The Course of Time*, book 1, lines 416–26:

> No being, once created rational,
> Accountable, endowed with moral sense,
> With sapience of right and wrong endowed,
> And charged, however fallen, debased, destroyed ;
> However lost, forlorn, and miserable ;
> In guilt's dark shrouding wrapped, however thick ;
> However drunk, delirious, and mad,
> With sin's full cup ; and with whatever damned,
> Unnatural diligence it work and toil,
> Can banish Virtue from its sight, or once
> Forget that she is fair.

Uly 14.12–13: by no exterior splendour is the prosperity of a nation more efficaciously asserted

This passage suggests a familiarity with the Preface to the English agriculturalist and social commentator Arthur Young's (1741–1820) *Travels During the Years 1787, 1788 and 1789, Undertaken more particularly with a View of ascertaining the Cultivation, Wealth, Resources, and National Prosperity, of the Kingdom of France* (London, 1792; Dublin, 1793), reading, in vol. 1 (of 2), p. vi, of the 1793 Dublin edition:

> How far have wealth and power and exterior splendour, from whatever cause they may have arisen, reflected back upon the people the prosperity they implied ? Very curious inquiries ; yet resolved insufficiently by those whose political reveries are spun by their fire-sides, or caught flying as they are whirled through Europe in post-chaises.

Uly 14.71–72: Some man that wayfaring was stood by housedoor at night's oncoming.

The section of this episode that aims stylistically to suggest the diction of the Anglo-Saxon tongue and in particular of Ælfric here contains a phrase, 'at night's oncoming', that occurs nearly verbatim, and apparently uniquely, in a nineteenth-century novel: the English author, magazine editor, and drama critic Frederick William Robinson's (1830–1901) *Little Kate Kirby* (London, 1873), where vol. 3 (of 3), chap. 10 ('In the Mist') begins, on p. 28, with: 'The mist about that day still lingered with me ; it did not pass away with my clearer knowledge, but deepened with the night's on-coming.'

Of the phrase 'at night's oncoming' SMT write: 'From Ælfric's [...] *Life of St Cuthbert*: "at night to the sea"'—not an obvious antecedent.

Uly 14.74–75: teeming mothers

SMT write: 'From Izaak Walton's (1593–1683) *The Compleat Angler*: "the teeming earth".' But for verbatim instances of Joyce's phrase, see, for example, a passage in the Anglican cleric, theologian, and poet Jeremy Taylor's (1613–1667) *The Rule and Exercises of Holy Dying*, first published in 1651 and with many editions thereafter, reading, in chap. 1 ('A General Preparation Towards a Holy and Blessed Death, By Way of Consideration'): 'And how many teeming mothers have rejoiced over their swelling wombs, and pleased themselves in becoming the channels of blessing to a family ; and the midwife hath quickly bound their heads and feet, and carried them forth to burial ?'

See also, with another instance of the phrase, *A short history of monastical orders in which the primitive institution of monks, their tempers, habits, rules, and the condition they are in at present, are treated of* (London, 1693), by the ordained Spanish secular priest, convert to Protestantism and, after his escape to London, anti-Catholic polemicist Antonio Gavin (fl. 1726), as 'Gabriel d'Emillianne', where a passage in chap. 14 on 'the Order of Gilbertines in England' reads on pp. 133–34:

> This Hermaphrodite Order, made up of both Sexes, did very soon bring forth Fruits worthy of it self ; these holy Virgins having got almost all of them big Bellies, which gave occasion to the following Verses:[27]
>
> > *Harum sunt quædam steriles, quædam parientes,*
> >   *Virgineoque tamen nomine cuncta tegunt.*
> > *Quæ pastoralis baculi dotatur honore,*
> >   *Illa quidem meliùs fertiliusque parit.*
> > *Vix etiam quævis sterilis reperitur in illis,*
> >   *Donec ejus ætas talia posse negat.*
>
> Tho' some are Barren Does, yet others,
> By Fryars help, prove teeming Mothers.
> When all to such Lewdness run,
> All's cover'd, under Name of Nun.
> Th' Abbess, in Honour as She' excells,
> Her Belly too, more often swells.
> If any She proves Barren still,
> Age is in fault, and not her will.

And, as a third example, see Sir Walter Scott's Waverly novel *The Pirate* (Edinburgh and London, 1822), chap. 4, p. 45:

---

27 The Latin lines (italicized in the original) are elsewhere—namely, in the English antiquarian, historian, topographer, and herald William Camden's (1551–1623) *Brittannia*, vol. 3, 'East Anglia and the Midlands', first published in English in 1610—reliably attributed to the Anglo-Norman satirist and poet Nigel de Longchamps (1130–1200), also known as Nigellus, a monk of Christ Church, Canterbury. The lines' English translation is presumably by Gavin.

> This eminent success reconciled Jasper to the dominion which his wife began to assume over him ; and which was much confirmed by her proving to be—let me see—what is the prettiest mode of expressing it ?—in the family way. On this occasion, Mrs. Yellowley had a remarkable dream, as is the usual practice of teeming mothers previous to the birth of an illustrious offspring. She " was a-dreamed," as her husband expressed it, that she was safely delivered of a plough, drawn by three yoke of Angus-shire oxen ; and being a mighty investigator into such portents, she sate herself down with her gossips, to consider what the thing might mean.

Uly 14.91: bloom of blushes

Joyce's phrase may have been suggested by a passage in Ouida's novel *Princess Napraxine* (London, 1884), vol. 2 (of 3), chap. 31, p. 305:

> Therefore his memory abided with her and moved her, and had power over her, and at times an irritable gnawing sense of something which might have been stole upon her. What could that child give him at Amyôt ? — white limbs, clear eyes, a rose-bloom of blushes ; but besides ? what sympathy, comprehension, inspiration ? what of the higher delights of the passions ?

Uly 14.97: bowels ruthful

See the English Hispanist, writer, and mining engineer Alexander James Duffield's (1821–1890) translation, from the Spanish originals of 1605 and 1606, of Miguel de Cervantes Saavedra's (1547?–1616) novel *The Ingenious Knight, Don Quixote De La Mancha* (London, 1881), with, in vol. 1 (of 3), part 2, chap. 11 ('Of what happened to Don Quixote among certain Goatherds'), p. 127:

> All was peace then, all amity, all concord. The painful share of the bended plough had not yet dared to open and search into the ruthful bowels of our first mother ; for she, without being forced, offered, in every part of her fertile and spacious bosom, all that could satisfy, sustain, and delight the children who then possessed her.

Uly 14.98: God's rightwiseness

In Wycliffe's Bible—the first translation of the entire Bible from the Latin Vulgate into Middle English, under the direction of the English theologians John Wycliffe (c. 1328–1384) and John Purvey (c. 1354–1421) in the late fourteenth century—Romans x 3 reads: 'For they not knowing God's rightwiseness, and seeking to make steadfast their own rightwiseness, be not subject to the rightwiseness of God.'

Joyce's phrase recurs in the anonymous play 'Hickscorner' in vol. 1 (of 12) of *A Select Collection of Old English Plays*—originally published by Robert Dodsley in 1744, the title page of the fourth edition (London, 1874–76) indicates—in a speech by the 'character' master Pity, addressing brother Perseverance, that begins on p. 151 with 'Sir, such as I can I shall show you :' and that ends on p. 152 with the following lines:

> The peril now no man dread will ;
> All is not God's law that is used in land ;
> Beware will they not, till death in his hand
> Taketh his sword, and smiteth asunder the life vein,
> And with his mortal stroke cleaveth the heart atwain :
> They trust so in mercy, the lantern of brightness,
> That no thing do they dread God's rightwiseness.

Another early version of the phrase occurs in Chaucer's 'The Parson's Tale', reading, on p. 267 of the Houghton Mifflin edition of *The Poetical Works of Geoffrey Chaucer* (Boston, 1879), vol. 2 (of 3):

> and as seith Seint Gregorie, that it aperteneth to the grete rightwisnesse of God, that nevere shal the peyne stynte, of hem that nevere wolde withdrawen hem fro synne hir thankes, but ay continue in synne, for thilke perpetueel wil to do synne shul they han perpetueel peyne.

Uly 14.329–30: like a curse of God ape

Gifford: 'Source and connotations unknown.' But perhaps not unknowable. One possibility: that Joyce's phrase was suggested by the Quran, chap. 7, verses 163–66, in which Allah punishes the Israelite inhabitants of a seaside town who have collected fish from the sea on a Sabbath by transforming them into apes.

Another possibility: that it points to Shakespeare's *The Taming of the Shrew*, II i 31–34, Katherine to Baptista, referring to Bianca: 'Nay, now I see | She is your treasure, she must have a husband ; | I must dance barefoot on her wedding-day, | And for your love to her lead apes in hell'—lines that may have inspired, or been inspired by, the first verse of a song entitled 'Hark! Wot ye what?' collected in the English lutenist and composer Robert Jones's (fl. 1577–1617) *A Musicall Dreame. Or the Fourth Booke of Ayres* (London, 1609) reading, in a modernized translation: 'Hark! Hark! wot ye what? nay faith, and shall I tell? | I am afraid | To die a maid. | And then lead Apes in hell. | O, it makes me sigh and sob with inward grief; | But if I can | But get a man, | He'll yield me some relief.'

See also the entry below on line 14.359's 'delights amorous'.

Uly 14.336–37: obedience in the womb

Gifford cites a passage from the *Maynooth Catechism* (Dublin, 1882) reading: 'By profession, members of the religious life publically assume the obligations of their state through the vows of poverty, chastity, and obedience.' But see also, by the English hymnwriter and theologian Frederick William Faber (1814–1863), *The Blessed Sacrament: or, The Works and Ways of God* (London, 1855), book 2, section 3 ('The Babe and the Host'), p. 174: 'The obedience in the womb to His Mother, to the appointed time, and to the future behests of all men, even sinners, enemies and executioners, presents an exact parallel to His obedience in the Blessed Sacrament'.

Uly 14.359: delights amorous

Thornton and Gifford have no comment on the phrase; SMT write: 'From Sir Thomas Overbury's (1581–1613) *Characters* (1614): "The flight of hawkes and chase of wilde beasts, either of them are delights noble."' But Joyce's phrase itself occurs nearly verbatim, as 'delight amorous', in the fifth (last) stanza of the song 'Harke al you ladies', collected in *A booke of ayres, set foorth to be song* [sic] *to the lute, orpherian, and base violl* (London, 1601), by the English poet, composer, and physician Thomas

Campion (1567–1620) and the English composer and musician Philip Rosseter (c. 1568–1623), which stanza reads: 'All you that loue, or lou'd before, | The Fairie Queene Proserpina | Bids you encrease that louing humour more: | They that yet haue not fed | On delight amorous, | She vowes that they shall lead | Apes in Auernus.' Subsequent reprintings of the poem, including in William Stanley Braithwaite's *The Book of English Verse* (Boston, 1906) and Frank Sidgwick's *The Cavalier To His Lady: Love-Poems of the XVIITH Century* (London, 1909), render the phrase as 'delights amorous', thus perfectly matching the phrase as it occurs in Joyce's 'Oxen'.

Uly 14.367–68: how thou settedst little by me

See, by the English soldier, statesman, and translator John Bourchier, Lord Berners (1467–1533), *The Book of Huon de Bordeaux, Adapted from French Sources, 1525–1533*, first printed by Wynkyn de Worde, 1534; second edition 1570, now lost; third edition by Thomas Purfoot, 1601; critical edition by the English biographer, writer, and critic Sir Sidney Lee (1859–1926) for the Early English Text Society, 1882–1887. Chapter 37 ('How Huon passed the fourth gate, and how he came in to the garden, whereas was the fountain, and of that he did here.') reads in part, on p. 26 of Lee's edition: 'Then he took his horn and blew it so fiercely that King Oberon heard it, being in his forest. And when he heard it he said, "Ah, good Lord," quod he, "I hear the false knight blow his horn, who setteth so little by me. For at the first gate that he passed he made a false lie. By the Lord that formed me, if he blow till the veins in his neck burst asunder he shall not be succoured for me, nor for no manner of mischief that may fall to him."'

Uly 14.448–49: he fell in with a certain whore of an eyepleasing exterior

SMT cite the English poet, courtier, scholar, and soldier Sir Philip Sidney's (1554–1586) *The Countess of Pembroke's Arcadia* (1593): 'all sorts of eye-pleasing flowers'. But the phrase 'eye-pleasing' also occurs in the English cavalier poet Sir John Suckling's (1609–1642) 'His Dream' (1638), an erotic poem that, as such, is more verbally and thematically apposite to the passage in 'Oxen' where the highlighted phrase occurs. Suckling's poem begins (lines 1–10):

> On a still, silent night, scarce could I number
> One of the clock, but that a golden slumber
> Had lockt my senses fast, and carried me
> Into a world of blest felicity,
> I know not how : first to a garden, where
> The apricock, the cherry, and the pear,
> The strawberry, and plum, were fairer far
> Than that eye-pleasing fruit that caus'd the jar
> Betwixt the goddesses, and tempted more
> Than fair Atlanta's ball, though gilded o'er.

and ends (lines 25–31):

> But here my gentle dream conveyed me
> Into the place where I most long'd to see,
> My mistress' bed ; who, some few blushes past
> And smiling frowns, contented was at last
> To let me touch her neck ; I, not content
> With that, slipt to her breast, thence lower went,
> And then—— I awak'd.

Uly 14.526: without bottom of reason

Joyce may have encountered the phrase 'bottom of reason' in any of several philosophical treatises. One such treatise was the English author and polymath Sir Thomas Browne's (1605–1682) *Hydriotaphia: Urne-Buriall, or, A Discourse of the Sepulchrall Urnes lately found in NORFOLK* (London, 1658), in chap. 1 of which Browne writes that all human burial practices were 'founded upon some Bottom of Reason' and reflect one or another of 'severall apprehensions of the most rational dissolution.' (*Works*, I, 137) Another was the English country gentleman and moral philosopher Abraham Tucker's (1705–1774) principal work, *The Light of Nature* (London, 1768–1777), in vol. 2 (of 3), chap. 17 ('Charity'), p. 285 of which he writes:

> If our general plan be well formed upon the solid bottom of reason and judgment, we may follow the impulse of inclination in executing the several parts : for we shall be doing the benefit to others at the seasons when we have them least in our thoughts.

Uly 14.553–54: he spoke French like a gentleman

Joyce's phrase occurs verbatim in the British historian and Whig politician Thomas Babington Macaulay's (1800–1859) *History of England from the Accession of James the Second* (London, 1848), vol. 3 (of 5), chap. 8, p. 142, where 'he' refers to Charles Talbot (1660–1718), fifteenth earl and first duke of Shrewsbury, and 'Lewis' to Louis XIV, King of France (1638–1715): 'He spoke French like a gentleman of Lewis's bedchamber, and Italian like a citizen of Florence.' Both the earl and the king were contemporaries of Daniel Defoe, whose writings (as has been noted) are frequently echoed in 'Oxen' from lines 530 to 650.

Uly 14.556: the use of the globes

This phrase, which denotes a standard pedagogical topic in eighteenth-century schoolrooms and seminaries, refers to terrestrial globes showing the geography of the earth's surface and celestial globes mapping the heavens. It also occurs verbatim in the titles of several contemporary treatises and textbooks, including, by Joseph Harris, British 'Teacher of the Mathematicks', *The Description and Use of the Globes, and the Orrery* (London, 1731 et seq.); Thomas Wright's *The Use of the Globes, or, The General Doctrine of the Sphere : Explaining and Demonstrating the Most Natural Propositions Relating to Astronomy, Geography, and Dialing : to which is Added, A Synopsis of the Doctrine of Eclipses* (London, 1740); and John Bransby's *The Use of the Globes : Containing, an Introduction to Astronomy and Geography; a Description of Globes and Maps; and a Variety of Problems Performed by the Globes, and by Calculation* (London, 1791; second, enlarged edition, 1808).

Uly 14.664–65: Well, let us hear of it, good my friend, said Mr Dixon.

For 'good my friend' SMT cite *Hamlet*, II ii 239–40, Hamlet to Guildenstern and Rosencrantz, which reads: 'What have you, my good friends, deserv'd at the hands of Fortune, that she sends you to prison hither?' But Joyce's phrase occurs verbatim and often elsewhere, including in *Romeo and Juliet*, V iii 124–26, Friar Lawrence to Balthasar: 'Bliss be upon you! Tell me, good my friend, | What torch is yond, that vainly lends his light | To grubs and eyeless skulls?'; in *Othello*, III i 29, Cassio to Clown: 'Do, good my friend.'; and, from his *Parleyings with Certain People of Importance in their Day* (London, 1887), in the closing lines of Robert Browning's poem 'With Bernard de Mandeville': 'Not I | More than yourself : so, good my friend, keep still | Trustful with—me ? with thee, sage Mandeville !'

Uly 14.666–67: accepted of the invitation

SMT write: 'After David Hume's (1711–76) *My Own Life*: "I accepted of it"'. But the phrase 'accepted of the invitation' occurs elsewhere verbatim, including in the Scottish biographer, diarist, and lawyer James Boswell's (1740–1795) *Life of Samuel Johnson, LL.D.* (London, 1791), vol. 2 (of 2), p. 40, where Boswell writes of Johnson: 'I accepted of the invitation, and had here another proof how amiable his character was in the opinion of those who knew him best'; in the Scottish writer Alexander Chalmers's (1759–1834) *The New General Biographical Dictionary*, revised and enlarged edition (London, 1814), vol. 14, s.v. FORSTER (George), p. 490: 'But soon after, the senate of Poland having offered him a chair in the university of Wilna, Forster accepted of the invitation'; and in Flavius Josephus, *Antiquities of the Jews*, in *The Works of Flavius Josephus the Jewish Historian*, as translated from the original Greek by William Whiston (London, 1737), book 13, chap. 7, section 2: 'He also sent ambassadors to Simon the Jewish High Priest, about a league of friendship and mutual assistance, who readily accepted of the invitation'.

Uly 14.670: conjugal vexations

Joyce's phrase previously occurred on at least three occasions: the first of these, in an essay by Samuel Johnson in *The Rambler* no. 39 for 31 July 1750, on 'The Unhappiness of women whether single or married', reading in part:

> The miseries, indeed, which many ladies suffer under conjugal vexations, are to be considered with great pity, because their husbands are often not taken by them as objects of affection, but forced upon

them by authority and violence, or by persuasion and importunity, equally resistless when urged by those whom they have been always accustomed to reverence and obey ; and it very seldom appears, that those who are thus despotick in the disposal of their children, pay any regard to their domestick and personal felicity, or think it so much to be enquired whether they will be happy, as whether they will be rich.

the second, in the Irish author Thomas Amory's (1691?–1788) quasi-autobiographical comic novel *The Life of John Buncle, Esq; containing Various Observations and Reflections, Made in several Parts of the World, and Many Extraordinary Relations* (London, part 1, 1756; and part 2, 1766), with in vol. 2 (of 2), part 2, section 1 ('The History of Orlando and Bellinda'), pp. 7–8:

> To reverence and obey (she said) was not required by any obligation, when men were unreasonable, and paid no regard to a wife's domestic and personal felicity ; nor would she give up her understanding to his weak determination, since custom cannot confer an authority which nature has denied : It cannot license a husband to be unjust, nor give right to treat her as a slave. If this was to be the case in matrimony, and women were to suffer under conjugal vexations, as she did, by his senseless arguments every day, they had better bear the reproach and solitude of antiquated virginity, and be treated as the refuse of the world, in the character of old maids.

and the third, in the Irish social philosopher and poet Anna Maria Winter's (1773–1837) *Thoughts on the Moral Order of Nature* (Dublin, 1831), vol. 3 (of 3), book 3, chap. 16 ('Thoughts on the Proper Remedy to be Accorded to the Husbands Who Are Tormented By Their Wives'), p. 295:

> It is easy for observers to assure themselves that the act of supreme power which honour would allow a justly and greatly incensed husband to execute, is one that would issue in freeing himself from his conjugal vexations, not in inflicting a positive punishment on his wife. When honorable minded men are harrassed by a consort's frowardness, they do not feel a wish to take advantage of their legal power to reduce her to reason by coercive measures ; they merely sigh to be disengaged from her. The detestation with which she inspires them, bears entirely on the bond which unites them to her, nowise on herself. They would willingly see her in the enjoyment of all the good luck possible, so she ceased to be a troublesome appendage of theirs.

Uly 14.714: applied himself to his dress

SMT write: 'From Richard Steele's (1672–1729) "Mr Bickerstaff Visits a Friend" in *The Tatler*: "applying herself to me".' There are, however, other pre-*Ulysses* phrases matching Joyce's more nearly verbatim. One such: from the Editor's Introduction to *The Works of John Locke in Nine Volumes* (London, 1824), twelfth edn, vol. 1: 'but returning [from Germany] to England again within the year, he applied himself with great vigour to his studies, and particularly to that of natural philosophy.' And another: from Dickens's *The Old Curiosity Shop* (London, 1841), chap. 66: 'Comforted by this intelligence, the patient applied himself to his food with a keen appetite'.

Uly 14.735: the most violent agitations of delight

Joyce's phrase occurs verbatim—and, it seems, uniquely pre-*Ulysses* other than in several collections reprinting the essay in which it appears—in Johnson's *The Rambler* no. 12, for 28 April 1750, where it is presented as having been sent to that journal by a female correspondent signing herself 'Zosima': 'They frequently turned their eyes upon me, and seemed to discover many subjects of merriment : for at every look they whispered, and laughed with the most violent agitations of delight.'

In one such collection, its constituent pieces gathered by Joseph Addison and published under the title *A Collection of Interesting Anecdotes, Memoirs, Allegories, Essays, and Poetical Fragments; Tending to Amuse the Fancy, and Inculcate Morality* (London, 1793), Johnson's essay, reprinted on pp. 111–16, is assigned the title 'The History of a Young Woman That Came to London for a Service'.

Uly 14.741–42: have the obligingness to pass him a flagon of cordial waters

The phrase 'have the obligingness to' (do something) appeared several times over the course of the nineteenth century, one early instance occurring in Frances Burney's once enormously popular novel *Camilla*, or, *A Picture of Youth* (London, 1796), vol. 4 (of 5), book 7, chap. 6 ('A Call of the House'), p. 78:

> The baronet now began an harangue upon the happiness that would accrue from these double unions, for which he assured them they should have double remembrances, though the same preparations would do for both, as he meant they should take place at the same time, provided Mr. Edgar would have the obligingness to wait for a fair wind, which he was expecting every hour.

Uly 14.742–43: questioning poise of the head

What seems to have been the only pre-*Ulysses*, all-but-verbatim instance of Joyce's phrase occurred in *Dudley. A Novel.* (London, 1888) by the Scottish writer Susan Richmond Lee (1854–1930) as 'Curtis Yorke', chap. 5 ('El Dorado!'), pp. 45–46:

> While he is thus occupied, the door opens, and admits a tall, soldierly-looking man of sixty-five or thereabouts, who bears a sufficient resemblance to Dudley to show that they are father and son. There is the same erect, well-knit, well-proportioned figure ; the same half-questioning poise of the head ; the same indescribable look about the mouth and eyes, denoting singular tenacity of idea ; a look deepening with the younger man, into tenacity of purpose as well.

Uly 14.747–48: There wanted nothing but this cup to crown my felicity.

Joyce could have borrowed the phrase 'crown my felicity' from any of a number of antecedent texts, the best known of which—and the most appropriate given the obstetrical motif permeating the episode—is the final sentence of Smollett's picaresque novel *The Adventures of Roderick Random* (London, 1748): 'I would have set out for London immediately after receiving this piece of intelligence, but my dear angel has been qualmish of late, and begins to grow remarkably round in the waist ; so that I cannot leave her in such an interesting situation, which I hope will produce something to crown my felicity.'

Uly 14.755–56: Gazing upon those features with a world of tenderness

What seems to have been the earliest of the many pre-Joyce instances of 'a world of tenderness' occurred in Defoe's *Roxana* (1724). In an edition of the novel published under its original title (see my comments above on *Uly* 13.7–18) and edited by George A. Aitken (London, 1895), the phrase occurs in chap. 13, on p. 178: '" Then, dear madam," said he, with a world of tenderness (and I thought I saw tears in his eyes), " allow me to repeat it, that I am a Christian, and consequently I do not allow what I have rashly, and without due consideration, done ; [...]"'—which, he goes on to say, was to have lain with her without benefit of wedlock.

But among the many post-*Roxana*, pre-*Ulysses* instances of the phrase, another that Joyce could have had in mind if and when he borrowed it—as it combines the phrase with the act of gazing—occurred (after its serialization in *Chambers's Journal* from January to July of that year) in *Lord Ulswater. A Novel.* (London, 1867) 'By the Author of "Lord Lynn's Wife," "Lady Flavia," &c.', namely, the English writer of ghost stories and sensational fiction John Berwick Harwood (1828–1899), with, in vol. 2 (of 3), chap. 2, p. 28:

> Her own thoughts, it might have been supposed, had any observer, to whom her antecedents were known, been present to note the expression of her compressed lips, and the lowering gloom of her dark eyes, dwelt more upon the vengeance which was in one scale of the balance than upon the profit in the other. Suddenly, her countenance cleared, as a cloud rolls away from a sunny sky, and there was a world of tenderness in her mellowed gaze, a world of tenderness in her voice, as she murmured : " It is for him, dear lad, for him !—my poor Jem !"

Uly 14.759: an artless disorder

SMT write: 'After Robert Herrick's (1591–1674) poem "Delight in Disorder" (1648), "A sweet disorder in the dress | Kindles in clothes a wantonness" (*Poetical Works*, vol. 1, p. 37).' But Joyce's phrase occurs verbatim and, it would seem, uniquely pre-*Ulysses* in *The East I Know*—a collection of short essays and poems by the French poet, essayist, dramatist, and diplomat Paul Claudel (1868–1955) translated for American and British readers by Teresa Frances and William Rose Benét

(New Haven and London, 1914), six years before 'Oxen of the Sun' was serialized in *The Little Review*—more specifically in its third essay 'The City at Night' (that is, Shanghai, where Claudel served as the French Consul), reading on p. 16:

> I go. And I carry the memory of a life congested, naïve, restless; of a city at the same time open and crowded, a single house with a multifold family. I have seen the city of other days, when, free of modern influences, men swarmed in an artless disorder; in fact it is the fascination of all the past that I am leaving, when, issuing out of the double gate in the hurly-burly of wheelbarrows and litters, in the midst of lepers and epileptics, I see the electric lights of the Concession shine.[28]

Uly 14.770–71: How mingled and imperfect are all our sublunary joys.

Thornton and Gifford are silent on this sentence; SMT provide the *OED*'s definition of 'sublunary', adding 'From Swift's *Tale of a Tub:* "the transitory state of all sublunary things".' Aptly, however, given the several French phrases in the long paragraph in which it occurs, Joyce's 'mingled and imperfect' seems more likely to have been inspired by a passage in the French philosopher, professor of philosophy at the University of Paris, and founder of 'eclecticism' Victor Cousin's (1792–1867) *Introduction à l'histoire de la Philosophie* or, as translated from the French by Henning Gotfried Linberg, *Introduction to the History of Philosophy* (Boston, 1832), lecture 1, pp. 13–14, reading:

> The most beautiful object in the world, the most charming figure is, in some respect, defective. How many miserable minutiæ connect beauty with matter ! Heroism itself, the greatest and the purest beauty, heroism, examined closely, appears sometimes pitiful. All that is actual, is mingled and imperfect. All existing beauty, whatever may be its kind or nature, fades when compared with the idea of beauty which it reveals.

---

28 *The Athenæum Journal of Literature, Science, and the Fine Arts* (London), no. 579 (1 Dec. 1838), p. 853, does, however, reprint a short, unsigned article from a recent *Heath's Picturesque Annual* which observes that the formal gardens of Versailles, designed by André Le Nôtre (1613–1700), the French landscape architect who was the principal gardener of King Louis XIV, 'are assuredly more appropriate to the precincts of a French palace, than the most picturesque and artless disorder of turf, foliage, and water.'

As for 'sublunary joys', that phrase occurs, among other pre-Joyce instances, in Young's *Night-Thoughts*, 'Night Ninth, The Consolation' (1745), lines 1690–93:

> As the chased hart, amid the desert waste,
> Pants for the living stream ; for Him who made her,
> So pants the thirsty soul, amid the blank
> Of sublunary joys.

in the German-British composer Georg Friedrich Händel's (1685–1759) oratorio *The Triumph of Time and Truth* (London, 1757), with words by the English librettist, classical scholar, and printer Thomas Morell (1703–1784), Act 2, section 40 (Recitative):

> Vain the delights of age or youth,
> Without the sanction and applause of Truth.
> And as the soul more bright appears
> Than the frail earthly form she wears,
> So much true pleasures, from this glass,
> All other sublunary joys surpass.

and in the English poet and Anglican hymnwriter William Cowper's (1731–1800) translation from the French, produced in 1782 and first published in 1806 as 'The Joy of the Cross', of a poem by the French aristocrat, Catholic mystic, Quietist, and poet Jeanne-Marie Bouvier de la Mothe-Guyon (1648–1717)—commonly known as Madame Guyon—the eighth of whose twelve stanzas reads:

> Souls once enabled to disdain
> Base sublunary joys, maintain
>   Their dignity secure ;
> The fever of desire is pass'd,
> And Love has all its genuine taste,
>   Is delicate and pure.

Uly 14.804: the humourous sallies

This rare phrase, and particularly rare when its second word is so-spelled, occurs pre-*Ulysses* in *The Book of the Courtier by Count Baldesar Castiglione* (1528) as translated from the Italian by Leonard Eckstein Opdycke (London, 1902), p. 153:

" Perhaps, my Lords, I might collect still many other occasions that give opportunity for humourous sallies : such as things said with shyness, with admiration, with threats, out of season, with excessive anger ; besides these, certain other conditions that provoke laughter when they occur : sometimes a kind of wondering taciturnity, sometimes mere laughter itself when untimely.["]

and in the British author and banker Kenneth Grahame's (1859–1932) children's novel *The Wind in the Willows* (London, 1908), chap. 8 ('Toad's Adventures'), p. 174:

The chaff and the humourous sallies to which he was subjected, and to which, of course, he had to provide prompt and effective reply, formed, indeed, his chief danger; for Toad was an animal with a strong sense of his own dignity, and the chaff was mostly (he thought) poor and clumsy, and the humour of the sallies entirely lacking. However, he kept his temper, though with great difficulty, suited his retorts to his company and his supposed character, and did his best not to overstep the limits of good taste.

Uly 14.828: a glorious incentive

For 'exercitations' in line 14.827, SMT note Oliver Goldsmith's use of the word, as 'exercitation' singular, in *The Citizen of the World, or Letters From a Chinese Philosopher, Residing in London, to His Friends in the East* (Dublin, 1762), where it occurs in his description of Louis XV in volume 1, letter 5. Unremarked by Thornton, Gifford, and SMT, the phrase 'a glorious incentive' in Joyce's next line occurs in volume 1, letter 13, pages 48–49, of the same work, where the citizen of the world, the fictional Lien Chi Altangi, reports what he said to 'a gentleman dressed in black' who had offered to escort him on his visit to Westminster Abbey:

" I was come to observe the policy, the wisdom, and the justice of the English, in conferring rewards upon deceased merit. If adulation like this, continued I, be properly conducted, as it can no ways injure those who are flattered, so may it be a glorious incentive to those who are now capable of enjoying it. It is the duty of every good government to turn this monumental pride to its own advantage to become strong in the aggregate from the weakness of the individual. If none but the truly great have a place in this awful repository, a temple like this will give the finest lessons of morality, and be a strong incentive to true ambition. I am told, that none have a place here but characters of the most distinguished merit." The man in black seemed impatient at my observations, so I discontinued my remarks, and we walked on together to take a view of every particular monument in order as it lay.

Uly 14.828–29: I cannot away with them.

An early instance of the phrase—after Isaiah i 13 ('Bring no more vain oblations; incense is an abomination unto me; the new moons and sabbaths, the calling of assemblies, I cannot away with; it is iniquity, even the solemn meeting.')—occurs in the New England Puritan cleric Samuel Mather's (1651–1728) *A Dead Faith Anatomized. A Discourse on the Nature, and the Danger, With the Deadly Symptoms of a Dead Faith in those who profess the Faith of Christ* (Boston, 1697), reading on p. 25 and referring to God (italics in the original): 'He calleth them *Vain, Iniquity, and Abomination* ; He saith, *I cannot away with them ; my Soul hateth them, they are a trouble to me, I am weary to bear them ; and when you make many Prayers, I will not hear.*'

See also *Mary Wollstonecraft Godwin* (London, 1885)—a biography of that English novelist (1797–1851) and the wife of Percy Bysshe Shelley by the American writer Elizabeth Robins Pennell (1855–1936)—chap. 3 ('Life as Governess, 1786–1788'), pp. 61–62, quoting a letter of 24 March 1788 from Mary in Dublin to her sister Everina Wollstonecraft reading, in part: 'I believe I told you before that as a nation I do not admire the Irish ; and as to the great world and its frivolous ceremonies, I cannot away with them ; they fatigue me.'[29]

The phrase also occurs in chap. 1 of *Tom Brown's School Days* (London, 1857), by the English lawyer, judge, politician, and author Thomas Hughes (1822–1896): 'I love vagabonds, only I prefer poor to rich ones; — couriers and ladies' maids, imperials and travelling carriages, are an abomination unto me — I cannot away with them.'

Uly 14.831: a puny child of clay

This rare phrase occurs verbatim in the English bookseller, antiquarian, and orientalist Edward Upham's (1776–1834) *Karmath. An Arabian Tale.*

---

[29] The passage is also quoted in *William Godwin: His Friends and Contemporaries* by C. Kegan Paul (London, 1876), vol. 1, p. 189.

(London, 1827), chap. 7, pp. 138–39: '" Shall we, the mighty of earth, who wield the elements, and know the secrets of nature, bend before a puny child of clay ? No !" exclaimed the furious Maholath, " let the hated race with whom we link our fate now perish.["]'

Minus the indefinite article, it also occurs in a translation from the German, by Walter Sichel, of four lines from Act 4 of the Austrian playwright Franz Seraphicus Grillparzer's (1791–1872) *Die Ahnfrau* [The Ancestress], an entry in the *Dictionary of Quotations (German)*, edited by Lilian Dalbiac (London, 1909), that reads on p. 377: 'Vainly little hands like children | Round the wheels of Fate we play : | Fate, whose chariot ploughs the thunder, | Brooks no puny child of clay.'

Uly 14.847: that age upon which it is commonly charged that it knows not pity

See Jessie Haynes's translation from the French (New York, 1902; London, 1904) of Victor Hugo's *Notre-Dame de Paris* (1831) as *The Hunchback of Notre Dame*, book 6, chap. 4 ('A Tear for a Drop of Water'), p. 229:

> The people—particularly in the Middle Ages—are to society what the child is in the family ; and as long as they are allowed to remain at that primitive stage of ignorance, of moral and intellectual nonage, it may be said of them as of childhood—" It is an age that knows not pity."

Uly 14.848–49: as full of extravagancies as overgrown children

While Philip Dormer Stanhope, Earl of Chesterfield's (1694–1773) posthumously published letter-essay 'On Passion' contains both the word 'extravagancy' and the phrase 'overgrown children'—though not the phrase 'full of extravagancies' or even the word 'extravagancies' plural—it is not unreasonable to suppose, as do SMT, that Joyce's phrase may owe something to that essay.

Nevertheless, 'full of extravagancies' itself occurs verbatim in a number of pre-Joyce works, among them Meric Casaubon's *A TREATISE PROVING Spirits, Witches, AND Supernatural Operations, BY PREGNANT*

INSTANCES AND EVIDENCES: Together with other Things worthy of Note (London, 1672), with, on p. 104 (italics in the original):

> My Author for [*Nicolaus*] *Remigius,* is one that calls himself *Philippus Ludwigus Elich,* in his *Dæmonomagia* : who is very full of quotations, out of good books, *I* confess, but otherwise, whether sober or no, when he wrote ; he is so full of extravagancies, *I* do not know.

and in the Scottish historian William Russell's (1741–1793) *History of Modern Europe: with an Account of the Decline and Fall of The Roman Empire: And a View of the Progress of Society, from the Rise of the Modern Kingdoms to the Peace of Paris, in 1763* etc (London, 1786), with, in vol. 2 (of 5), part 1, letter 58, pp. 173–74:

> Dantè, the father of Italian poetry, flourished in the beginning of the fourteenth century. His *Inferno*, though full of extravagancies, is one of the greatest efforts of human genius.

As for 'overgrown children', that phrase, while rare, also occurs pre-Joyce in Mary Wollstonecraft's *A Vindication of the Rights of Woman: With Strictures on Political and Moral Subjects* (London, 1792), chap. 2 ('The Prevailing Opinion of a Sexual Character Discussed'), p. 39 (italics in the original):

> Though, to reason on Rousseau's ground, if man did attain a degree of perfection of mind when his body arrived at maturity, it might be proper, in order to make a man and his wife *one*, that she should rely entirely on his understanding ; and the graceful ivy, clasping the oak that supported it, would form a whole in which strength and beauty would be equally conspicuous. But, alas ! husbands, as well as their helpmates, are often only overgrown children ; nay, thanks to early debauchery, scarcely men in their outward form—and if the blind lead the blind, one need not come from heaven to tell us the consequence.

Uly 14.849: their tumultuary discussions

SMT cite the *OED*'s definition of 'tumultuary' as 'disordered, haphazard' and continue: 'From Edward Gibbon's (1737–94) *Decline of the Roman Empire*: "By their tumultuary election".' As for Joyce's phrase, it occurs verbatim in the *London and Edinburgh Philosophical Magazine and Journal of Science*, vol. 10, no. 59 (Feb. 1837), on p. 144 of an article entitled

'Address of His Royal Highness the President [of the Royal Society], delivered at the Anniversary Meeting, Nov. 30, 1836':

> Such extraordinary meetings being strictly domestic, and confined to the Fellows of the Society only, appear to me not merely to offer a sufficient security against any great mismanagement of the affairs of the establishment, but likewise to protect your ordinary meetings from those irregular and somewhat tumultuary discussions on matters of business, or personal conduct, which might otherwise be in danger of arising.

In 1836, the President of the Society was Prince Augustus Frederick, Duke of Sussex (1773–1843), the sixth son and ninth child of King George III and his queen consort, Charlotte of Mecklenburg-Strelitz.

Uly 14.866: a habit of mind which he never did hold with

SMT cite as an antecedent the phrase 'I hold with the Persian' in the English essayist and poet Charles Lamb's (1775–1834) *Essays of Elia* (London, 1823). But there are many instances of personal pronouns followed, as here, by 'never did hold with', including, in *The Cornhill*, vol. 7, no. 38 (London, 1899), p. 272, a passage from chap. 33 ('Jim Pembury Makes a Mistake') of the Scottish novelist S[amuel]. R[utherford]. Crockett's (1859–1914) serialized novel *Little Anna Mark*: 'I never did hold with this cant of mercy'; and also including, in chap. 3 ('The Building of the Sphere') of the English writer H[erbert]. G[eorge]. Wells's (1866–1946) *The First Men in the Moon* (London, 1901), this from p. 53:

> " How would you like a trip to the moon ? " I cried.
> " I never did hold with them ballooneys," she said, evidently under the impression that this was a common excursion enough. " I wouldn't go up in one—not for ever so."

Uly 14.870: a precipitate and inglorious retreat

SMT cite Samuel Johnson's 'A Garret and Its Tenants'—in *The Rambler* no. 161 for 1 Oct. 1751—with '...was forced to make a precipitate retreat from this quarter of the town'. There are, however, several instances of antecedent works in which Joyce's phrase occurs verbatim.

One such, by Percie Enderbie, Gent. (d. 1670), was *Cambria Triumphans, or, Brittain in its perfect lustre; shevving the origin and antiquity of that illustrious nation* etc (London, 1661), book 8, with, on p. 407 of the third edition (London, 1805):

> The winter coming on, and having suffered much by a furious attack which the Welsh had made from the mountains, Henry once again relinquished the field to Llewelyn ; and, instead of punishing a revolting vassal, he himself, with the broken remains of his army, was obliged to make a precipitate and inglorious retreat to Chester.

Another, from *Hogg's Instructor*—a periodical edited by the Scottish publisher James Robert Hogg (1806–1888) and featuring serialized novels and short stories—vol. 3 (Edinburgh and London, 1854), is an anonymous novella called 'The Struggle', reading, in chap. 1, p. 318: 'Gertrude had found this last homily quite too much for her patience, and had made a precipitate and inglorious retreat.'

A third, from *The English Illustrated Magazine* (London), vol. 23, no. 201 (July 1900), 'The Haunt of the Water-Rail' by Herbert W[inckworth]. Tompkins (1867–c. 1914), reading on p. 218: 'The hare, not being as sensible of the privileges of human friendship as were the hares of the poet Cowper, beat a precipitate and inglorious retreat.'

Uly 14.871: mettlesome youth

Instances of this phrase occur in the Scottish scholar, lawyer, humanist, and educator John Stuart Blackie's (1809–1895) *Musa Burschicosa: A Book of Songs for Students and University Men* (Edinburgh, 1869) with, in 'Some Book-Worms Will Sit and Will Study', stanza 5, lines 1–4, on p. 94: 'Beside her old wheel when 't is birring, | A spinster may sit and may croon, | But a mettlesome youth should be stirring, | Like Hermes with wings to his shoon'; and in Everett-Green's *Fallen Fortunes: Being the Adventures of a Gentleman of Quality in the Days of Queen Anne* (London, 1903) with, in chap. 13 ('The Hero of the Hour'), p. 253: '"He is a mettlesome youth, and deserves the praise of the town."'

Uly 14.879: the bounty of the Supreme Being

SMT cite Henry St John, 1st Viscount Bolingbroke's 'Letter to Windham': 'will of the Supreme Being'. But Joyce's six-word phrase occurs verbatim in, and apparently only in, a passage of the Methodist theologian and Anglican minister John William Fletcher's (1729–1785) 'General Observations on the Redemption of Mankind by Jesus Christ', reprinted in several editions of *The Works of the Rev. John Fletcher, Late Vicar of Madeley* including in vol. 9 (of 9) of the 1860 London edition, 335–48, where the excerpt below appears on p. 336:

> Is it not strange that such a plan, formed by the love, the justice, the wisdom, and the bounty of the Supreme Being, executed by the incarnate Word, confirming a great number of prophecies ; — a plan which has the admiration of angels, and of millions of pious persons for so many ages ; which hath comforted such multitudes of penitents, in the most frightful circumstances ; and hath made so many martyrs to triumph under the greatest torture, and even sing in the cold arms of death : — is it not strange, I say, that such a plan should be the constant topic of ridicule to Socinians and Deists ?

Uly 14.882: a frigid genius

Before Joyce's use of it, this phrase seems to have occurred verbatim only once, in Goldsmith's *Citizen of the World*, letter 39, p. 175: 'Of the truth of this maxim in every language, every fine writer is perfectly sensible from his own experience, and yet to explain the reason would be perhaps as difficult as to make a frigid genius profit by the discovery.'

With a definite in place of the indefinite article, the phrase also occurred in Samuel Johnson's 'Observations on the Oriental Eclogues' of the English poet William Collins (1721–1759), posthumously collected in Johnson's *The Works of the Poets of Great Britain and Ireland; with Prefaces Biographical and Critical* (London, 1800), and reading on p. 48: 'In consequence of these peculiarities, so ill adapted to the frigid genius of the North, Mr. Collins could make but little use of it as a precursor for his oriental eclogues ; and even in his third eclogue, where the subject is of a similar nature, he has chosen rather to follow the mode of the Doric and the Latin pastoral.'

Uly 14.886: I must acquaint you

While SMT cite Cowper's essay 'On Conversation', with 'but as I must acquaint them', Joyce's phrase occurs verbatim in (among other instances) Shakespeare's *The Second Part of Henry the Fourth* (aka *2 Henry IV*), IV i 6–8, Archbishop Scroop to Lord Hastings and others: 'My friends and brethren in these great affairs, | I must acquaint you that I have receiv'd | New-dated letters from Northumberland'; and in Fielding's picaresque novel *The History of Tom Jones, a Foundling* (London, 1749), vol. 2 (of 4), book 7 ('Containing three Days'), chap. 8 ('Containing Scenes of Altercation, of no very uncommon Kind.'), p. 36 (italics in the original): '"Since you make such a Return to my Civility," said the other, ["]I must acquaint you, Mrs. *Honour*, that you are not so good as me.["]'

Uly 14.935: some faded beauty

For this phrase SMT cite Junius's 'Letter to the Duke of Grafton: "in the arms of *faded beauty*" (*Letters of Junius*, vol. 1, p. 148)'. But Joyce's three-word phrase occurs verbatim from time to time elsewhere including, most notably, in a passage from Lord William Pitt Lennox's (1799–1881) serialized novel *Ernest Atherley; or, Scenes at Home and Abroad*, published (and, it appears, only published) in vols. 21 and 22 (1852 and 1853) of *The Sportsman's Magazine of Life in London and the Country* (London). The passage in question, on p. 329 of the July 1853 issue, reads (italics in the original):

> There is no happiness, however, without some alloy ; illnature, envy, hatred, malice, and uncharitableness, will find their way into all society, and Dublin was not exempt from the general rule. Some faded beauty pronounced Mrs. Atherley to be " horribly made up ;" a disappointed spinster declared her to be an "awful flirt ;" an antiquated piece of nobility, with three " impossible" daughters, anathematized her as a " heartless coquette ;" a dashing widow, anxious to renew a matrimonial lease, assured her friends that there had been strange reports about Kilkenny Kate ; a lady, whose hair, according to her own statement, was " sweet auburn," certainly not " the *loveliest* of

the *plain*," asserted that she knew the artist who dyed the bride's hair every day before dinner. The personal remarks were perfectly innocuous : not so the slanders against my wife's inward graces, which, added to my extravagancies, were duly reported to my parents.

Uly 14.1007: in obedience to an inward voice

SMT write: 'Perhaps from Joseph Conrad's [...] *Lord Jim* (1900): "pushing out into the unknown in obedience to an inward voice".' Another possibility in which the same phrase occurs, also verbatim—and that, moreover, aptly describes Leopold Bloom no less than Walt Whitman— occurs in the American naturalist and nature essayist John Burroughs's (1837–1921) *Whitman: A Study* (Boston, 1896; London, 1897), with, on p. 86 of both editions:

> There are no more precious and tonic pages in history than the records of men who have faced unpopularity, odium, hatred, ridicule, detraction, in obedience to an inward voice, and never lost courage or good-nature. Whitman's is the most striking case in our literary annals,—probably the most striking one in our century outside of politics and religion. The inward voice alone was the oracle he obeyed:
> " My commission obeying, to question it never daring. "

Uly 14.1034–35: The lonely house by the graveyard is uninhabited.

Gifford and SMT both cite the Irish author J[oseph]. Sheridan Le Fanu's (1814–1873) three-volume historical novel *The House by the Churchyard* (London, 1863). But see also the American novelist and short-story writer Mrs Mary J. Holmes's (1825–1907) *Edna Browning; or, The Leighton Homestead. A Novel.* (New York and London, 1872), with, in chap. 8 ('The Brave Little Woman'), p. 66:

> All this Edna knew was in store for her whenever the state of the roads would admit of her aunt's journey to town with her butter, eggs, and poultry ; but, aside from these, there was the dreadful possibility of being taken from school and compelled to pass the dreary winter in that lonely house by the graveyard, with no companions but the cat and her own gloomy thoughts, unless it were the balls of carpet-rags she hated so terribly.

Uly 14.1065: child of shame

From a parenthetical passage in *Ulysses* reading '(she is a poor waif, a child of shame, yours and mine and of all for a bare shilling and her luckpenny)', the phrase 'child of shame' previously occurred in the anonymous poem 'Fast and Humiliation; or, Sick Beasts *v.* Sick Paupers' published in *Punch*, vol. 50 (7 Apr. 1866), p. 142, the tenth (of eleven) stanza of which reads:

> Now 'tis a babe, the child of shame, forsaken and foredone ;
> The pauper wet-nurse has her own, and her milk is scant for one.
> " 'Tis dead ! "—"No, 'tis so slow to die ! "—" For the grave let's have it drest ! "
> " What's the odds of a few minutes ? —Who's Hillocks, to protest,
> And disturb the lady-matron while she has friends to tea,
> All because little Green ain't dead when dead she ought to be ! "

'The Child of Shame' recurs as the title of a poem on pp. 26–28 of a volume entitled *Weak Moments* (London, 1879) by the pseudonymous 'XOC'. In that poem, an infant born out of wedlock is cast by its mother into a raging river to drown, after which the mother leaps in herself.

In a comment on Joyce's phrase, SMT declare it to be 'From Defoe's [...] *Colonel Jack*: "son of shame".'

Uly 14.1069: entwined in nethermost darkness

Joyce's 'nethermost darkness' occurs in the English Spasmodic poet Philip James Bailey's (1816–1902) *Festus*, first published anonymously in 1839, then reissued in a revised and expanded second edition of some forty thousand lines in 1845. In the poem's tenth edition (London, 1877), the phrase 'nethermost darkness' occurs in book 11, p. 166:

> Minds still which know by proof
> What those could but assume, that all these rocks,
> Hand-wrought of One, these solid fires ; the air
> Nebulous, commixed with starry spore, and earth's
> Waters, with unborn continents heavy, all
> The rude original seen in nature, here,
> Being ordered, now, informed, all procreant mate
> Of heaven ; these crude products of matter, once
> Like firstlings on the axis, altarwise,

> Laid, of the globe, earth's testimony still stand
> To her creative God ; who, in the heart
> Of nethermost darkness, his miraculous name
> Scores legible, as upon the sun's broad brow,
> Mid blaze chaotic, and liquescent plains
> Of ever-seething flame, where sink and rise
> Alp-blebs of fire, vast, vagrant ; name which reads
> Perfection infinite in all ways ; all names
> Other of gods, obliterates.

The phrase recurs, less esoterically, in a passage in Grant Allen's novel *In All Shades* (London, 1886; rvsd edn London and Edinburgh, 1899)— having first been serialized from 2 January to 24 September 1886 in *Chambers's Journal*—reading in chap. 23, pp. 165–66, of the 1899 edition:

> And Dr. Whitaker ? On he rode, the lightning terrifying his little mountain pony at every flash, the rain beating down upon him mercilessly with equatorial fierceness, the darkness stretching in front of him and below him, save when, every now and then, the awful forks of flame illumined for a second the gulfs and precipices that yawned beneath in profoundest gloom. Yet he still rode on, erect and heedless, his hat now lost, bareheaded to the pitiless storm, cold without and fiery hot at heart within. He cared for nothing now—for nothing—for nothing. Nora had put the final coping-stone on that grim growth of black despair within his soul, that palace of nethermost darkness which alone he was henceforth to inhabit.

Uly 14.1073: the bride of darkness

Unremarked by Thornton, Gifford, and SMT, Joyce's phrase previously occurred as the final line of the fifth section of Tennyson's poem *Demeter and Persephone* (1889):

> Last as the likeness of a dying man,
> Without his knowledge, from him flits to warn
> A far-off friendship that he comes no more,
> So he, the God of dreams, who heard my cry,
> Drew from thyself the likeness of thyself
> Without thy knowledge, and thy shadow past
> Before me, crying 'The Bright one in the highest
> Is brother of the Dark one in the lowest,
> And Bright and Dark have sworn that I, the child
> Of thee, the great Earth-Mother, thee, the Power

> That lifts her buried life from gloom to bloom,
> Should be for ever and for evermore
> The Bride of Darkness.'

Uly 14.1074: No, Leopold. Name and memory solace thee not.

The last will of the English philosopher and statesman Francis Bacon, 1st Viscount St Alban (1561–1626), as recorded by James Spedding, Robert Leslie Ellis, and Douglas Denon Heath in their edition of *The Works of Francis Bacon*, vol. 7 (London, 1874), chap. 10, p. 539, reads in part: 'For my name and memory, I leave it to men's charitable speeches, and to foreign nations, and the next ages.' See also a phrase Bloom is far more likely to have known, the Hebrew curse *Yimakh shemo v'zikhro*: 'May his name and memory be erased'.

Uly 14.1075: That youthful illusion of thy strength was taken from thee

Pointing, perhaps, to a passage in George Eliot's *The Mill on the Floss* (London, 1860), vol. 1 (of 3), book 1 ('Boy and Girl'), chap. 8 ('Mr Tulliver Shows His Weaker Side'), p. 136:

> Mrs Tulliver had lived thirteen years with her husband, yet she retained in all the freshness of her early married life a facility of saying things which drove him in the opposite direction to the one she desired. Some minds are wonderful for keeping their bloom in this way, as a patriarchal gold-fish apparently retains to the last its youthful illusion that it can swim in a straight line beyond the encircling glass. Mrs Tulliver was an amiable fish of this kind, and, after running her head against the same resisting medium for thirteen years, would go at it again to-day with undulled alacrity.

Uly 14.1078: The voices blend and fuse in clouded silence

Although it turns up from time to time elsewhere, the phrase 'clouded silence' seems most likely to have come to Joyce's attention from a reading of Charlotte Brontë's *Villette* (London, 1853), where a passage in vol. 3 (of 3), chap. 32 ('M. Paul'), p. 57 reads:

> If, at last, he let the neophyte sleep, it was but a moment ; he woke him suddenly up to apply new tests ; he sent him on irksome errands when he was staggering with weariness ; he tried the temper, the sense, and the health ; and it was only when every severest test had been applied and endured, when the most corrosive aquafortis had been used, and failed to tarnish the ore, that he admitted it genuine and, still in clouded silence, stamped it with his deep brand of approval.

Uly 14.1088: the ghosts of beasts

SMT note: 'After Odysseus's men kill the cattle of the sun god Helios in the *Odyssey*, they are haunted by the dead animals (XII.393–96)'. As for Joyce's phrase itself, that occurs verbatim in at least three pre-*Ulysses* works:

First of the three, in the British cultural anthropologist Edward B[urnett]. Tylor's (1832–1917) *Primitive Culture: Researches into the Development of Mythology, Philosophy, Religion, Art, and Custom* (London, 1871), vol. 1 (of 2), chap. 11 ('Animism'), p. 424: 'the Hovas of Madagascar know that the ghosts of beasts and men, dwelling in a great mountain in the south called Ambondrombe, come out occasionally to walk among the tombs or execution-places of criminals.'

Next, in John Ruskin's *Modern Painters* (London, 1873), vol. 3, part 4 ('Of Many Things'), chap. 13 ('Of Classical Landscape'), p. 188: 'Thus, meadows of asphodel are prepared for the happier dead ; and even Orion, a hunter among the mountains in his lifetime, pursues the ghosts of beasts in these asphodel meadows after death.'

And third, in the Scottish poet, novelist, folklorist, and literary critic Andrew Lang's (1844–1912) *The Book of Dreams and Ghosts* (London, 1897), chap. 7 ('More Ghosts with a Purpose'), p. 155:

> We now, in accordance with a promise already made, give an example of the ghosts of beasts ! Here an explanation by the theory that the consciousness of the beast survives death and affects with a hallucination the minds of living men and animals, will hardly pass current. But if such cases were as common and told on evidence as respectable as that which vouches for appearances of the dead, believers in these would either have to shift their ground, or to grant that [quoting Pope's *Essay on Man* (1733–34), lines 111–112]

> Admitted to that equal sky,
> Our faithful dog may bear us company.

Uly 14.1161: The gods too are ever kind

Among the handful of pre-*Ulysses* versions of the phrase, see the English poet and physician Sir Richard Blackmore's (1654–1729) *Prince Arthur. An Heroick Poem. In Ten Books.* (London, 1695), book 7, p. 202: 'Neglect these Dreams, the Gods are ever kind | To the best Troops, and to th' undaunted Mind'; and, in *All the Year Round*, vol. 18 (7 July 1877), 'The Fortunes of Nara. An Old Japanese Story.', chap. 1, p. 440: 'Yet think not that Kaimiri hath deceived thee. The gods are ever kind to those who carry into their worldly actions true hearts and honest consciences.'

Uly 14.1164–65: Warily, Malachi whispered, preserve a druid silence.

For the apparently only pre-Joyce instance of 'a druid silence', with or without the indefinite article, see, by the Irish novelist E[dith]. Œ[none]. Somerville (1858–1949) and her cousin the novelist Violet Florence Martin (1862–1915)—together, 'Martin Ross'—*Some Irish Yesterdays* (London, 1906), with, in the final lines of 'Hunting Mahatmas', p. 89: 'The Mahatma maintained a Druid silence ; it was not for him to comment on the eternal supremacy of Mind over Matter.'

Uly 14.1167: the incorruptible eon of the gods

In the Editor's Preface to the Greek bishop of Lyon Saint Irenæus's (c. 130–c. 202) *Libros quinque adversus Haereses* [Against heresies, book five] (Cambridge, 1857), the English cleric and academic W[illiam]. Wigan Harvey (1810–1883) writes, on p. lxxxv (italics in the original):

> The mundane *Sophia* or *Nus*, finding no rest either in heaven or earth, invoked the help of the Maternal Spirit, and obtained from the First Man, or Incorruptible Æon, that Christ should be sent to her aid, and being united with her, should by a combined descent upon Jesus at his baptism, form that Ecclesia on earth, which had an eternal counterpart in the union of Christ with the Father, Son, and Spirit in heaven.

See also *The Wedding-Song of Wisdom*, by the English historian, writer, editor, translator, and Theosophist G[eorge]. R[obert]. S[tow]. Mead (1863–1933)—issued by The Theosophical Publishing Society (London and Benares, 1906)—with, on p. 71:

" At these things the Rulers and the Father of Jesus (that is, the Father of his body, the Demiurge or Former of the physical world, which they equated with the Jewish idea of God) grew angry and set to work to have him killed. The moment this was brought about the Christ - together-with - Wisdom departed into the Incorruptible Æon (Eternity), while it was the Jesus who suffered the death of crucifixion[."]

Uly 14.1174: preposterous surmise

Among the handful of pre-*Ulysses* instances of this phrase, what seems to be the earliest occurs in the English playwright and theatrical manager William Dimond's (1781–1830) *The Broken Sword, A Grand Melo-Drama, Interspersed with Songs, Chorusses, &c.*, second edn (London, 1816), Act 2, sc. 4, p. 39: 'Claudio. And is this your motive for suspicion ? Vain and preposterous surmise ! Rigolio, the bravest and best of heroes, become the assassin of an innocent boy !—too monstrous even for reply.'; and the next earliest a year later in *Sermons, Chiefly on Devotional Subjects* (London, 1817) by the Rev. Archibald Bonar, Minister of Cramond, Edinburgh, vol. 2 (of 2), with, in sermon 1 ('Preached before the Society incorporated by Royal Charter, for the Benefit of the Sons of the Clergy of the Established Church of Scotland, in St Andrew's Church, Edinburgh, May 23, 1800.'), 1–36, the following on p. 24: 'There cannot be a more unjust or a more preposterous surmise, than the contemptuous sarcasm of unthinking men, who affect to hold out covetousness and indolence as the stimulating motives with the ministers of Christ for undertaking the pastoral office.'

Uly 14.1207: the stigmata of early depravity and premature wisdom

'Early depravity' was a common phrase and concept in the theological-religious, political, sociological, and medical literature of the eighteenth and nineteenth centuries. Pre-Joyce instances of 'premature wisdom', less so. But the latter include a brief item in *The Irish Penny Journal*, vol. 1, no. 32 (6 Feb. 1841), p. 256: 'PREMATURE WISDOM. The premature wisdom of youth resembles the forced fruit of our hot-houses ; it looks like the natural production, but has not its flavour or raciness.'; another, in a passage in *Disease in Childhood, Its Common Causes, and Directions for Its Management* (London, 1852), by the English surgeon and obstetrician Robert Ellis (1823–1885), reading on p. 163:

> But religious teaching was never known to do a child bodily
> harm. However great may be our power of opening up a child's
> mind, and filling it at a very early age with premature wisdom, we are
> powerless as regards its heart, save as instruments in His hands who
> alone can open that wild and wayward casket of the soul.

another, in *The Saturday Review of Politics, Literature, Science, and Art* (London), vol. 31, issue 812, for 20 May 1871, an anonymous article on pp. 628–29 entitled 'Idea-Mongers' with, in its final paragraph:

> If a man simply seeks for men to speak well of him, premature wisdom
> is certainly the height of folly. Before his views are adopted, he is
> laughed at; after they are adopted, he is forgotten. Any one who has
> stirred much in controversy must have lived to hear his own sayings
> quoted to him as the last new discovery of the newest light. Yet the
> poor "idea-monger," the old fogy who has been so silly as to think of
> a thing before other people, may have been doing some practical good
> all the same. He may have done something to teach the newest light,
> though the newest light may know nothing about him. But if a man
> simply wants immediate credit and immediate influence, he will avoid
> the folly of premature wisdom ; he will never think of things before
> other people ; he will wait and find out what is in the mind of the
> public at large in a vague and unformed shape ; he will lick it into a
> better shape, and put it forth to an admiring world as the words of the
> newest and deepest wisdom. Verily he hath his reward, but to our taste
> the reward of Roger Bacon is better worth having.

and another, in the popular English novelist Mary Mackay's, as 'Marie Corelli' (1855–1924) theologically, philosophically, and mystically themed novel *The Mighty Atom* (London, 1896), chap. 1, pp. 8–9:

> The window was open, and in the room beyond it a small boy sat at
> a school-desk reading, and every now and then making pencil notes
> on a large folio sheet of paper beside him. He was intent upon his

work,—yet he turned quickly at the sound of the bird's song and
listened, his deep thoughtful eyes darkening and softening with a
liquid look as of unshed tears. It was only for a moment that he thus
interrupted his studies,—anon, he again bent over the book before
him with an air of methodical patience and resignation strange to see
in one so young. He might have been a bank clerk, or an experienced
accountant in a London merchant's office, from his serious old-
fashioned manner, instead of a child barely eleven years of age;
indeed, as a matter of fact, there was an almost appalling expression of
premature wisdom on his pale wistful features;—the "thinking furrow"
already marked his forehead,—and what should still have been the
babyish upper curve of his sensitive little mouth, was almost though not
quite obliterated by a severe line of constantly practised self-restraint.

Uly 14.1218–19: stained by the mire of an indelible dishonour

While the phrase 'an indelible dishonour' had previously occurred
from time to time elsewhere, Joyce in employing it here may have had
in mind Sir Walter Scott's story 'The Two Drovers', the second tale in his
Chronicles of the Canongate, First Series (Edinburgh and London, 1827),
about a dispute over pasturage between two cattle drovers and friends,
the Scotsman Robin Oig M'Combich, with his Highlander's strong
sense of honor, and the hot-tempered Harry Wakefield, a Yorkshireman.
The dispute leads to a fist fight in which Wakefield knocks M'Combich
down, after which M'Combich returns, kills Wakefield, is tried by an
English jury, and executed. As the narrator says near the end of the story:

> The facts of the case were proved in the manner I have related
> them ; and whatever might be at first the prejudice of the audience
> against a crime so un-English as that of assassination from revenge, yet
> when the rooted national prejudices of the prisoner had been explained,
> which made him consider himself as stained with indelible dishonour,
> when subjected to personal violence ; when his previous patience,
> moderation, and endurance, were considered, the generosity of the
> English audience was inclined to regard his crime as the wayward
> aberration of a false idea of honour rather than as flowing from a heart
> naturally savage, or perverted by habitual vice.

Uly 14.1221: voluptuous loveliness

Among the several instances of the phrase appearing in print over the course of the nineteenth century, one of the two with which Joyce seems most likely to have crossed paths occurs in Macaulay's previously cited *History of England* (1848), vol. 2, chap. 4, pp. 2–3, speaking of the final days of King Charles the Second (1630–1685):

> The King sate there chatting and toying with three women, whose charms were the boast, and whose vices were the disgrace, of three nations. Barbara Palmer, Duchess of Cleveland, was there, no longer young, but still retaining some traces of that superb and voluptuous loveliness which twenty years before overcame the hearts of all men. There too was the Duchess of Portsmouth, whose soft and infantine features were lighted up with the vivacity of France. Hortensia Mancini, Duchess of Mazarin, and niece of the great Cardinal, completed the group.

and the other, in Ouida's previously cited *Folle-Farine* (1871), vol. 1, chap. 2, p. 136:

> She had the hues of his youth about her ; in that blood-red light, amongst the blood-red flowers, she made him think of women's forms that he had seen in all their grace and their voluptuous loveliness clothed in the red garment of death, and standing on the dusky red of the scaffold as the burning mornings of the summers of slaughter had risen over the land.

15. 'Circe'

***Uly* 15.518–19: I am not on pleasure bent. I am in a grave predicament.**

Gifford: 'Source unknown.' But both the phrase 'not on pleasure bent' and its affirmative counterpart 'on pleasure bent' may be ultimately traceable to Cowper's comic ballad 'The Diverting History of John Gilpin' (1782), stanza 8 of which reads: 'John Gilpin kissed his loving wife, | O'erjoyed was he to find | That though on pleasure she was bent, | She had a frugal mind.'

The phrase 'not on pleasure bent' itself seems first to have occurred verbatim in the English travel writer Richard Ford's (1796–1858) *Gatherings From Spain* (London, 1846), chap. 21, reading on pp. 297–98:

> The *plaza* is the focus of a fire, which blood alone can extinguish ; what public meetings and dinners are to Britons, reviews and razzias to Gauls, mass or music to Italians, is this one and absorbing bull-fight to Spaniards of all ranks, sexes, ages, for their happiness is quite catching ; and yet a thorn peeps amid these rosebuds ; when the dazzling glare and fierce African sun calcining the heavens and earth, fires up man and beast to madness, a raging thirst for blood is seen in flashing eyes and the irritable ready knife, then the passion of the Arab triumphs over the coldness of the Goth : the excitement would be terrific were it not on pleasure bent ; indeed there is no sacrifice, even of chastity, no denial, even of dinner, which they will not undergo to save money for the bull-fight.

Another early instance of the phrase occurs on p. 42 of Dinah Maria Craik's essay 'A City at Play' as first published in *Macmillan's Magazine*, vol. 18, no. 103 (May 1868), 40–47; and on p. 99 of the essay as collected in her *Fair France, Impressions of a Traveller* (London, 1871), in both of which, comparing the British to the French public, Craik writes:

> But on its "general holidays" the brightest of them, say a royal marriage or funeral—for both come alike to the too-rare holiday-makers—the British public is a somewhat sullen animal, which takes its pleasures with a solemn rapacity, knowing they are but few, and is rather hard to deal with, tenacious of affront, obnoxious to harsh rule, prone to grumble loudly at its voluntary hardships. Besides, a large proportion of it is not "on pleasure bent" at all, but pursuing its vocation, whether of pocket-picking, seat-letting, or orange and cake-selling, with a business-like pertinacity, never turned aside by such a small thing as amusement.

As for Bloom's 'I am in a grave predicament', the phrase 'a grave predicament' occurs as the title of chap. 5 of the children's story author and, later, novelist Mrs [Mary Louisa] Molesworth's (1839–1921) *The Old Pincushion, or, Aunt Clotilda's Guests* (London, 1889). Among several other instances at least as early as 1874, it also occurs in R. S. Scott's translation of Honoré de Balzac's novella *Une Fille d'Éve* (1839) as *A Daughter of Eve* (London, 1897), with, on p. 101:

> Raoul, instead of having his suspicions roused by this accommodating reception, was only vexed that he had not asked for more. This is the way with men of the greatest intellectual power ; they see only matter for pleasantry in a grave predicament, and reserve their wit for writing books, as though afraid there might not be enough of them to go round if applied to daily life.

Uly 15.521: your cock and bull story

Not noted by Thornton, Gifford, or SMT, the now familiar phrase 'cock and bull story' originated in the closing passage of the Anglo-Irish novelist and cleric Laurence Sterne's (1713–1768) *The Life and Opinions of Tristram Shandy, Gentleman* (York, 1759–1767), reading:

> L – – d! said my mother, what is this story about? – –
> A Cock and a Bull, said Yorick – – . And one of the best of its kind, I ever heard.

Uly 15.559: cruel naughty creature

In lines 15.558–59, where Bloom playfully calls Mrs Breen 'you cruel naughty creature', he, Joyce, or both may have had in mind any of several instances of 'cruel naughty', one as early as *Lessons for Children from Three to Four Years Old* (Dublin, 1814) by Anna Letitia Barbauld (1743–1825), with, on p. 90, 'There was cruel naughty boy once—I will tell you a story about him'; another in the English novelist, short story writer, and biographer Elizabeth Gaskell's (1810–1865) Gothic tale 'The Old Nurse's Story', first published on pp. 11–20 of the extra Christmas number of Dickens's *Household Words* in December 1852, with, on p. 17:

> " What is the matter with my sweet one ?" cried Dorothy, as I bore in Miss Rosamond, who was sobbing as if her heart would break.
> " She won't let me open the door for my little girl to come in ; and she'll die if she is out on the Fells all night. Cruel, naughty Hester," she said, slapping me ; but she might have struck harder, for I had seen a look of ghastly terror on Dorothy's face, which made my very blood run cold.["]

or an instance of 'cruel creature', as in Dickens's *The Life and Adventures of Nicholas Nickleby* (London, 1839), chap. 24 ('Of the Great Bespeak for Miss Snevellicci, and the First Appearance of Nicholas Upon Any Stage'), p. 292:

> " Oh you cruel creature, to read such things as those. I'm almost ashamed to look you in the face afterwards, positively I am," said Miss Snevellicci, seizing the book and putting it away in a closet. " How careless of Led ! How could she be so naughty ! "

See also the two instances of 'naughty, cruel creature' discussed in the following entry.

Uly 15.562: Naughty cruel I was!

When in line 559, as noted above, Bloom calls Mrs Breen a 'cruel naughty creature', she squeezes his arm, simpers, and replies 'Naughty cruel I was!' Like Bloom's 'cruel naughty', Mrs Breen's 'naughty cruel' had previously occurred several times in mid-nineteenth-century novels, including two in which 'naughty cruel' is immediately followed by 'creature'.

The first of these, by the English author and Shakespeare scholar Mary Victoria Cowden Clarke (1809–1898), was *The Iron Cousin: or, Mutual Influence*, new edition (London, 1862), with, in chap. 30, p. 242:

> " Evviva !" she exclaimed. " Tell us all the particulars. This is indeed something worth hearing ! The Iron Cousin defeated ! Enchanting ! "—" Kate, Kate ! " said Miss White, in a soft, deprecating tone ; then turning to Fermor, she added : " Yes, Mr. Worthington, pray do tell us all about it ; we shall all sympathize with your mortification, though this naughty, cruel creature pretends to rejoice."

The second instance, by the American author Mary Virginia Hawes Terhune (1830–1922), as 'Marion Harland', occurs in her novel *Moss-Side* (New York, 1857; London, 1858), chap. 22, p. 339 of both editions: " Naughty, cruel creature ! how can I forgive you ? If I were less attached to you, I would take my leave without another word. Where have you been ? what have you been doing, that I have not heard of you ?"

Uly 15.643: Soon got, soon gone.

Pre-*Ulysses* instances of this proverbial phrase include, among others, the statement of a vagrant in Mayhew's *London Labour and the London Poor*, enlarged edn (London, 1861), vol. 3 (of 4), reading, on p. 381:

> To the second letter that I sent home my mother sent me an answer herself. She sent me a sovereign. She told me that my father was the same as when I first left home, and it was no use my coming back. She sent me the money, bidding me get some clothes and seek for work. I didn't do as she bade. I spent the money—most part in drink. I didn't give any heed whether it was wrong or right. Soon got, soon gone ; and I know they could have sent me much more than that if they had pleased.

It also occurs—in Yeats's *Per Amica Silentia Lunae* (London, 1918)—in the essay 'Anima Hominis', section 5, pp. 31–32:

> He only can create the greatest imaginable beauty who has endured all imaginable pangs, for only when we have seen and foreseen what we dread shall we be rewarded by that dazzling unforeseen wing-footed wanderer. We could not find him if he were not in some sense of our being and yet of our being but as water with fire, a noise with silence. He is of all things not impossible the most difficult, for that

only which comes easily can never be a portion of our being, "Soon got, soon gone," as the proverb says. I shall find the dark grow luminous, the void fruitful when I understand I have nothing, that the ringers in the tower have appointed for the hymen of the soul a passing bell.

Uly 15.711–12: even *Leo ferox* there, the Libyan maneater

Gifford: 'Unknown.' *Leo ferox*—fierce or ferocious lion—is, however, a common phrase in Latin and Christian literature, occurring, for example, in the Roman author and grammarian Aulus Gellius's (125–180 CE) tale of 'Androcles and the Lion'; and in the commentary on Jeremiah of the Italian Dominican friar, philosopher, theologian, and jurist Thomas Aquinas (1225–1274), the latter reading in part: 'primo significans culpae magnitudinem: facta est mihi hereditas, scilicet populus, quasi leo, ferox ad impugnandam me' [First, signifying the magnitude of their guilt: my inheritance, the people, has become for me like a lion, fierce to attack me].

Joyce's 'Libyan maneater' may have been suggested by Dryden's translation of Virgil's *Aeneid*, book 12, lines 9–16:

> As, when the swains the Libyan lion chase,
> He makes a sour retreat, nor mends his pace ;
> But, if the pointed javelin pierce his side,
> The lordly beast returns with double pride :
> He wrenches out the steel ; he roars for pain ;
> His sides he lashes, and erects his mane :
> So Turnus fares : his eyeballs flash with fire ;
> Through his wide nostrils clouds of smoke expire.

or perhaps by such a work as the American general and sometime prison warden Charles McCormick Reeve's (1847–1947) *How We Went and What We Saw: A Flying Trip Through Egypt, Syria, and the Aegean Islands* (New York and London, 1891), with, in chap. 21 ('Beyrout, St. George, and the Dog River.'), p. 278:

> As the weeping maiden was wending her way sorrowfully towards the lake, who should she chance to meet but George, riding along as unconcernedly as if there was no man-eating monster in all Libya.

Uly 15.775–76: I am a man misunderstood.

Unremarked by Thornton, Gifford, and SMT, this phrase from Bloom's hallucinatory plea to the jury echoes verbatim a line from the French poet Charles Baudelaire's (1821–1867) *Les Fleurs du Mal* (Paris, 1857), and specifically from the poem therein called 'Le Vin d'Assassin' as translated by 'O.' in *The Oxford Magazine. A Weekly Newspaper and Review*, vol. 1, no. 17, for 24 Oct. 1883, p. 329. There, as 'From Baudelaire. "The Murderer's Wine."'—with its first line, 'Ma femme est morte, je suis libre.' as epigraph—the poem reads (italics in the original):

Now I am free : my wife is dead.
    Now I can drink, and drink to filling.
Christ ! how her screaming racked my head
    When I came in without a shilling !

I am as happy as a king.
    O the sweet air and splendid sky !
We had just such a day of spring
    When we went loving, she and I.

And I am racked with a demon drought.
    How much would you suppose would slake it
Of Liquor ? For a real bout
    Her coffin-full would do, I take it.

Why, for I tossed her down a well ;
    Down in the deep well-hole I set her ;
And one by one the flags they fell ;
    And now please God I will forget her.

By all the sweet oaths that we swore,
    Nor aught on earth may turn aside,
So to be friends as once before
    Upon our love's fair mad noontide,

On a dark place at evening
    I begged her meet me, and she came,
And saw no madness in the thing.
    All in our way are mad the same.

She still was beautiful to see,
    But tired, tired now ! and I
Loved here too well for her to be,

> And therefore did I bid her *Die.*
>
> I am a man misunderstood.
> > Which of these silly sots would think
> In his sick midnights, if he could,
> > To spin himself a shroud of drink ?
>
> No armour like a drunken bout !
> > As little as an iron wheel
> Turning around, spring in, spring out,
> > Knows it how real love doth feel,
>
> With all her sable sorceries,
> > Her terrors and their demon train,
> Her deadly flasks, her raining eyes,
> > Her skeleton and creaking chain.
>
> Now I am free and left alone,
> > Dead drunk this evening I will be.
> Without a pang, without a groan,
> > Upon the ground I 'll flatten me
>
> And sleep as sound as an old dog.
> > The waggon driving heavily,
> Laden with boulder and with log,
> > And the cart dragging slowly by
>
> May crush my guilt-oppressèd brow
> > Or split me like a cloven sod !
> *That* for them ! *That* for Satan, now !
> > *That* for God's altar ! *That* for God !

Uly 15.814–15: in accurate morning dress

Part of the parenthetical, sartorial description of Mr Philip Beaufoy, Joyce's phrase matches nearly verbatim a phrase in the Irish novelist and raconteur Charles Lever's (1806–1872) novel *Davenport Dunn: A Man of Our Day* (London, 1859), vol. 2 (of 2), chap. 71 ('At Rome'), p. 611, spoken by Lady Lackington and referring to Mr Spicer:

> " The absurd notion that he is a sporting character is the parent of so many other delusions ; he fancies himself affluent, and, stranger still, imagines he's a gentleman." And the idea so amused her Ladyship, that she laughed aloud at it.

> " Mr. Spicer, my Lady," said a servant, flinging wide the door, and in a most accurate morning dress, every detail of which was faultless, that gentleman bowed his way across the room with an amount of eagerness that might possibly exact a shake of the hand, but, if unsuccessful, might easily subside into a colder acceptance. Lady Lackington vouchsafed nothing beyond a faint smile, and the words, " How d'ye do ?" as with a slight gesture she motioned to him the precise chair he was to seat himself on. Before taking his place, Mr. Spicer made a formal bow to Lady Grace, who, with a vacant smile, acknowledged the courtesy, and went on with her work.

Lady Grace's dismissive view of Mr Spicer's pretensions to affluence and gentility—he is in fact a confidential betting-agent of low birth—is echoed in Mr Beaufoy's own dismissive view, in lines 820–25, of Bloom's pretensions to being a gentleman and an author (italics in the original): 'No, you aren't. Not by a long shot if I know it. I don't see it, that's all. No born gentleman, no-one with the most rudimentary promptings of a gentleman would stoop to such particularly loathsome conduct. One of those, my lord. A plagiarist. A soapy sneak masquerading as a *littérateur*.'

Uly 15.1100–01: You have lashed the dormant tigress in my nature into a fury.

Gifford and others cite *Venus in Furs* (1870), a novella by the Austrian author Leopold von Sacher-Masoch (1836–1895), in which, Gifford writes, 'Wanda repeatedly complains that Severin has corrupted her by awakening "Dangerous potentialities that were slumbering" in her (p. 129) and transforming her into a "lioness" (p. 116).' The highlighted sentence, spoken (Joyce indicates) by The Honourable Mrs Mervyn Talboys and directed at Bloom, may also point to a passage by the London-born, Eton-educated, prolific and once-popular novelist and short-story writer W[illiam]. E[dward]. Norris (1847–1925) in his novel *The Right Honourable Gentleman* (London, 1913), chap. 25 ('Sisterly Remonstrances'), p. 216, which begins:

> " Still alive and unhurt ?" asked Mrs. Marlowe, appearing without delay in the doorway through which Lily had just retired. " All my compliments and felicitations ! I was holding myself in readiness to fly to your assistance, but as no shrieks came, I suppose you must have pacified the lady. How did you manage it ?"

" Oh, she wasn't violent," answered Madeline, who was looking a little tired ; " I didn't expect her to be."

" You didn't ? Well, you know her and I don't ; but I should have thought violence might be expected, and she certainly produced the effect of a dormant tigress upon me. Besides, if she wasn't going to be violent, why did she come here at all ?"

Uly 15.1189–90: Her artless blush unmanned me.

Early instances of 'her artless blush' occur in Smollett's play *The Regicide: or, James the First, of Scotland. A tragedy.* (London, 1749), Act I, scene 8, Angus to Eleonora:

> Remember, *Eleonora*, from what Source
> Thine Origin is drawn.—Thy Mother's Soul
> In Purity excell'd the snowy Fleece
> That cloaths our northern Hills !—her youthful Charms,
> Her artless Blush, her Look severely sweet,
> Her Dignity of Mien and Smiles of Love
> Survive in thee—Let me behold thee too
> Her Honour's Heiress—

and in the English composer Samuel Howard's (c. 1710–1782) setting of the anonymous poem *The Queen of May* (1754), which begins 'Ev'ry Nymph and Shepherd bring | Tributes to the Queen of May', and stanza 2 of which reads:

> Now the fair Narcissus blows,
> With his sweetness now delights ;
> By his side the Maiden-Rose,
> With her artless blush invites ;
> Such, so fragrant , and so gay,
> Is the blooming Queen of May.

The phrase 'artless blush' minus the possessive pronoun occurs in William Hamilton of Bangour's poem called 'Song', collected in James Paterson's *Poems and Songs of William Hamilton of Bangour* (Edinburgh, 1850), written in 1724, beginning 'Ah the shepherd's mournful fate', and the second stanza of which reads:

> The tender glance, the redd'ning cheek,
> O'erspread with rising blushes,

> A thousand various ways they speak,
> A thousand various wishes.
> For oh ! that form so heavenly fair,
> Those languid eyes so sweetly smiling,
> That artless blush, and modest air,
> So fatally beguiling.

Uly 15.1247: My master's voice!

Gifford writes: 'The advertising trademark of Victrola (a phonograph) depicted a seated dog, listening at the horn of a gramophone, with the legend "His Master's Voice."' True, but among prior, verbatim instances of Joyce's phrase, one occurs in Emily Brontë's (1818–1848), as 'Ellis Bell', poem 'The Prisoner. A Fragment.' from *Poems by Currer, Ellis, and Acton Bell* (London, 1846), pp. 76–79, stanza 7: '" My master's voice is low, his aspect bland and kind, | But hard as hardest flint, the soul that lurks behind ; | And I am rough and rude, yet not more rough to see | Than is the hidden ghost that has its home in me."'

Another: in Charlotte Brontë's (as 'Currer Bell') *The Professor. A Tale.* (London, 1857), vol. 2 (of 2), chap. 23, p. 158, in stanza 16 of a poem beginning on p. 151: 'Yet, when my master's voice I heard | Call, from the window, " Jane ! " | I entered, joyful, at the word, | The busy house again.'

In the 12 February 1876 issue of *All the Year Round*, a story called 'Keane Malcombe's Pupil'—republished in 1880 under the title 'Mabel Meredith's Love Story'—by the then first-time English author Bertha Jane Grundy (1837–1912) as 'Bertha Leith Adams', chap. 2 (of 7) has on p. 480: [']There is a quiver in my master's voice, for is not the " corner " going to be left empty again?[']; and, two paragraphs later: 'Grave and silent we walk home, for my master's voice and words have sobered us.'

A final, also pre-Victrola instance occurs in Stevenson's Gothic novella *The Strange Case of Doctor Jekyll and Mr. Hyde* (London, 1886), chap. 8 ('The Last Night'), p. 72:

> ' Sir,' he said, looking Mr. Utterson in the eyes, ' was that my master's voice ? '
> ' It seems much changed,' replied the lawyer, very pale, but giving look for look.

Uly 15.1258–59: Dignam's dead and gone below.

Thornton, Gifford, and SMT, among others, cite the children's singing game 'Old Roger Is Dead' as the source of 'dead and gone below', though the phrase does not occur there. It does, however, do so verbatim in Stevenson's adventure novel *Treasure Island* (London, 1883), part 6 ('Captain Silver'), chap. 31 ('The Treasure-Hunt—Flint's Pointer'), p. 265:

> " I saw him dead with these here deadlights," said Morgan. " Billy took me in. There he laid, with penny-pieces on his eyes."
> " Dead—ay, sure enough he's dead and gone below," said the fellow with the bandage ; " but if ever sperrit walked, it would be Flint's. Dear heart, but he died bad, did Flint !"

Uly 15.1267–68: Kisses chirp amid the rifts of fog.

Joyce may have owed the phrase 'kisses chirp' to the English author—mostly of historical novels for children—Emily Sarah Holt (1836–1893), whose *Imogen: A Story of the Mission of Augustine* (London, 1876), has, in chap. 4 ('Rather Uncomfortable'), p. 95: 'One of the new-comers, a tall woman with sallow complexion and black hair, took Cynedreth in her arms, and treated her to a succession of little chirping kisses on both cheeks.'

Another possibility, though birds, not kisses, do the chirping: Swinburne's *Poems and Ballads: Second Series.* (London, 1878), where stanza 23 of the poem 'At a Month's End'—previously published in vol. 1, no. 2 (Apr. 1871) of a short-lived London journal called *The Dark Blue*—reads on p. 42: 'Ah, too soon shot, the fool's bolt misses ! | What help ? the world is full of loves ; | Night after night of running kisses, | Chirp after chirp of changing doves.'

Uly 15.1321: You'll know me the next time.

Zoe's words to Bloom here—and Bella's identical words to him in line 15.3481—echo verbatim a phrase in the Canadian dime novelist May Agnes Fleming's (1840–1880) *Pride and Passion* (New York and London, 1882), chap. 1 ('The Mermaid'), p. 19:

> " Well, Grizzle, my old friend," said that gentleman with a sneer, " you'll know me the next time, won't you ? Can't I prevail on you

to come in, and sit down, and make yourself as miserable as possible while you stay. How have you been since I saw you last, my dear ? You can't think how I have been pining for you ever since, my love."

The same phrase also occurs in John Buchan's adventure novel *The Thirty-Nine Steps* (Edinburgh and London, 1915), chap. 5 ('The Adventure of the Spectacled Roadman'), where it comes at the end of a paragraph beginning on p. 116:

> " Are you Alexander Turnbull ? " he asked. " I am the new County Road Surveyor. You live at Blackhopefoot, and have charge of the section from Laidlaw-byres to the Riggs ? Good ! A fair bit of road, Turnbull, and not badly engineered. A little soft about a mile off, and the edges want cleaning. See you look after that. Good-morning. You'll know me the next time you see me."

Uly 15.1356: Mankind is incorrigible.

Not quite verbatim, but perhaps suggested by an item in *The Collected Works of William Hazlitt*—the English essayist, drama and literary critic, painter, social commentator, and philosopher (1778–1830)—edited by A[lfred]. R[ayney]. Waller and Arnold Glover (London, 1902–1904), vol. 11 (of 12), 'Fugitive Writings, Part 1' (of 2), 'Common Places', first published in *The Literary Examiner* (London) from September to December 1823, with, in entry number 76, on p. 557: 'Mankind are an incorrigible race. Give them but bugbears and idols—it is all that they ask ; the distinctions of right and wrong, of truth and falsehood, of good and evil, are worse than indifferent to them.'

Or perhaps inspired by another not-quite-verbatim item in *The Busy Body, or Men and Manners, Edited by Humphrey Hedgehog, Esq.*—in actuality, the English printer, editor, and author John Agg (1783–1855)—vol. 2 (London, 1817), where an essay called 'The New Club" reads in part, on p. 19:

> ["]But my great stroke was a plough and a composition, with which I proposed so to manure the crown lands, for the cultivation of flax, that in a few years we should be sure to have lace and cambric finer than they are to be found in Flanders : but this was treated as an impracticable chimera ; so, after the many other attempts altogether as unsuccessful, having thrown away about thirty thousand pounds on my vagaries, and found the follies of mankind incorrigible, I stopped short,

and am now determined to invent nothing but what may give a zest to our wine and a spur to our hilarity."

A third possibility, also not quite verbatim: in Joseph Conrad's *The Mirror of the Sea* (New York and London, 1906), a collection of autobiographical essays and anecdotes from his seafaring days published in various magazines between 1904 and 1906, with, in section 22, on pp. 119–20:

> In his own time a man is always very modern. Whether the seamen of three hundred years hence will have the faculty of sympathy it is impossible to say. An incorrigible mankind hardens its heart in the progress of its own perfectability.

Uly 15.1580: Expel That Pain (medic)

One of the 'cheap reprints of the World's Twelve Worst Books' (*Uly* 15.1577–78). Gifford comments: 'Unknown'; SMT: 'Apparently fictitious (but, potentially, useful).' The phrase may have originated in *Mr. Dampier's Voyages and Descriptions* (London, 1705) by Captain William Dampier (1652–1715), vol. 2 (of 2), part 2 ('Containing an Account of the Bay of *Campeachy* in the *West-Indies*, and Parts adjacent'), chap. 2, p. 64:

> Here are also a sort of Spiders of a prodigious size, some near as big as a Man's fist, with long small Legs like the Spiders in *England*, they have two Teeth, or rather Horns an Inch and a half, or two Inches long, and of a proportionable bigness, which are black as Jett, smooth as Glass, and their small end sharp as a Thorn ; they are not strait but bending. These Teeth we often preserve. Some wear them in their Tobacco pouches to pick their Pipes. Others preserve them for Tooth-Pickers, especially such as were troubled with the Toothach ; for by report they will expel that pain, tho' I cannot justifie it of my own Knowledge.

Uly 15.1580–81: Infant's Compendium of the Universe (cosmic)

Gifford: 'Unknown'; SMT: 'Apparently fictitious', adding that 'Bloom does own two books on astronomy', which they name. Joyce's fictitious title is based, it would seem, on a passage in the *Exameron* (or *Hexameron*)—'On the Six Days'—an exegetical work written c. 386–390 by Saint Ambrose, theologian, statesman, and Bishop of Milan (c. 339–c. 397), reading, at IX, 75, in one modern translation, 'man is the summit and, as it were, compendium of the universe and the supreme beauty of Creation'; and, in another, 'The human person is the peak and the compendium of the universe, and the highest beauty of the whole of creation.'

Uly 15.1583: Songs that Reached Our Heart (melodic)

Gifford: 'Unknown.' SMT: 'After the titles of various song anthologies, such as *Harps of Gold: Songs which Reach the Heart* (1909)'. But see also 'Songs of the Populace', an essay by the British writer and journalist Clarence Rook (1862–1915) published c. 1915 in the left-of-center *Daily Chronicle* (London), the final paragraph of which, as subsequently reprinted in two US-based publications, ends:

> There should be a collector who would make a sort of diary of the "songs that reached our heart," and set them out in full, as they appealed year by year. If possible he should append the names of the writers and composers. That would demand considerable research. The singers are easy to find.

Uly 15.1584: Pennywise's Way to Wealth (parsimonic)

Gifford: 'Unknown, but with the comic inversion of the proverb: Penny-wise is pound-foolish.' See, however, 'The Way to Wealth or Father Abraham's Sermon', an essay by the American writer, printer, polymath, and statesman Benjamin Franklin (1706–1790), first published as the untitled preface to the 1758 edition of *Poor Richard's Almanack*; later reprinted as *Franklin's Way to Wealth; or, "Poor Richard Improved"* (London, 1810).

Uly 15.1600: My more than Brother!

Gifford: 'Echoes Tennyson's *In Memoriam* (1850) 10:16–20: "My friend, the brother of my love; || My Arthur, whom I shall not see | Till all my widow'd race be run; | Dear as the mother to the son, | More than my brothers are to me.' Joyce's phrase occurs verbatim, however, in Byron's *The Bride of Abydos. A Turkish Tale.* (London, 1813), canto 11, stanza 22, lines 495–96: 'Another—and another—and another— | " Oh ! fly—no more—yet now my more than brother !"' and in other works by, among others, John Hoole (1727–1803), James Hogg, Samuel Taylor Coleridge, Rev. William Wickenden (1794–1864), Alfred Austin (1835–1913), and Jack London (1876–1916).

Uly 15.1686: New worlds for old.

Title of a book by H. G. Wells (London, 1908) on what he deemed to be the nature and future of socialism. The passage in Joyce goes on to provide Bloom's take on the same topic, including 'Free money, free rent, free love and a free lay church in a free lay state.'

Uly 15.2117: What went forth to the ends of the world

SMT cite their comment on *Uly* 9.1042–44, where they note that the Belgian poet and playwright Maurice Maeterlinck's (1862–1949) *La Sagesse et la destinée* (1899) has a passage reading in part, as translated: 'If Judas go forth to-night, it is towards Judas his steps will tend'. But Joyce's phrase here seems more likely to have been inspired by two scriptural verses: Psalm xix 4, reading 'Their line is gone out through all the earth, and their words to the end of the world.'; and Romans x 18, reading: 'But I say, Have they not heard? Yes verily, their sound went into all the earth, and their words unto the ends of the world.'

Uly 15.2126: God help your head

See Swift's satirical pamphlet 'The RIGHT of PRECEDENCE between *Physicians* and *Civilians* Enquir'd into.' (Dublin and London, 1720), pp. 17–18, reading in part (italics in the original):

> and when we see some Men less Courageous, Witty, or Learn'd, than others, we shou'd pity their bad Stomachs or Indigestion, rather than

their Incapacity or Indisposition of Brain : I am so sensible of this, that I have of many Years disus'd, as an Absurdity, that Saying to a simple Fellow ——*God help your Head* ; but I wish him, with more Propriety, a good Stomach, or a better Dinner.

Uly 15.2153: through the gathering darkness

Of the several instances and versions of the phrase in nineteenth-century literature, one of the handful that Joyce seems most likely to have had in mind occurs in the English poet and cultural critic Matthew Arnold's (1822–1888) 'Rugby Chapel' (1867)—a somber tribute to his father Dr Thomas Arnold, headmaster of that school, who had died suddenly at the age of forty-seven twenty years earlier and was buried in the school chapel. The poem begins:

> Coldly, sadly descends
> The autumn-evening. The field
> Strewn with its dank yellow drifts
> Of wither'd leaves, and the elms,
> Fade into dimness apace,
> Silent;—hardly a shout
> From a few boys late at their play!
> The lights come out in the street,
> In the school-room windows;—but cold,
> Solemn, unlighted, austere,
> Through the gathering darkness, arise
> The chapel-walls, in whose bound
> Thou, my father! art laid.

Another possibility: Grahame's *The Wind in the Willows*, where the phrase occurs in chap. 3 ('The Wild Wood'), on p. 57:

> He had patiently hunted through the wood for an hour or more, when at last to his joy he heard a little answering cry. Guiding himself by the sound, he made his way through the gathering darkness to the foot of an old beech tree, with a hole in it, and from out of the hole came a feeble voice, saying 'Ratty! Is that really you?'

Uly 15.2160: *L'homme primigène!*

Although the passage in which this phrase occurs seems clearly to have been inspired by Victor Hugo's novel *L'Homme qui rit* (1869), the phrase itself occurs not there but in the Dutch sinologist and field naturalist Gustaaf (or Gustave) Schlegel's (1843–1903) *Uranographie Chinoise, ou Preuves Directes Que l'Astronomie Primitive Est Originaire de La Chine, et Qu'elle a Été Empruntée Par Les Anciens Peuples Occidentaux à la Sphère Chinoise*—that is, 'Chinese uranography, or, direct evidence that early astronomy originated in China, and that it was borrowed by ancient western peoples from the Chinese sphere' (The Hague and Leiden, Netherlands, 1875), with, on p. 262 (italics in the original): 'Ce qui confirme encore notre hypothèse sur l'identité de l'homme primigène *Pouan-kou* avec l'astérisme Étoile de l'homme, c'est que cet astérisme se trouve justement au dessus du centre de la grande constellation boréale de la *Tortue noire*, et que *Pouan-kou* et toujours représenté accompagné de la *tortue divine*, qui se trouve à ses pieds.'—that is, 'What further confirms our hypothesis on the identity of the primigenous [original] man *Pouan-kou* with the Star of Man asterism is that this asterism finds itself precisely above the center of the large boreal constellation of the Black Turtle, and that *Pouan-kou* is always represented accompanied by the *divine turtle*, located at his feet.'[30]

Uly 15.2167–68: Nebulous obscurity occupies space

The most familiar of the handful of pre-*Ulysses* literary instances of the phrase 'nebulous obscurity' occurs—after the tale's initial publication in the May 1838 issue of *The United States Magazine and Democratic Review* (Washington, D.C.)—in vol. 2 (of 2) of Hawthorne's *Twice-Told Tales* (Boston, 1842), where the first of the four stories comprising 'Legends of the Province House'—'Howe's Masquerade'—pp. 1–23, has, at the beginning of its final paragraph:

> When the truth-telling accents of the elderly gentleman were hushed, I drew a long breath and looked round the room, striving, with the best energy of my imagination, to throw a tinge of romance and historic grandeur over the realities of the scene. But my nostrils snuffed up a scent of cigar-smoke, clouds of which the narrator had emitted by way of visible emblem, I suppose, of the nebulous obscurity of his tale.

---

30 Pouan-kou is elsewhere identified as 'the *Sovereign Man*, the divine artificer and Demiourgos, who lived in the time of the primal chaos and formed the universe.' See 'On the Mythic Aspects of Ancient and Medieval Chronology', part 2', by 'L[uke]. B[urke].', in the Jan. 1866 issue of the London-based *Ethnological Journal: A Monthly Record of Ethnological Research and Criticism*, p. 305.

Given Joyce's quoted phrase in its entirety, however, it seems more likely, though by no means certain, that he had in mind a work by the British inventor, precision-tool manufacturer, engineer, architect, author, and educational philanthropist (among other pursuits) William Ford Stanley (1829–1909) entitled *Notes on the Nebular Theory in Relation to Stellar, Solar, Planetary, Cometary, and Geological Phenomena* (London, 1895). In that book—the reviews of which, in *Nature* and other scientific journals, generally dismissed it as ill-informed, speculative, and stylistically impenetrable—Stanley offered his views, as an amateur cosmologist and mathematician, in general support of the French astronomer and mathematician Pierre-Simon Laplace's suggestion (1796) that the Sun and its planets were formed when a rotating nebula cooled, collapsed, and condensed into rings that eventually became the solar system as we know it. It was a 'period of nebulous obscurity of the sun caused by an absorption band across the sun's disc,' Stanley claimed on p. 214, followed by a 'period of dull nebulous light and heat lasting from the early part of the condensation of the Venus-zone,' that eventually led to the formation of [Venus] as a nebulous planet.

Uly 15.2332: Meretricious finery to deceive the eye.

'Meretricious finery' is a topic addressed by the French theologian, pastor, and leading Protestant reformist John Calvin (1509–1564) in his *Commentary on Hosea* (Geneva, 1557), including on Hosea ii 2 (italics in the original):

> Then God says, *Let her take away her fornications*. But the phrase, *Let her take away from her face and from her breasts*, seems singular; and what does it mean? because women commit fornication neither by the face nor by the breasts. It is evident the Prophet alludes to meretricious finery; for harlots, that they may entice men, sumptuously adorn themselves, and carefully paint their face and decorate their breasts.

The phrase recurs six years later in Foxe's *Actes and Monuments* (his *Book of Martyrs*) where it is applied explicitly to the Roman Catholic Church:

> The Church of Rome is a new and upstart communion, built up of the spoils of religion, reason, human right, and social affection. In the protestant churches alone, we hail and revere the grey hairs of

age and of ancient times, and we rise and venerate the august and holy form. All that our Reformers did, and all we desire to do, is to detach the meretricious finery and fantastic rags wherewith the Lady of Babylon has decked out the church, and marred her fair aspect, and present her as the apostles did, bright with the signatures of primeval truth, arrayed in the robes and adorned by the likeness of Jesus, and inlaid with the inner glories of the Holy Spirit.

Uly 15.2380: a chapter of accidents

Early instances or variants of Joyce's phrase occur in Smollett's *Humphry Clinker*, where, in vol. 1 (of 2) of the second edition (London, 1771), p. 13, a letter dated 6 April from Lydia Melford to her friend Lætitia Willis reads in part: 'let us trust to time and the chapter of accidents; or rather to that Providence which will not fail, sooner or later, to reward those that walk in the paths of honour and virtue.'; and as the title of a play by the English novelist, playwright, and educator Sophia Lee (1750–1824), *The Chapter of Accidents: a Comedy, in Five Acts, as it is performed at the Theatre-Royal in the Hay-Market* (London, 1780). Two later instances of the phrase occur in Hughes's *Tom Brown's School Days*, as the title of chap. 9, 'A Chapter of Accidents'; and as the title of the book *A Chapter of Accidents; or, The Mother's Assistant, in Cases of Burns, Scalds, Cuts, Etc* (London, 1860), by the anonymous author of *A Woman's Secret* and *Woman's Work*.

Brewer's *Dictionary of Phrase and Fable* defines 'chapter of accidents' as unforeseen events. 'To trust to the chapter of accidents is to trust that something unforeseen may turn up in your favour.'

Uly 15.2413: reiterated coition

This rare phrase seems first to have occurred in the Scottish physician Robert Couper's (1750–1818) *Speculations on the Mode and Appearances of Impregnation in the Human Female* (Edinburgh and London, 1789), with, on p. 44, in the first of the book's two instances of the phrase: 'If an afflux of blood to these parts was always to be attended with these alleged effects, what violence must the ovaria be exposed to, by reiterated coition, and by every return of the menstrual discharge?'; then on p. 60, in the second instance: 'And we may add farther, that when the consent and power of procreation begins to fail on the part of the female, the crenulations of the vagina are then always visibly decayed, whether affected by the advances of age, or by imprudently reiterated coition.' The latter passage also appears in the article on 'Conception' in the *Encyclopaedia Londinensis, or, Universal Dictionary of Arts, Sciences, and Literature* (London, 1810), which article, though unsigned, Couper may also have written.

Uly 15.2436–37: Stay, good friend.

Among other pre-*Ulysses* instances of the phrase, see Schiller's five-act, seventy-five-scene republican tragedy *Die Verschwörung des Fiesco zu Genua* (Frankfurt and Leipzig, 1783), anonymously translated from the German as *Fiesco, or The Conspiracy of Genoa* (London and Edinburgh, 1841), Act 1, scene 9, p. 18, with: '*Fiesco* (*seizing him ; calls with a loud voice.*)—Stephano ! Drullo ! Antonio ! (*seizing the Moor by the throat.*)— Stay, good friend ! Infernal knavery ! (*Enter servants.*) Remain and answer me ! You have bungled the thing sadly ; whom have you to ask for your hire ?'

Uly 15.2457: Instinct rules the world.

Both Gifford and SMT cite William Ross Wallace's 'What Rules the World?': 'They say that man is mighty, | He governs land and sea; | He wields a might scepter | O'er lesser powers that be; | And the hand that rocks the cradle | Is the hand that rules the world.' Joyce's phrase, however, occurs verbatim pre-*Ulysses* in two novels, first in the English novelist, essayist, and feminist Mona Caird's (1854–1932) *The Daughters of Danaus* (London, 1894), chap. 22, which ends, on pp. 211–12:

> " This hero-worship blinds you. Depend upon it, he is not without the primitive instinct to kill."
> " There are individual exceptions to all savage instincts, or the world would never move."
> " Instinct rules the world," said Miss Du Prel. " At least it is obviously neither reason nor the moral sense that rules it."
> " Then why does it produce a Professor Fortescue now and then ? "
> " Possibly as a corrective."
> " Or perhaps for fun," said Hadria.

and next in the English novelist and poet Ethel Sidgwick's (1877–1970) *Succession: A Comedy of the Generations* (London, 1913), chap. 7 ('The Penalty'), p. 224:

> " I have quarrelled with Madame," wrote Savigny finally. " I knew I should, before we got through. She has her plan, cut out and ready, clean as you please, not an allowance made anywhere for other people's ideas. The way these females think their instinct rules the world. Instinct ? It is the cunning of the weak, developed by a few centuries' experience on slightly better lines than Eve's was, that is all.["]

Uly 15.2516: All is not well.

Unremarked by Thornton, Gifford, and SMT, this phrase occurs in *Hamlet*, I ii 254–57, where in the scene's final lines the grieving prince, now alone, says: 'My father's spirit—in arms! All is not well, | I doubt some foul play. Would the night were come! | Till then sit still, my soul. [Foul] deeds will rise, | Though all the earth o'erwhelm them, to men's eyes.'

Uly 15.2690: And the breath of the balmy night

As SMT note, Stanislaus Joyce recalled the song of which this is the third of four quoted lines as one sung by his father, and Simon Daedalus sings the four lines in *Stephen Hero*, but, they add, the song is otherwise unknown. Coincidentally or not, this line from the song matches nearly verbatim a phrase in the last sentence of a tale in the French novelist Alphonse Daudet's (1840–1897) short-story collection *Lettres de mon moulin* (Paris, 1869) translated by Katharine Prescott Wormeley as *Letters from My Mill; To which are added Letters to an Absent One* (Boston, 1900). The story, 'At Milianah. Notes of Travel.' in Wormeley's version, ends on p. 152 with: 'All this is floating in the moonrays to the soft breath of the balmy night.'

Uly 15.2702–03: I'm very fond of what I like.

Not noted by Thornton, Gifford, SMT, or others, Zoe's phrase perfectly matches the first line of a music-hall song performed by Harry Champion (stage name of the English music-hall composer, singer, and comedian William Henry Crump, 1865–1942), words and music by the English songwriter Gren Forbes (pseudonym of Arthur Stroud). The first verse and chorus of the song, called 'I Want Meat', as transcribed from a 1925 audio recording by Champion (available at the link cited below)[31] that begins with Champion singing 'In My Old White Spats'), read:

> I'm very fond of what I like, and what I like, I like.
> When they tell me to eat more fruit, my inside goes on strike.
> The roast beef of old England's good enough for me today,
> And when my dinnertime comes round, you're sure to hear me say:
>
> *Chorus*
> I want meat. I want meat.
> Meat, meat, meat, meat, meat.
> I like it cold. I like it hot.
> Like it in a stew in the old Dutch pot.
> Leg of pork, a leg o' lamb,
> Juicy steak, a slice of ham.
> I don't want fruit from Alabam'
> I want meat, meat, meat.

Uly 15.2864: I promise never to disobey.

Gifford notes that 'In *Venus in Furs* (pp. 90–91) Severin signs the "agreement" that makes him Wanda's servant-slave, Gregor; the agreement, of course, involves a similar promise.' Along with that and the antecedents cited by SMT—a reader's letter sent to the fetish magazine *Bits of Fun* published in the 7 August 1920 issue, a copy of which issue Frank Budgen sent to Joyce at Joyce's request; and the oath of Entered Apprentices (also cited by Gifford) that was part of the Masonic initiation rite—see Musgrave Heaphy's (1843–1910) *Glimpses and Gleams* (London, 1884), in the last of whose seven stories, 'The Blue Scarf'—reminiscent of Grahame's *The Wind in the Willows*, though that book was not published until 1908—the highlighted phrase occurs verbatim on p. 151:

---

31 'Harry Champion - In My Old White Spats / I Want Meat (1925)', uploaded by VintageBritishComedy, 18 June 2012, YouTube, https://youtu.be/YBOi_QEGma8?si=fmQtho9U7G75p6Ia&t=202

" Mistress Toad," said he, " we must do what we can to get this little Boy well, although he is a Human Being, for he has shown kindness to one that is dear to us."

" If you will only do that, I promise never to disobey again as long as I live ; I will never even go out of your sight unless you give me permission," said the young Frog eagerly.

The London-born Thomas Musgrave Heaphy, his obituary states, was in 1874 'appointed scientific adviser, engineer and inspector to the Phœnix Fire Office, and was the author of the Phœnix rules for electric-light and power installations.' *Glimpses and Gleams* seems to have been his only work of prose fiction.

Uly 15.2866: You little know what's in store for you.

Gifford writes: 'Wanda repeatedly makes similar remarks to Severin in [Sacher-Masoch's] *Venus in Furs*'; SMT specifically compare Bella/Bello's 'You little know what's in store for you' to Wanda's 'You shall know me! (p. 151)'. But see also Arnold Heath's (perhaps a pseudonym; personal details unknown) novel *Edith's Marriage* (London, 1868), vol. 2 (of 3), chap. 1, pp. 23–24, where, on the latter page the highlighted phrase occurs verbatim:

> " They must have been very busy about some one's character, or I should not have got away without a regular examination," said he to himself. " However, I am all right now, and shall be off by the next train. Ha ! ha ! my friend Fred, you little know what's in store for you, but I'm afraid your blissful ignorance will be rudely enlightened before very long."

The same phrase also occurs in *Sweet, Not Lasting* (London, 1874), a novel by the otherwise unknown Annie B. Lefurt, with, in chap. 9 ('Love's Young Dream'), the following exchange on p. 140 (italics in the original):

> " Have you seen Miss Dorcas Sandiland since you took to the water-dog business ?" asked young Bennett.
> " No, and I don't want to," growled Bertie, who was as little disposed to cultivate her acquaintance as he could possibly be. A fellow-feeling has not *always* the effect of making us " wondrous kind."

"Ah ! you little know what's in store for you *there*. I have it on good authority she means to honour you with an embrace the first time she meets you."

Uly 15.2966: Now for your punishment frock.

The 'punishment frock' that Bella/Bello threatens to use on Bloom—or one like it—made another literary appearance five years before Joyce wrote 'Circe'. *The Daughter of a Soldier: A Colleen of South Ireland* (London, 1915), by Elizabeth Thomasina Meade Smith as 'Mrs. L. T. Meade', chap. 25 ('Fuzzy-Wuzzy') has the following dialogue on pp. 312–13:

> " Daisy," said Maureen, " she has come to tell you that she is very, very sorry."
> " I am indeed, most truly," said Henrietta, and there was absolute conviction in her voice.
> " Then of course I forgive you, Fuzzy darling—darling! It was your trying to take off our dearest Maureen that hurt my very soul."
> Here she touched Maureen with infinite love and tenderness on the shoulder.
> " I quite forgive our Henny," she said.
> " Then, my dear Henrietta," said Mrs. Faithful, " there is an end of the matter. You have expressed sorrow and are quite forgiven. Maureen, darling, take her upstairs and remove her punishment frock. We sincerely trust there will not be a repetition of this terrible scene."

Uly 15.2990: Little jobs that make mother pleased, eh?

Joyce had been working for a year on the 'Circe' episode and had just written out, or was about to write out, the latest of several fair copies of the episode when, in January 1921, an advertisement in that month's issue of *The Strand Magazine*, vol. 61, no. 36, seems to have caught his eye. There, on page 63 of the issue's advertising section, was an advert for The "FLUXITE" Soldering Set, a product of FLUXITE Ltd. of Bermondsey, England. FLUXITE, the advert declared,

> can be used by father, sonny, or the maid, and think of the heavy plumber's bills it will save. Every day there is some job for FLUXITE,

and after all there is a great pleasure in doing those many little jobs that make mother pleased and keep money in your pocket.

Adverts for The "FLUXITE" Soldering Set had been placed in *The Strand Magazine* once or twice a year since 1910, and would be placed there a total of six times in 1921 alone. But no two FLUXITE adverts were ever exactly alike, and I have found no other advert for FLUXITE in that or any other publication containing the phrase 'little jobs that make mother pleased'. It would seem, then, that it was this advert in this issue of this publication that inspired Joyce's use of the phrase as he continued to work on the 'Circe' episode in and well beyond January 1921.

Uly 15.3481: You'll know me the next time.

See note on line 15.1321.

Uly 15.4029-30: exaggerated grace

Unremarked by Thornton, Gifford, and SMT, Joyce's phrase, in a sentence reading 'Stephen, arming Zoe with exaggerated grace, begins to waltz her round the room', may have been suggested to him by a passage in Honoré de Balzac's novel *La Cousine Bette* (Paris, 1846)—the first episode in Balzac's *La Comédie humaine*—in which the title character, an unmarried middle-aged woman in mid-nineteenth-century Paris, aided and abetted by the young, unhappily married Valérie Marneffe, sets out to destroy her extended family by seducing and tormenting its male members. In the Caxton Edition of Balzac's *The Human Comedy* (London, 1896), vol. 1, *Cousin Bette*, as translated by George Burnham Ives, reads on p. 127:

> Madame Marneffe bowed gracefully, and was as proud of her success as the baron of his.
> " Where the devil was she coming from so early?" he asked himself, while he watched the undulating movement of her dress, to which she imparted a somewhat exaggerated grace. " Her face is too tired to be returning from the baths, and her husband is waiting for her. It's very puzzling and furnishes much food for thought."

Other novels in which Joyce's phrase occurs include M. E. Braddon's *The Fatal Three* (London, 1890), p. 249; Edmund Gosse's *The Secret of Narcisse* (London, 1892), p. 57; and Anne Douglas Sedgwick's *Paths of Judgement* (London, 1904), p. 131.

Uly 15.4227: The intellectual imagination!

SMT write that Stephen's phrase echoes Matthew Arnold's reference to 'imaginative reason' in the lecture on 'Pagan and Medieval Religious Sentiment' (1864) collected in his *Essays in Criticism: First Series* (1865), p. 212. The phrase occurs verbatim, however, in the title of the English poet, short-story writer, novelist, and essayist Walter de la Mare's (1873–1956) long essay *Rupert Brooke and the Intellectual Imagination* (London, 1919), in which essay the phrase is also extensively repeated and discussed.

Uly 15.4672: A chasm opens with a noiseless yawn.

What seems the only pre-Joyce instance of 'noiseless yawn'—it is also present in Joyce's *Stephen Hero*—occurs in *Adrian Rome* (London, 1899), the second of two collaborative novels by Ernest Dowson and Arthur Moore, chap. 1, p. 11:

> After Lord Hildebrand had polished his eyeglass to his satisfaction, and had buttoned a pair of loose but otherwise entirely unimpeachable grey kid gloves, he settled himself more comfortably in his seat, and relaxed his immobile features, first in a noiseless yawn, which displayed a set of suspiciously perfect teeth, and then into a smile at once indulgent and conciliatory.

Uly 15.4692: goddess of unreason

Commenting on Joyce's phrase—which occurs in a sentence reading, in lines 15.4691–93, 'On the altarstone Mrs Mina Purefoy, goddess of unreason, lies, naked, fettered, a chalice resting on her swollen belly.'— Gifford writes, in a note echoed by SMT: 'Black Mass is traditionally celebrated with the body of a naked woman as the altar. As "goddess of unreason," she is an inversion of the "Goddess of Reason," an abstraction set up in 1793 by the French Revolutionists to take the place of the Christian God as the supreme deity.' To this may be added that Joyce's phrase occurs verbatim in a handful of pre-*Ulysses* works.

One of these, entitled 'Popery in Paris' and signed 'J. R. L.', appears in the April 1867 issue (vol. 45) of *The Evangelical Magazine and Missionary Chronicle*, a London-based Protestant publication, and reads on p. 195, referring to Paris's Metropolitan Cathedral, Nôtre Dame, during and after its seizure and sacking by an anti-Catholic mob during the French Revolution (italics in the original):

> Such were the revolutionary orgies in the so-called Temple of Reason. It is now, and, indeed, long has been restored to its original papal worship, but might be said paradoxically to be at present consecrated to the Goddess of Unreason—for such may the Virgin of Immaculate Conception be styled. How remarkable is the union of high intellect and gross superstition in this age, and in this building ! Here, annually, on [the Feast of the Immaculate Conception, a Roman Catholic observance], meet some of the *literati* of Paris, and many of its municipal authorities and officers. Can one suppose that these men really believe in the papal dogma respecting the Virgin ? And yet here also weekly meet many devout females, and of course the members of the priesthood, who do apparently believe this gross fable and this palpably human invention. Yes, this is preached and believed in the very same old " Temple of Reason," now certainly become a Temple of Unreason !

Another was in a story by the American-British author Henry James (1843–1916) called 'Guest's Confession', published in the October 1872 (vol. 30, no. 180) and November 1872 (vol. 30, no. 181) issues of *The Atlantic Monthly* (Boston), and reading, on p. 386 of the former:

> I was discomposed and irritated, and all for no better reason than that Edgar was coming. What was Edgar that his comings and goings should affect me ? Was I, after all, so excessively his younger brother ? I would turn over a new leaf ! I almost wished things would come to a crisis between us, and that in the glow of exasperation I might say or do something unpardonable. But there was small chance of my quarrelling with Edgar for vanity's sake. Somehow, I didn't believe in my own egotism, but I had an indefeasible respect for his. I was fatally goodnatured, and I should continue to do his desire until I began to do that of some one else. If I might only fall in love and exchange my master for a mistress, for some charming goddess of unreason who would declare that Mr. Musgrave was simply intolerable and that was an end of it !

A third was in an essay by Peter Struthers entitled 'South Africa and Imperialism', published in *The Westminster Review* (London), vol. 156, no. 2 (Aug. 1901), 119–32, and reading, on p. 131, after asking whether any patriotic Briton would accept an invasion by, and subordination to, the German Emperor even if he promised to leave Great Britain free to manage her own internal affairs:

> Any thinking man can see that that is a most illogical position, and yet that is practically how many so-called patriots reason regarding the South African Republic. The revolutionary Parisians worshipped the Goddess of Reason. The patriotic British Jingoes worship the Goddess of Unreason. For my part, I prefer the Goddess of Reason. When we see men who glory in the deeds of Wallace and Bruce, those great guerilla leaders, foam at the mouth when De Wet and Botha, men of the same noble strain, receive their due meed of praise, we see how pseudo-patriotism prevents its devotees from recognising the truth.

16. 'Eumaeus'

Uly 16.22: the distinctly fetid atmosphere of the livery stables

See, by Emmet Densmore, M.D. (1837–1911), *How Nature Cures: comprising A New System of Hygiene ; also The Natural Food of Man: A Statement of the Principal Arguments Against the Use of Bread, Cereals, Pulses, Potatoes, and All Other Starch Foods* (London and New York, 1892), with, in chap. 4 ('Sleep and Hygienic Aids'), on pp. 88–89, what appear to be the only two pre-*Ulysses* instances of 'distinctly fetid atmosphere':

> Even those who are in the greatest fear of a draught, and who have become accustomed to living in close and unventilated apartments, are still able to feel the difference between a distinctly fetid atmosphere and a room that is reasonably free from impurities. Any of our readers who have been in the life-long habit of sleeping in close bedrooms—and who have supposed that this course is a necessary safeguard—and who are content in the impure atmosphere of a church, a theatre, or a living room badly ventilated, are still able to perceive that an escape from a distinctly fetid atmosphere is a great gain in comfort.

Uly 16.55: with internal satisfaction

Joyce's phrase occurred several times in imaginative literature over the course of the nineteenth century, perhaps most notably in an early, anonymous English translation of Alexandre Dumas's *The Count of Monte Christo* [sic] (London, 1848), with, in vol. 2 (of 3), chap. 48 ('The Dappled Greys'), p. 133:

> The count witnessed all this with internal satisfaction, and a smile stole over his features as he thought that such a child bade fair to realize one part of his hopes ; while Madame de Villefort reprimanded her son with a gentleness and moderation very far from conveying the least idea of a fault having been committed.

It also occurred, also notably, in Isabel F. Hapgood's translation from the Russian, as collected in his *St. John's Eve and Other Stories* (New York, 1886), of the Ukrainian playwright, short-story writer, and novelist Nikolai Gogol's (1809–1852) 'The Cloak' (1842)—better known in other, later translations as 'The Overcoat'—with, on p. 347: 'Meantime Akakiy Akakievitch went on with every sense in holiday mood. He was conscious every second of the time, that he had a new cloak on his shoulders ; and several times he laughed with internal satisfaction.'[32]

Uly 16.62: disgustingly sober

Although it occurred from time to time elsewhere—mostly in periodicals, mostly in America—Joyce seems most likely to have encountered this phrase in the English journalist, author, and promoter of the Volunteer Force (a citizen army) Alfred Bate Richards's (1820–1876) *So Very Human: A Tale of the Present Day* (London, 1873), vol. 1 (of 3), chap. 15 ('A Tilt in the Escurial'), p. 251:

> The vengeance which the Fates meditated that eventful evening was of the smallest and the paltriest kind. A puny little wandering Nemesis, bent on mortal mischief, had, as we have recorded, drawn thither, by some invisible string, the elegant Phil Cousens and his companion at that particular time. Phil himself was, as he said, disgustingly sober, but his companion was in the first stage of Circean enchantment. He had already drunk the blood of the monkey, and a single glass of the Escurial brandy initiated him into the lion stage.

---

32 In chap. 9, 'Farrington, the Scrivener, Revisited: "Counterparts"', of her *Suspicious Readings of Joyce's 'Dubliners'* (Philadelphia: University of Pennsylvania Press, 2003) 122–39, p. 122, Margot Norris writes that Herman Melville's short story 'Bartleby, the Scrivener' has already been remarked as an analogue for Joyce's 'Counterparts', adding: 'And I would suggest consideration also of Gogol's story "The Overcoat," about a scrivener crazed by the theft of his new coat. There is, alas, no evidence that Joyce read either story'. The presence of the rare phrase 'with internal satisfaction' both here in *Ulysses* and in Hapgood's translation of Gogol's tale, although less than conclusive, may constitute such evidence.

Uly 16.223–24: in every deep, so to put it, a deeper depth

As Thornton and SMT note, the ultimate source of the highlighted phrase is probably Satan's speech in Milton's *Paradise Lost*, 4.73–78: 'Me miserable ! which way shall I fly | Infinite wrath and infinite despair ? | Which way I fly is Hell ; myself am Hell ; | And, in the lowest deep, a lower deep | Still threatening to devour me opens wide, | To which the Hell I suffer seems a Heaven.'

But near-verbatim antecedents of Joyce's phrase, with 'so to put it' replaced by "there is", seem to have occurred only twice before his use of it, once in an article entitled 'Nails and Chains' by the Non-Subscribing Presbyterian Church of Ireland minister, journalist, land leaguer, and home ruler Rev. Harold Rylett (1851–1936) published in the December 1889 issue of *The English Illustrated Magazine*, 163–75, aimed at eliciting sympathy for the women and children employed in the hand-made chain and nail trades of late-nineteenth-century England, with, on p. 168: 'In every deep there is a deeper depth, and we have not touched bottom in the nail trade until we have seen how spike nails are made'; and again in *Sanity and Insanity* (London, 1895), by the British psychiatrist, expert on forensic psychiatry and insanity, and debunker of spiritualism Charles Mercier (1851–1919), chap. 11 ('The Forms of Insanity'), reading, on pp. 296–97: 'In every deep there is a deeper depth, and even in idiocy there are degrees of defect, some being less and some more severely affected.'

Uly 16.253: to seek misfortune

Only a handful of instances of this phrase seem to have occurred pre-*Ulysses*, two of them in English translations of French fiction.

The first of the two: in the French journalist, novelist, poet, playwright, and librettist Joseph Méry's (1797–1866) *La Guerre du Nizam* (Paris, 1847), as translated 'from the thirty-fifth Paris edition' by O. Vibeur under the title *Through Thick and Thin: or, "La Guerre du Nizam"* (New York and Paris, 1874)—an Anglo-Indian tale reissued as an anonymous work under the title *Only Caprice* by the same publisher (G. W. Carleton, New York) in 1879—in the first section of which ('Octavia's Whims'), chap. 1 ('A

Wedding-Bell in Smyrna'), p. 41, the Englishman Sir Edward Klerbbs is taking leave of the young French widow Countess Octavie de Verzon:

> " I dread happiness, madame ; I dread it as an unknown enemy."
> " And what are you seeking, then, throughout the world ? "
> " Misfortune ! I like things that are easily found."
> The countess threw her head back with a swan-like undulation ; her black curls left uncovered her brow and her temples, and her eyes, fixed on Sir Edward's face, shone with a lustre full of tenderness and seduction. She selected the most velvety notes within the compass of her voice ; it sounded something like the suave and mysterious orchestra accompaniment to the final trio in the *Comte Ory*.
> " One goes far to seek misfortune, Sir Edward," she said, " when the happiness that one does not seek lies sometimes within reach.["]

The second of the two: in chap. 8 of the French novelist Georges Ohnet's (1848–1918) *Serge Panine* (Paris, 1881) as translated by Jessie Hamilton (Manchester and London, 1883) under the title *Serge Panine; or, Can You Blame Her?*—and as later issued in a nearly identical but more widely available translation under the title *Prince Serge Panine* (London, 1885)—where, on p. 86 of the 1883 edition, the eponymous Prince Panine is talking to Madame Desvarennes, with whose daughter Micheline the prince is in love:

> Madame Desvarennes became thoughtful. " What a strange thing life is ! " said she. " I did not want you for a son-in-law, and now you are behaving so well towards me that I am full of remorse. Oh, I see now what a dangerous man you are, if you captivate other women's hearts as you have done mine." She looked at the Prince fixedly, and said in her clear commanding voice, with a shade of gaiety : " Now, I hope you will reserve all your powers of charming for my daughter. No more flirting, eh ? She loves you ; she would be jealous, and you would get into hot water with me ! Let Micheline's life be happy, without a cloud—blue, always blue sky ! "
> " That will be easy," said Serge. " To be unhappy I should have to seek misfortune ; and I certainly shall not do that."

A third instance of the same phrase occurred in Hayward Porter's translation into English of the French poet and critic Nicolas Boileau Despréaux's (1636–1711) 'Satire X' in *The Satires of Boileau Despréaux and his 'Address to the King'* (Glasgow, 1904), reading, on p. 93:

> ' With much devotion to the Saints she oft repairs,
> She reads Rodriguez, formulates long mental prayers,
> She goes about to seek misfortune far and wide ;
> To visit hospitals and prisons is her pride ['.]

Uly 16.529: a bit of bounce

The phrase 'a bit of bounce'—signifying a rhetorical flourish or threat display, mainly for effect—occurred several times, mainly in periodical literature, in the half-century before Joyce's use of it in *Ulysses*. One such instance: in the novella 'The Winning Hazard', by the English writer Frederick Talbot (fl. 1870s–1880s), published in *Chambers's Journal*, vol. 8, Christmas Extra Double Number (24 Dec. 1870), 1–32, with, in chap. 16 ('To-morrow! Oh, that's sudden! Spare him, spare him!'), the following passage on p. 26:

> ' Look here, miss : we've not been asleep in the matter. We've filed a bill, and got a receiver appointed, and there'll be a meeting at his office—it's old Nails the lawyer, you know—there'll be a meeting at his office a Monday at noon. Now your feyther—ax your pardon, I mean your uncle—he must be there with t' brass. But if he can't bring brass, he may bring a note ee your handwriting, summat after this fashion : " Dear Mr Good, I accept you as my husband ;" and then *we'll* square it for you. Good'll write a cheque for the money, and there'll be an end of it.'
> ' And if he brings neither note nor money ?'
> ' Why, then, the law must take its course.'
> ' I think I understand. Then you'll leave us now without more ado till Monday ?'
> ' Ay, miss.'
> ' Then why did you bring the constable ?'
> ' That were a bit of bounce, miss, more than aught else. Only we thought if th' old gent turned nasty, why we'd be nasty too.'

and again in the novel *The Voyage of the "Pulo Way": A Record of Some Strange Doings at Sea* (London, 1898), by the Australian author Carlton Dawe (1865–1935), with, in chap. 7 ('Piracy on the High Seas'), p. 101:

> It was a bit of bounce, and yet not altogether bounce. I knew the men were desperate, and that they would not hesitate to sacrifice me if I endeavoured to thwart them. The alternative was therefore given me— and yet what an alternative ! To join them, even against my will, would

be to make me equally guilty in the eyes of the law. Not to join them meant that there was no room for me aboard the *Pulo Way*. Therefore the bounce was not all bounce ; there was a deadly seriousness underlying it as befitted such an occasion, which I think Macshiel was quick to see. Or perhaps the knowledge that between him and a bullet there was only the lining of my coat may have quickened his perception.

Uly 16.588: chamber of horrors

The phrase seems first to have been employed in 1843 when Madame Tussaud referred in an advert to a room in her family's wax museum—a room previously called at various times the Separate Room, the Dead Room, and the Black Room—as its Chamber of Horrors. Thanks especially to several subsequent print and cartoon mentions and appearances of it in *Punch*—one notable example being a cartoon captioned 'TIME'S WAXWORKS' in the 31 December 1881 issue, in which Father Time shows Mr Punch around Madame Tussaud's and Mr Punch says, pointing to the figure of an Irish terrorist carrying blunderbuss, knife, pistol, and dynamite, "HA! YOU'LL HAVE TO PUT HIM INTO THE CHAMBER OF HORRORS!"— 'chamber of horrors' soon gained wide currency as a catch phrase with a life of its own independent of its connection to Madame Tussaud's.

Uly 16.607: took the civilised world by storm

An early instance of the phrase occurs in the January 1855 issue of *The Edinburgh Review*, vol. 101, no. 205, pp. 191–220, in an unsigned article with the running title 'Mount Athos and its Monasteries' reviewing three books—including the Oxford don George Ferguson Bowen's *Mount Athos, Thessaly, and Epirus: a Diary of a Journey from Constantinople to Corfu* (London, 1852); the artist Edward Lear's *Journals of a Landscape Painter* (London, 1851); and the Right Hon. the Earl of Carlisle's *Diary in Turkish and Greek Waters* (London, 1854)—where, on p. 207, commenting on the victory of the Greek over the Persian fleet at the battle of Salamis, and of its army over Persia's at the battle of Plataea, the reviewer writes: 'And it is a lasting and wonderful monument of that novel influence which issued from an obscure corner of Asia, took the civilised world by storm, and has held possession of it ever since.'

Uly 16.634: find out the secret for himself

Gifford, SMT, and others cite Henry Wadsworth Longfellow's poem 'The Secret of the Sea" (1841)' with '"Would'st thou," so the helmsman answered, | "Learn the secret of the sea? | Only those who brave its dangers | Comprehend its mystery!"' (lines 29–32).' Joyce's phrase occurs verbatim, however, in a handful of pre-*Ulysses* works.

One such work: 'Tom Crosthwaite's Motto', by 'Uncle Maurice', in *The Juvenile Magazine* (London), vol. 5 (Nov. 1881), chap. 11, p. 162: 'Mr. Barker had furnished him with only the barest directions for the purpose, being anxious that Tom should find out the secret for himself if possible, and Tom had determined that before the night was over the difficulty should be solved and mastered.'

And another: *Kilmeny of the Orchard* (London, 1910), a romance novel by the Canadian author—best known for her *Anne of Green Gables* (London, 1908)—L[ucy]. M[aud]. Montgomery (1874–1942), with, in chap. 5 ('A Phantom of Delight'), p. 68: 'If he had to ask any one it should be Mrs. Williamson; but he meant to find out the secret for himself if it were at all possible.'

Uly 16.986: a forcible-feeble philippic

SMT note the *OED*'s definition of 'forcible feeble' as 'feeble but making a great presence of vigour', but not the phrase's Shakespearean origin in 2 *Henry the Fourth*, III ii 164–68, Falstaff to Feeble: 'I would thou wert a man's tailor, that thou mightst mend him and make him fit to go. I cannot put him to a private soldier that is the leader of so many thousands. Let that suffice, most forcible Feeble.'

17. 'Ithaca'

Uly 17.23: inherited tenacity

This pseudo-scientific term—which occurs with some frequency in late-nineteenth-century treatises purporting to explain why people having certain physical, psychological, and/or other characteristics tend to survive and flourish while others lacking such characteristics often do not—also turns up on occasion in literary contexts. One such occasion is the English novelist George Gissing's (1857–1903) introduction to Dickens's *The Old Curiosity Shop and Master Humphrey's Clock* (London, 1901), p. xv: 'Dickens, an Englishman and an artist, clings to the ancient with inherited tenacity, yet assails its abuses with the keenest gusto.'

The phrase recurs in the British whaler, lecturer, and writer of sea stories Frank T. Bullen's (1857–1915) short story "Light Ho, Sir!", first published under that title by Crowell (New York), along with another Bullen story ('My Night Watch is Over'), in 1901, later collected in his *Light Ho, Sir! And Other Sketches* (London, 1913), published by the Religious Tract Society. In both appearances, the story's fifth paragraph reads:

> Now it is no part of my present plan, even if I had the necessary material, to trace Johnny's career from the gutters of —— until he found himself in the position of boy on board a North Country collier brig, being then, as he supposed, about thirteen years of age. By some inherited tenacity of constitution he had survived those years of starvation, cold, and brutality, and was, upon going to sea, like a well-seasoned rattan, without an ounce of superfluous flesh upon him, and with a capacity for stolid endurance almost equalling a Seminole Indian.

Uly 17.233–34: in fresh cold neverchanging everchanging water

Possibly suggested by the last two lines of Tennyson's poem 'To the Duke of Argyll', written in 1881, first published in *Tiresias and Other Poems* (London, 1885), p. 194, and reading in its entirety:

> O Patriot Statesman, be thou wise to know
> The limits of resistance, and the bounds
> Determining concession ; still be bold
> Not only to slight praise but to suffer scorn ;
> And be thy heart a fortress to maintain
> The day against the moment, and the year
> Against the day ; thy voice, a music heard
> Thro' all the yells and counter-yells of feud
> And faction, and thy will, a power to make
> This ever-changing world of circumstance,
> In changing, chime with never-changing Law.

Uly 17.322: corrugated his brow

Gifford notes that 'Odysseus's brow is repeatedly "corrugated" as he witnesses the state of affairs in his besieged home'. Among the handful of other pre-*Ulysses* instances of the same phrase, see—in *The Modern Pythagorean: A Series of Tales, Essays, and Sketches, by the late Robert Macnish, LL.D.*, surgeon, physician, philosopher, and writer (1802–1837), vol. 2 of 2 (Edinburgh and London, 1838)—'The Metempsychosis', 1–55, with, on p. 44: '" Then, fool," said he, while a frown perfectly unnatural to him corrugated his brow, and his eyes shot forth vivid glances of fire—" then, fool, I leave you to your fate. You shall never see me again."'; and—by the English novelist, poet, and youngest of the Brontë sisters, Anne Brontë (1820–1849) as 'Acton Bell'—in *The Tenant of Wildfell Hall* (London, 1848), chap. 38 ('The Injured Man'), p. 289: 'He continued gazing from the window while I spoke, and did not answer, but, stung by the recollections my words awakened, stamped his foot upon the floor, ground his teeth, and corrugated his brow, like one under the influence of acute physical pain.'

Instances of 'corrugated brow' minus the possessive pronoun occur in Emily Brontë's (as 'Ellis Bell') novel *Wuthering Heights* (London,

1847), vol. 2 (of 3), chap. 9, p. 185: '" Well, Linton," murmured Catherine, when his corrugated brow relaxed. " Are you glad to see me? Can I do you any good?"'; also in the American novelist E[mma]. D[orothy]. E[liza]. N[evitte]. Southworth's (1819–1899) *Allworth Abbey; or, Eudora* (New York, 1876)—after its serialization as 'Eudora' in *The London Journal*, beginning with vol. 34, no. 855 (29 June 1861)—chap. 2 ('Horrible Suspicions'), p. 54: 'Mr. Montrose withdrew his hand from his corrugated brow, raised his troubled eyes to the speaker, and awaited his further words.'; and in Robert Browning's 'The Two Poets of Croisic' (1878), stanza 146, ending: 'To do a sister's office and laugh smooth | Thy corrugated brow — that scowls forsooth !'

Uly 17.580–81: infinite possibilities [...] of the modern art of advertisement

Bloom's view of advertising as conveyed by Joyce was not without precedent. An article printed under the title 'A Notable Advertisement' in *The Gas World* (London), a trade journal, vol. 57, no. 1461 (20 July 1912), p. 77, reads in part:

> There was, until comparatively recently, very little about gas to advertise. There was only the flat-flame burner for light ; and although even this was, as a rule, badly done, there was not much likelihood that advertising in the newspapers would help matters. People either wanted gas light, or they did not ; and there was an end of the question. It is, of course, the pressure of competition and the variety of the services gas is now competent to render—always as one of several expedients equally open to the public for choice—that warrant the calling in of the modern art of advertisement to commend this particular service to the favourable attention of the community.

Uly 17.1055–56: a parenthesis of infinitesimal brevity

Although 'infinitesimal brevity' occurs from time to time elsewhere, mainly in scientific or technical publications, Joyce's application of the phrase to 'the years, threescore and ten, of allotted human life' may point to a passage in the fifth and subsequent editions of *Esoteric Buddhism*

(London, 1885 et seq.) by A[lfred]. P[ercy]. Sinnett (1840–1921), President of the London Lodge of the Theosophical Society—one of the first books seeking to explain Theosophy as promulgated by the Society to the general public—reading, on p. 128 of the 1885 edition:

> Again, while Kama loca periods may thus be prolonged beyond the average from various causes, they may sink to almost infinitesimal brevity when the spirituality of a person dying at a ripe old age, and at the close of a life which has legitimately fulfilled its purpose, is already far advanced.

In Buddhist and Theosophical belief, *Kama loca* denotes a posthumous, transitional plane of existence analogous to the Christian notion of Purgatory.

The phrase occurs again pre-Joyce in a footnote to the Anglican divine, scholar, hymnodist, poet, and translator E[dward]. H[ayes]. Plumptre's (1821–1891) edition of *The Commedia and Canzoniere of Dante Alighieri: A New Translation* (London, 1887), vol. 2 (of 2), p. 54, commenting, with reference to the *Summa Theologica* (iii, *Supp.* 84, 3) of the Italian Dominican friar, priest, theologian, and philosopher Saint Thomas Aquinas (1225–1274), on a passage in Plumptre's translation beginning on line 28 ('The minister of Nature, chief in might'):

> In this [Dante] was in accord with Aquinas, who discusses the question whether the saints in heaven move in time, and answers it in the affirmative ; the time, however, being imperceptible on account of its extreme, infinitesimal brevity.

Uly 17.1623: an innate love of rectitude

What may have been the earliest verbatim instance of the highlighted phrase occurs in *The Friend of Youth. Translated from the French of M. Berquin* (London, 1788)—that is, of the French children's author Arnaud Berquin (1747–1791), best known for his *L'Ami des Enfans* (London, 1782)—which includes, in vol. 1 (of 2), a closet drama entitled 'Charles II. A Drama in Five Acts', with, in Act 4, scene 13, at p. 199, the following speech by Lord Wyndham to the King:

> What is your happiness or mine? it is the happiness of a whole people, that should occupy your thoughts. Led astray by the violence of their

passions, but ever ready, from an innate love of rectitude, to return to the ways of justice and honour, they must be indebted to you alone for such a reformation : they will soon come and supplicate your return. Whenever that happens, grant their desire ; return, not as a conqueror, but as a father : my blood, then, will not cry out to you for vengeance, but for mercy, liberty, and love.

The phrase recurs, again verbatim, in *Sermons on Various Subjects* (London, 1827) by Aubrey George Spencer (1795–1872)—first bishop of the Anglican Diocese of Newfoundland and Bermuda; also bishop of Jamaica—sermon 17 of which ('On the Danger of Minor Offences') reads, on p. 180: 'For our abhorrence and correction of many flagrant offences, we are indebted not always to the virtues, but sometimes to the very vices of humanity ; not to an innate love of rectitude, but to a strong and overruling principle of selfishness.'

And recurs again in *College Debts. A Novel.* (London, 1870) 'By An Oxford M. A.'—elsewhere identified as the Anglican curate and author John Cox Boyce (1827–1889)—vol. 1 (of 2), chap. 8 ('Lord Forester'), pp. 124–25:

> " My dear fellow, a little worldly wisdom is a most wholesome thing. One cannot get through this kind of life without it."
>
> Grantley swallowed the reply which was rising to his lips. Impetuous and careless himself, he had yet an innate love of rectitude, and Osborne's speech seemed to him to testify either that University life, in his case, had blunted the edge of noble, unselfish principles, or that his character lacked altogether the ballast of high aims and good purposes to keep it the better in temptation.

Uly 17.1631–32: all perpetuators of international animosities

Among other pre-Joyce instances of the latter phrase, the lead editorial in the 'Topics of the Day' section of *The Spectator* (London) for the week ending 21 February 1903 is headed 'International Animosities' and begins, on p. 280, with the following:

> Mr. Balfour and Sir Henry Campbell-Bannerman have both during the past week lectured the British Press, including, no doubt, the *Spectator*, on its recklessness in stirring up international animosities,—the allusion, of course, being to the way in which the German Alliance

has been criticised, and to the plain speaking in regard to Germany's policy and her aspirations towards this country. The Prime Minister, quoted with approval by Sir Henry Campbell-Bannerman, used the following words :—" Let us remember that the old idea of Christendom should still be our idea ; that all those nations who are in the forefront of civilisation should learn to work together by practical means for the common good, and that nothing could militate against the realisation of that great ideal so conclusively as the encouragement of these international bitternesses, these international jealousies, these international dislikes."

Arthur Balfour (1848–1930), the British statesman and Conservative politician, served as Prime Minister of the United Kingdom from 1902 to 1905; Sir Henry Campbell-Bannerman (1836–1908) served as Leader of the Liberal Party from 1899 to 1908, and would succeed Lord Balfour as Prime Minister in 1905.

Another instance of the phrase: in the American economist and sociologist Thorstein Veblen's (1857–1929) *An Inquiry into the Nature of Peace and the Terms of Its Perpetuation* (New York and London, 1917), with, in chap. 4 ('Peace Without Honour'), p. 140:

> The "nation," without the bond of dynastic loyalty, is after all a make-shift idea, an episodic half-way station in the sequence, and loyalty, in any proper sense, to the nation as such is so much of a make-believe, that in the absence of a common defense to be safeguarded any such patriotic conceit must loose [sic] popular assurance and, with the passing of generations, fall insensibly into abeyance as an archaic affectation. The pressure of danger from without is necessary to keep the national spirit alert and stubborn, in case the pressure from within, that comes of dynastic usufruct working for dominion, has been withdrawn. With further extension of the national boundaries, such that the danger of gratuitous infraction from without grows constantly less menacing, while the traditional régime of international animosities falls more and more remotely into the background, the spirit of nationalism is fairly on the way to obsolescence through disuse.

Uly 17.1632: domestic conviviality

Among other pre-Joyce instances of this phrase, the earliest seems to have occurred in a book with the odd title *The Odd Volume; or, Book of Variety* (London, Dublin, and Edinburgh, 1835), illustrated by Robert

Seymour and Robert Cruikshank with engravings by Samuel Slader, in which the anonymous tale 'The March of Mind', on pages 96–99, ends with the following two paragraphs (italics in the original):

> Of poor Thomas, my account, I grieve to say, must be equally disheartening. An epic poem, on which he had been some months engaged, having not only failed, but even contributed to introduce its publisher to ready-furnished lodgings in the Fleet, he is now driven to the necessity of jobbing for minor periodicals, thereby adding one more to the already swollen catalogue of those who, mistaking the *ignis fatuus* of vanity for the sober radiance of intellect, start off prematurely on the voyage of life, without pilot to steer, compass to direct, or ballast to steady their course.
>
> When I called on the young man, a few mornings since, I was much struck with his more than usually picturesque condition. Being always fond of air, he had hired a back attic, overlooking two charming gardens filled with clothes'-lines, and commanding a distant view of some brick-fields, a pig, and an Irish hodman from Carrickfergus. His wife was seated at the fire, watching a leg of mutton as it pirouetted before the grate, at the end of a bit of whipcord : Fernando, her eldest boy, was riding with manifest ecstacy on the back of an old chair : and her two other darling babes, Alphonso and Eleonora, were fast asleep, on a turn-up bedstead, in an adjoining room. Close by Thomas, who was busy writing reviews at a deal table with three legs, was an elderly cotton shirt, hanging to dry on a small wooden horse, quite a pony in its dimensions ; and at the further end of the room, near the door, stood a pot of half-and-half, a pen'orth of pickled cabbage in a tea-cup, a twopenny French roll, a black horn dinner knife, and a fork with two prongs, both of which were broken. On observing these evident symptoms of domestic conviviality, I abruptly hastened my departure ; but, on my return home by way of Crutched-Friars, could not refrain from stopping an instant in order to survey my old friend's establishment. It was in the most deplorable condition possible. The voice of its till was mute ; the very fixtures themselves were removed ; and advertisements, three deep, specifying in large red characters the virtues of Daffy's Elixir, were posted up, on door, wall, and window-shutter. Altogether, the scene was of the most affecting character, and forcibly impressed on my mind the calamities attendant on what Shakspeare calls " ill-judged ambition."

Another early, less colorful instance of the phrase: in the Scottish lawyer, judge, and literary figure Henry Cockburn's (1779–1854) *Memorials of His Time* (Edinburgh, 1856), chap. 1, p. 41: 'I doubt if from the year 1811, when I married, I have closed above one day in the month, of my town life, at home and alone. It is always some scene of domestic conviviality, either in my own house or in a friend's. And this is the habit of all my best friends.'

A third instance: in the Anglican priest, hagiographer, antiquarian, scholar, and writer Sabine Baring-Gould's (1834–1924) *An Old English Home and Its Dependencies* (London, 1898), with, in chap. 11 ('The Village Doctor'), p. 260: 'I suppose my grandmother considered that after every great Christian festival or domestic conviviality my programme was overfull, for the leaden spoon and the quart bottle of castor oil invariably appeared on the scene upon the morrow.'

And, as a fourth and final example, the phrase recurs in *Landmarks* (London, 1914), a collection of short, fictional pieces by the prolific English humorist, author, scholar (especially on Charles Lamb), and editor (of *Punch*) E[dward]. V[errall]. Lucas (1868–1938), chap. 14 ('Showing How One Who Should Much Longer Have Retained His Divinity Lost It'), p. 90:

> Dinner was to be at half-past six sharp, on account of the
> great meeting, and Rudd, for the first time in his life, saw a row of
> champagne bottles in his father's house. Not that Mr. Sergison was
> a teetotaller ; but hitherto sherry, claret and port had represented
> the utmost he had attemped for state occasions, and claret alone for
> ordinary domestic conviviality. It seemed, Mrs. Sergison explained to
> Rudd, that legislators expect champagne.

18. 'Penelope'

Uly 18.7: too much old chat

This idiomatic expression previously occurred in the Anglo-Irish poet and novelist—and daughter of William Alexander, the Anglican Lord Bishop of Derry and Raphoe, later Archbishop of Armagh and Primate of All Ireland—Eleanor [Jane] Alexander's (1857–1939) *Lady Anne's Walk* (London, 1903), a collection of prose sketches having to do, directly or indirectly, with Lady Anne Beresford (1779–1842), sister of Primate J. G. Beresford and third daughter of George Beresford, first Marquis of Waterford. In *Ulysses*, the passage in which the phrase occurs, in which Molly recalls Mrs Riordan, reads: 'she had too much old chat in her about politics and earthquakes and the end of the world'; in *Lady Anne's Walk*, chap. 22 ('Her Last Appearance'), on p. 239, Alexander imagines a conversation between Lord Protector Oliver Cromwell and the Archbishop of Canterbury in which the latter observes to the former: 'There has been too much "old chat" already about sunrises and sunsets, especially the latter, with which—not being early saints—we are the most familiar.'

Uly 18.8–9: let us have a bit of fun

One of a handful of prior instances of Molly's phrase occurs in *Wine and Walnuts; or, After Dinner Chit-Chat* (London, 1823), by the writer, illustrator, and painter William Henry Pyne (1769–1843) as 'Ephraim Hardcastle, Citizen and Dry-Salter' (London, 1823), vol. 2 (of 2), chap. 21 ('The Devil Tavern'), p. 298: '" Let us have a bit of fun with the old sinner," said Quin.'

A second instance: in *Pickwick Abroad; or, The Tour in France* (London, 1839)—after its incomplete serialization in *The Monthly Magazine of Politics, Literature, and the Belles Lettres* (London) between December 1837 and June 1838—by the British author and journalist G[eorge]. W[illiam]. M[acArthur]. Reynolds (1814–1879), chap. 40 ('The Honesty of the Landlord at the Principal Hotel in Amiens' etc.), p. 336, in a passage that may have suggested itself to Joyce because of the role reversal—Bloom asking Molly, in an unprecedented request, to bring him his breakfast in bed, rather than the other way round—with which episode 18 begins (italics in the original):

> " Well, Snodgrass,—I tell you what it is," cried the Count, starting as if a very sudden idea had struck him ; " let us have a bit of fun. I am tired of always being a lord—and you are anxious to try it. Now—I'll tell you what we'll do. During the remainder of the journey you shall be the Count, and I will be Mr. Snodgrass. What say you ?"
>
> Mr. Snodgrass had a great deal to say against the propriety of this arrangement ; but all his objections were over-ruled by the Count, who laughed heartily at the joke, and declared, in a peculiar style of aristocratic eloquence, that it was " the rummest go *he'd* ever known in the whole course of *his* life."

Uly 18.408: turning and turning

Joyce produced the earliest known draft of the 'Penelope' episode in June 1921; Yeats's poem 'The Second Coming', written in 1919, was first published in the November 1920 issue of *The Dial*, then collected in his *Michael Robartes and the Dancer*, published by The Cuala Press (Churchtown, Dundrum) in February 1921. The passage in 'Penelope' where the highlighted phrase occurs—'better leave this ring behind want to keep turning and turning to get it over the knuckle'—may thus have contained a deliberate, perhaps playful echo of the first line of Yeats's recently published poem: 'Turning and turning in the widening gyre'.

Uly 18.766: in every hole and corner

This phrase occurs in a passage in which Molly Bloom recalls the day eighteen years past when, sixteen years old and still living in Gibraltar, she unexpectedly received a letter from her early flame the British naval officer Lieutenant Mulvey—whose first name she can now barely recall:

'an admirer he signed it I nearly jumped out of my skin [...] but I never thought hed write making an appointment I had it inside my petticoat bodice all day reading it up in every hole and corner while father was up at the drill'[.]

The phrase 'in every hole and corner' occurred with some frequency in the decades before *Ulysses*. One early instance: in the first verse of a broadside ballad under the title 'Father Mathew, and the Pledge'[33] published in Scotland c. 1842, during or after a visit there by Father Mathew on a temperance crusade of the British isles: 'Father Mathew is come to town, | To sober you all tis his desire then, | Five million of drunkards he did reform, | In every hole and corner of Ireland, | Wherever he goes he does propose, | For to reclaim each rank and station, | Give them a good blow out at the pump, | And banish away intoxication[.]'

Two more instances of the phrase followed in 1859, the first of these in *Popular Tales From the Norse* (Edinburgh, 1859), with translations by George Webbe Dasent (1817–1896), British lawyer and translator of folk tales, where the second paragraph of the anonymous tale 'Katie Woodencloak'—about a widowed King who marries a monstrous widowed Queen after his beloved first wife's death—reads in part, on p. 411: 'Well, after a time he fell into war with another King, and went out to battle with his host, and then the stepmother [of the Princess, his daughter] thought she might do as she pleased ; and so she both starved and beat the Princess, and was after her in every hole and corner of the house.'; and the second in George Eliot's first novel, *Adam Bede* (Edinburgh and London, 1859), vol. 3 (of 3), book 5, chap. 40 ('The Bitter Waters Spread'), p. 102:

> Bartle hurried away from the Rectory, evading Carrol's conversational advances, and saying in an exasperated tone to Vixen, whose short legs pattered beside him on the gravel,
> " Now, I shall be obliged to take you with me, you good-for-nothing woman. You'd go fretting yourself to death if I left you—you know you would, and perhaps get snapped up by some tramp ; and you'll be running into bad company, I expect, putting your nose in every hole and corner where you've no business ; but if you do anything disgraceful I'll disown you—mind that, madam, mind that ! "

---

33   A facsimile of the ballad may be accessed on the National Library of Scotland website at https://digital.nls.uk/74892652. The 'Mathew' of the title is an apparent error for 'Mathews', as the name appears several times in the text of the ballad.

Uly 18.768–69: the old stupid clock

This phrase, which occurs in a passage reading 'and I wanted to put on the old stupid clock to near the time he was the first man kissed me under the Moorish wall', echoes verbatim a phrase from 'Under the Hazel Tree', a popular ballad with words by the British librettest, author, and adapter of French operettas H[enry]. B[rougham]. Farnie (1836–1889) and music by composer P[asquale]. D. Guglielmo (1810–1873), the sheet music for which was published by C. H. Ditson (New York) in 1867. The song's lyrics read, in their entirety:

I promised that I'd wait for him
    Beneath the hazel tree
Our signal lamp, it was agreed
    The evening star should be,
But oh the sun goes on as if
    He ne'er meant going down
It seems a twelve-month since we met
    This morning in the town,
I've shaken our old stupid clock
    To hurry on the night,
It never was of much account
    And now it's stopp'd out-right.
I wish I knew the thief of time
    I'd ask I'd ask him but to steal
The next few hours And I for one
    Their loss should never feel.

Chorus
Oh! lovers who appoint to meet
    At closing of the day,
Remember in December,
    That you'll have to wait in May.

I tried to read a novel
    and I tried to hum a song
But the novel was not novel and
    The music sounded wrong,
And so it just occur'd to me
    That I might go and see,
If nuts were coming plenteously
    Upon the hazel tree,
Beneath the spreading branches then

> Who should I chance to find,
> But one who'd wandered there he said,
> In much my frame of mind,
> And there we sat and there we vowed
> Beneath the silent, silent moon,
> That evening stars had better rise,
> Just in the afternoon.
>
> *Chorus*

Uly 18.896: I could have been a prima donna

Molly's 'I could have been a prima donna only I married him' may have been suggested by the English novelist, biographer, and editor (of *The Christian World Magazine and Family Visitor*) Emma Jane Worboise's (1825–1887) novel *The Grey House at Endlestone* (London, 1877), chap. 11 ('From Hilda's Diary'), p. 117 (italics in the original): 'Complimentary, is it not, after being flattered into the persuasion that I was one of the best pianistes, and one of the finest singers, in London drawing-room society—that I might have been a *prima donna* had I chosen ?'

Uly 18.987: immediately if not sooner

From a passage in which Molly recalls the promises Bloom made to her about their approaching marriage and honeymoon: 'O how nice I said whatever I liked he was going to do immediately if not sooner'. The phrase, while sometimes attributed to the American humorist Charles Farrar Browne (1834–1867), as 'Artemus Ward'—who wrote, in *Artemus Ward His Book* (New York, 1862), p. 211, 'Of course they git throwed eventooually, if not sooner'—first occurred at least as early as 1833 (a year before Browne was born), in 'The Last Duel I Had a Hand In', by C. O'Donoghue, Late Ensign 18th Royal Irish', *Fraser's Magazine*, vol. 8, no. 44 (Aug. 1833), 156–67, with, on p. 164: 'He was determined to fight ; right or wrong, fight he must, and fight he would—immediately, if not sooner.' By the time Joyce wrote *Ulysses*, the expression had become idiomatic and its origin long since forgotten—perhaps including by Joyce himself.

Uly 18.1260: that's the way his money goes

Molly's phrase matches nearly verbatim a line occurring in several versions of a traditional English song, country dance, or nursery rhyme known as 'Pop Goes the Weasel', one such version of which reads:

> Half a pound of tuppenny rice,
>   Half a pound of treacle.
> That's the way the money goes,
>   Pop! Goes the weasel.
>
> Up and down the City road,
>   In and out the Eagle,
> That's the way the money goes,
>   Pop! Goes the weasel.
>
> Every night when I go out,
>   The monkey's on the table,
> Take a stick and knock it off,
>   Pop! Goes the weasel.
>
> A penny for a spool of thread
>   A penny for a needle,
> That's the way the money goes,
>   Pop! Goes the weasel.
>
> All around the cobbler's bench,
>   The monkey chased the weasel;
> The monkey thought 'twas all in fun,
>   Pop! Goes the weasel.

Uly 18.1335: where poetry is in the air

With or without the initial 'where', this phrase occurred verbatim and apparently uniquely pre-Joyce in an essay by Maud Diver on 'The Indian Woman as Poet' first published in Ada Ballin's *Womanhood, The Magazine of Woman's Progress and Interests—Political, Legal, Social, and Intellectual—and of Health and Beauty Culture* (London) and later collected, along with other of Diver's *Womanhood* essays, in *The Englishwoman in India* (Edinburgh and London, 1909). In a discussion of Mrs Sarojini Naidu of Hyderabad (1879–1949), a prominent Indian poet, feminist, and political activist, Diver wrote, on p. 196 of the book:

Of herself and her own talent it has been said, that " no one could, if she would, speak more intimately and with greater authority on questions of female education and emancipation in India. But it must be remembered that she is a porcelain poetess. Into her art she introduces Brahminical instincts and antecedents. ' The best or nothing,' she says to herself. That she will one day enter the sanctuary of poetry is believable, since she has avoided the pitfalls of many minor poets—she has never been extreme or eccentric. She lives in a city where poetry is in the air, surrounded by love, beauty, and admiration ; and her influence behind the Purdah is very great."

Select Bibliography

The following list includes the principal annotated editions of Joyce's *Dubliners*, *A Portrait of the Artist as a Young Man*, and *Ulysses*, and a selection of book-length studies further documenting their allusive content.

Bauerle, Ruth, *The James Joyce Songbook* (New York: Garland Publishing, 1982).

Bowen, Zack, *Musical Allusions in the Works of James Joyce: Early Poetry Through 'Ulysses'* (Albany: State University of New York Press, 1974).

Gifford, Don, *Joyce Annotated: Notes for 'Dubliners' and 'A Portrait of the Artist as a Young Man'*, second edition, revised and enlarged (Berkeley: University of California Press, 1982).

Gifford, Don with Robert J. Seidman, *'Ulysses' Annotated*, second edition (Berkeley: University of California Press, 1988).

Hodgart, Matthew J. C. and Mabel P. Worthington, *Song in the Works of James Joyce* (New York: Columbia University Press, 1959).

Joyce, James, *Dubliners*, with an introduction and notes by Terence Brown (New York: Penguin Books, 1993).

Joyce, James, *Dubliners*, an illustrated edition with annotations, edited by John Wyse Jackson and Bernard McGinley (New York: St. Martin's Press, 1993).

Joyce, James, *Dubliners*, edited by Robert Scholes and A. Walton Litz (New York: Penguin Books, 1996).

Joyce, James, *Dubliners*, edited with an introduction and notes by Jeri Johnson (Oxford: Oxford University Press, 2000).

Joyce, James, *Dubliners*, edited by Margot Norris, text edited by Hans Walter Gabler with Walter Hettche (New York: W. W. Norton, 2006).

Joyce, James, *A Portrait of the Artist as a Young Man*, text, criticism, and notes edited by Chester G. Anderson (New York: Viking Press, 1968).

Joyce, James, *A Portrait of the Artist as a Young Man*, edited with an introduction and notes by Jeri Johnson (Oxford: Oxford University Press, 2000).

Joyce, James, *A Portrait of the Artist as a Young Man*, edited with an introduction and notes by Seamus Deane (New York: Penguin Books, 2003).

Joyce, James, *A Portrait of the Artist as a Young Man*, edited by John Paul Riquelme, text edited by Hans Walter Gabler with Walter Hettche (New York: W. W. Norton, 2007).

Joyce, James, *A Portrait of the Artist as a Young Man*, annotations by Marc A. Mamigonian and John Turner (London: Alma Books, 2014).

Joyce, James, *Ulysses*, edited with an introduction and notes by Jeri Johnson (Oxford: Oxford University Press, 1993).

Joyce, James, *The Cambridge Centenary 'Ulysses': The 1922 Text with Essays and Notes*, edited by Catherine Flynn (Cambridge: Cambridge University Press, 2022), https://doi.org/10.1017/9781009027007

Slote, Sam, Marc A. Mamigonian, and John Turner, *Annotations to James Joyce's 'Ulysses'* (Oxford: Oxford University Press, 2022), https://doi.org/10.1093/actrade/9780198864585.book.1

Thornton, Weldon, *Allusions in 'Ulysses': An Annotated List* (Chapel Hill: University of North Carolina Press, 1968).

Index of Antecedent Writers and Works Discussed

The antecedent works listed below, along with their authors' names (where known) and their dates of first publication, each contain one or more phrases or short passages of two or three to as many as several words that are identical or very nearly so to phrases or short passages in *Dubliners*, *A Portrait of the Artist as a Young Man*, or *Ulysses*. The latter works are identified here, as in the main text, by abbreviated book title (as *Dub*, *Por*, or *Uly*); then full or abbreviated story title (for *Dubliners*), chapter number (for *Portrait*), or episode number (for *Ulysses*); then line number(s) as they appear in, respectively, the Norton Critical Edition of *Dubliners*, edited by Margot Norris, with text edited by Hans Walter Gabler with Walter Hettche (New York and London: W. W. Norton, 2006); the Norton Critical Edition of *A Portrait of the Artist as a Young Man*, edited by John Paul Riquelme, with text edited by Hans Walter Gabler with Walter Hettche (New York and London: W. W. Norton, 2007); and *Ulysses, The Corrected Text*, edited by Hans Walter Gabler with Wolfhard Steppe and Claus Melchior, First American Edition (New York: Random House, 1986). For the convenience of readers primarily interested in new textual parallels identified in one or the other of the three Joyce works discussed in this study, the index begins, as does the main text, with new textual parallels found in *Dubliners*, followed, in turn, by those found in *Portrait* and then *Ulysses*.

For readers' further convenience, the following is a list, in alphabetical order, of the full titles, subtitles (if any), and principal locations of all periodicals cited in this study:

All the Year Round (London)

Aunt Judy's Magazine (London)

Belgravia: A London Magazine aka *Belgravia: An Illustrated London Magazine* (London)

Bentley's Miscellany (London)

Blackwood's Edinburgh Magazine aka *Blackwood's Magazine* (Edinburgh and London)

Boys of the World; a Journal for Prince and Peasant and its supplement *Boys of the World Story-Teller* (London)

Cassell's Little Folks: The Magazine for Boys and Girls (London)

Chambers's Edinburgh Journal (Edinburgh, later London); from 1854, *Chambers's Journal of Popular Literature, Science, and Art*; from 1897, *Chambers's Journal*

Cosmopolis, an International Monthly Review (London and New York)

Fraser's Magazine for Town and Country (London)

Fun (London)

Good Words (Edinburgh and London)

Happy Hour Stories (London)

Harper's Magazine (New York)

Harper's Weekly, A Journal of Civilization (New York)

Hogg's Instructor (Edinburgh and London)

Hood's Magazine and Comic Miscellany (London)

Horlick's Magazine. And Home Journal for Australia, India and the Colonies (London)

Household Words (London)

Lippincott's Monthly Magazine (Philadelphia and London)

London Society, A Monthly Magazine of Light and Amusing Literature etc (London)

Macmillan's Magazine (London)

Meliora: A Quarterly Review of Social Science in its Ethical, Economical, Political and Ameliorative Aspects (London)

Nature (London)

Once a Week (London)

Philosophical Transactions of the Royal Society (London)

Pick-Me-Up (London)

Punch, or The London Charivari (London)

St. Nicholas: Scribner's Illustrated Magazine for Girls and Boys (New York)

Tales, A Magazine of the World's Best Fiction (New York)

The Athenaeum: Journal of English and Foreign Literature, Science, and the Fine Arts (London)[1]

The Atlantic Monthly, Devoted to Literature, Art, and Politics (Boston)

The Bee: Being Essays On the Most Interesting Subjects (London)

The Bible Treasury: A Monthly Magazine of Papers on Scriptural Subjects (London)

The Boy's Own Paper (London)

The Bulletin (Sydney)

The Century Magazine aka *The Century Illustrated Monthly Magazine* (New York and London)

---

1 With changes of ownership, editorship, and editorial focus this journal's subtitle changed several times over the course of the nineteenth century including, from the initial *Literary and Critical Journal* (1828) to, among others, *Journal of Literature, Science, and the Fine Arts*; *Journal of English and Foreign Literature, Science, and the Fine Arts*; and *Journal of Literature, Science, The Fine Arts, Music, and the Drama*.

The Christian Examiner and Church of Ireland Magazine (Dublin)

The Christian Lady's Magazine (London)

The Christian Witness and Church Members' Magazine (London)

The Conservator (Philadelphia)

The Contemporary Review (New York and London)

The Cornhill Magazine (London)

The Daily Chronicle (London)

The Dark Blue (London)

The Dollar Monthly Magazine (Boston)

The Dublin University Magazine (Dublin)

The Edinburgh Review, or The Critical Journal (Edinburgh)

The English Illustrated Magazine (London)

The Evangelical Magazine and Missionary Chronicle (London)

The Examiner (London)

The Expositor (London)

The Family Herald; or, Useful Information and Amusement for the Million (London)

The Family Reader (London)

The Fortnightly Review (London and New York)

The Freemasons' Quarterly Review (London)

The Gas World (London)

The Girl's Own Paper (London)

The Gospel Magazine (London)

The Graphic. An Illustrated Weekly Newspaper (London)

The Halfpenny Journal: A Weekly Magazine for All Who Can Read (London)

The Halfpenny Marvel (London)

The Illuminated Magazine (London)

The International Review (New York)

The Irish Monthly: A Magazine of General Literature (Dublin)

The Irish Penny Journal (Dublin)

The Juvenile Magazine (London)

The Knickerbocker, or, New-York Monthly Magazine (New York)

The Lady's Companion and Monthly Magazine (London)

The Lady's Magazine, or Entertaining Companion for the Fair Sex (London)

The Leeds Times, a weekly newspaper published from 1833 to 1901 (Leeds, West Yorkshire)

The Literary Examiner (London)

The Literary Gazette and Journal of Belles Lettres, Science, and Art (London)

The London and Edinburgh Philosophical Magazine and Journal of Science (London)[2]

The London Journal: and Weekly Record of Literature, Science, and Art (London)

The Meteor (London)

The Month, A Catholic Magazine and Review (London and Dublin)

The Monthly Magazine of Politics, Literature, and the Belles Lettres (London)

The Monthly Packet of Evening Readings for Members of the English Church (London)

---

2 Published under that title from 1832 to 1840; and subsequently under the title *The London, Edinburgh, and Dublin Philosophical Magazine and Journal of Science*.

The Motherwell Times (Motherwell, Lanarkshire, Scotland)

The Musical World (London)

The National Magazine (London)

The National Review (London)

The Nautical Magazine and Naval Chronicle: A Journal of Papers on Subjects Connected With Maritime Affairs (London)

The New Monthly Belle Assemblée; A Magazine of Literature and Fashion, Under the Immediate Patronage of Her Royal Highness the Duchess of Kent (London)

The New Monthly Magazine and Literary Journal (London)[3]

The Oxford Magazine: A Weekly Newspaper and Review (Oxford)

The Pall Mall Magazine (London)

The People's Magazine: An Illustrated Miscellany for Family Reading (London)

The Pioneer. A Literary and Critical Magazine (Boston)

The Public Advertiser (London)

The Quiver: An Illustrated Magazine for Sunday and General Reading (London, Paris, and New York)

The Railway Signal, or Lights Along the Line. A Journal of Evangelistic and Temperance Work on All Railways (London)

The Rambler (London)

The Saturday Review of Politics, Literature, Science, and Art (London)

The Scots Magazine (Edinburgh)

---

3   From 1814 to 1820 operating as *The New Monthly Magazine and Universal Register*; from 1821 as *The New Monthly Magazine and Literary Journal*; from 1837 as *The New Monthly Magazine and Humorist*; from 1853 as *The New Monthly Magazine*; from 1882 to 1884 as *The New Monthly*.

The Shamrock (Dublin)

The Sketch: A Journal of Art and Actuality (London)

The Smart Set (New York)

The Spectator (London)

The Sphere: An Illustrated Newspaper for the Home (London)

The Sportsman's Magazine of Life in London and the Country (London)

The Star Chamber (London)

The Strand Magazine: An Illustrated Monthly (London)

The Tatler (London)

The United States Magazine and Democratic Review (Washington, D.C.)

The Westminster Review (London)

The Wide World Magazine: An Illustrated Monthly of True Narrative: Adventure[,] Travel[,] Customs and Sport (London)

The Workers' Republic (Dublin)

The Yellow Book: An Illustrated Quarterly (London)

The Young Lady's Magazine of Theology, History, Philosophy and General Knowledge, embracing Literature, Science, and Art (London)

Truth (London)

Womanhood, The Magazine of Woman's Progress and Interests (London)

Young Folks; A Boys' and Girls' Paper of Instructive and Entertaining Literature (London)

Young Ireland: An Irish Magazine of Entertainment and Instruction (Dublin)

In *Dubliners*

Adams, Francis William Lauderdale
'To England' in his *Songs of the Army of the Night* (London, 1894)
    Dub, Ivy Day, line 526, p. 34

Anonymous
Beowulf, An Epic Poem, transl. Wackerbarth (London, 1849)
    Dub, Ivy Day, line 529, p. 35

History of Scotland in *Moore's Dublin Edition* (1796) of the *Encyclopædia Britannica*
    Dub, Race, lines 4–5, p. 11

'Recollections of an Old Umbrella', publ. Nov. 1830 in *The New Monthly Magazine*
    Dub, Counterparts, line 179, p. 27

Review publ. Feb. 1834 in *The Christian Examiner* of Thomas Taylor's *Life of William Cowper, Esq.*
    Dub, Araby, line 219, p. 7

'Social Prayer', publ. 1861 in *The Christian Witness*
    Dub, Race, lines 6–7, p. 12

'The British Umbrella', publ. 12 July 1862 in *The Spectator*
    Dub, Mother, line 310, p. 41

'The Coiner's Fate', publ. 1 Dec. 1869 in *Boys of the World Story-Teller*
    Dub, Cloud, line 21, p. 19

'The Great Work', signed 'W.P.J.', publ. Sept. 1891 in *Macmillan's Magazine*
    Dub, The Dead, line 945, p. 47

The History of Little Goody Two-Shoes (London, 1765)
    Dub, Cloud, line 88, p. 22

'The Moral Umbrella' in *Popular American Readings in Prose and Verse* (London, 1893)
    Dub, Mother, line 310, p. 41

Armin, Robert
Foole upon Foole, or, Six sortes of sottes (London, 1605)
  Dub, Cloud, line 88, p. 22

Bible (King James Version)
Job ii 2
  Dub, Mother, line 2, p. 39

Isaiah lii 2
  Dub, Cloud, line 101, p. 23

Broderip, Frances Freeling
Way-side Fancies (London, 1857)
  Dub, Gallants, lines 328–29, p. 16

Burke, Edmund
An Appeal from the New to the Old Whigs (London, 1791)
  Dub, Grace, line 443, p. 45

Campbell, Major Calder
'The Phantasmal Reproof', publ. Apr. 1844 in *Hood's Magazine*
  Dub, Ivy Day, line 533, p. 36

Coleridge, Samuel Taylor
'On Receiving an Account That His Only Sister's Death Was Inevitable' (1794), first publ. in his collected works (London, 1834)
  Dub, Cloud, line 106, p. 23

Craufurd, Rev. Alexander H[enry].
'Spiritual Loneliness and Its Remedy' in his *Seeking for Light. Sermons.* (London, 1879)
  Dub, Painful, line 145, p. 30

De Quincey, Thomas
'The Palimpsest of the Human Brain' publ. Spring–Summer 1845 in *Blackwood's*
  Dub, Cloud, line 70, p. 21

De Vere, Aubrey Thomas
'King Ethelbert of Kent and Saint Augustine' in his *Legends of the Saxon Saints* (London, 1879)
   Dub, Ivy Day, line 529, p. 35

Dickens, Charles
Great Expectations (London, 1861)
   Dub, Cloud, line 88, p. 22

Disraeli, Benjamin
'The Dunciad of To-day. A Satire.', publ. April–June 1826 in *The Star Chamber*
   Dub, Ivy Day, line 542, p. 37

Eliot, George
The Lifted Veil, first publ. anonymously in *Blackwood's* (July 1859); republished separately and by name (London, 1878).
   Dub, Cloud, lines 52–53, p. 20

Elizabeth I, Queen
'The doubt of future foes exiles my present joy' (c. 1568–71)
   Dub, Cloud, lines 52–53, p. 20

Evans, Mary Anne
See Eliot, George

Ferguson, Samuel
Hibernian Nights' Entertainment, Third Series: The Rebellion of Silken Thomas (Dublin and London, 1887)
   Dub, Ivy Day, line 542, p. 37

Fletcher, John
The Loyal Subject, or, The Faithful General (London, 1647)
   Dub, Cloud, line 88, p. 22

Fletcher, Robert
'Our Present Sorrow, and our Present Joy' (1603)
   Dub, Cloud, lines 52–53, p. 20

Fleury, Rev. C[harles]. M[arlay].
Thirty Sermons, on the Life of David, and on the Twenty-Third and Thirty-Second Psalms (Dublin, 1847)
  Dub, Sisters, line 181, p. 3

Freeman, E[dward]. A[ugustus].
'Saalburg and Saarbrücken', publ. Nov. 1872 in *Macmillan's Magazine*
  Dub, Mother, line 339, p. 42

Fullom, S[tephen]. W[atson].
The Mystery of the Soul (London, 1865)
  Dub, Gallants, lines 328–29, p. 16

Galt, John
  The Majolo: A Tale (London, 1816)
  Dub, Cloud, line 21, p. 19

Gentleman, Francis
'Fable XI. The Birth Day' in his *Royal Fables* (London, 1766)
  Dub, Ivy Day, line 545, p. 38

Goldsmith, Oliver
'Of the Opera in England', publ. 24 Nov. 1759 in Goldsmith's *The Bee*
  Dub, Painful, lines 71–72, p. 29

Green, John Richard
  A Short History of the English People (London, 1874)
  Dub, Race, lines 4–5, p. 11

Hamilton of Gilbertfield, William
The Life and Heroick Actions of the Renoun'd Sir William Wallace etc. (Edinburgh, 1722)
  Dub, Ivy Day, line 523, p. 34

Howard, Blanche Willis
Guenn. A Wave on the Breton Coast (Boston and New York, 1883)
  Dub, Mother, line 310, p. 41

Howard, Edward
'The Canon with Two Consciences', publ. Mar. 1839 in *The New Monthly Magazine*
  Dub, Encounter, line 50, p. 5

Kaler, J[ames]. O[tis].
'A Journey On Snowshoes: The Adventures of Two Boys in an Arctic Clime', publ. 2 Apr. 1881 in *Young Ireland* (1881)
  Dub, Ivy Day, line 206, p. 33

Lever, Charles James
A Day's Ride: A Life's Romance (London, 1863)
  Dub, Painful, lines 71–72, p. 29

Maugham, W[illiam]. Somerset
The Making of a Saint: A Romance of Mediæval Italy (London, 1898)
  Dub, Counterparts, line 179, p. 27

Mellor, Rev. E[noch].
'Paul's Computation', publ. Mar. 1877 in *The Evangelical Magazine*
  Dub, Grace, line 797, p. 45

Oliphant, Mrs Margaret
Young Musgrave, serialized Jan.–Dec. 1877 in *Macmillan's Magazine*; then publ. in book form
(London, 1877)
  Dub, Gallants, line 19, p. 15

Ollier, Charles
'The Night-Shriek: A Tale for December', publ. Dec. 1841 in *Bentley's Miscellany*
  Dub, Eveline, lines 1–2, p. 9

Ouida
Folle-Farine (London, 1871)
  Dub, Araby, line 219, p. 7

Pardoe, Julia
Speculation (London, 1834)
  Dub, Gallants, line 19, p. 15

Payne, Will
Mr. Salt: A Novel (Boston and New York, 1903)
  Dub, Race, line 96, p. 13

Pollok, Robert
The Course of Time: A Poem, in Ten Books (London, 1827)
  Dub, Cloud, lines 52–53, p. 20

Ponsonby, Lady Emily Charlotte
Oliver Beaumont and Lord Latimer (London, 1873)
    Dub, Cloud, line 106, p. 23

Ramé, Maria Louise
See Ouida

Reade, Charles
The Cloister and the Hearth: A Tale of the Middle Ages, serialized 2 July–1 Oct. 1859 in *Once a Week*; then publ. in book form (London, 1861)
    Dub, Painful, line 338, p. 31

Richardson, David Lester
'The Final Toast: A Masonic Song' (1852)
    Dub, Ivy Day, line 535, p. 36

Robertson, John George
'Current German Literature', publ. Mar. 1897 in *Cosmopolis, An International Monthly Review*
    Dub, The Dead, line 945, p. 47

Shakespeare, William
The Merchant of Venice
    Dub, Mother, line 150, p. 40

Smith, Charles
The Mosiad, or Israel Delivered; a Sacred Poem (London, 1815)
    Dub, Ivy Day, line 523, p. 34

Smith, Charlotte
'Sonnet XLV. On leaving a part of Sussex' in her *Elegiac Sonnets and Other Poems* (Worcester, 1795)
    Dub, Cloud, line 106, p. 23

Stevenson, Robert Louis
The Black Arrow: A Tale of the Two Roses, serialized June–Oct. 1883 in *Young Folks*; then publ. in book form (London, 1888)
    Dub, Ivy Day, line 526, p. 34

Tennyson, Alfred
'A Dream of Fair Women' (1832)
Dub, The Dead, line 945, p. 47

'Ode to Memory' (1830)
Dub, Cloud, line 106, p. 23

Thistlethwaite, James
'THE CONSULTATION. *A Mock Heroic, In Four Cantos*' (Bristol, 1775)
Dub, Ivy Day, line 542, p. 37

Tolstoy, Leo
Resurrection, transl. Maude (London, 1900)
Dub, Grace, lines 42 and 172–73, p. 43

Townsend, Virginia F[rances].
'The Temptation and the Triumph', publ. May 1857 in *The Lady's Companion*
Dub, Ivy Day, line 533, p. 36

Wordsworth, William
'I heard (alas, 'twas only in a dream)' (1819)
Dub, Ivy Day, line 538, p. 37

The Prelude; Or, Growth of a Poet's Mind (London, 1850)
Dub, Cloud, lines 52–53, p. 20

In *A Portrait of the Artist as a Young Man*

A.L.O.E.
The Haunted Room. A Tale. (London, 1876)
   Por 1.427–28, p. 52

Anderson, Lt. Col. Joseph
Recollections of a Peninsular Veteran (London, 1913)
   Por 1.1325–28, p. 58

Anonymous
   'No Peace with Rome', publ. Apr. 1848 in *The Gospel Magazine*
   Por 1.1075–76, p. 57

   The Arabian Nights' Entertainments
   Por 2.105, p. 64

   'The Lamentation of the Rev. Father Campbell' (n.p., n.d.)
   Por 1.985–86, p. 56

Balzac, Honoré de
'Peace in the House' in *La Comédie humaine*, ed. G. Saintsbury (London, 1896)
   Por 2.245, p. 66

Barrow, Frances Elizabeth
The Wife's Stragatem: A Story for Fireside and Wayside (New York and London, 1862)
   Por 1.427–28, p. 52

Bennett, Arnold
Clayhanger (London, 1910)
   Por 2.245, p. 66

Byron, George Gordon, Lord
'Childish Recollections' (1807)
   Por 2.92, p. 63

'Elegy On Thyrza' (1811)
   Por 5.2729, p. 78

Cavendish, William George Spencer, Sixth Duke of Devonshire
Remarks in the House of Lords (1829)
Por 1.1075–76, p. 57

Coleridge, Samuel Taylor
Remorse: A Tragedy, in Five Acts (London, 1813)
Por 4.783–84, p. 73

Conrad, Joseph
'Gaspar Ruiz: The Story of a Guerilla Chief', serialized July–Oct. 1906 in *The Pall Mall Magazine*; collected in Conrad's *A Set of Six* (London, 1908)
Por 3.849, p. 71

'Typhoon', serialized Jan.–Mar. 1902 in *The Pall Mall Magazine*; collected in Conrad's *Typhoon and Other Stories* (London, 1903)
Por 2.245, p. 66

Dibdin, Charles
Hannah Hewit: or, The Female Crusoe (London, 1792)
Por 2.105, p. 64

Dickens, Charles
A Tale of Two Cities (London, 1859)
Por 2.20, p. 61

Doyle, Sir Arthur Conan
The Sign of the Four, first publ. Feb. 1890 in *Lippincott's Monthly Magazine*, then in book form (London, 1890)
Por 4.783–84, p. 73

Dumas *père*, Alexandre
Marceau's Prisoner, first publ. June–Dec. 1892 in *The Strand Magazine*
Por 2.313–14, p. 67

Emerson, Ralph Waldo
'Art', essay in his *Society and Solitude: Twelve Chapters* (Boston and London, 1870)
Por 4.783–84, p. 73

Goethe, Johann Wolfgang von
Faust, a Tragedy (1808), transl. Swanwick (London, 1879) and/or Latham (London, 1905)
   Por 2.839, p. 69

Hardy, Thomas
Jude the Obscure (London, 1895)
   Por 2.622, p. 68

Ibsen, Henrik
When We Dead Awaken: A Dramatic Epilogue in Three Acts, transl. Archer (London, 1900)
   Por 5.2729, p. 78

Jacobs, Joseph
'Jack and his Golden Snuff-Box' and 'The Well of the World's End', both in his *English Fairy Tales* (London, 1890)
   Por 1.1, p. 51

James, Howard W.
'Swallowing a Fortune', publ. June 1865 in *The Dollar Monthly Magazine* (Boston)
   Por 1.1325–28, p. 58

Johnstone, Christian Isobel
Clan-Albin: A National Tale (London, 1815)
   Por 5.1299, p. 75

Lawrence, D[avid]. H[erbert].
The Trespasser (London, 1912)
   Por 2.622, p. 68

Lynam, William Francis
'Mick M'Quaid's Spa', publ. 16 Feb. 1878 in *The Shamrock*
   Por 1.840–41, p. 55

MacDonald, George
The Vicar's Daughter: An Autobiographical Story (London, 1872)
   Por 5.1329–30, p. 77

Madden, R[ichard]. R[obert].
   Literary Remains of The United Irishmen of 1798 (Dublin, 1887)
      Por 1.985–86, p. 56

Malan, Rev. A[rthur]. N[oel].
   'The Dis-Order of the Bath', publ. 31 Oct. 1891 in *The Boy's Own Paper*
      Por 2.118, p. 65

Mayhew, Henry
   London Labour and the London Poor (London, 1851)
      Por 1.1, p. 51

Moore, George
   Vain Fortune (London, 1895)
      Por 5.1299, p. 75

Oliphant, Mrs Margaret
   The Ladies Lindores, serialized Apr. 1882–May 1883 in *Blackwood's*; then publ. in book form (Edinburgh and London, 1883)
      Por 1.1325–28, p. 58

Paine, Ralph D[elahaye].
   'Corporal Sweeney, Deserter', first publ. Sept. 1904 in *The Century Magazine*
      Por 1.1052, p. 57

Peard, Frances Mary
   'Under the Mountain', first publ. July 1871 in *The Cornhill Magazine*; later in Peard's *A Madrigal and Other Stories* (London, 1876)
      Por 5.213, p. 75

Peterson, Charles Jacobs
   Wilfred Montressor: or the Secret Order of the Seven (New York, 1848)
      Por 5.2729, p. 78

Rowe, Richard
   Picked Up in the Streets, or, Struggles for Life Amongst the London Poor (London, 1880)
      Por 1.823, p. 53

Shakespeare, William
Antony and Cleopatra
   Por 2.93, p. 63

Smith, Dexter and J[ohn]. R[ogers]. Thomas
'Kate O'Shane' (1858)
   Por 2.20, p. 61

Stevenson, Robert Louis
Vailima Letters (London and Chicago, 1895)
   Por 1.1325–28, p. 58

Swinburne, Algernon Charles
'Giordano Bruno 9 June 1889' in his *Astrophel and Other Poems* (London, 1894)
   Por 5.2218–19, p. 77

Symons, Arthur
Essay on Joris-Karl Huysmans publ. Mar. 1892 in *The Fortnightly Review*; later in Symons's *The Symbolist Movement in Literature* (London, 1899)
   Por 5.1299, p. 75

Thackeray, William Makepeace
The Irish Sketch-Book (London, 1843)
   Por 1.823, p. 53

Tolstoy, Leo
Resurrection, transl. Maude (London, 1900)
   Por 2.93, p. 63

Tucker, Charlotte Maria
See A.L.O.E.

Williams, Richard D'Alton
'The Dying Girl' (1851), collected in *The Poems of Richard D'Alton Williams* (Dublin, 1894)
   Por 2.20, p. 61

In *Ulysses*

Adams, Bertha Leith
'Keane Malcolmbe's Pupil', publ. Feb. 1876 in *All the Year Round*
Uly 15.1247, p. 344

Adams, Mrs Hugh (née Evelyn Wills)
'The Town Twin', publ. Sept. 1903 in *The Pall Mall Magazine*
Uly 13.154–55, p. 262

Ælfric, Abbot
See Thurston, Herbert, S.J.

Agg, John
'The New Club' in *The Busy Body, or Men and Manners, Edited by Humphrey Hedgehog, Esq.* (London, 1817)
Uly 15.1356, p. 346

Aïde, Charles Hamilton
Rita: An Autobiography (London, 1858)
Uly 13.172, p. 263

Alcott, Louisa May
Little Men, or Life at Plumfield with Jo's Boys (Boston, 1871; London, 1872)
Uly 6.88, p. 132

Little Women, or Meg, Jo, Beth and Amy (Boston, 1869; London, 1872)
Uly 5.217, p. 124

Alexander, Eleanor Jane
Lady Anne's Walk (London, 1903)
Uly 18.7, p. 379

Allardyce, Alexander
Earlscourt, A Novel of Provincial Life, serialized Jan. 1893–Jan. 1894 in *Blackwood's*; then publ. in book form (Edinburgh, 1894)
Uly 13.24–25, p. 254

Index of Antecedent Writers and Works Discussed

Allen, Grant

'An Episode in High Life', publ. Dec. 1882 in *Belgravia*
Uly 13.690–91, p. 286

In All Shades (London, 1886; rvsd edn London and Edinburgh, 1899)
Uly 14.1069, p. 326

Post-Prandial Philosophy (London, 1894)
Uly 3.9, p. 95

Allen Jr., Thomas Gaskell

'From St. Paul's to Pekin by Rail', publ. July 1898 in *The Wide World Magazine*
Uly 13.637–38, p. 285

A.L.O.E.

Harry Dangerfield, the Poacher (Edinburgh and London, 1860)
Uly 13.7, p. 250

Ambrose, Bishop of Milan, Saint

The *Exameron* or *Hexameron* (c. 386–390)
Uly 15.1580–81, p. 347

Amory, Thomas

The Life of John Buncle, Esq. (London, Part 1, 1756, Part 2, 1766)
Uly 14.670, p. 310

Anonymous

Account of a naval engagement between the *Nemesis* and Chinese 'war junks' in *The Nautical Magazine and Naval Chronicle for 1841* (London)
Uly 12.1858, p. 243

A Chapter of Accidents; or, The Mother's Assistant, in Cases of Burns, Scalds, Cuts, Etc (London, 1860)
Uly 15.2380, p. 353

'A Cold Love Letter' in George Cruikshank's *Table-Book* (London, 1845)
Uly 1.152–53, p. 84

'Address of His Royal Highness the President [of the Royal Society]',
publ. Feb. 1837 in *The London and Edinburgh Philosophical Magazine*
    Uly 14.849, p. 320

Advertisement for the Fluxite Soldering Set, printed Jan. 1921 in *The Strand Magazine*
    Uly 15.2990, p. 358

'Alice in Blunderland (On the Ninth of November)', publ. 22 Nov. 1890 in *Punch*
    Uly 6.1033, p. 148

'A Notable Advertisement', publ. 20 July 1912 in *The Gas World*
    Uly 17.580–81, p. 373

'A Soiree at Monsieur Guizot's', publ. Dec. 1840 in *The New Monthly Magazine*
    Uly 13.415–16, p. 272

Batrachomuomachia: or, The Battle of the Frogs and Mice, transl. Parnell (London, 1717)
    Uly 4.186, p. 113

'Bernard M'Shane', collected in Tom M'Lachlan's *Thoughts in Rhyme* (Glasgow, 1884)
    Uly 4.112–13, p. 111

'Canvassing for Death' (1883)
    Uly 6.124, p. 133

'Chamber of Horrors' in *Punch* (passim)
    Uly 16.588, p. 368

'Concerts', publ. 13 Feb. 1847 in *The Musical World*
    Uly 12.650–51, p. 236

'Curfew', publ. Aug. 1843 in *The Illuminated Magazine*
    Uly 2.16, p. 89

'Description of Jamaica' (1731)
    Uly 9.1170, p. 195

'Eastbourne, Queen of Watering-Places', publ. 23 Aug. 1899 in *The Sketch*
   Uly 13.3–4, p. 248

Edwy and Elgiva: A Romance of the Olden Time (London, 1868)
   Uly 13.734–35, p. 289

'Essence of Parliament. Extracted from the Diary of Toby, M.P.', publ. 13 Feb. 1892 in *Punch*
   Uly 7.875–76, p. 164

'Execution of Probert', publ. 26 June 1825 in *The Examiner*
   Uly 12.525, p. 235

'Fast and Humiliation; or, Sick Beasts *v.* Sick Paupers', publ. 7 Apr. 1866 in *Punch*
   Uly 14.1065, p. 326

'Father Mathew, and the Pledge' (c. 1842)
   Uly 18.766, p. 380

'Floats and Flies', publ. 9 Nov. 1881 in *Fun*
   Uly 1.152–53, p. 84

'Her "Day of Rest." (The Song of the Shop-Girl.)', publ. 8 Apr. 1893 in *Punch*
   Uly 13.2–3, p. 247

'Hickscorner' in Dodsley's *Select Collection of Old English Plays* (London, 1744)
   Uly 14.98, p. 305

High Treason: A Romance of the Days of George the Second (London, 1902)
   Uly 4.514, p. 118

'How many miles to Dublin town?' (1915)
   Uly 9.415–17, p. 187

'Idea-Mongers', publ. 20 May 1871 in *The Saturday Review*
   Uly 14.1207, p. 331

'If Women Bet, What Do They Bet?', publ. 13 Oct. 1855 in *Punch*
    Uly 13.241–42, p. 267

Inscription on 'The National Monument to the Forefathers' in Boston (1889)
    Uly 7.508–09, p. 155

'International Animosities', publ. 21 Feb. 1903 in *The Spectator*
    Uly 17.1631–32, p. 375

'"International Vanities" No. VIII. – Glory', publ. Dec. 1874 in *Blackwood's*
    Uly 11.698, p. 224

'Katie Woodencloak' in *Popular Tales From the North*, ed. Dasent (Edinburgh, 1859)
    Uly 18.766, p. 380

'Liszt at the Piano' in L. Ramann's *Franz Liszt, Artist and Man. 1811–1840.* (London, 1882)
    Uly 11.601, p. 223

'Matrimonial Biology', publ. 17 July 1852 in *Punch*
    Uly 13.241–42, p. 267

'May his name and memory be erased' (n.d.)
    Uly 14.1074, p. 328

Memorial essay on the death of 'His Royal Highness, the Grand Master' of the Freemasons, publ. 30 Sept. 1837 in *The Freemasons' Quarterly Review*
    Uly 10.188, p. 207

'Mount Athos and its Monasteries', publ. Jan. 1855 in *The Edinburgh Review*
    Uly 16.607, p. 368

'My Doctor', publ. 30 Dec. 1893 in *Pick-Me-Up*
    Uly 5.15–16, p. 121

'My Professional Work', publ. 5 Jan. 1897 in *The Girl's Own Paper*
    Uly 13.15–17, p. 252

'Nights At Mess', publ. June 1835 in *Blackwood's*
   Uly 8.40, p. 168

'Obligations of Literary Men' (Cincinnati, 1846)
   Uly 7.623, p. 159

'On Feasting', publ. June 1840 in *The Christian Lady's Magazine*
   Uly 13.637–38, p. 285

'On the Affectation of Faults and Imperfections', publ. 5 Oct. 1709 in *The Tatler*; repr. in *Steele: Selections* (Oxford, 1885)
   Uly 9.950, p. 190

'Outlawed', publ. 20 May 1893 in *All the Year Round*
   Uly 13.368–70, p. 269

'Personal Recollections of Thomas Campbell, Esq.', publ. May 1845 in *The Dublin University Magazine*
   Uly 12.1552–53, p. 240

'Popery in Paris', publ. Apr. 1867 in *The Evangelical Magazine*
   Uly 15.4692, p. 360

'Pop Goes the Weasel' (n.d.)
   Uly 18.1260, p. 384

'Premature Wisdom', publ. 6 Feb. 1841 in *The Irish Penny Journal*
   Uly 14.1207, p. 331

'Quarter-Day; or, Demand and No Supply', publ. 30 Mar. 1895 in *Punch*
   Uly 1.449, p. 86

'Recollections of the Burschenschaft of Germany', publ. Apr. 1846 in *The Dublin University Magazine*
   Uly 13.286–87, p. 268

'Rus in Urbe' by 'Ruricola', publ. Jan. 1895 in *The Month, A Catholic Magazine and Review*
   Uly 11.144–45, p. 218

'Self-Culture' in vol. 9, no. 35, of *Meliora* (1866)
   Uly 7.623, p. 159

'"SHE–THAT–OUGHT–NOT–TO–BE–PLAYED!"
A Story of Gloomy Gaiety', publ. 15 Sept. 1888 in *Punch*
   Uly 7.917, p. 159

*The Captive of Valence; or The Last Moments
of Pius VI* (London, 1804)
   Uly 12.1820, p. 241

'The Child of Shame' in *Weak Moments* (London, 1879)
   Uly 14.1065, p. 326

'The End of an Escapade', publ. Mar. 1903 in *The English Illustrated
Magazine*
   Uly 13.116, p. 260

'The Fortunes of Nara. An Old Japanese Story.', publ. 7 July 1877 in
All the Year Round
   Uly 14.1161, p. 330

'The French Peasant Girl' in vol. 1 (1838) of *The Young Lady's
Magazine*
   Uly 13.734–35, p. 289

'The Maniac, Or Once One Is Two', publ. 14 June 1834 in *The People's
Magazine*
   Uly 13.977, p. 297

'The March of Mind' in *The Odd Volume; or, Book of Variety* (London,
Dublin, and Edinburgh, 1835)
   Uly 17.1632, p. 376

The Merry Devill of Edmonton (London, 1608)
   Uly 6.67–68, p. 131

'The Queen of May' (n.d.)
   Uly 15.1189–90, p. 343

The Rose, a Comic Opera in Two Acts (London, 1773)
   Uly 13.655, p. 285

'The Shakespeare Night', publ. Jan. 1848 in *The New Monthly Belle
Assemblée*
   Uly 12.650–51, p. 236

'The Struggle' in vol. 3 (1854) of *Hogg's Instructor* (Edinburgh and London)
   Uly 14.870, p. 321

'The Two Widows' in vol. 4 of *The National Magazine* (London, 1863)
   Uly 13.172, p. 263

'Time's Waxworks', publ. 31 Dec. 1881 in *Punch*
   Uly 16.588, p. 368

'Tom Crosthwaite's Motto', publ. Nov. 1881 in *The Juvenile Magazine*
   Uly 16.634, p. 369

'Where friends are met for cheerful mirth', publ. 1840 in *The Meteor*
   Uly 10.1082–83, p. 214

'Why People Cough At Church', publ. 2 Mar. 1899 in *Truth*
   Uly 13.106, p. 259

'Yimakh shemo v'zikhro' (Hebrew curse) (n.d.)
   Uly 14.1074, p. 328

Aquinas, Saint Thomas
Commentary on *Jeremiah* (n.d.)
   Uly 15.711–12, p. 339

Archer, William
'The Drama in the Doldrums', publ. 1 Aug. 1892 in *The Fortnightly Review*
   Uly 10.1074–75, p. 213

Armstrong, James
'The Kielder Hunt' in his *Wanny Blossoms: A New Book of Border Songs and Ballads* (Carlisle, 1876)
   Uly 3.19–20, p. 96

Arnold, Edwin
'The Entry Into Heaven' in his *Indian Idylls: from the Sanscrit of the Mahâbharâta* (London, 1883)
   Uly 8.730, p. 179

Arnold, Matthew
'Rugby Chapel' (1867)
Uly 15.2153, p. 350

Augustine of Hippo, Saint
Commentary on Matthew vii 7
Uly 6.917, p. 148

Aulus Gellius
'Androcles and the Lion' (n.d.)
Uly 15.711–12, p. 339

Austen, Jane
Mansfield Park (London, 1814)
Uly 11.213, p. 220

Bacon, Francis
Last will, in *The Works of Francis Bacon* (London, 1874)
Uly 14.1074, p. 328

Badcock, John (as 'Jon Bee')
Entry on 'Hell' in his *Slang. A Dictionary of the Turf, the Ring, the Chase* (London, 1823)
Uly 10.559, p. 208

Bailey, Philip James
Festus (London, 1839 et seq)
Uly 14.1069, p. 326

Baillie, Joanna
Rayner: A Tragedy (London, 1805)
Uly 5.461–62, p. 129

Balzac, Honoré de
A Daughter of Eve, transl. Scott (London, 1897)
Uly 15.518–19, p. 335

'La Bourse' as 'The Purse' in *At the Sign of the Cat and Racket*, transl. Bell (London, 1895)
Uly 13.83–84, p. 257

La Cousine Bette, transl. Ives (London, 1896)
   Uly 15.4029–30, p. 359

Barbauld, Anna Letitia
   Lessons for Children from Three to Four Years Old (Dublin, 1814)
   Uly 15.559, p. 337

Barham, Richard Harris
   The Ingoldsby Legends; or, Mirth and Marvels (London, 1840)
   Uly 6.673, p. 144

Baring-Gould, Sabine
   An Old English Home and Its Dependencies (London, 1898)
   Uly 17.1632, p. 376

Barlee, Ellen
   Helen Lindsay; or, The Trial of Faith (London, 1859)
   Uly 6.533, p. 143

'Baroness von Beck'
   See Racidula, Wilhelmine

Baudelaire, Charles
   'Le Vin d'Assassin' as 'The Murderer's Wine', transl. by 'O.', publ. 24 Oct. 1883 in *The Oxford Magazine*
   Uly 15.775–76, p. 340

Beatson, R[obert?].
   'On Female Power', publ. Oct. 1782 in *The Lady's Magazine*
   Uly 10.601–02, p. 209

Beecher, Henry Ward
   'The Name Above Every Name' (1870)
   Uly 13.209–10, p. 266

Beerbohm, Max
   'Whistler's Writing', publ. May 1904 in *The Pall Mall Magazine*
   Uly 7.232, p. 152

Berquin, Arnaud
   Charles II. A Drama in Five Acts (London, 1788)
   Uly 17.1623, p. 374

Bible (Douay-Rheims Version)
Old Testament
    Judges xiv 3
        Uly 9.539, p. 187

    Ecclesiastes iv 11
        Uly 6.554–55, p. 144

Bible (King James Version)
Old Testament
    2 Samuel i 6
        Uly 2.16–17, p. 91

    Psalm xix 4
        Uly 15.2117, p. 349

    Ecclesiastes iv 11
        Uly 6.554–55, p. 144

    Jonah i 17 and ii 10
        Uly 8.495, p. 175

New Testament
    Matthew vii 16
        Uly 11.149–50, p. 218

    Matthew xvi 18
        Uly 3.501, p. 109

    Luke vi 44
        Uly 11.149–50, p. 218

    Romans x 18
        Uly 15.2117, p. 349

    2 Peter iii 3
        Uly 2.83–85, p. 93

Bingley, William
    Entry on 'Porpesse' in his *Animal Biography* (London, 1805)
        Uly 11.144–45, p. 218

Blackie, John Stuart
'Some Book-Worms Will Sit and Will Study' in his *Musa Burschicosa* (Edinburgh, 1869)
>*Uly* 14.871, p. 322

Blackmore, Richard
Prince Arthur. An Heroick Poem. In Ten Books. (London, 1695)
>*Uly* 9.934 and 14.1161, pp. 188 and 330

Blake, Mrs [Edith Osborne]
The Realities of Freemasonry (London, 1879)
>*Uly* 13.691, p. 287

Blake, William
'The Rime of the Ancient Mariner' (1834)
>*Uly* 1.273–74, p. 86

Blashfield, Evangeline Wilbour
Portraits and Backgrounds: Hrotsvitha, Aphra Behn, Aïssé, Rosalba Carriera (New York, 1917)
>*Uly* 3.212–13, p. 103

Blavatsky, H[elena]. P[etrovna].
The Secret Doctrine: The Synthesis of Science, Religion and Philosophy (London, 1888)
>*Uly* 3.157, p. 102

Blitz, Julia
Digger Dick's Darling, and Other Tales (London, New York, and Melbourne, 1888)
>*Uly* 13.87–88, p. 257

Boileau Despréaux, Nicolas
'Satire X' in *The Satires of Boileau Despréaux*, transl. Porter (Glasgow, 1904)
>*Uly* 16.253, p. 365

Bonar, Rev. Archibald
Sermons, Chiefly on Devotional Subjects (London, 1817)
>*Uly* 14.1174, p. 331

Boswell, James
The Life of Samuel Johnson, LL.D. (London, 1791)
Uly 14.666–67, p. 310

Bourchier, John, Lord Berners
The Book of Huon de Bordeaux; Adapted From French Sources (n.p., 1534)
Uly 14.367–68, p. 307

Bowring, Edgar Alfred
See Goethe, Johann Wolfgang von

Boyce, John Cox
College Debts. A Novel. (London, 1870)
Uly 17.1623, p. 374

Braddon, Mary Elizabeth
Joshua Haggard's Daughter (London, 1876)
Uly 8.333, p. 172

The Christmas Hirelings (London, 1894)
Uly 3.88, p. 99

Three Times Dead; or, The Secret of the Heath, first publ. in book form (London, 1860); later serialized in *The Halfpenny Journal*, 1 Aug. 1864–28 Nov. 1865
Uly 5.15–16, p. 121

Brame, Charlotte Marie
See Clay, Bertha M.

Bransby, John
The Use of the Globes (London, 1791)
Uly 14.556. p. 309

Brewer, E[benezer]. Cobham
Dictionary of Phrase and Fable (London, 1895)
Uly 7.874–75, p. 164

Bridges, Robert
'The Voice of Nature' in *The Shorter Poems of Robert Bridges* (London, 1890)
    Uly 6.136, p. 135

Broderip, Frances Freeling
'The Jewel Princess' in *The Daisy and Her Friends: Simple Tales and Stories for Children* (London, 1869)
    Uly 13.162, p. 262

Brome, Richard
The Queenes Exchange, A Comedy (London, 1657)
    Uly 8.730, p. 179

Brontë, Anne
The Tenant of Wildfell Hall (London, 1848)
    Uly 17.322, p. 372

Brontë, Charlotte
Shirley (London, 1849)
    Uly 13.616, p. 282

The Professor. A Tale. (London, 1857)
    Uly 15.1247, p. 344

Villette (London, 1853)
    Uly 14.1078, p. 328

Brontë, Emily
'And like myself lone, wholly lone' in *The Complete Poems of Emily Brontë*, ed. Shorter (London, 1910)
    Uly 6.136, p. 135

'The Prisoner. A Fragment.' in *Poems by Currer, Ellis, and Acton Bell* (London, 1846)
    Uly 15.1247, p. 344

Wuthering Heights (London, 1847)
    Uly 17.322, p. 372

Broughton, Rhoda
Not Wisely, But Too Well (London, 1867 and 1875)
Uly 6.252, p. 139

Browne, Marie Hedderwick
'A Mother's Grief' in her *A Spray of Lilac, and Other Poems and Songs* (London and Edinburgh, 1892)
Uly 13.764, p. 293

Browne, Sir Thomas
Hydriotaphia: Urne-Buriall (London, 1658)
Uly 14.526, p. 308

Browning, Elizabeth Barrett
Aurora Leigh (London, 1856)
Uly 11.312, p. 221

Browning, Robert
King Victor and King Charles (London, 1842)
Uly 13.691, p. 287

'The Two Poets of Croisic' in his *La Saisiaz: The Two Poets of Croisic* (London, 1878)
Uly 17.322, p. 372

'With Bernard de Mandeville' in his *Parleyings with Certain People of Importance in their Day* (London, 1887)
Uly 14.664–65, p. 309

Buchan, John
Greenmantle (London and Boston, 1916)
Uly 13.805, p. 294

The Thirty-Nine Steps (Edinburgh and London, 1915)
Uly 15.1321 and 3481, pp. 345 and 359

Bullen, Frank T[homas].
'Light Ho, Sir!' in his *Light Ho, Sir! and Other Sketches* (London, 1913)
Uly 17.23, p. 371

Bulwer-Lytton, Edward
Eugene Aram. A Tale. (London, 1832)
Uly 8.638, p. 176

Eugene Aram, a Tragedy (London, 1833)
Uly 8.638, p. 176

Kenelm Chillingly: His Adventures and Opinions (London, 1878)
Uly 13.421–22, p. 273

Rienzi: The Last of the Roman Tribunes (London, 1835)
Uly 6.1033, p. 148

Burbank, A[lfred]. S[tevens].
Guide to Historic Plymouth: Localities and Objects of Interest (Plymouth, Mass., 1895)
Uly 7.508–09, p. 155

Burgess, Alexander
The Book of Nettercaps (Dundee, 1875)
Uly 8.495, p. 175

Burnett, Frances Hodgson
The Fortunes of Philippa Fairfax (London, 1888)
Uly 13.11, p. 251

Burney, Frances
Camilla, or, A Picture of Youth (London, 1796)
Uly 14.741–42, p. 312

Memoirs of Doctor Burney (London, 1832)
Uly 7.874–75, p. 164

Burns, Robert
'Auld Lang Syne' (1788)
Uly 9.1202, p. 196

'Tam O'Shanter' (1791)
Uly 10.548, p. 208

Burroughs, John
Whitman: A Study (Boston, 1896; London, 1897)
Uly 14.1007, p. 325

Bury, Lady Charlotte Campbell
The Devoted (Paris, 1836)
   Uly 12.161–62, p. 231

The History of a Flirt. Related by Herself. (London, 1840)
   Uly 13.655, p. 285

Byron, George Gordon, Lord
Hours of Idleness (London, 1807)
   Uly 11.312, p. 221

The Bride of Abydos. A Turkish Tale. (London, 1813)
   Uly 15.1600, p. 348

The Corsair, A Tale. (London, 1814)
   Uly 7.682, p. 160

The Giaour (London, 1813)
   Uly 5.563–64, p. 130

'The Prisoner of Chillon' in *The Prisoner of Chillon and Other Poems* (London, 1816)
   Uly 13.690–91, p. 286

Caillard, Emma Marie
'The Divine Sacrifice', publ. Feb. 1895 in *The Contemporary Review*
   Uly 10.1074–75, p. 213

Caird, Mona
The Daughters of Danaus (London, 1894)
   Uly 15.2457, p. 354

Calvin, John
Commentary on *Hosea* (Geneva, 1557)
   Uly 15.2332, p. 352

Cameron, William
'Speak Not to Me of War', publ. 18 Mar. 1910 in *The Motherwell Times*
   Uly 2.16–17, p. 91

Campion, Thomas and Philip Rosseter
'Harke, al you ladies' in *A booke of ayres* (London, 1601)
   Uly 14.359, p. 306

Capes, Bernard
The Great Skene Mystery (London, 1907)
Uly 7.232, p. 152

Carbery, Ethna
'Páistín Fionn' in *The Four Winds of Eirinn* (Dublin, 1902)
Uly 12.70–71, p. 229

Carey, Rosa Nouchette
Heriot's Choice: A Tale, serialized July 1877–Oct. 1879 in *The Monthly Packet*; then publ. in book form (London, 1879)
Uly 13.213, p. 266

Carle, Richard
Jumping Jupiter (1910)
Uly 6.87–88, p. 131

Carlyle, Thomas
On Heroes, Hero-worship and the Heroic in History (London, 1841)
Uly 7.315, p. 153

Carr, Francis
Left Alone; or, The Fortunes of Phillis Maitland (London, 1879)
Uly 8.333, p. 172

Carr, Helen and Gabrielle
See Wood, Lady Emma Caroline

Carson, Joseph
'Address to His Majesty King George the Fourth' (Newry, 1831)
Uly 13.746, p. 292

Carter, August
'Denizens of the Aqueous Kingdom', publ. 6 Jan. 1887 in *Nature*
Uly 12.74, p. 230

Carter, Mary E[lizabeth].
Mrs. Severn (London, 1889)
Uly 13.421–22, p. 273

Cary, H[enry]. F[rancis].
The Vision: or, Hell, Purgatory, and Paradise (London, 1814)
Uly 14.8–9, p. 301

Casaubon, Meric
A TREATISE PROVING Spirits, Witches, AND Supernatural Operations (London, 1672)
Uly 14.848–49, p. 319

Translation of *The Meditations of Marcus Aurelius* (London, 1634)
Uly 13.375–76, p. 270

Castiglione, Baldassare
The Book of the Courtier (1528), transl. Opdycke (London, 1902)
Uly 14.804, p. 316

Castle, Egerton
Consequences (London, 1891)
Uly 13.576, p. 279

The Light of Scarthey: A Romance (London, 1895)
Uly 13.578–79, p. 280

Catullus
Poem 45 (Acmen Septimius suos amores)
Uly 4.186, p. 113

Caunter, Rev. John Hobart
Sermon 19, on Matthew v 9, from his *Sermons on the Lord's Prayer and the Eight Beatitudes* (London, 1849)
Uly 7.804–05, p. 162

Cervantes Saavedra, Miguel de
The Ingenious Knight, Don Quixote De La Mancha, transl. Duffield (London, 1881)
Uly 14.97, p. 304

Chalmers, Alexander
The New General Biographical Dictionary (London, 1814)
Uly 14.666–67, p. 310

Chaucer, Geoffrey
 'The Parson's Tale' in his *Canterbury Tales* (c. 1392)
  Uly 14.98, p. 305

Chekhov, Anton
 'Gusev', in his *The Witch and Other Stories*, transl. Garnett (London, 1918)
  Uly 12.59, p. 228

Chesterton, G[ilbert]. K[eith].
 What's Wrong With The World (London, 1910)
  Uly 8.684–85, p. 178

Chetwind (or Chetwynd), John
 Anthologia historica (London, 1674)
  Uly 10.807, p. 211

Chézy, Wilhelmine Christiane von
 See Weber, Carl Maria von

Cicero
 De Natura Deorum, transl. Brooks (London, 1896)
  Uly 11.1104, p. 226

Clarke, Mary Victoria Cowden
 The Iron Cousin: or, Mutual Influence (new edn, London, 1862)
  Uly 15.562, p. 337

Claudel, Paul
 The East I Know, transl. Benét (New Haven and London, 1914)
  Uly 14.759, p. 314

Clay, Bertha M.
 'A Weak Woman' in the Jan. 1902 issue of *Happy Hour Stories*
  Uly 9.345–46, p. 183

 A Woman's Temptation, serialized 12 June–16 Sept. 1875 in *The Family Reader*; later publ. in book form (New York, 1880)
  Uly 13.764, p. 293

Clifton, Harry
'The Wedding of Biddy McGrane'
Uly 4.112–13, p. 111

Clowes, Evelyn May
See Mordaunt, Elinor

Cobbett, William
'Advice to a Father' in his *Advice to Young Men* etc (London, 1829)
Uly 9.1094–95, p. 193

Cockburn, Henry
Memorials of His Time (Edinburgh, 1856)
Uly 17.1632, p. 376

Collins, Wilkie
Man and Wife (London, 1870)
Uly 8.333, p. 172

Collins, Wilkie and Charles Dickens
The Lazy Tour of Two Idle Apprentices, serialized 3 Oct.–31 Oct. 1857 in *Household Words*; and 31 Oct.–28 Nov. 1857 in *Harper's Weekly*; later publ. in book form (London, 1890)
Uly 10.94, p. 201

Colman the Elder, George
The Spleen, or, Islington Spa: A Comick Piece in Two Acts (Dublin, 1776)
Uly 13.1110–11, p. 299

Connolly, James
'Home Thrusts' column attacking Daniel Tallon in the 20 Aug. 1898 issue of *The Workers' Republic*
Uly 7.315, p. 153

Conrad, Joseph
The Mirror of the Sea (New York and London, 1906)
Uly 15.1356, p. 346

Corelli, Marie
The Mighty Atom (London, 1896)
    Uly 14.1207, p. 331

Corfield, Clara Lavinia
See Temple, Crona

Cornwall, Barry
'The Nights' in his *English Songs, and Other Small Poems* (London, 1832)
    Uly 7.560, p. 156

'The Portrait on My Uncle's Snuff-Box. An Anecdote', first publ. in *The Keepsake for 1828* (London, 1827); later collected in his *Essays and Tales in Prose* (Boston, 1853)
    Uly 8.344–45, p. 174

Couper, Robert
Speculations on the Mode and Appearances of Impregnation in the Human Female (Edinburgh and London, 1789)
    Uly 15.2413, p. 353

Courthope, W[illiam]. J[ohn].
The Marvellous History of King Arthur in Avalon (London, 1904)
    Uly 6.852–53, p. 147

Cousin, Victor
Introduction to the History of Philosophy, transl. Linberg (Boston, 1832)
    Uly 14.770–71, p. 315

Cowper, William
'The Diverting History of John Gilpin', first publ. 1782 in *The Public Advertiser*; then in Cowper's *The Task: A Poem, in Six Books* (London, 1785)
    Uly 15.518–19, p. 335

'The Joy of the Cross' (1806)
    Uly 14.770–71, p. 315

Craik, Dinah Maria
'A City at Play' in her *Fair France, Impressions of a Traveller* (London, 1871)
   Uly 15.518–19, p. 335

'My Christian Name', first publ. 1 June 1850 in *Chambers's Edinburgh Journal*; later collected in her *Poems* (London, 1866)
   Uly 9.1202, p. 196

Young Mrs. Jardine, serialized Jan.–Dec. 1879 in *Good News*; then publ. in book form (London, 1879)
   Uly 13.242, p. 267

Crawford, F[rancis]. Marion
Saracinesca (Edinburgh and London, 1887)
   Uly 13.600, p. 281

Crockett, S[amuel]. R[utherford].
Little Anna Mark, serialized Jan.–Dec. 1899 in *The Cornhill*; then publ. in book form (London, 1900)
   Uly 14.866, p. 321

Croly, George
Salathiel. A Story of the Past, the Present, and the Future (New York and Philadelphia, 1828; London, 1829)
   Uly 3.308–09, p. 105

Crowne, John
The History of Charles the Eighth of France (London, 1671); repr. in his *Dramatic Works* (Edinburgh and London, 1873)
   Uly 4.447–49, p. 116

Cunningham, Sir Henry Stewart
Late Laurels, serialized Apr. 1863–Feb. 1864 in *Fraser's Magazine*; then publ. in book form (London, 1864)
   Uly 13.733–34, p. 288

Dampier, William
Mr. Dampier's Voyages and Descriptions (London, 1705)
   Uly 15.1580, p. 347

Danby, Frank
Twilight (London, 1916)
    Uly 4.511, p. 117

Dance, George
A Chinese Honeymoon (1899)
    Uly 13.24–25, p. 254

Darlow, Thomas Herbert
'The Implicit Promise of Perfection' in *The Expositor*, vol. 9 (1894)
    Uly 12.202, p. 232

Darragh, Redmond
'Ralph Brandon's Love', publ. 23 Apr. 1881 in *The Shamrock*
    Uly 4.511, p. 117

Dasent, George Webbe
Three To One, or, Some Passages Out of the Life of Amicia Lady Sweetapple, serialized Oct. 1871–Sept. 1872 in *Belgravia*; then publ. in book form (London, 1872)
    Uly 6.772, p. 146

Daudet, Alphonse
Lettres de mon moulin (1869) as *Letters from My Mill*, transl. Wormeley (Boston, 1900)
    Uly 15.2690, p. 355

L'Immortel (1888) as *The Immortal*, transl. Ives (Boston, 1899)
    Uly 1.198–99, p. 85

Davidson, John
'A Ballad of a Nun' in his *Ballads and Songs* (London, 1894)
    Uly 9.1221–22, p. 197

A Full and True Account of the Wonderful Mission of Earl Lavender (London, 1895)
    Uly 10.121, p. 202

Dawe, W[illiam]. Carlton
The Voyage of the "Pulo Way", A Record of Some Strange Doings at Sea (London, 1898)
    Uly 16.529, p. 367

Defoe, Daniel
Roxana: The Fortunate Mistress (London, 1724)
Uly 13.17–18 and 14.755–56, pp. 253 and 314

de la Mare, Walter
Rupert Brooke and the Intellectual Imagination (London, 1919)
Uly 15.4227, p. 360

Deland, Margaret Wade Campbell
'At the Stuffed-Animal House' in her *Dr. Lavendar's People* (New York and London, 1903)
Uly 13.745, p. 292

Delitzsch, Franz
Biblical Commentary on the Prophecies of Isaiah, transl. Martin (Edinburgh, 1874)
Uly 10.822, p. 212

d'Emillianne, Gabriel
A Short History of Monastical Orders (London, 1693)
Uly 14.74–75, p. 302

Densmore, Emmet, M.D.
How Nature Cures (New York and London, 1892)
Uly 16.22, p. 363

Dickens, Charles
Dombey and Son (London, 1848)
Uly 5.461–62, p. 129

Hard Times.—For These Times (London, 1854)
Uly 6.533, p. 143

Little Dorrit (London, 1857)
Uly 1.6, p. 83

Our Mutual Friend (London, 1864–65)
Uly 7.602, p. 158

The Battle of Life: A Love Story (London, 1846)
Uly 12.1351, p. 239

The Chimes: A Goblin Story (London, 1844)
    Uly 6.1033, p. 148

The Lazy Tour of Two Idle Apprentices
    See entry above under Collins, Wilkie and Charles Dickens
    Uly 10.94, p. 201

The Life and Adventures of Nicholas Nickleby (London, 1839)
    Uly 15.559, p. 337

The Mystery of Edwin Drood, in *The Mystery of Edwin Drood and Other Stories* (London, c. 1870)
    Uly 4.186, p. 113

The Old Curiosity Shop (London, 1841)
    Uly 14.714, p. 312

The Personal History of David Copperfield (London, 1850)
    Uly 8.77–78 and 13.600, pp. 169 and 281

Dietzgen, Josef
The Positive Outcome of Philosophy, transl. Untermann (Chicago, 1906)
    Uly 10.181–82, p. 205

Dimond, William
The Broken Sword; A Grand Melo-Drama, second edn (London, 1816)
    Uly 14.1174, p. 331

Diver, Maud
Captain Desmond, V.C. (Edinburgh and London, 1910; rvsd edn, New York and London, 1914)
    Uly 13.576, p. 279

'The Indian Woman as Poet', first publ. in the periodical *Womanhood*; later collected in Diver's *The Englishwoman in India* (Edinburgh and London, 1909)
    Uly 18.1335, p. 384

Dostoevsky, Fyodor
Crime and Punishment, transl. Garnett (London, 1914)
    Uly 13.624, p. 283

Douglas, Lord Alfred
    Dedicatory poem in *Sonnets By Lord Alfred Douglas* (London, 1909)
        Uly 10.866, p. 213

Doveton, F[rederick]. B[rickdale].
    'Scorned' in his *Snatches of Song* (London, 1880)
        Uly 13.578–79, p. 280

Dowson, Ernest Christopher, and Arthur Collins Moore
    A Comedy of Masks (London, 1893)
        Uly 3.2–3, p. 95

    Adrian Rome (London, 1899)
        Uly 15.4672, p. 360

Drewry, Edith Stewart
    'A Prize Worth Winning', publ. 12 Apr. 1879 in *The London Journal*
        Uly 4.514, p. 118

Dryden, John
    'Annus Mirabilis' (London, 1667)
        Uly 1.273–74, p. 86

    The State of Innocence, and Fall of Man (London, 1677)
        Uly 8.543, p. 175

    Verse translation of Virgil's *Aeneid* (London, 1697)
        Uly 15.711–12, p. 339

    Verse translation of Virgil's *Georgics* (London, 1697)
        Uly 9.1221–22, p. 197

Duffett, Thomas
    'Gratitude to Fidelia' in his *New Poems, Songs, Prologues and Epilogues* (London, 1676)
        Uly 10.601–02, p. 209

Dumas, Alexandre
    The Count of Monte-Cristo, anonymous translations (London, 1848; New York, 1894)
        Uly 13.616 (New York) and 16.55 (London), pp. 282 and 363, respectively

Edgeworth, Maria
The Absentee (London, 1812)
Uly 10.486, p. 207

Eliot, George
Adam Bede (Edinburgh and London, 1859)
Uly 18.766, p. 380

The Mill on the Floss (London, 1860)
Uly 14.1075, p. 328

Ellis, Robert
Disease in Childhood (London, 1852)
Uly 14.1207, p. 331

Emerson, Ralph Waldo
'To Rhea' in his *Poems* (Boston, 1847)
Uly 12.70–71, p. 229

Enderbie, Percie
Cambria Triumphans (London, 1661)
Uly 14.870, p. 321

Erskine, Thomas
Armata: A Fragment (London, 1817)
Uly 13.3–4, p. 248

Evans, Mary Ann
See Eliot, George

Evans, Rev. Robert Wilson
'The Conversion of Manaen' in his *Parochial Sermons* (London, 1855)
Uly 7.776, p. 161

Everett-Green, E[velyn].
Esther's Charge: A Story for Girls (Edinburgh, 1899)
Uly 13.735, p. 290

Fallen Fortunes (London, 1903)
Uly 14.871, p. 322

Ewing, Juliana Horatia
Jan of the Windmill: A Story of the Plains, serialized Nov. 1872–Oct. 1873 in *Aunt Judy's Magazine*; then publ. in book form (London, 1896)
Uly 10.181–82, p. 205

Faber, Frederick William
The Blessed Sacrament: or, The Works and Ways of God (London, 1855)
Uly 14.336–37, p. 306

Fabyan, Robert
New Chronicles of England and France (London, 1515)
Uly 12.335, p. 234

Farley, Philip
Criminals of America; or, Tales of the Lives of Thieves (New York, 1876)
Uly 11.973, p. 225

Farnie, H. B. and P. D. Guglielmo
'Under the Hazel Tree' (1867)
Uly 18.768–69, p. 382

Farnol, Jeffery
Beltane the Smith (London, 1915)
Uly 12.215, p. 233

Ferguson, D. M.
Evan Bane; A Highland Legend: and Other Poems (London, 1832)
Uly 13.597, p. 280

Ferguson, Sir Samuel
'The Abdication of Fergus Mac Roy' in his *Lays of the Western Gael, and Other Poems* (London, 1865)
Uly 7.682, p. 160

Fielding, Henry
The History of Amelia (London, 1752)
Uly 11.213, p. 220

The History of Tom Jones, a Foundling (London, 1749)
Uly 14.886, p. 324

Fitchett, John
King Alfred: A Poem (London, 1841–42)
Uly 9.245, p. 182

Fitzgerald, F. Scott
'May Day', first publ. July 1920 in *The Smart Set*
Uly 1.6, p. 83

Fleming, May Agnes
One Night's Mystery (New York and London, 1876)
Uly 13.576, p. 279

Pride and Passion (New York and London, 1882)
Uly 15.1321, p. 345

Fletcher, Rev. John William
'General Observations on the Redemption of Mankind by Jesus Christ' in his *Works* (London, 1860)
Uly 14.879, p. 323

Foote, Mary Hallock
'The Eleventh Hour', publ. Jan. 1906 in *The Century*
Uly 11.79, p. 217

Forbes, G[ren].
'I Want Meat' (c. 1865)
Uly 15.2702–03, p. 355

Ford, Richard
Gatherings From Spain (London, 1846)
Uly 15.518–19, p. 335

Foxe, John
Actes and Monuments (London, 1563) aka *Foxe's Book of Martyrs*
Uly 13.375–76 and 15.2332, pp. 270 and 352

Frankau, Julia
See Danby, Frank

Franklin, Benjamin
'The Way to Wealth or Father Abraham's Sermon'
in *Poor Richard's Almanack* (Philadelphia, 1758); later in Franklin's
Way to Wealth; or "Poor Richard Improved" (London, 1810)
Uly 15.1584, p. 348

Fraser, Mrs Hugh and J. Crawford Fraser
Her Italian Marriage (London, 1915)
Uly 13.162, p. 262

French, Arthur W[ells].
'Little Sweetheart Come and Kiss Me' (1872)
Uly 13.858–59, p. 295

Gardenstone, Francis Garden, Lord
Miscellanies in Prose and Verse (Edinburgh, 1792)
Uly 10.734–35, p. 210

Gaskell, Mrs Elizabeth
'The Old Nurse's Story', publ. Christmas 1852 in *Household Words*
Uly 15.559, p. 337

Gaunt, Mary Eliza Bakewell
'Christmas Eve at Warwingie', first publ. Jan. 1891 in *The English
Illustrated Magazine*; later in Gaunt's *The Moving Finger*
(London, 1895)
Uly 13.3, p. 248

Gavin, Antonio
See d'Emillianne, Gabriel

Georgiana, Lady Chatterton
Lost Happiness; or, The Effects of a Lie (London, 1845)
Uly 13.17–18, p. 253

Giberne, Agnes
Enid's Silver Bond (London, 1898)
Uly 13.742–43, p. 290

Gissing, George
Introduction to the 1901 London edn of Dickens's
The Old Curiosity Shop and Master Humphrey's Clock
    Uly 17.23, p. 371

Workers in the Dawn (London, 1880)
    Uly 5.76–77, p. 123

Goethe, Johann Wolfgang von
Faust: A Tragedy (1808), transl. Blackie, second edn (London, 1880)
    Uly 13.851–52, p. 295

'The Doubters and the Lovers', transl. Bowring, in *The Poems of Goethe* (London, 1853)
    Uly 9.1221–22, p. 197

Gogol, Nikolai Vasilievich
'The Cloak' aka 'The Overcoat' in his *St. Johns Eve and Other Stories*, transl. Hapgood (New York, 1886)
    Uly 16.55, p. 363

Goldsmith, Oliver
The Citizen of the World (Dublin, 1762)
    Uly 14.828 and 882, pp. 317 and 323

Grahame, Kenneth
The Wind in the Willows (London, 1908)
    Uly 14.804 and 15.2153, pp. 316 and 350

Grant, James
The King's Own Borderers. A Military Romance. (London, 1865)
    Uly 13.17–18, p. 253

Greene, Robert
Greene's Groats-worth of Witte (London, 1592)
    Uly 3.177, p. 103

Grillparzer, Franz Seraphicus
Die Ahnfrau (1817), cited in L. Dalbiac's *Dictionary of [German] Quotations* (London, 1909)
    Uly 14.831, p. 318

Grundy, Bertha Jane
See Adams, Bertha Leith

Guevara, Luis Vélez de
El Diablo Cojuelo (Madrid, 1641)
Uly 13.851–52, p. 295

Haggard, H[enry]. Rider
The People of the Mist (London, 1894)
Uly 2.16–17, p. 91

Hall, Agnes C.
See St. Clair, Rosalia

Hamilton of Bangour, William
'Ah the shepherd's mournful fate' in his *Poems and Songs*, ed. Paterson (Edinburgh, 1850)
Uly 15.1189–90, p. 343

'To Lady Mary Montgomery' in his *Poems on Several Occasions*, third edn (Edinburgh, 1760)
Uly 11.601, p. 223

Hardcastle, Ephraim
Wine and Walnuts; or, After Dinner Chit-Chat (London, 1823)
Uly 18.8–9, p. 379

Hardy, Thomas
Desperate Remedies (London, 1871)
Uly 13.412–13, p. 271

'The To-be-forgotten' in his *Wessex Poems and Other Verses; Poems of the Past and the Present* (New York and London, 1901)
Uly 4.256, p. 115

The Woodlanders (London, 1887)
Uly 1.152–53, p. 84

Hare, Julius Charles, and Augustus William Hare
Guesses at Truth by Two Brothers (London, 1827)
Uly 7.215–16, p. 152

Harland, Marion
Moss-Side (New York, 1857; London, 1858)
   Uly 15.562, p. 337

Harraden, Beatrice
The Guiding Thread (New York and London, 1916)
   Uly 13.105, p. 259

Harrington, Sir John
'On the games that have been in request at the court' in his *Epigrams Both Pleasant and Serious* (London, 1615)
   Uly 12.1596, p. 240

Harris, Joseph
The Description and Use of the Globes, and the Orrery (London, 1731)
   Uly 14.556, p. 309

Harrison, Constance Cary
The Anglomaniacs, serialized June–Sept. 1890 in *The Century Magazine*; then publ. in book form (London, 1890)
   Uly 4.514, p. 118

Harrison, Henry Sydnor
Queed (Boston, New York, and London, 1911)
   Uly 13.422–23, p. 274

Harvey, W[illiam]. Wigan
Preface to Irenaeus's *Against Heresies* (Cambridge, 1857)
   Uly 14.1167, p. 330

Harwood, John Berwick
Lord Ulswater. A Novel. (London, 1867)
   Uly 14.755–56, p. 314

Hawker, Robert Stephen
'Dupath Well' in his *Cornish Ballads and Other Poems* (Oxford and London, 1869)
   Uly 2.16–17, p. 91

Hawthorne, Nathanael
'Dr. Heidegger's Experiment' in vol. 1 of his *Twice-Told Tales* (Boston, 1842)
   Uly 13.548–49, p. 276

'Howe's Masquerade' in vol. 2 of his *Twice-Told Tales* (Boston, 1842)
Ulys 15.2167–68, p. 351

'The Birth-Mark' in his *Mosses from an Old Manse* (London, 1846)
Ulys 13.415–16, p. 272

Haydn, Joseph
Der krumme Teufel (1751–52)
Ulys 13.851–52, p. 295

Haynie, James Henry
Paris, Past & Present (New York, 1902)
Ulys 7.599, p. 158

Hazlitt, William
'Common Places', publ. 29 Nov. 1823 in *The Literary Examiner*
Ulys 15.1356, p. 346

'Mr. Wordsworth' in his *Spirit of the Age: or Contemporary Portraits*, second edn (London, 1825)
Ulys 9.356, p. 184

Heaphy, Thomas Musgrave
'The Blue Scarf' in his *Glimpses and Gleams* (London, 1884)
Ulys 15.2864, p. 356

Hearn, Lafcadio
Glimpses of Unfamiliar Japan, First Series (London, 1894)
Ulys 8.730, p. 179

Heath, Arnold
Edith's Marriage (London, 1868)
Ulys 15.2866, p. 357

Herbert, Victor, and Glen MacDonough
'Ask Her While the Band is Playing' (1909)
Ulys 13.439–41, p. 275

Higginson, Thomas Wentworth
'The Disappearance of Ennui' in his *Book and Heart: Essays on Literature and Life* (New York, 1897)
Ulys 9.938, p. 189

Hine, Muriel
Half in Earnest (London, 1910)
Uly 13.742–43, p. 290

Hogg, James Robert
'The Brownie of the Black Haggs' in his *Tales and Sketches, by the Ettrick Shepherd* (Glasgow, Edinburgh, and London, 1837)
Uly 3.19–20, p. 96

Hollingshead, John
My Lifetime (London, 1895)
Uly 12.544, p. 236

Holmes, Mrs Mary J.
Edna Browning; or, The Leighton Homestead (New York and London, 1872)
Uly 14.1034–35, p. 325

Holmes, Oliver Wendell
Essay, publ. Oct. 1879 in *The International Review*, on Sir Edwin Arnold's *The Light of Asia; or, The Great Renunciation* (London, 1879)
Uly 9.2–3, p. 181

Holt, Emily Sarah
Imogen: A Story of the Mission of Augustine (London, 1876)
Uly 15.1267–68, p. 345

Hood, Basil, and Walter Alfred Slaughter
'Won't you come to Margate?' (1895)
Uly 3.21–22, p. 97

Hood, Thomas
'The Dream of Eugene Aram, the Murderer' (London, 1831)
Uly 8.638, p. 176

Horstius, Jacob (aka James) Merlo
The Paradise of the Christian Soul (London, 1850)
Uly 10.172 and 13.209–10, pp. 203 and 266

Hughes, Thomas
Tom Brown's School Days (London, 1857)
Uly 14.828–29 and 15.2380, pp. 318 and 353

Hugo, Victor
Les Misérables, transl. Wraxall (London, 1862)
Uly 6.467, p. 142

L'Homme qui rit, transl. Young as *The Man Who Laughs* (New York, 1869) and as *By the King's Command* (London, 1875)
Uly 11.79, p. 217

Notre-Dame de Paris, transl. Haynes as *The Hunchback of Notre Dame* (New York, 1902; London, 1904)
Uly 14.847, p. 319

Humphreys, Samuel
LETTERS from the Marchioness de M*** (London, 1735)
Uly 10.601–02, p. 209

Huneker, James
Ivory Apes and Peacocks (New York and London, 1915)
Uly 7.448, p. 154

Hungerford, Mrs Margaret Wolfe
An Unsatisfactory Lover (London, 1894)
Uly 8.269, p. 170

Doris (London, 1885)
Uly 13.412–13 and 742–43, pp. 271 and 290

Hunt, Sir Aubrey de Vere
The Duke of Mercia, an historical drama (London, 1823)
Uly 13.597, p. 280

Hyam, Lord Mark
'An English Girl (Seen on Lac Leman)' in his
Moods & Memories: A Volume of Verse
(London, 1916)
Uly 8.62–63, p. 169

Ibsen, Henrik
Brand (1866), transl. Wilson (London, 1891)
Uly 3.132–33, p. 100

Little Eyolf (1894), transl. Archer (London, 1895)
   Uly 13.188–89, p. 264

When We Dead Awaken (1899), transl. Archer (London, 1900)
   Uly 10.807, p. 211

Ingoldsby, Thomas
   See Barham, Richard Harris

Jacobs, W[illiam].
   The Self-Instructing Latin Classic (London, 1841)
      Uly 4.447–49, p. 116

James, Henry
   'Guest's Confession', publ. Oct.–Nov. 1872 in *The Atlantic Monthly*
      Uly 15.4692, p. 360

Jelley, Symmes M[ajor].
   Shadowed to Europe: A Chicago Detective on Two Continents (Chicago and New York, 1885)
      Uly 13.87–88, p. 257

Johns, Rev. B. G.
   'The Sense of Touch' in vol. 8 (1873) of *The Quiver*
      Uly 7.215–16, p. 152

Johnson, Grace Leslie Keith
   See Keith, Leslie

Johnson, Henry
   All for Number One, or, Charlie Russell's Ups and Downs: A Story for Boys and Girls (London, 1888)
      Uly 8.39, p. 168

Johnson, Samuel
   'Observations on the Oriental Eclogues' of William Collins in Johnson's *The Works of the Poets of Great Britain and Ireland* (London, 1800)
      Uly 14.882, p. 323

   'The History of a Young Woman That Came to London for a Service' (London, 1750)
      Uly 14.735, p. 312

'The Unhappiness of Women Whether Single or Married',
publ. 31 July 1750 in *The Rambler* (London)
   Uly 14.670, p. 310

Jones, Arthur Llewelyn
   See Machen, Arthur

Jones, Robert
   'Hark! Hark! wot ye what?' in *A Musicall Dreame. Or the Fourth Booke of Ayres* (London, 1609)
   Uly 14.329–30, p. 305

Jonson, Ben
   The Alchemist (London, 1612)
   Uly 8.61, p. 169

Josephs, Matthew
   'Grief' in his *Wonders of Creation and Other Poems* (London, 1876)
   Uly 9.1036, p. 191

Keats, John
   Endymion: A Poetic Romance (London, 1818)
   Uly 12.69, p. 229

Keble, Rev. John
   The Christian Year: Thoughts in Verse for the Sundays and Holidays Throughout the Year (London, 1827)
   Uly 13.624, p. 283

Keith, Leslie
   Venetia's Lovers: An Uneventful Story (London, 1884)
   Uly 9.345–46, p. 183

Kelly, William
   'On 2 Thessalonians—Chapter iii. 10–15', publ. Nov. 1883 in *The Bible Treasury: A Monthly Magazine of Papers on Scriptural Subjects*
   Uly 10.183, p. 206

King, John
   'The Siren' in his *Rustic Pictures and Broken Rhymes* (London, 1874)
   Uly 13.4–5, p. 249

King, Katharine Douglas
'Lucretia', publ. July 1896 in *The Yellow Book*
Uly 13.735, p. 290

King, William
The Transactioneer, With some of his Philosophical Fancies in Two Dialogues (London, 1700)
Uly 7.47, p. 151

Kipling, Rudyard
Kim (London, 1901)
Uly 5.217 and 13.597, pp. 124 and 280

Kraus, Karl
Die Fackel (Vienna, 1899)
Uly 12.1351, p. 239

Landon, Letitia Elizabeth
See 'L.E.L.'

Landor, Walter Savage
Imaginary Conversations of Greeks and Romans (London, 1853)
Uly 3.9, p. 95

Lane, Martha A[llen]. L[uther].
'Prince Ahmed and Peribanou' in her *Arabian Nights' Entertainment: Stories from The Thousand and One Nights Told for Young People* (Boston, New York, and London, 1915)
Uly 9.938, p. 189

Lang, Andrew
The Book of Dreams and Ghosts (London, 1897)
Uly 14.1088, p. 329

Leal, Frederick
Wynter's Masterpiece, serialized 31 Oct. 1891–6 Feb. 1892 in *The Leeds Times*; then publ. in book form (London, 1892)
Uly 6.126–27, p. 134

Lecky, William Edward Hartpole
'On an Old Song', first publ. Feb. 1885 in *Macmillan's Magazine*; later coll. in his *Poems* (London, 1891)
Uly 9.352, p. 184

Ledwidge, Francis
'Evening Clouds' in his *Songs of Peace* (London, 1917)
Uly 10.181–82, p. 205

Lee, Sophia
The Chapter of Accidents: a Comedy, in Five Acts (London, 1780)
Uly 15.2380, p. 353

Lee, Susan Richmond
See Yorke, Curtis

Lefurt, Annie B.
Sweet, Not Lasting (London, 1874)
Uly 15.2866, p. 357

Le Gallienne, Richard
'London Beautiful' in his *New Poems* (London and New York, 1910)
Uly 3.212–13, p. 103

L.E.L.
'Sketch Second', publ. 19 Jan. 1822 in *The Literary Gazette*
Uly 7.682, p. 160

Lennox, Lord William Pitt
Ernest Atherley; or, Scenes at Home and Abroad, serialized 1852–53 in *The Sportsman's Magazine*
Uly 14.935, p. 324

Le Queux, William
A Secret Service: Being Strange Tales of a Nihilist (London, 1896)
Uly 13.564, p. 278

The Closed Book: Concerning the Secret of the Borgias (London, 1904)
Uly 13.154–55, p. 262

Lesage, Alain René
Le Diable Boiteux: or, the Devil Upon Two Sticks (London, 1708)
Uly 13.851–52, p. 295

L'Estrange, Sir Roger
'Of Anger' in his *Seneca's Morals by Way of Abstract*, eleventh edn (London, 1718)
Uly 9.950, p. 190

Lever, Charles James
Charles O'Malley, The Irish Dragoon (Dublin and London, 1841)
Uly 6.522–23, p. 142

Davenport Dunn: A Man of Our Day (London, 1859)
Uly 15.814–15, p. 341

Locke, John
Editor's Introduction to his nine-volume *Works* (London, 1824)
Uly 14.714, p. 312

Lodge, Sir Oliver Joseph
The Survival of Man: A Study in Unrecognized Human Faculty (London, 1909)
Uly 7.915, p. 165

Lofft, Capel
Self-Formation; or, The History of an Individual Mind (London, 1837)
Uly 9.1094–95, p. 193

Longfellow, Henry Wadsworth
'The Two Angels' in his *Courtship of Miles Standish, and Other Poems* (London, 1853)
Uly 7.560, p. 156

Longfellow, Samuel
'The Homestead' (c. 1839)
Uly 9.245, p. 182

Lucas, Annie
Léonie; or, Light Out of Darkness (London, 1875)
Uly 13.193–94, p. 265

Lucas, Edward Verrall
Landmarks (London, 1914)
Uly 17.1632, p. 376

Lucas, Edward Verrall, and Charles Larcom Graves
Wisdom while you wait: Being a foretaste of the glories of the 'Insidecompletuar Britanniaware.' (London, 1903)
Uly 11.906, p. 225

Lucian of Samosata
'Dialogues of the Gods', transl. Fowler (Oxford, 1905)
Ully 6.456, p. 141

Luther, Martin
Table Talk, transl. of the *Tischreden* (1566)
Ully 10.174, p. 204

Lydgate, John
The Fall of Princes, written c. 1431–38
Ully 3.412, p. 106

Macaulay, Thomas Babington
The History of England from the Accession of James the Second (London, 1848)
Ully 14.553–54 and 1221, pp. 309 and 334

MacDonald, George
A Book of Strife, in the Form of the Diary of an Old Soul (London, 1909)
Ully 9.374–75, p. 185

Donal Grant (London, 1883)
Ully 13.624, p. 283

Lilith: A Romance (London, 1895)
Ully 6.456, p. 141

Rampolli: Growths From a Long-Planted Root (London, 1897)
Ully 13.1–2, p. 245

MacDonough, Glen
See Herbert, Victor

MacGregor, Robert Guthrie
Indian Leisure. Petrarch. On the Character of Othello. etc (London, 1854)
Ully 9.1202, p. 196

Machen, Arthur
'A Fragment of Life' in *The House of Souls*, serialized in the first four issues of *Horlick's Magazine* (1904); then publ. in book form (London, 1906)
Uly 12.59, p. 228

Mackay, Charles
New Light on Some Obscure Words and Phrases in the Works of Shakspeare and His Contemporaries (London, 1884)
Uly 7.578, p. 157

'The Wood-Nymph' in his *Songs and Poems* (London, 1834)
Uly 7.560, p. 156

Mackay, Mary
See Corelli, Marie

Mackie, Charles
The Castles of Mary Queen of Scots, third edn (London, 1835)
Uly 13.396, p. 271

Maclaren, Alexander
'How to Work the Work of God' in *The Wearied Christ and Other Sermons* (London, 1893)
Uly 13.1110–11, p. 299

'The Resurrection of Dead Souls' in his *St. Paul's Epistle to the Ephesians* (London, 1909)
Uly 11.461, p. 223

MacManus, Anna Johnston
See Carbery, Ethna

Macnish, Robert
'The Metempsychosis' in his *Modern Pythagoreans: A Series of Tales, Essays, and Sketches* (Edinburgh and London, 1838)
Uly 17.322, p. 372

MacPherson, James
Fingal, An Ancient Epic Poem (London, 1762)
Uly 2.16–17, p. 91

'The Hunter' in his *Poems of Ossian, &c.* (Edinburgh, 1805)
Uly 9.934, p. 188

Maillard, Annette Marie
Miles Tremenhere (London, 1853)
Uly 13.422–23, p. 274

Malcolm of Poltalloch, John
'The Waters of Oblivion' in the 1830 edn of *Forget Me Not* (London)
Uly 5.365, p. 126

Malling, Mathilda
Daggryning (1902), anon. transl. as *Daybreak* in the June 1906 issue of *Tales, A Magazine of the World's Best Fiction*
Uly 13.690–91, p. 286

Manzoni, Alessandro
I promessi sposi (1827), anon. transl. as *The Betrothed* (London, Edinburgh, and Dublin, 1834)
Uly 12.738–39, p. 237

Marcus Aurelius
See Casaubon, Meric

Mario, Alberto
The Red Shirt. Episodes. (London, 1865)
Uly 13.1–2, p. 245

Markham, Edwin
'A Lyric of the Dawn' in *The Man with the Hoe and Other Poems* (New York, 1899; London, 1900)
Uly 13.104, p. 258

Marlowe, Christopher
The Tragical History of the Life and Death of Doctor Faustus (London, 1604 and 1616)
Uly 8.329, p. 172

The Troublesome Raigne and Lamentable Death of Edward the Second (London, 1594)
Uly 12.335, p. 234

Marryat, Captain [Frederick]
Japhet in Search of a Father (London, 1836)
Uly 13.578–79, p. 280

Marston, John
The History of Antonio and Mellida (London, 1602), as coll. in his *Works*, ed. Bullen (London, 1887)
Uly 5.461–62, p. 129

Martial (Marcus Valerius Martialis)
Epigram 11.104, transl. Ker in vol. 2 of his *Martial, Epigrams* (Cambridge, Mass., 1920)
Uly 10.1082–83, p. 214

Martin, John
'Sadak in Search of the Waters of Oblivion' (painting, 1812)
Uly 5.365, p. 126

Martyn, Frederic
A Holiday in Gaol (London, 1903)
Uly 13.637–38, p. 285

Mather, Samuel
A Dead Faith Anatomized (Boston, 1697)
Uly 14.828–29, p. 318

Matheson, Annie
'Christ's Invitation' in her *Selected Poems: Old and New* (London, 1899)
Uly 13.1–2, p. 245

Maturin, Charles Robert
Manuel: A Tragedy, in Five Acts (London, 1817)
Uly 9.245, p. 182

Maughan, Janet
The Co-Heiress (London, 1866)
Uly 13.286–87, p. 268

Maunder, Samuel
Entry on 'porpoise' in his *Treasury of Natural History* (London, 1848; rvsd edn 1870)
Uly 11.144–45, p. 218

Maxwell, William Hamilton
Captain O'Sullivan; or, Adventures, Civil, Military, and Matrimonial, of a Gentleman on Half Pay (London, 1846)
Uly 12.332, p. 233

Mayhew, Henry
London Labour and the London Poor, rvsd edn (London, 1861)
Uly 15.643, p. 338

Mead, G[eorge]. R[obert]. S[tow].
The Wedding-Song of Wisdom (London and Benares, 1906)
Uly 14.1167, p. 330

Meade, L. T.
Frances Kane's Fortune (London, 1890)
Uly 13.511, p. 275

The Daughter of a Soldier: A Colleen of South Ireland (London, 1915)
Uly 15.2966, p. 358

Mellish, Joseph Charles
See Schiller, Friedrich

Melville, Herman
White-Jacket; or, The World in a Man-of-War (London, 1850)
Uly 13.188–89, p. 264

Mercier, Charles Arthur
Sanity and Insanity (London, 1895)
Uly 16.223–24, p. 365

Meredith, George
Diana of the Crossways (London, 1885)
Uly 2.17, p. 92

Méry, Joseph
La Guerre du Nizam (Paris, 1847), transl. Vibeur as *Through Thick and Thin: or, "La Guerre du Nizam"* (New York and Paris, 1874)
Uly 16.253, p. 365

Millington, Rev. T. S.
'A Great Mistake', publ. 19 Dec. 1885 in *The Boy's Own Paper*
Uly 3.308–09, p. 105

Milton, John
Paradise Lost (1674 version), book 2
Uly 5.365, p. 126

Paradise Lost (1674 version), book 4
Uly 12.70–71, p. 229

Paradise Lost (1674 version), book 10
Uly 8.543, p. 175

Mitford, Mary Russell and Charles Packer
Sadak and Kalasrade, or, The Waters of Oblivion (opera, 1835)
Uly 5.365, p. 126

M'Lachlan, Tom
'Bernard M'Shane' in his *Thoughts in Rhyme* (Glasgow, 1884)
Uly 4.112–13, p. 111

Molesworth, Mrs [Mary Louisa]
Hathercourt Rectory (London, 1878)
Uly 13.412–13, p. 271

'"The Blue Dwarfs" An Adventure in Thüringen', first publ. 1882 in *The Churchman*; later in *Aunt Judy's Annual Volume* (London, 1882)
Uly 4.179, p. 112

The Old Pincushion, or, Aunt Clotilda's Guests (London, 1889)
Uly 15.518–19, p. 335

Montaigne, Michel de
'Of Vanitie' in *The Essayes of Michael Lord of Montaigne*, transl. Florio (London, 1603)
Uly 3.490, p. 108

Montgomery, L[ucy]. M[aud].
Kilmeny of the Orchard (London, 1910)
Uly 16.634, p. 369

Montgomery, Robert
The Age Reviewed: A Satire: In Two Parts (London, 1827)
Uly 12.69, p. 229

Moore, Arthur
See Dowson, Ernest

Moore, Frank Frankfort
A Gray Eye or So (London, 1893)
Uly 13.24–25, p. 254

Mordaunt, Elinor
The Processionals (London, 1918)
Uly 9.1087, p. 192

'Morell, Sir Charles'
See Ridley, James Kenneth

Morell, Thomas
The Triumph of Time and Truth (London, 1757)
Uly 14.770–71, p. 315

Mühlbach, Luise
Mohammed Ali and His House: An Historical Romance,
transl. Coleman (New York, 1872)
Uly 5.36, p. 122

Mundt, Klara (or Clara)
See Mühlbach, Luise

Murdoch, Alex[ander]. G[regor].
'The Flittin' Day' in his *Lilts on the Doric Lyre* (Glasgow, 1873)
Uly 3.19–20, p. 96

Murray, Eustace Clare Grenville
*That Artful Vicar: The Story of What a Clergyman Tried
to Do for Others and Did for Himself* (London, 1879)
Uly 13.106, p. 259

The Russians of To-Day (London, 1878)
    Uly 7.804–05, p. 162

Murray, Sir James A. H., et al
A New English Dictionary on Historical Principles
(London, 1919)
    Uly 10.807, p. 211

Napier, Mark
Memorials and Letters Illustrative of the Life and Times of John Graham of Claverhouse, Viscount Dundee
(Edinburgh and London, 1862)
    Uly 7.578, p. 157

Nashe, Thomas
Pierce Penilesse his Supplication to the Divell (London, 1592)
    Uly 10.807, p. 211

Norris, W[illiam]. E[dward].
The Right Honourable Gentleman (London, 1913)
    Uly 15.1100–01, p. 342

O'Brien, Frances Marcella 'Attie'
Won by Worth, posthumously serialized Dec. 1891–July 1892 in
The Irish Monthly
    Uly 13.976, p. 296

O'Donoghue, C.
'The Last Duel I Had a Hand In', publ. Aug. 1833 in
Fraser's Magazine
    Uly 18.987, p. 383

Ohnet, Georges
Serge Panine, transl. Hamilton (Manchester and London, 1883)
    Uly 16.253, p. 365

Oliphant, Mrs Margaret
Madonna Mary (London, 1867)
    Uly 13.1–2, p. 245

The Son of His Father (London, 1886 and 1887)
    Uly 13.549, p. 277

Oppenheim, E[dward]. Phillips
Mr. Lessingham Goes Home (London, 1918)
Uly 13.116, p. 260

Orred, Meta
'Rest' in her *Poems* (London, 1874)
Uly 13.2, p. 246

O'Ryan, Julia M.
'John Richardson's Relatives', serialized July 1874–Nov. 1875 in *The Irish Monthly*
Uly 5.76–77, p. 123

O'Shaughnessy, Arthur W. E.
'Chaitivel; or, the Lay of Love's Unfortunate' in his *Lays of France (Founded on the Lays of Marie)* (London, 1872)
Uly 9.1202, p. 196

Otway, Thomas
The Soldier's Fortune. A Comedy (London, 1681)
Uly 9.1094–95, p. 193

Ouida
Folle-Farine (London, 1871)
Uly 11.312, 13.742–43, and 14.1221, pp. 221, 290, and 334

Princess Napraxine (London, 1884)
Uly 14.91, p. 304

Pangborn, Frederic Werden
Alice, or The Wages of Sin (New York, 1883)
Uly 13.746, p. 292

Parker, Joseph
Tyne Folk: Masks, Faces, and Shadows (London, 1896)
Uly 13.745, p. 292

Paterson, A[ndrew]. B[arton]. 'Banjo'
'The City of Dreadful Thirst', first publ. Dec. 1899 in *The Bulletin* (Sydney); later coll. in his *Rio Grande's Last Race and Other Verses* (Sydney, 1902; London, 1904)
Uly 3.153–54, p. 100

Patton-Bethune, Florence
Debonnair Dick (London and Sydney, 1892)
Uly 1.198–99, p. 85

Payne, John
Translation (London, 1886) of Boccaccio's *Decameron*
Uly 12.448–49, p. 235

Pennefather, Catherine as 'C.P.'
'Gather up the Fragments.': Notes of Bible Classes.
(London, 1869)
Uly 11.149–50, p. 218

Pennell, Elizabeth Robins
Mary Wollstonecraft Godwin (London, 1885)
Uly 14.828–29, p. 318

Petrarca, Francesco
'Canzone IV', transl. Robert Guthrie MacGregor in his
Indian Leisure. Petrarch. On the Character of Othello. etc (London, 1854)
Uly 9.1202, p. 196

Phillpotts, Eden
Children of the Mist (London, 1898)
Uly 10.559, p. 208

Plautus
Amphitryon, transl. Thornton (London, 1769)
Uly 6.759, p. 145

Plumptre, E[dward]. H[ayes].
Translation (London, 1887) of *The Commedia and Canzoniere of Dante Alighieri*
Uly 17.1055–56, p. 373

Pollok, Robert
The Course of Time: A Poem, in Ten Books. (London, 1827)
Uly 14.8–9, p. 373

Pound, Ezra
'In Durance', in his *Personae* (London, 1909)
Uly 9.1202, p. 196

Procter, Bryan Waller
See Cornwall, Barry

Purcell, Mrs
The Orientalist, or, Electioneering in Ireland; a Tale, by Myself (London, 1820)
Uly 6.88, p. 132

Pyle, Howard
'The Crafty Fox', publ. Feb. 1877 in *St. Nicholas* (New York)
Uly 7.804–05, p. 162

Pyne, William Henry
See Hardcastle, Ephraim

Quarles, Francis
Emblemes (London, 1634)
Uly 12.335, p. 234

Quran
Quran 7:163–66
Uly 14.329–30, p. 305

Racidula, Wilhelmine, as 'Baroness von Beck'
Personal Adventures during The Late War of Independence in Hungary (London, 1850)
Uly 12.1820, p. 241

Radziwill, Princess Catherine
See Ebenthal, Hildegarde

Ramé, Maria Louise
See Ouida

Rankin, J[eremiah]. E[ames].
'Tell Me More, Still More of Jesus' in *Gospel Bells* (Chicago, 1880) and other hymnals
Uly 3.132–33, p. 100

Reeve, Charles McCormick
How We Went and What We Saw: A Flying Trip Through Egypt, Syria, and the Aegean Islands (New York and London, 1891)
    Uly 15.711–12, p. 339

Reeve, Rev. J[ohn]. W[illiam].
Doctrine and Practice: Lectures Preached in Portman Chapel, London (London, 1861)
    Uly 13.6–7, p. 249

Reid, Ellis
'My Mistress', publ. Dec. 1898 in *London Society*
    Uly 13.7, p. 250

Reid, Mayne
'Among the Palmettoes, An Adventure in the Swamps of Louisiana', in Reid's *The Pierced Heart and Other Stories* (London, 1885)
    Uly 9.1040, p. 191

The Wood-Rangers: or, The Trappers of Sonora (London, 1860)
    Uly 13.118–19 and 548–49, pp. 260 and 276

Reynolds, G[eorge]. W[illiam]. M[acArthur].
Pickwick Abroad; or, The Tour of France (London, 1839)
    Uly 18.8–9, p. 379

Reynolds, John Hamilton
The Press, or Literary Chit-Chat. A Satire. (London, 1822)
    Uly 6.88, p. 132

Rice, Rosa A.
'Why Not To-Night?', publ. Mar. 1889 in *The Railway Signal, or Lights Along The Line*
    Uly 13.136–37, p. 261

Richards, Alfred Bates
So Very Human: A Tale of the Present Day (London, 1873)
    Uly 16.62, p. 364

Richards, Laura E[lizabeth].
Fernley House (Boston, 1901)
Uly 5.76–77 and 13.616, pp. 123 and 282

Richardson, Dorothy M[iller].
Backwater (London, 1916)
Uly 13.4–5, p. 249

Pointed Roofs (London, 1915)
Uly 11.166, p. 219

Ridley, James Kenneth
'Sadak and Kalasrade' in his *Tales of the Genii* (London, 1764)
Uly 5.365, p. 126

Ritchie, David G[eorge].
Natural Rights: A Criticism of Some Political and Ethical Conceptions (London and New York, 1903)
Uly 7.553, p. 156

Rittenberg, Max
Every Man His Price (London, 1914)
Uly 6.772, p. 146

Robinson, Frederick William
Little Kate Kirby (London, 1873)
Uly 14.71–72, p. 302

Rochester, John Wilmot, Earl of
'The Imperfect Enjoyment' (before 1680)
Uly 4.186, p. 113

Rook, Clarence
'Songs of the Populace', publ. c. 1915 in the *Daily Chronicle*
Uly 15.1583, p. 348

Rose, George
See Sketchley, Arthur

Rosenberg, Isaac
Moses: A Play (London, 1916), later coll. in
Poems by Isaac Rosenberg (London, 1922)
    Uly 4.256, p. 115

Ross, Helen Halyburton
The Isles of Destiny, serialized 20 Aug.–8 Oct. 1904 in *Chambers's Journal*
    Uly 13.11, p. 251

Ross, Martin
Some Irish Yesterdays (London, 1906)
    Uly 14.1164–65, p. 330

Rossetti, Christina
'Songs in a Cornfield' (1866), coll. in her *Poems* (London and New York, 1901)
    Uly 13.188–89, p. 264

Rousseau, Jean-Jacques
The Reveries of the Solitary Walker (London, 1782 et seq)
    Uly 9.1087, p. 192

Royce, Josiah
The Philosophy of Loyalty (New York, 1908)
    Uly 7.553, p. 156

Runciman, James
The Chequers: Being the Natural History of a Public-house set forth in A Loafer's Diary (London, 1888)
    Uly 1.449, p. 86

Ruskin, John
Modern Painters (London, 1873)
    Uly 14.1088, p. 329

'Sir Joshua and Holbein', publ. Mar. 1860 in *The Cornhill*
    Uly 11.418, p. 221

'Water Colour Societies', coll. in Ruskin's *Works*, ed. Cook and Wedderburn (London, 1904)
    Uly 11.418, p. 221

Russell, Rev. Matthew
'Augustus Law, S. J. [:] Notes in Remembrance', publ. Aug. 1886 in *The Irish Monthly*
    Uly 6.126–27, p. 134

Russell, William
History of Modern Europe (London, 1786)
    Uly 14.848–49, p. 319

Rutherford, Samuel
Christ Dying and Drawing Sinners to Himselfe (London, 1647)
    Uly 3.88, p. 99

Rylett, Rev. Harold
'Nails and Chains', publ. Dec. 1889 in *The English Illustrated Magazine*
    Uly 16.223–24, p. 365

Rymer, James Malcolm
Edith Heron, or, The Earl and the Countess (London, 1862)
    Uly 13.733–34, p. 288

Saint-Evremond, Charles de
Quoted without attribution in T. Nixon's *Maxims, Observations & Reflections on Morality and Religion* (London, Nottingham, and Sheffield, 1806)
    Uly 9.950, p. 190

Schiller, Friedrich
Don Carlos, transl. Boylan (London, 1872)
    Uly 13.691, p. 287

Fiesco, or The Conspiracy of Genoa, anon. transl. (London and Edinburgh, 1841)
    Uly 15.2436–37, p. 354

Mary Stuart, A Tragedy, transl. Mellish (London, 1801)
    Uly 12.738–39, p. 237

Schlegel, Gustave
Chinese Uranography (The Hague and Leiden, Netherlands, 1875)
    Uly 15.2160, p. 350

Schürer, Emil

A History of the Jewish People in the Time of Jesus Christ,
transl. Macpherson (Edinburgh, 1890)
    Uly 10.188, p. 207

Scott, Michael

Tom Cringle's Log, serialized between 1829 and 1833 in *Blackwood's*;
then publ. in book form (Edinburgh and London, 1833)
    Uly 6.88 and 252, pp. 132 and 139

Scott, Sir Walter

Guy Mannering; or The Astrologer (Edinburgh, 1815)
    Uly 6.917, p. 148

Ivanhoe: A Romance (Edinburgh, 1819)
    Uly 2.17 and 8.322, pp. 92 and 171

*The Journal of Sir Walter Scott, from the original manuscript
at Abbotsford* (Edinburgh, 1890)
    Uly 11.698, p. 224

The Pirate (Edinburgh and London, 1822)
    Uly 14.74–75, p. 302

'The Two Drovers' in *Chronicles of the Canongate,
First Series* (Edinburgh and London, 1827)
    Uly 14.1218–19, p. 333

Selby, Angelica

In the Sunlight: A Tale of Mentone (London, 1892)
    Uly 13.735, p. 290

Shakespeare, William

Coriolanus
    Uly 2.17, p. 92

Hamlet, Prince of Denmark
    Uly 15.2516, p. 355

Julius Caesar
    Uly 2.17 and 9.356, pp. 92 and 184

Macbeth
   Uly 7.602, p. 158

Othello
   Uly 14.664–65, p. 309

Pericles, Prince of Tyre (with George Wilkins)
   Uly 2.17, p. 92

Romeo and Juliet
   Uly 12.1596 and 14.664–65, pp. 240 and 309

The Merchant of Venice
   Uly 12.31–32, p. 227

The Second Part of Henry the Fourth
   Uly 14.886 and 16.986, pp. 324 and 369

The Second Part of Henry the Sixth
   Uly 8.40, p. 168

The Taming of the Shrew
   Uly 14.329–30, p. 305

Sheldon, Lurana W.
   'What Bliss!' (1907)
   Uly 13.439–41, p. 275

Shelley, Mary Wollstonecraft
   Lives of the Most Eminent Literary and Scientific Men of Italy, Spain, and Portugal (London, 1835–37)
   Uly 6.351, p. 140

Shelley, Percy Bysshe
   'Sadak the Wanderer. A Fragment.' in *The Keepsake for 1828* (London)
   Uly 5.365, p. 126

   The Cenci. A Tragedy, in Five Acts (London, 1819)
   Uly 7.602, p. 158

   The Revolt of Islam (London, 1818)
   Uly 5.563–64, p. 130

Sidgwick, Ethel
Succession: A Comedy of the Generations (London, 1913)
Uly 15.2457, p. 354

Sidney, Sir Philip
The Countess of Pembroke's Arcadia (London, 1590)
Uly 9.1221–22, p. 197

Sinnett, A[lfred]. P[ierce].
Esoteric Buddhism, fifth edn (London, 1885)
Uly 17.1055–56, p. 373

Sketchley, Arthur
Mrs. Brown on the Royal Russian Marriage (London, 1874)
Uly 8.17–18, p. 167

Skinner, Rev. James
Cœlestia. The Manual of St Augustine (London, 1881)
Uly 9.1170, p. 195

Smith, Elizabeth Thomasina Meade
See Meade, L. T.

Smith, Horace
Arthur Arundel, A Tale of the English Revolution (London, 1844)
Uly 10.121, p. 202

Smith, Sarah
See Stretton, Hesba

Smith, Thomas
The Retrospective Tutors' Assistant (London, 1839)
Uly 6.149–50, p. 136

Smollett, Tobias
The Adventures of Roderick Random (London, 1748)
Uly 14.747–48, p. 313

The Expedition of Humphry Clinker (London, 1771)
Uly 10.486 and 15.2380, pp. 207 and 353

The Regicide: or, James the First, of Scotland. A tragedy.
(London, 1749)
Uly 15.1189–90, p. 343

Sollas, W[illiam]. J[ohnson].
'On the Cranial and Facial Characters of the Neanderthal Race', publ. 1 Jan. 1908 in *Philosophical Transactions of the Royal Society*
Uly 2.39, p. 92

Somerville, E[dith]. Œ[none]. and Violet Florence Martin
See Ross, Martin

Southworth, E.D.E.N.
Allworth Abbey; or, Eudora, serialized 29 June–12 Oct. 1861 in *The London Journal*; later publ. in book form (Philadelphia, 1865; New York, 1876)
Uly 17.322, p. 372

Speed, John
The Histoire of Great Britaine Vnder the Conqvests of The Romans, Saxons, Danes and Normans, second edn (London, 1623)
Uly 3.412, p. 106

Spencer, Aubrey George
'On the Danger of Minor Offences' in his *Sermons on Various Subjects* (London, 1827)
Uly 17.1623, p. 374

Spenser, Edmund
Book 1 ('The Legend of the Knight of the Red Crosse') in *The Faerie Queene* (London, 1590, 1596)
Uly 11.154, p. 219

Stanley, William Ford
Notes on the Nebular Theory etc (London, 1895)
Uly 15.2167–68, p. 351

Stannard, Henrietta Eliza Vaughan
See Winter, John Strange

St. Clair, Rosalia

Clavering Tower. A Novel. In Four Volumes. (London, 1822)
 Uly 12.161–62, p. 231

The First and Last Years of Wedded Life, vol. 3 (London, 1827)
 Uly 12.161–62, p. 231

Stebbing, Grace

That Bother of a Boy (London, 1888)
 Uly 13.549, p. 277

Steele, Richard

'On the Affectation of Faults and Imperfections' (London, 1709); repr. in *Steele: Selections from the Tatler, Spectator and Guardian*, ed. Dobson (Oxford, 1885)
 Uly 9.950, p. 190

Sterling, John

'The Last of the Giants', first publ. 4 June 1828 in *The Athenæum*; repr. in *Essays and Tales by John Sterling*, ed. Hare (London, 1848)
 Uly 12.174, p. 232

Sterne, Laurence

The Life and Opinions of Tristram Shandy, Gentleman (York, 1759–1767)
 Uly 15.521, p. 336

Stevenson, Robert Louis

'Pan's Pipes' in his *Virginibus Puerisque and Other Papers* (London, 1881)
 Uly 9.539, p. 188

The Strange Case of Doctor Jekyll and Mr. Hyde (London, 1886)
 Uly 15.1247, p. 344

Treasure Island (London, 1883)
 Uly 15.1258–59, p. 345

Stowe, Harriet Beecher

Uncle Tom's Cabin; or, Life Among the Lowly (London, 1852)
 Uly 8.344–45 and 10.174, pp. 174 and 204

Stretton, Hesba
Alone in London (London, 1869)
Uly 13.242, p. 267

Strindberg, August
Inferno (1897), transl. Field (London, 1912)
Uly 6.772, p. 146

Struthers, Peter
'South Africa and Imperialism', publ. Aug. 1901 in *The Westminster Review*
Uly 15.4692, p. 360

Suckling, Sir John
'His Dream' (1638)
Uly 14.448–49, p. 307

Swift, Jonathan
A Tale of a Tub, Written for the Universal Improvement of Mankind (London, 1704)
Uly 1.6, p. 83

'The Right of Precedence Between Physicians and Civilians Enquir'd into' (Dublin and London, 1720)
Uly 15.2126, p. 349

Swinburne, Algernon Charles
Atalanta in Calydon. A Tragedy. (London, 1865; rvsd edn London, 1892)
Uly 9.376–78, p. 186

'At a Month's End', first publ. Apr. 1871 in *The Dark Blue*; coll. in his *Poems and Ballads: Second Series* (London, 1878)
Uly 15.1267–68, p. 345

Symmons, Charles
'Life of the Poet' (Chiswick, 1826)
Uly 8.543, p. 175

Talbot, Frederick
'The Winning Hazard' in the Christmas 1870 issue of
Chambers's Journal
Uly 16.529, p. 367

Tasso, Torquato
Ecco Mormorar L'Onde (1590)
Uly 12.70–71, p. 229

Taylor, E[rnest]. A[rchibald].
Paris, Past and Present (London, Paris, and New York, 1915)
Uly 7.599, p. 158

Taylor, Jeremy
The Rule and Exercises of Holy Dying (London, 1651)
Uly 14.74–75, p. 302

Temple, Crona
The Glorious Return: A Story of the Vaudois (London, 1889)
Uly 13.764, p. 293

Tennyson, Alfred
'Demeter and Persephone' (1889)
Uly 14.1073, p. 327

'In Love, if Love be Love', from the 'Merlin and Vivien' episode of
Idylls of the King (1859)
Uly 3.452, p. 107

'To the Duke of Argyll' (1885)
Uly 17.233–34, p. 372

'Will Waterproof's Lyrical Monologue' (1842; rvsd 1853)
Uly 5.461–62, p. 129

Terhune, Mary Virginia Hawes
See Harland, Marion

Thackeray, William Makepeace
The History of Pendennis: His Fortunes and Misfortunes, His Friends and His Greatest Enemy (London, 1850)
Uly 6.1033, p. 148

Vanity Fair: A Novel Without a Hero (London, 1848)
    Uly 11.213, p. 220

Thayer, Stephen Henry
    'The Dead Year' in his *Songs of Sleepy Hollow and Other Poems* (New York and London, 1886)
    Uly 8.638, p. 176

Thomas à Kempis
    The Imitation of Christ (c. 1418–1427)
    Uly 13.1110, p. 299

Thompson, Francis
    'Poet and Anchorite' in his *Sister Songs: An Offering to Two Sisters* (London, 1895)
    Uly 9.539, p. 188

Thomson, James
    'Winter' in *The Seasons* (London, 1730)
    Uly 10.1082–83 and 12.69, pp. 214 and 229

Thornbury, George Walter
    'Fair and Foul Circassians', publ. 31 Dec. 1859 in *All the Year Round*
    Uly 6.759, p. 145

Thurston, Herbert, S.J.
    Lent and Holy Week (London, 1904)
    Uly 3.501, p. 109

Tolstoy, Leo
    Anna Karenina, transl. Garnett (London, 1901)
    Uly 4.511, p. 117

    Anna Karenina, transl. Dole (New York, 1886; rvsd edn, London, 1889)
    Uly 13.412–13, p. 271

Tompkins, Herbert W[inckworth].
    'The Haunt of the Water-Rail', publ. July 1900 in *The English Illustrated Magazine*
    Uly 14.870, p. 321

Index of Antecedent Writers and Works Discussed 473

Towle, George M[akepeace].
The Story of Magellan or the First Voyage Round the World
(London, 1896)
Uly 13.118–19, p. 260

Traubel, Horace
Review in the Mar. 1915 issue of *The Conservator* of Paul Rohrbach's
German World Policies (New York, 1915)
Uly 12.1351, p. 239

Trollope, Anthony
Barchester Towers (London, 1857)
Uly 13.188–89, p. 264

Sir Harry Hotspur of Humblethwaite (London, 1871)
Uly 12.31–32, p. 227

The Macdermots of Ballycloran (London, 1847)
Uly 6.228, p. 137

Tucker, Abraham
The Light of Nature (London, 1768–1777)
Uly 14.526, p. 308

Tucker, Charlotte Maria
See A.L.O.E.

Turgenev, Ivan
Smoke, transl. Hapgood (New York, 1903; London, 1905)
and Garnett (London, 1906)
Uly 13.80 (Garnett) and 13.549 (Hapgood), pp. 256 and 277

'The District Doctor' in *A Sportsman's Sketches*,
transl. Garnett (London, 1895)
Uly 5.254, p. 125

Tylor, Edward B.
Primitive Culture (London, 1871)
Uly 14.1088, p. 329

Tyrrell, Henry
Woman: And Her Failings (London, 1857)
Uly 5.36, p. 122

Underhill, George F[rederick].
In At The Death: A Tale of Society (London, 1888)
    Uly 8.344–45, p. 174

Upham, Edward
Karmath. An Arabian Tale. (London, 1827)
    Uly 14.831, p. 318

Vandenhoff, George
The Art of Elocution, third edn (London, 1862)
    Uly 11.418, p. 221

Veblen, Thorstein
An Inquiry into the Nature of Peace and the Terms of Its Perpetuation (London, 1917)
    Uly 17.1631–32, p. 375

Vizetelly, Ernest Alfred
See Zola, Émile

Wallace, Edgar
The Man Who Knew (Boston, 1918; London, 1919)
    Uly 13.415–16, p. 272

Warden, Florence
A Witch of the Hills (London, 1888)
    Uly 13.742–43, p. 290

Warden, Gertrude
Her Fairy Prince, serialized July–Oct. 1895 in *The Family Herald*; then publ. in book form (London, 1896)
    Uly 8.333, p. 172

Warren, Samuel
Passages from the Diary of a Late Physician, serialized Aug. 1830–Aug. 1837 in *Blackwood's*; selections publ. in a three-vol. edn (London, 1832)
    Uly 13.172, p. 263

Webb, Will
'An HYMENÆUM, Or Bridal-Sonet' (London, 1663)
Uly 13.655, p. 285

Weber, C. M. von, and Wilhelmine Christiane von Chézy
Euryanthe (1823), libretto as transl. by A. Schloss
Uly 13.8, p. 251

Wells, H[erbert]. G[eorge].
New Worlds for Old (London, 1908)
Uly 15.1686, p. 349

The First Men in the Moon (London, 1901)
Uly 14.866, p. 321

Whistler, James Abbot McNeill
The Gentle Art of Making Enemies (London, 1890; rvsd edn 1892)
Uly 7.608, p. 159

Whiston, William
'Antiquities of the Jews', from his transl. (London, 1737) of the works of Flavius Josephus
Uly 11.154 and 14.666–67, pp. 219 and 310

White, J[ames]. Edson
'Two Kinds of Service' in *The King's Daughter and Other Stories for Girls* (n.p., 1910)
Uly 13.375–76, p. 270

Whiting, Sydney
Heliondé; or, Adventures in the Sun (London, 1855)
Uly 13.564, p. 278

Whittier, John Greenleaf
'The Prophecy of Samuel Sewall' (1859)
Uly 13.421–22, p. 273

Williamson, C[harles]. N[orris]. and A[lice]. M[uriel]. Williamson
A Soldier of the Legion (New York, 1914)
Uly 13.193–94, p. 265

Wilmot, John
See Rochester, John Wilmot, Earl of

Wilson, J. Arbuthnot
See Allen, Grant

Winter, Anna Maria
Thoughts on the Moral Order of Nature (Dublin, 1831)
Uly 14.670, p. 310

Winter, John Strange
A Born Soldier (London, 1894)
Uly 13.600, p. 281

Bootles' Baby. A Story of the Scarlet Lancers (London, 1891)
Uly 13.21–22, p. 254

Wister, Owen
Lady Baltimore (New York and London, 1906)
Uly 13.578–79, p. 280

Wollstonecraft, Mary
A Vindication of the Rights of Woman: With Strictures on Political and Moral Subjects (London, 1792)
Uly 14.848–49, p. 319

Wolseley, Viscount
Corrafin (London, 1878)
Uly 8.269, p. 170

Wood, Lady Emma Caroline and Anna Caroline Steele
'Sleep comes not through the dreary hours of night'
in their *Ephemera* (London, 1865)
Uly 9.245, p. 182

Youth On The Prow (London, 1879)
Uly 6.252, p. 139

Worboise, Emma Jane
The Grey House at Endlestone (London, 1877)
Uly 18.896, p. 383

Wordsworth, William
Guilt and Sorrow: or, Incidents upon Salisbury Plain (London, 1842)
   Uly 4.256, p. 115

'I Wandered Lonely as a Cloud' (1807)
   Uly 13.12, p. 252

Wright, Thomas
The Use of the Globes (London, 1740)
   Uly 14.556, p. 309

Wycliffe, John
Romans x 3 in *Wycliffe's Bible* (1382)
   Uly 14.98, p. 305

Wyndham, Sir William
'It is an old maxim, That every man has his price, if you can but come up to it', quoted in *The Bee* (1734)
   Uly 6.772, p. 146

Wynne, Catherine Simpson
Margaret's Engagement (London, 1867)
   Uly 13.162, p. 262

Yates, Edmund Hodgson
A Waiting Race (London, 1872)
   Uly 6.351, p. 140

Yeats, William Butler
'Aedh Tells of the Perfect Beauty' (1899)
   Uly 10.94, p. 201

'Anima Hominis' in *Per Amica Silentia Lunae* (London, 1918)
   Uly 15.643, p. 338

'The Second Coming' (1920)
   Uly 18.408, p. 380

Yonge, Charlotte Mary
'The Caged Lion', publ. Apr. 1869 in *The Monthly Packet of Evening Readings for Members of the English Church*
    Uly 7.804–05, p. 162

Yorke, Curtis
Dudley. A Novel. (London, 1888)
    Uly 14.742–43, p. 313

Young, Arthur
Travels During the Years 1787, 1788 and 1789 (London, 1792; Dublin, 1793)
    Uly 14.12–13, p. 302

Young, Edward
The Complaint : or Night-Thoughts on Life, Death, & Immortality (London, 1742–1745)
    Uly 14.770–71, p. 315

Yriarte (or Iriarte), Tomás de
'The Parrots and the Monkey', transl. Rockliff, first publ. Aug. 1839 in *Blackwood's*
    Uly 9.374–75, p. 185

Zola, Émile
Au Bonheur des Dames, transl. by Vizetelly as *The Ladies' Paradise* (London, 1886)
    Uly 12.738–39, p. 237

La Bête Humaine, transl. by Vizetelly as *The Monomaniac* (London, 1901)
    Uly 3.279, p. 104

Travail, Vizetelly's preface to his transl. of, as *Work* (London, 1901)
    Uly 13.655, p. 285

About the Team

Alessandra Tosi was the managing editor for this book.

Lucy Barnes proofread and indexed the manuscript.

Jeevanjot Kaur Nagpal designed the cover. The cover was produced in InDesign using the Fontin font.

Annie Hine typeset the book in InDesign. The main text font is Tex Gyre Pagella and the heading font is Californian FB.

The conversion to the PDF and HTML editions was performed with open-source software and other tools freely available on our GitHub page at https://github.com/OpenBookPublishers.

Jeremy Bowman created the EPUB.

Hannah Shakespeare was in charge of marketing.

This book was peer-reviewed by two anonymous referees. Experts in their field, these readers donated their time to help ensure the academic rigour of our books. We are grateful for their generous and invaluable contributions.

This book need not end here...

Share

All our books — including the one you have just read — are free to access online so that students, researchers and members of the public who can't afford a printed edition will have access to the same ideas. This title will be accessed online by hundreds of readers each month across the globe: why not share the link so that someone you know is one of them?

This book and additional content is available at
https://doi.org/10.11647/OBP.0429

Donate

Open Book Publishers is an award-winning, scholar-led, not-for-profit press making knowledge freely available one book at a time. We don't charge authors to publish with us: instead, our work is supported by our library members and by donations from people who believe that research shouldn't be locked behind paywalls.

Join the effort to free knowledge by supporting us at
https://www.openbookpublishers.com/support-us

We invite you to connect with us on our socials!

BLUESKY	MASTODON	LINKEDIN
@openbookpublish.bsky.social	@OpenBookPublish@hcommons.social	open-book-publishers

Read more at the Open Book Publishers Blog
https://blogs.openbookpublishers.com

You may also be interested in:

Genetic Inroads into the Art of James Joyce
Hans Walter Gabler

https://doi.org/10.11647/OBP.0325

Text Genetics in Literary Modernism and Other Essays
Hans Walter Gabler

https://doi.org/10.11647/OBP.0120

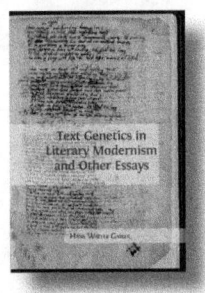

Tennyson's Poems: New Textual Parallels
R. H. Winnick

https://doi.org/10.11647/OBP.0161

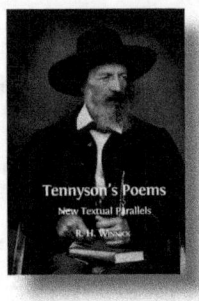

www.ingramcontent.com/pod-product-compliance
Lightning Source LLC
Chambersburg PA
CBHW052040220426
43663CB00012B/2389